Grammatical Interfaces in HPSG

Studies in Constraint-Based Lexicalism

The aim of this series is to make work in various nonderivational, lexicalist approaches to grammar available to a wide audience of linguists. In approaches of this kind, grammar is seen as the interaction of constraints from multiple dimensions of linguistic substance, including information about syntactic category, grammatical relations, and semantic and pragmatic interpretation.

Studies in
Constraint-Based Lexicalism

Grammatical Interfaces in HPSG

edited by

Ronnie Cann, Claire Grover & Philip Miller

CSLI
PUBLICATIONS
Center for the Study of
Language and Information
Stanford, California

CSLI Publications
Center for the Study of Language and Information
Leland Stanford Junior University
Printed in the United States
05 04 03 02 01 1 2 3 4 5

Library of Congress Cataloging-in-Publication Data

Grammatical interfaces in HPSG / edited by Ronnie Cann, Claire Grover & Philip Miller.
p. cm. -- (Studies in constraint-based lexicalism ; 8)
Chiefly papers presented at the 6th HPSG conference, held Aug. 1999, University of Edinburgh.
Includes bibliographical references and indexes.
ISBN 1-57586-314-6 (paper : alk. paper) -- ISBN 1-57586-313-8 (cloth : alk. paper)
1. Head-driven phrase structure grammar--Congresses. I. Cann, Ronnie. II. Grover, Claire, 1958- III. Miller, Philip H., 1959- IV.Series.

P158.4 .G73 2001
415--dc21

00-065836

∞ The acid-free paper used in this book meets the minimum requirements of the American National Standard for Information Sciences – Permanence of Paper for Printed Library Materials, ansi z39.48-1984.

Please visit our web site at
http://cslipublications.stanford.edu/
for comments on this and other titles, as well as for changes and corrections by the authors, editors and publisher.

Contents

Contributors vii

Introduction xi
Ronnie Cann, Claire Grover and Philip Miller

1 **Incorporation in Danish: Implications for Interfaces** 1
Ash Asudeh and Line Hove Mikkelsen

2 **Incorporating Contracted Auxiliaries in English** 17
Emily M. Bender and Ivan A. Sag

3 **Negation in Colloquial Welsh** 33
Robert D. Borsley and Bob Morris Jones

4 **Argument Realization and Dutch R-Pronouns: Solving Bech's Problem without Movement or Deletion** 51
Gosse Bouma

5 **Syntactic Transparency of Pronominal Affixes** 77
Berthold Crysmann

6 **From Argument Raising to Dependent Raising** 97
Kordula De Kuthy and W. Detmar Meurers

7 **The Nature of Pragmatic Information** 113
Georgia M. Green

8 **The Morphosyntax of Lai Relative Clauses** 137
Andreas Kathol

9 Grammatical Interfaces in Korean Relatives 153
JONG-BOK KIM AND BYUNG-SOO PARK

10 Prosodic Constituency in HPSG 169
EWAN KLEIN

11 A Head-Driven Account of Long-Distance Case Assignment 201
ROBERT MALOUF

12 German Particle Verbs and the Predicate Complex 215
STEFAN MÜLLER

13 A Constraint-Based Semantics for Tenses and Temporal Auxiliaries 231
FRANK VAN EYNDE

14 Spanish Psychological Predicates 251
CARL VOGEL AND BEGOÑA VILLADA

15 A Bistratal Approach to the Prosody-Syntax Interface in Japanese 267
KEI YOSHIMOTO

Subject Index 283

Name Index 289

Contributors

ASH ASUDEH: Linguistics Department, Stanford University, Margaret Jacks Hall, Building 460, Stanford, CA 94305-2150, USA, asudeh@csli.stanford.edu

EMILY M. BENDER: Department of Linguistics, University of California at Berkeley, 1203 Dwinelle Hall, Berkeley CA 94720-2650, USA, ebender@socrates.berkeley.edu

ROBERT D. BORSLEY: Department of Language and Linguistics, University of Essex, Wivenhoe Park, Colchester CO4 3SQ, UK, rborsley@essex.ac.uk

GOSSE BOUMA: Alfa-informatica, Groningen University, Postbus 716, 9700 AS Groningen, The Netherlands, gosse@let.rug.nl

RONNIE CANN: Department of Theoretical and Applied Linguistics, University of Edinburgh, 40 George Square, Edinburgh EH8 9LL, UK, ronnie@ling.ed.ac.uk

BERTHOLD CRYSMANN: Deutsches Forschungszentrum für Künstliche Intelligenz (DFKI) GmbH, Stuhlsatzenhausweg 3, 66123 Saarbrücken, Germany, berthold.crysmann@dfki.de

KORDULA DE KUTHY: SFB 340, Seminar für Sprachwissenschaft, Universität Tübingen, Kleine Wilhelmstr. 113, 72074 Tübingen, Germany, kdk@sfs.nphil.uni-tuebingen.de

GEORGIA M. GREEN: Department of Linguistics, University of Illinois, 4088 Foreign Language Building, 707 S. Mathews St., Urbana, IL 61801, USA, g-green@uiuc.edu

CLAIRE GROVER: Division of Informatics, University of Edinburgh, 2 Buccleuch Place, Edinburgh EH8 9LW, UK, claire.grover@ed.ac.uk

ANDREAS KATHOL: Department of Linguistics, University of California at Berkeley, 1203 Dwinelle Hall, Berkeley CA 94720-2650, USA, kathol@socrates.berkeley.edu

JONG-BOK KIM: School of English, Kyung Hee University, 1 Hoegi-dong, Dongdaemoon-gu, Seoul 130-702, Korea, jongbok@khu.ac.kr

EWAN KLEIN: Division of Informatics, University of Edinburgh, 2 Buccleuch Place, Edinburgh EH8 9LW, UK, ewan.klein@ed.ac.uk

ROBERT MALOUF: Alfa-informatica, Groningen University, Postbus 716, 9700 AS Groningen, The Netherlands, malouf@let.rug.nl

W. DETMAR MEURERS: Department of Linguistics, Ohio State University, Oxley Hall, 1712 Neil Avenue, Columbus, OH 43210-1298, USA, dm@ling.ohio-state.edu

LINE HOVE MIKKELSEN: Department of Linguistics, University of California at Santa Cruz, Stevenson College, 1156 High Street, Santa Cruz, CA 95064, USA, mikkelse@ling.ucsc.edu

PHILIP MILLER: SILEX, Université Lille 3, BP 149, 59653 Villeneuve d'Ascq cedex, France, miller@univ-lille3.fr

BOB MORRIS JONES: Department of Education, University of Wales, Aberystwyth, Ceredigion SY23 2AX, UK, bmj@aber.ac.uk

STEFAN MÜLLER: Deutsches Forschungszentrum für Künstliche Intelligenz (DFKI) GmbH, Stuhlsatzenhausweg 3, 66123 Saarbrücken, Germany, stefan.mueller@dfki.de

Byung-Soo Park: School of English, Kyung Hee University, 1 Hoegi-dong, Dongdaemoon-gu, Seoul 130-702, Korea, byspark@khu.ac.kr

Ivan A. Sag: Linguistics Department, Stanford University, Margaret Jacks Hall, Building 460, Stanford, CA 94305-2150, USA, sag@csli.stanford.edu

Frank Van Eynde: Centre for Computational Linguistics, University of Leuven, Maria Theresiastraat 21, 3000 Leuven, Belgium, frank.vaneynde@ccl.kuleuven.ac.be

Begoña Villada: Alfa-informatica, Groningen University, Postbus 716, 9700 AS Groningen, The Netherlands, villada@let.rug.nl

Carl Vogel: Computational Linguistics Lab, Computer Science Department, O'Reilly Institute, Trinity College, University of Dublin, Dublin 2, Ireland, vogel@tcd.ie

Kei Yoshimoto: Graduate School of International Cultural Studies, Tohoku University Kawauchi, Aoba-ku, Sendai 980-8576, Japan, kei@intcul.tohoku.ac.jp

Introduction

Ronnie Cann, Claire Grover and Philip Miller

Research carried out in the last decade of the twentieth century has increasingly shown the importance of the interaction of different components of the grammar in defining grammaticality. For example, concepts from lexical semantics, such as participant roles and lexical aspect, play a role in many frameworks in defining the well-formedness of constructions such as passive, perfect, and other aspectual constructions (Verkuyl, 1993). Work on the information structure of sentences requires reference not only to morpho-syntax, but also to prosody and pragmatics (Engdahl and Vallduví, 1996). It has thus become a matter of some importance to be able to handle interactions between the various traditional grammatical components, phonology (particularly prosody), morphology, syntax, semantics and pragmatics, and so the study of the interfaces between these components has come to have increasing significance. Furthermore, as illustrated by the papers in this volume and many others, analyzing a problem in a way that involves principles from two different components of linguistic theory interacting at an interface often leads to a simpler global explanation than if the analysis had been couched within a single component.

Head-driven Phrase Structure Grammar (Pollard and Sag, 1994) provides an elegant solution to the problem of analyzing interactions between different grammatical components. Since there is only a single information type in the theory, the attribute-value pair, the way information is encoded for all linguistically significant components must be of the same sort. Furthermore, since all such information forms part of a single linguistic object, the sign, it is in principle possible (and indeed easy) to share information between different levels that represent linguistic properties from different components. Ensuring that information is

Grammatical Interfaces in HPSG.
Ronnie Cann, Claire Grover and Philip Miller.

properly propagated as signs are built up is not so straightforward, but presents an interesting and illuminating view of the nature of grammatical interfaces. Specifically, constraints must be imposed on the sharing of information within the sign in order to enforce certain classical interface interaction principles, such as the Principle of Phonology-Free Syntax (PPFS) of Zwicky and Pullum (1986). The papers in this volume explore interface phenomena in one way or another within HPSG with respect to a range of constructions and languages and between various grammatical components.

The Papers

A number of papers in this volume look at the interface between phonology and syntax. Klein and Yoshimoto both explore the mismatch in structure between constituent structure and phonological (especially prosodic) phrasing. Klein (ch. 10) explores how prosodic constituency can be built up recursively in parallel with the construction of syntactic phrases. He develops the PHON attribute of signs to allow for structured representations in the form of metrical trees. The latter, of type *mtr*, are defined by two attributes: DOM, a prosodic domain, whose value is a list of prosodic elements (phonological words or metrical trees), and DTE (designated terminal element, after Liberman and Prince 1977) whose value is a single prosodic element and which indicates the most prominent daughter in the metrical tree. Following Zwicky's (1982) treatment of unaccented function words as *leaners*, Klein singles out a special subtype of metrical tree, *mtr(lnr)*, which consists of one or more leaners combined with a prosodic word to form a prosodic phrase. By contrast, metrical trees whose root does not immediately dominate a leaner are of type *mtr(full)*. A parametrised operation on prosodic units is defined, which broadly speaking combines a list of prosodic elements into one of the two subtypes of metrical tree, either *mtr(lnr)* or *mtr(full)*. This operation over metrical trees is then constrained to operate with respect to certain (syntactic) construction types, thus providing a recursive definition of phonological structure which is directly linked to the construction of syntactic structure. This approach accommodates a range of possible prosodic patterns, including well-known mismatches between prosodic and syntactic structure.

The introduction of a metrical grid into the PHON attribute is also proposed in Asudeh and Mikkelsen (ch. 1), but for rather different purposes from Klein. The paper is concerned with the analysis of noun incorporation in Danish which is characterised by the combination of a noun phrase and a verb into a single phonological phrase where the verb is de-accented. Their approach expands PHON to include information about different stress levels such as word, foot, and syllable. A description level lexical rule (Meurers, 1995) applies to full verbs and outputs a verb that is de-accented at the word level. Additionally, the lexical rule provides information about the semantic and pragmatic effects of the construction. For noun incorporation to be well-formed in Danish, the incorporated noun phrase must be non-specific and the resulting predicate must denote some sort of 'institutionalized' action. The former constraint is captured by requiring the incorporating verb to select for a 'lite' (Abeillé and Godard, 2000) nominal complement which is constrained to be a nominal phrase with a predicative head but no specifier and whose CONTENT is non-specific but with a referential index. The pragmatic requirement is handled within the background value of the CONTEXT by requiring the incorporated noun phrase to be the undergoer of some *institutionalized-rel.* Although the authors do not provide a full analysis of the semantics and pragmatics of the construction, the analysis they propose shows clearly how natural it is within HPSG to define the interaction of all the different components, phonology, syntax, semantics and pragmatics in determining the limits of grammaticality within this construction.

The paper by Yoshimoto (ch. 15) considers the interaction between phonology and syntax with respect to Japanese. He draws attention to the fact that 'accentual phrases' consisting of a substantive element and a grammatical morph may cut across significant syntactic boundaries. On the other hand, constituent structure remains important for determining certain aspects of pitch prominence in Japanese which are sensitive to whether a phrase is syntactically left or right branching. Yoshimoto proposes a feature P-STR that provides a link from the word order domain (DOM) of Kathol (1995) to the phonology proper. Values for P-STR are determined by a principle that constructs an output phonological structure from the head's P-STR and the order domain of a complement or adjunct, in effect translating orderings into phonological structures. The relation between constituent structure and the 'metrical boost' with certain types of adnominal adjunction is handled by propagating the directionality of branching from constituent structure to phonological structure, again illustrating how, within HPSG, relations between grammatical levels can be stated in a natural and effective way.

Three papers in the collection involve interactions between morphology and syntax. Bender and Sag (ch. 2) provide an analysis of contracted auxiliaries in English. The paper takes issue with Sadler (1997) which provides an account of the phenomenon within LFG, proposing that expressions like *you'll* are essentially noun phrases with an incorporated auxiliary verb. Bender and Sag criticize this approach on empirical and theoretical grounds. In particular, they point out that the treatment of contracted auxiliaries as subject noun phrases undermines many of the foundational principles of HPSG, such as the Head Feature Principle and the Valence Principle (Pollard and Sag, 1994). Instead, the authors provide an analysis which reverses that of Sadler (1997) and Barron (1998) and treat contracted auxiliary forms as verbs with an incorporated pronominal subject. A lexical rule of Pronoun Incorporation takes two signs, one of which is a finite auxiliary and outputs a single sign with an empty SUBJ value and a PHON value that is some function of the two input phonologies (a function which is undefined for all values of PHON except those of the relevant sort, i.e. PHON values of the pronouns and the auxiliaries). The rule also introduces the LOCAL value of the input pronoun as the first member of the ARG-ST of the output and assigns it the type *affix* to prevent it from being realized in the output COMPS list. This elegant analysis covers all the facts adduced to support the LFG analysis, but also automatically accounts for the fact that the constructions in which the contracted and uncontracted forms of auxiliaries can appear are identical, modulo the incorporated subject.

The paper by Crysmann (ch. 5) also explores the relation between syntax and morphology, this time in relation to the pronominal affixes in European Portuguese. These clitics are clearly affixal in nature (showing gaps in the paradigm, having morphological idiosyncrasies and being able to appear between a stem and a tense/agreement morpheme) and yet their appearance as enclitics or proclitics depends, not on the morphological form of the host, but on the appearance of certain elements before the verb. Crysmann provides evidence that complementizers, *wh*-expressions, negation and monotone decreasing quantifier phrases all induce obligatory proclisis. The conditioning environment for proclisis thus involves not just syntax (position and category) but also semantics (properties of quantifiers). Using Minimal Recursion Semantics (Copestake et al., 1998) to model monotonicity, clitic placement in European Portuguese is defined by three implicational constraints that relate elements in the domain list in the preverbal domain to the order of clitic and verb in the verbal domain, according to the types of the former. This is achieved by specifying that the word order domain is ordered according to three TOPO values: *pre* (pre-verbal), *post* (post-verbal) and *vc* (verbal cluster). An element that has value [TOPO *pre*] and that is also a *wh*-word, a monotone decreasing quantifier or a lexical marker requires a noun in the verbal cluster to precede the head verb. These constraints necessarily refer to syntactic and semantic information to constrain a morphological operation on clitic placement.

Another construction that involves a relation between syntax and morphology appears in the Sino-Tibetan language Lai. Relative clauses in Lai may be formed using one of two relative markers, *mii* and *tuu*, that follow the predicate of the embedded clause in which there is a missing element (in externally headed relative clauses). In his paper (ch. 8), Kathol argues that the gap is strictly local (i.e. cannot be in a clause embedded in the relative clause itself) and is best analyzed as a null pronoun, a subtype of *nom-obj*. He analyses the relative marker as a nominal element that takes a relative clause as complement and binds the index of the covert pronoun in that clause, through structure sharing. A minor modification of this approach allows him also to analyze internally headed relative clauses in the same way. The difference between the two relative markers is that *mii* can license subject and non-subject dependencies within the relative clause, whereas *tuu* only licenses subject dependencies in transitive constructions. The author uses an ERG feature which picks out the transitive subject and requires *tuu* to bind only the index of the XP that provides the value of this attribute. Interestingly from the point of view of grammatical interfaces, in Lai, subject dependencies within a relative clause are associated with a morphological difference in the verb compared with dependencies involving other grammatical functions. This is accounted for by postulating two morphological constraints on signs which require a head verb to have one morphological form if its relative value is structure-shared with the first element in ARG-ST and to be of another form, if the relative value on the verb is not the same. Using these very simple grammatical devices, Kathol captures a range of what appear to be complex morphosyntactic effects within this little studied language.

The paper by Kim and Park (ch. 9) is also concerned with relative clauses, this time in Korean. However, their concern is not so much with the interaction between morphology and syntax (although the authors note interesting facts with regard to the morphosyntax of this construction), but principally between syntax and semantics. Having provided a general analysis for Korean relatives with subject, complement and adjunct dependencies, they turn to a discussion of the apparent ability of the language to permit relativization of a specifier. Thus, the Korean equivalent of [*father goes to college*] *boy* ('boy whose father goes to college') is grammatical. Instead of treating this as an instance of a gap being licensed in a specifier position, they relate such relative clauses to double nominative constructions, the hypothesis being that a relative with an apparent specifier gap is acceptable just in case the relative clause itself could be expressed with a double nominative (which the authors interpret as a focus construction). One of the constraints on the double nominative construction is that the semantic relation between the two nominative marked noun phrases must be one of 'subordination' where this property holds of part-whole, hierarchical and taxonomic relations (inter alia). Thus, 'father' and 'child' instantiate a subordinate relation while 'president and 'professor' do not. This semantic constraint holds of the apparent possessive relativization strategy in Korean and so, argue Kim and Park, these constructions are best analysed as instantiating nominative relative dependencies rather than genitive ones. Korean relative clauses thus illustrate the importance of the interaction of different levels of information to define grammaticality.

The papers by Green (ch. 7) and van Eynde (ch. 13) are concerned with matters encoded as part of the CONTEXT attribute of a sign. Green provides an overview of the sorts of information than can be encoded withing an HPSG, as well as a discussion of which sorts really should be. She argues that the pragmatic information encoded in signs is different in kind from other, more specifically linguistic, information. In particular, background information encoded in the CONTEXT|BKGR attribute does not have to be consistent, unlike information encoded elsewhere in the sign, since pragmatic information has to do with the relation between the user of the sign and the act of using the sign. This means, for example, that the background attribute does not encode facts but attitudes towards propositions. Green discusses the general properties of sentence final particles in Chinese and Japanese, discourse markers in English and honorifics and provides the sketch of an analysis for illocutionary force within HPSG. The paper ends with a proposal that the projection of pragmatic information is not the problem that it is usually portrayed as being. If background information contains contradictory information, then, Green suggests, this is not a linguistic problem but a problem for hearers: how to induce a rational interpretation from an inconsistent set of propositions. This allows her to propose a CONTEXT Inheritance Principle that simply propagates background information by the union of the CONTEXT|BKGR values of all daughters and the head of a phrase.

Tense is the topic of van Eynde's contribution (ch. 13). The author provides a constraint based semantics for Dutch tenses and temporal auxiliaries which combines ideas from Davidson, Reichenbach and Discourse Representation Theory. He proposes that verbs should carry an INDEX value which acts like a Davidsonian event variable and is linked in the CONTENT value of a verbal sign to a temporal location. This in turn links to CONTEXT values where BACKGROUND information provides information about the relations between event time (the time at which the verb index is located), reference time and utterance time, as in Reichenbach and as developed in DRT. An analysis is provided of the present and past tenses in Dutch which feeds into an account of the perfect and future constructions. In order to account for the difference between a fully aspectual use of the perfect and the simple past-time interpretation, van Eynde proposes a distinction between two sorts of local object: *substantive* and *nonsubstantive.* This is reminiscent of, but not the same as the functional/lexical distinction in transformational (and other) frameworks. It is similar in that nonsubstantive items lack the CONTENT attribute, but unlike in that it is not tied to functional categories, such as ASPECT and TENSE, but to lexical items. Hence, *hebben* has a substantive instantiation as the aspectual, perfect, auxiliary as well as a non-substantive one to signal past-time perfect. This innovation ensures that the past-time auxiliary is exempt from the temporal constraints associated with substantive verbs and so can straightforwardly express its contribution to the interpretation of the sign by background information specified in its lexical entry. By invoking relations between CONTENT and CONTEXT in this way, this HPSG analysis provides an elegant and motivated account of a significant part of the Dutch tense-aspect system.

The constraint-based formalism of HPSG and its specification of well-formed signs means that the notion of interface goes beyond the obvious interactions between what have traditionally been regarded as different components of the grammar, phonology, morphology, syntax, semantics and pragmatics. Thus, one can consider all interactions between different attributes of the sign as in some sense interface relations. The difference between the interface between (say) syntax and semantics and that between valence and ARG-ST is thus really one of embeddedness within the sign, between what one might call 'macro-attributes', at the highest levels of the sign, and 'micro-attributes' within these domains. The remaining papers in this volume deal with structure-sharing and other relations between elements in SYNSEM and more particularly within the SYNSEM|LOCAL attribute.

One of these 'micro' interface relations that has become increasingly important is the relation between argument structure and/or a dependents list and valence. Although originally introduced to handle binding effects, ARG-ST has become increasingly used to mediate between valence and CONTENT in those constructions where there is a mismatch in the elements that feature as values of the valence attributes and those that function as part of the argument structure of a predicate. Bouma exploits the dissociation of these attributes in his paper on Bech's problem (ch. 4). Extraction out of a PP in Dutch is permitted only if the extracted element is an R-pronoun, an expression that can also function as a locative adverbial. The pronoun *er* can, however, also function as the subject in impersonal passives constructions. The problem discussed in the paper is that there are sentences in which *er* acts both as the subject of an impersonal passive and simultaneously as the extracted object of a preposition. Bouma solves the problem through the use of a DEPS list and Argument Extension and Realization Principles for prepositions as well as verbs which indicate how DEPS mediates between ARG-ST and valence. *Er* is treated as a sort of adverbial which may appear in the dependents attribute and then be projected into the valence list through the argument realisation principles. Verbs whose DEPS list contains an R-pronoun are permitted to bind a gap introduced by a preposition and in impersonal passives and existential constructions this may be realized as the value of SUBJ thus leading to function amalgamation.

The problem of partial fronting in German has been successfully treated in HPSG by using 'argument raising' prior to fronting (Pollard 1996; Müller 1997; Meurers 1999, *inter alia*). Argument raising is modelled by allowing a predicate to inherit onto its COMPS list elements from the COMPS list of one of its arguments. The canonical relations underlying this kind of reshuffling are preserved by means of the ARG-ST list, thus the use of ARG-ST as the interface between valence and semantics is once again crucial. De Kuthy and Meurers (ch. 6) show that it is not always arguments that are left behind in partial fronting in German—in some cases adjuncts or even a mixture of arguments and adjuncts are left behind. In order to provide a unified analysis of both the argument and the adjunct cases, they adopt the adjunct-as-complements analysis of Bouma et al. (2001) which utilises a DEPS list to encode a wider set of dependents than ARG-ST encodes. Thus De Kuthy and Meurers replace argument raising with 'dependent raising' and show that all cases of partial fronting can be given a uniform analysis.

In his paper (ch. 12) Müller also deals with word order in German, specifically the status of preverbs of particle verbs. Unlike De Kuthy and Meurers, Müller uses Reape's word order domains (Reape, 1996), encoded using the feature DOM to account for some of the word order permutations in German. He argues that preverbs are separate elements which form part of the verbal complex (where verbal complex elements are selected by the verb by means of the valence feature VCOMP). This enables him to present an analysis which requires no new mechanisms but which accounts for a wide range of particle verb data including fronting of the particle.

The paper by Vogel and Villada (ch. 14) takes issue with the now widely accepted proposal put forward in (Borsley, 1989) that there should be a SUBJ feature to distinguish this grammatical function from other complements. Considering data from psychological predicates in

Spanish, the authors argue that the notion of subject is too problematic to be considered to be explanatory in any meaningful sense. Their argument centers around patterns of agreement with such predicates in Spanish with respect to subject-verb and clitic agreement. Looking further at existential expletive (there) constructions in English, they conclude that there is no unequivocal sense in which these constructions can be said to have subjects and that other properties of clauses are more important and explanatory than this notion. These properties, they argue, are agreement and linearization. They propose two features, POS (position) and AGRC (agreement controller) which are used as the basis for analyses of linearization and of control and raising constructions in Spanish which make no reference to subjecthood. By these two features and a number of revised LP and ID rules and two principles, Raising and Control, Vogel and Villada are able to eschew the SUBJ attribute and revert to the SUBCAT list ordered by obliqueness of earlier days.

Malouf (ch. 11) looks at long distance case concord in some Australian aboriginal languages. In these languages the modifier of a head may bear, not only a case-marking that signals its own dependency with the head, but also a case-marking that signals the dependency of its head on some other head. So, multiple case-marking is permitted in these languages and the phenomenon is non-local. Such constructions are discussed extensively in Nordlinger (1998) which uses inside-out conditions in Lexical Functional Grammar to handle the data. The analysis proposed in the paper, however, shows that such inside-out constraints are not necessary in HPSG as long as the CASE feature is generalized so that it has as value a list of morphosyntactic cases, rather than a single value as generally assumed. A Case-Concord Principle is defined as a constraint on the DEPS list. This appends the case of a head onto some dependent which may itself bear case to indicate its function as a modifier. A Case-Realization Principle then relates the value of the case attribute to its morpho-phonological realization. In the Australian aboriginal languages cited by Malouf, this will give rise a series of morphs agglutinated to the stem. Malouf suggests, however, multiple cases may still be assigned to words in other languages, such as Classical Armenian and Gothic, which allow only a single case morph per stem, the morphology of the language determining which value is realized in particular constructions. He also discusses the fact that semantic case values may be stacked but are not semantically potent on the dependents of a head. It is proposed that variations of Argument Structure Extension can be used to ensure that the semantic information of a case value is instantiated in the CONTENT of a head but not on any of its dependents.

Borsley and Morris Jones (ch. 3) is the paper least concerned with interface matters. In it, the authors provide an account of certain aspects of main clause negation in modern colloquial Welsh. The authors present data that show that negative verbs in Welsh must be followed by some negative element. This element may be a negated subject, object or a post subject adverbial, *dim*. The latter is argued to be, not a premodifier of some predicative phrase, but a complement of the finite verb and evidence is adduced from facts about distribution and initial mutation. To account for these data, Borsley and Morris Jones propose that negative verbs carry a [NEG +] specification and that their related negative complements are marked [NC +], i.e. as carrying negative concord. The restrictions on the relation between the verbal head and its negative complements and between the latter and other elements in the COMPS list need to be given a general statement as they apply to all negative verbs whatever their valence. They discuss, but reject, an approach using lexical rules, since these appear to miss simple generalizations. Instead, the authors propose two general lexical constraints that require a negative verb to have an [NC +] complement and that require a negative adverbial to appear in a COMPS list with a non-negative subject and without any object NPs. These two simple constraints account for the apparently complex data associated with main clause negation in spoken Welsh.

Acknowledgements

Many of the papers in this collection were presented at the sixth HPSG conference held at the University of Edinburgh in August 1999 hosted by the Human Communication Research Centre and the Department of Theoretical and Applied Linguistics with additional financial support from the British Academy.

We would like to thank the following people for reviewing papers for this volume: Dora Alexopoulou, Emily Bender, Bob Borsley, Gosse Bouma, Jo Calder, Frank van Eynde, Howard Gregory, Steve Harlow, Andreas Kathol, Ewan Klein, Dimitra Kolliakou, Marc Moens, Stephen Nightingale, Adam Przepiórkowski, Mike Reape, Peter Sells, Maggie Tallerman, Anthony Warner, Arnold Zwicky.

We are also grateful to Frank Keller for his invaluable help in formatting this volume.

References

Abeillé, A. and D. Godard. 2000. French word order and lexical weight. In R. D. Borsley, ed., *The Nature and Function of Syntactic Categories*, pages 325–360. New York: Academic Press.

Barron, J. 1998. *Have* contraction: Explaining "trace effects" in a theory without movement. *Linguistics* 36(2):223–251.

Borsley, R. 1989. An HPSG Approach to Welsh. *Journal of Linguistics* 25:333–54.

Bouma, G., R. Malouf, and I. A. Sag. 2001. Satisfying constraints on extraction and adjunction. *Natural Language and Linguistic Theory* 19:1–65.

Copestake, A., D. Flickinger, and I. Sag. 1998. Minimal recursion semantics. An introduction. Proceedings of ESSLLI 10, Saarbrücken.

Engdahl, E. and E. Vallduví. 1996. Information packaging in HPSG. In C. Grover and E. Vallduví (eds.), *Studies in HPSG*: Edinburgh Working Papers in Cognitive Science, 1–31.

Kathol, A. 1995. *Linearization-Based German Syntax*. Ph.D. thesis, Ohio State University.

Liberman, M. and A. Prince. 1977. On stress and linguistic rhythm. *Linguistic Inquiry* 8:249–336.

Müller, S. 1997. Yet another paper about partial verb phrase fronting in German. Research Report RR-97-07, DFKI, Saarbrücken. A shorter version appeared in *Proceedings of the 16th Conference on Computational Linguistics (COLING-96).*

Meurers, W. D. 1995. Towards a semantics for lexical rules as used in HPSG. In *Proceedings of the ACQUILEX II Workshop on the Formalisation and Use of Lexical Rules*, pages 1–20. Cambridge, UK. Also presented at the First Conference on Formal Grammar, Barcelona, 1995.

Meurers, W. D. 1999. *Lexical Generalizations in the Syntax of German Non-Finite Constructions*. Ph.D. thesis, Seminar für Sprachwissenschaft, Universität Tübingen, Tübingen. Available as Volume 145 in Arbeitspapiere des SFB 340, 2000.

Nordlinger, R. 1998. *Constructive Case: Evidence from Australian Languages*. Stanford: CSLI Publications.

Pollard, C. and I. Sag. 1994. *Head-Driven Phrase Structure Grammar*. University of Chicago Press and CSLI Publications.

Pollard, C. J. 1996. On head non-movement. In H. Bunt and A. van Horck, eds., *Discontinuous Constituency*, Natural language processing, pages 279–305. Berlin, New York: Mouton de Gruyter.

Reape, M. 1996. Getting things in order. In H. Bunt and A. van Horck, eds., *Discontinuous Constituency*, pages 209–253. Berlin, New York: Mouton de Gruyter. 1996.

Sadler, L. 1997. English auxiliaries as tense inflections. Version of November, 1997. To appear in the *Special Issue of Essex Research Reports produced on the occasion of the retirement of Keith Brown.*

Verkuyl, H. 1993. *A Theory of Aspectuality. The Interaction between Temporal and Atemporal Structure*, vol. 64 of *Cambridge Studies in Linguistics*. Cambridge University Press.

Zwicky, A. M. 1982. Stranded *to* and phonological phrasing in English. *Linguistics* 20(1/2):3–57.

Zwicky, A. M. and G. K. Pullum. 1986. The principle of phonology-free syntax: introductory remarks. In A. M. Zwicky, ed., *Interfaces*, vol. 32 of *Ohio State University Working Papers in Linguistics*, pages 63–91. Ohio State University Department of Linguistics.

1

Incorporation in Danish: Implications for Interfaces

ASH ASUDEH AND LINE HOVE MIKKELSEN

1.1 Introduction

Syntactic noun incorporation (SNI) in Danish is a phenomenon that has reflexes in phonology, syntax, semantics and pragmatics. In contrast with morphological noun incorporation, which involves compounding of an N stem and a V stem to yield a larger, derived V stem (Mithun, 1984, 847), SNI does not involve any overt word order perturbation or overt morphology, but is rather expressed prosodically. However, SNI shares essential semantic and pragmatic characteristics of morphological noun incorporation (in particular, Mithun's (1984) type I incorporation).

Although there is a large body of descriptive work on SNI (see Rischel and Basbøll (1995) and references cited there), there have been few attempts to give a formal analysis of the phenomenon (a notable exception is Hentze (1996)). As an information-theoretic, sign-based framework, HPSG is especially well-suited for a formal treatment of SNI that simultaneously captures generalizations in all four areas as well as interactions between them. Building on work by Abeillé and Godard (2000). Bird and Klein (1994), and Meurers (1995, 1999), we propose a lexical account of SNI that introduces non-trivial extensions to HPSG phonology. However, we follow the descriptive literature on the Danish phenomenon in using the term 'syntactic noun incorporation'.

1.2 The Data

The (a) sentences below are examples of SNI, while the (b) and (c) sentences show contrasts with ordinary object DPs. Following Nedergaard Thomsen (1992), we use $_{\circ}$ to indicate reduced stress and ˈ to indicate

Grammatical Interfaces in HPSG.
Ronnie Cann, Claire Grover and Philip Miller.

a word with regular word stress. For simplicity we indicate stress at the left edge of a word. Phonological phrasing is indicated using square brackets.[1] Note that we use 'phonological phrase' as a general term for a phonological constituent, not as a name for a particular phonological constituent of a particular size (i.e., we are not making claims about Phonological Phrases versus Intonational Phrases or Intermediate Phrases, etc.).

(1) a. Min nabo [$_p$ k̥øbte 'hus] sidste år.
My neighbour bought house last year
'My neighbour did house-buying last year.'
∼'My neighbour bought a house last year.'

b. Min nabo [$_p$ 'købte] [$_p$ et 'hus] sidste år.
My neighbour bought a house last year
'My neighbour bought a house last year.'

c. Min nabo [$_p$ 'købte] [$_p$ 'hus.et] sidste år.
My neighbour bought house.DEF last year
'My neighbour bought the house last year.'

(2) a. Har du [$_p$ r̥edt 'seng]?
Have you made bed
'Did you bed-make?'
∼'Did you make your bed?'

b. Har du [$_p$ 'redt] [$_p$ din 'seng]?
Have you made your bed
'Did you make your bed?'

c. Har du [$_p$ 'redt] [$_p$ 'seng.en]?
Have you made bed.DEF
'Did you make the bed?'

There are two things to note here. First, the main purpose of the prosodic bracketing is to show that in the SNI cases, (1a) and (2a), the verb and its object are part of the same phonological phrase, whereas in the other cases they are in separate phrases. Second, the semantic differences between the (a) and (b) sentences do not readily translate into English. We have attempted to indicate the relevant distinctions by giving two translations for the (a) cases. We return to this in more detail in section 1.2.3 below.

[1] We use '∼' to indicate closest idiomatic English translation, '*' for syntactic ungrammaticality, '#' for pragmatic anomaly, '=' for possible interpretation, and '≠' for impossible interpretation.

1.2.1 Phonology

The standard phonological characterization of Danish SNI is in terms of "unit accentuation" (Jespersen, 1934; Rischel, 1983). As the term indicates, the verb and its incorporated element form a single stress group, whose main stress falls on the incorporated noun. We analyze this property as the result of phonological phrasing and concomitant destressing of the verb. The exact degree of stress loss, and the number of stress levels in Danish generally, has been extensively debated in the literature (Fischer-Jørgensen, 1983; Basbøll, 1995); we remain agnostic about these issues here.

One further complication is due to contrastive stress, which may override the normal SNI destressing of the verb:

(3) A: K̥øbte Peter 'hus sidste år?
B: Nej, han '**solgte** 'hus sidste år.
A: 'Did Peter buy a house last year?'
B: 'No, he **sold** a house last year.'

In this example, the contrastive stress on *solgte* obscures the normal SNI destressing. As (3A) shows, the verb can be nonadjacent to its incorporated object; this is further discussed in the next section.

1.2.2 Syntax

There are three essential syntactic properties of SNI. First, in contrast to morphological incorporation, the incorporated element is a phrase, not a word. In particular, we argue that it is a special kind of unsaturated noun phrase (of the type *lite*; Abeillé and Godard 2000). Second, there is no adjacency requirement on the linearization of the verb and the incorporated phrase. Third, the incorporated object reduces the valence of the verb by saturating an argument position.

That the incorporated element is a phrase and not a word is supported by the fact that it can take adjectival modification and can be a conjunction:

(4) a. Min nabo [$_p$ k̥øbte 'nyt 'hus] sidste år.
My neighbour bought new house last year

b. Min nabo [$_p$ k̥øbte (både) 'hus og 'bil] sidste år.
My neighbour bought (both) house and car last year

However, the incorporated element cannot be a full noun phrase. In particular, it may not contain a specifier (article, numeral, or quantifier) or a relative clause (restrictive or nonrestrictive, extraposed or not):[2]

[2]The status of other postnominal modifiers and complements is not entirely clear, so we leave them aside here.

(5) a. * Min nabo [$_p$ købte et 'hus / hus.et / to hus.e / nogle hus.e] sidste år.
My neighbour bought a house / house.DEF / two house.PLU / some house.PLU last year

b. * Min nabo [$_p$ købte 'hus som kostede over en million] sidste år.
My neighbour bought house which cost over one million last year

c. * Min nabo [$_p$ købte 'hus] sidste år som kostede over en million.
My neighbour bought house last year which cost over one million

There are two qualifications to this characterization of incorporable noun phrases. Modification of plural nouns is usually better; this may be related to the fact that bare plurals are generally possible. Also, adjectival modification is only allowed insofar as it does not interfere with the pragmatic restriction on the institutionalized interpretation of the SNI construction (see section 1.2.4).

The second syntactic characteristic also sets SNI apart from morphological incorporation: adjacency of the verb and the incorporated element is neither necessary nor sufficient for SNI. Nonadjacency occurs in interrogative subject verb inversion (see example (3A) above) and when adverbials intervene between the verb and the incorporated element, as in the following example (Herslund, 1997, (10d)).

(6) Julie [$_p$ læser 'fandeme også 'altid 'amerikanske 'tegneserier].
Julie reads bloody also always American cartoons
'Julie always freakin' reads American cartoons.'

And, even when adjacency is respected, a noun carrying the definite suffix cannot be incorporated:

(7) * Min nabo [$_p$ købte 'huset] sidste år.
My neighbour bought house-DEF last year

Finally, the incorporated object saturates an argument slot of the verb, such that the result of incorporating an object cannot take another object argument:

(8) * Min nabo [$_p$ købte 'hus] villa sidste år.
My neighbour bought house-DEF villa last year

A transitive verb like *købte* is thus detransitivized and acts as an intransitive. This latter property holds for compounding, but not classificatory, morphological incorporation (Gerdts, 1998, 88–89).

1.2.3 Semantics

The basic characterization of the semantics of SNI, going back to Jespersen (1934), is that the resulting, complex predicate has "semantic and conceptual unity" (Nedergaard Thomsen, 1995, 151). The incorporated nominal also has a different (more restricted) semantics than an unincorporated object.

First, the incorporated nominal is interpreted as nonspecific in reference. As indicated by the data in (9), the incorporated element must take narrow scope with respect to the intensional verb.

(9) Min bror vil gerne [$_p$ købe 'hus].
My brother will PARTICLE buy house
='My brother wants to buy a house (any house).'
≠'There is a house that my brother wants to buy.'

Although, we do not equate specificity with wide scope, we do believe that the *consistent* narrow scope readings of incorporated objects indicate that they are nonspecific (see Van Geenhoven 1998 for this and related tests).[3]

1.2.4 Pragmatics

One commonly discussed pragmatic restriction on SNI is that the resulting predicate must denote an action that is "institutionalized" (Rischel, 1983). In other words, the denotation of the incorporated verb phrase must be an action or event which is conventionally associated with a certain structure or set of activities. A similar point is made by Mithun (1984, 848), with respect to morphological incorporation. Contrast (1a) above with (10) below.[4]

[3]However, conversational implicature may give rise to a specific reading in certain cases. This is exemplified in (1), where the question is normally taken as asking whether the addressee made his/her own bed.

(1) Har du [$_p$ redt 'seng]?
Have you made bed
'Did you bed-make?'

It is possible to think of situations where this implicature does not hold. For example, if (1) is part of a checklist for a practical exam for hospital orderlies, the question would only be asking whether the orderly made a bed, as per the exam requirements. There would be no implicature that it is the orderly's own bed.

[4]A reviewer provided examples (a) and (b) to show that similar pragmatic restrictions hold for bare nominal complements of prepositions in English; note the contrast

(10) # Min nabo [$_P$ købte 'blyant] igår.
My neighbour bought pencil yesterday

Furthermore, the incorporated object has different discourse anaphoric properties from an unincorporated object. First, the incorporated element cannot be anaphorically dependent on a preceding NP:

(11) Jeg [$_P$ skrev 'brev$_i$] til Pia og idag [$_P$ fik hun 'brev$_{*i/j}$].
I wrote letter to Pia and today got she letter

~'I wrote a letter to Pia and today she got (another) letter.'

This has not been observed in the literature on SNI, but has been noted for morphological incorporation in West Greenlandic (Bittner, 1994).

Second, incorporated noun phrases generally do not license discourse anaphora (i.e., no subsequent pronominal can be anaphorically dependent on the incorporated element). However, as illustrated in (12), there is lexical variation with regard to this.

(12) a. Vita [$_P$ købte 'hus$_i$] sidste år. Det$_i$ ligger i Hals.
Vita bought house$_i$ last year. It$_i$ lies in Hals.

~'Vita bought a house last year. It is in Hals.'

b. Rikke forsøgte [$_P$ at rede 'hår$_i$]. ?# Det$_i$ var helt filtret efter cykelturen.
Rikke tried to comb hair$_i$. It$_i$ was all tangled after bike.ride.DEF

~'Rikke tried to comb her hair. It was all tangled up after the bike ride.'

c. Mikkel [$_P$ holdt 'forelæsning$_i$]. # Den$_i$ var spændende.
Mikkel held lecture$_i$. It$_i$ was interesting.

We think this phenomenon is comparable to what we call inferential pronominalization, where there is no overt antecedent for the pronoun:

(13) a. Peter got married last July. She's an architect.

b. # Peter got adopted last July. She's an architect.

---

with (c):

(1) a. Mary stayed in bed. (usual activity, sleeping, etc.)

b. Mary stayed in the bed. (hiding during hide and seek)

c. Mary stayed in *(the) room.

Danish shows a similar contrast for prepositional complements, but we have not investigated these (or the English examples) and their relation to SNI systematically.

Similarly to the SNI cases in (12), the possibility of inferential pronominalization in the English examples above depends on lexical factors. Although we can reasonably infer a female participant in both marriage and adoption, only the first sentence is felicitous.

We conclude that syntactically incorporated nominals in Danish do not license discourse anaphora. This sets SNI apart from the kind of morphological incorporation found in West Greenlandic, where incorporated nominals do license discourse anaphors, as argued by Van Geenhoven (1998, 47–9).

In our HPSG analysis, we do not attempt to directly account for these discourse properties. We think that these phenomena are best handled in a dynamic semantic framework, perhaps along the lines of Van Geenhoven (1998). Note that the lack of discourse transparency in SNI is consistent with the impossibility of the incorporated element heading a relative clause, in which the relative pronoun is anaphorically dependent on the head of the relative clause.

1.3 Danish SNI in the Typology of Incorporation

As discussed throughout the previous section, Danish SNI shares a number of characteristics with type I incorporation (sample languages given below) in Mithun's (1984) typology:

1. The incorporated nominal is interpreted non-specifically.
2. The resulting predicate must denote an institutionalized activity.
3. Incorporated nominals do not have a determiner.
4. The incorporated nominal must be a patient, location or instrument argument of the incorporating verb.[5]

What sets Danish apart from other type I incorporating languages is the way the incorporation is expressed. The closest analog to SNI is "omposition by juxtaposition", which is found, for example, in certain Oceanic (e.g., Mokilese, Yapese, and Samoan) and Mayan (e.g., Mam, Kanjobal) languages (Mithun, 1984, 849–853). In this kind of incorporation construction the verb and the incorporated nominal are juxtaposed but remain phonologically separate units, whereas in Danish the verb and its incorporated nominal form a single phonological unit. Also, in certain cases modifiers to the verb or the noun may intervene between the verb and the incorporated nominal (see section 1.2.2).

[5]In Danish, only patients/themes can incorporate. For reasons of space, we have not discussed this specific property, but it holds in all the examples given and is further supported by the incorporation of arguments of unaccusatives in intransitive expletive sentences.

1.4 Formal Analysis

Following Abeillé and Godard (2000, 334), we use a multiple-inheritance type hierarchy to cross-classify the type *sign* for weight and phrasality.[6]

(14)

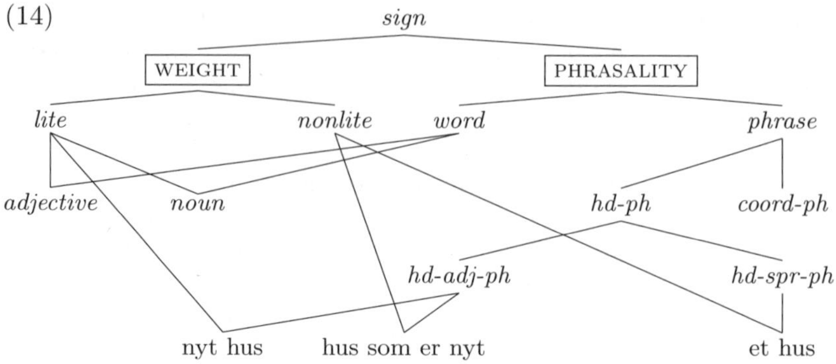

Adjectives and common nouns are specified as *lite* in the lexicon. Clausal postnominal modifiers are *nonlite*. Phrases of type *hd-adj-ph* and *coord-ph* inherit their weight values from their daughters in the following manner (adapted from Abeillé and Godard 2000, 333):

(15) a. $\begin{bmatrix} \textit{head-adjunct-phrase} \wedge \textit{lite} & \\ \text{HEAD-DAUGHTER} & \textit{lite} \\ \text{NON-HEAD-DAUGHTERS} & \langle [\textit{lite}] \rangle \end{bmatrix}$

b. $\begin{bmatrix} \textit{coordinated-phrase} \wedge \textit{lite} & \\ \text{NON-HEAD-DAUGHTERS} & \textit{list(lite)} \end{bmatrix}$

The constraints are stated in such a way that these phrases are *lite* if and only if all of their daughters are *lite*. In other words, conjoined noun phrases are *lite* iff both conjuncts are *lite*, and head-modifier phrases are *lite* iff the modifier is *lite* (the head noun is lexically specified as *lite*; see (14) above). Since relative clauses are *nonlite*, noun phrases containing a relative clause will never be *lite*. Together with the restriction that incorporated elements must be *lite*, introduced in (16) below, this accounts for the ban on relative clauses in SNI.

We use a description level lexical rule (DLLR) (Meurers, 1995, 1999) to state the lexical relationship between normal transitive verbs and SNI verbs. For readability, we further articulate the structure of the

[6]Abeillé and Godard (2000) introduce the term 'weight' to characterize a property of linguistic expressions (words and phrases) that influences both word order (e.g., *lite* elements must precede *nonlite* elements within a certain domain) and combinatorial syntax (e.g., a *lite* modifier may only combine with a *lite* head).

incorporated element—the value of RESULT|SS|LOC|CAT|COMPS—in (18) below.

(16)
$$\begin{bmatrix} \textit{sni-dllr} & \\ \text{RESULT} & \begin{bmatrix} \textit{sni-v-lxm} & \\ \text{PHON} & \begin{bmatrix} \textit{p-word} & \\ \text{SEGMENTS} & \boxed{6}\,\textit{nelist} \\ \text{LEXICAL-STRESS} & \begin{bmatrix} \textit{metrical-grid} & \\ \text{WORD-LEVEL} & \textit{elist} \\ \text{FOOT-LEVEL} & \boxed{4} \\ \text{SYL-LEVEL} & \boxed{5} \end{bmatrix} \end{bmatrix} \\ \text{SS} \mid \text{LOC} & \begin{bmatrix} \text{CAT} \mid \text{COMPS} & \left\langle \begin{bmatrix} \textit{noun} \wedge \textit{lite} \end{bmatrix}_{\boxed{2}}, \ldots \right\rangle \\ \text{CONT} & \boxed{3} \\ \text{CONX} \mid \text{BKGR} & \left\{ \begin{bmatrix} \textit{institutionalized-rel} & \\ \text{UNDERGOER} & \boxed{2} \end{bmatrix} \right\} \end{bmatrix} \end{bmatrix} \\ \text{SOURCE} & \begin{bmatrix} \textit{trans-v-lxm} & \\ \text{PHON} & \begin{bmatrix} \textit{p-word} & \\ \text{SEGMENTS} & \boxed{6}\,\textit{nelist} \\ \text{LEXICAL-STRESS} & \begin{bmatrix} \textit{metrical-grid} & \\ \text{WORD-LEVEL} & \textit{nelist} \\ \text{FOOT-LEVEL} & \boxed{4} \\ \text{SYL-LEVEL} & \boxed{5} \end{bmatrix} \end{bmatrix} \\ \text{SS} \mid \text{LOC} & \begin{bmatrix} \text{CAT} \mid \text{COMPS} & \left\langle \text{NP}_{\boxed{2}}, \ldots \right\rangle \\ \text{CONT} & \boxed{3} \end{bmatrix} \end{bmatrix} \end{bmatrix}$$

This captures three of the SNI facts lexically, but before discussing these we have to explain our extensions to the PHONOLOGY feature. Following the string-based approach of Bird and Klein (1994, 62) and Monachesi (1999, 72), we assume the partition for *phon* to be:

(17) $\textit{phon} \rightarrow \textit{utterance} \vee \textit{p-phrase} \vee \textit{p-word} \vee \textit{foot} \vee \textit{syl(lable)} \vee \textit{segment}$

One of the features appropriate for *phon* is SEGMENTS, with the value *list(segments)*. The SEGMENTS value of a *syllable* is a list of *segment* objects representing the segments that make up the syllable being modelled. Similarly, the SEGMENTS value of a *foot* is a list of *segment* objects representing the segments that make up the foot in question. To ensure that the linear order of SEGMENTS is preserved when building larger phonological constituents out of smaller ones, we use the list append operator, ⊕, such that the SEGMENTS list of a *foot* is the append of the SEGMENTS lists of the *syllable* objects that make up that foot, and so on.

The feature LEXICAL-STRESS is declared for objects of type *p-word*. Its value is an object of type *metrical-grid*, which encodes stress placement up to the level of the phonological word, according to the grid representation proposed for metrical phonology (Liberman and Prince, 1977; Hayes, 1995). The value of each of the three features SYL-LEVEL, FOOT-LEVEL, and WORD-LEVEL is *list(syl)*. For each of these features, if a syllable is present on the feature's list value, it bears stress at that level. If a syllable is on the WORD-LEVEL list, it must also be on the FOOT-LEVEL list, and if it is on the FOOT-LEVEL list, it must be on the SYL-LEVEL list (cf. the 'Continuous Column Constraint' of Hayes 1995, 34). This can be formalized with a pair of implicational constraints.

We can now return to three SNI facts captured by (16). First, the stress reduction on the verb is indicated in the value of the feature LEXICAL-STRESS. Since the SNI verb is unstressed at the word level, the rule indicates that its WORD-LEVEL feature is an empty list. As indicated by coindexing the values in SOURCE and RESULT, the foot and syllable level stress remain the same (see Fischer-Jørgensen 1983).

Second, we introduce a new kind of relation, *institutionalized-rel*, to capture the pragmatic restrictions on SNI discussed above. Since the 'institutionalized reference' restriction never applies to the subject (i.e., the subject is free to vary), the restriction must be imposed only on the verb plus its incorporated, direct object. We achieve the required effect by coindexing the incorporated object with the UNDERGOER of the *institutionalized-rel*, which is in the BACKGROUND of the incorporating verb's CONTEXT. The pragmatic restriction can then apply such that the incorporated nominal must be participating in some kind of institutionalized activity, as required.

Third, the DLLR in (16) captures the special subcategorization requirements of incorporating verbs, namely that the incorporated nominal must be of type *lite*. Furthermore, we propose that nonspecific reference of the incorporated nominal arises as a consequence of the nominal being both *lite* and predicative, as illustrated in (18).

(18)
$$\begin{bmatrix} \textit{lite} \wedge \textit{noun} & \\ \text{CAT} & \begin{bmatrix}\text{HEAD} & \begin{bmatrix}\text{PRD} & + \end{bmatrix}\\ \text{SPR} & \langle [\,] \rangle\end{bmatrix} \\ \text{CONT} & \begin{bmatrix} \textit{content} & \\ \text{SPECIFIC} & - \\ \text{INDEX} & \textit{ref}\end{bmatrix}\end{bmatrix}$$

This move is supported by the ocurrence of *lite* predicative nouns in other syntactic configurations in Danish. For example, nominal complements of copulas and predicative nominals in resultative constructions are never specific in reference.

(19) a. Hun er lærer.
She is teacher.
'She is a teacher.'

b. Han blev valgt til president.
He was elected to president.
'He was elected president.'

It is important to note that using description level lexical rules in this manner will allow the standard linearization principles of Danish to apply. In particular, subject verb inversion in interrogatives and adverb placement will occur as usual (Hentze, 1996).

To account for the conditions on phonological phrasing, we propose a general mechanism for calculating phrasing in parallel with syntactic combination. Using the value of the SEGMENTS feature for individual words, we augment the combinatorial schemas to add phrasing information to the SEGMENTS value of phrasal categories. Crucially, words do not have phrasing information. We introduce the special boundary segments '[' and ']'. Although these will be on the SEGMENTS list, they are in effect the phonological representation of pauses, and are not phonemes. Prosodic bracketing will allow domain restrictions on certain phonological processes to be stated directly on the SEGMENTS list. Asudeh (1999) provides preliminary experimental evidence for one such process, namely lengthening of the final rhyme before a phonological phrasing boundary.

For purposes of illustration, consider the augmented *hd-comp-ph* schema in (20), based on Sag (1997).

(20)
$$\begin{bmatrix} \textit{hd-comp-ph} & \\ \text{PHON} \mid \text{SEGMENTS} & \langle\, [\, \rangle \oplus \boxed{1} \oplus \boxed{2} \oplus \ldots \oplus \boxed{n} \oplus \langle\,]\, \rangle \\ \text{COMPS} & \langle\rangle \\ \text{HD-DTR} & \begin{bmatrix} \text{PHON} \mid \text{SEGMENTS} & \boxed{1} \\ \text{COMPS} & \left\langle \boxed{3}, \ldots, \boxed{m} \right\rangle \end{bmatrix} \\ \text{NON-HD-DTRS} & \left\langle \begin{bmatrix} \text{PHON} \mid \text{SEGS} & \boxed{2} \\ \text{SYNSEM} & \boxed{3} \end{bmatrix}, \ldots, \begin{bmatrix} \text{PHON} \mid \text{SEGS} & \boxed{n} \\ \text{SYNSEM} & \boxed{m} \end{bmatrix} \right\rangle \end{bmatrix}$$

The effect of the segment concatenation operation, represented by the infixed $\oplus$ operator is illustrated in (21) below. Crucially, we assume that the various schemas differ in how they affect phonological phrasing. In particular, *hd-subj-ph*, *hd-spr-ph*, and *hd-comp-ph* introduce bracketing, whereas *hd-adj-ph* does not introduce bracketing:

(21) a.

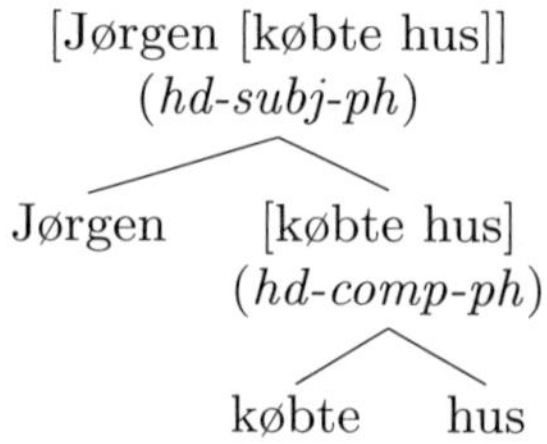

b.

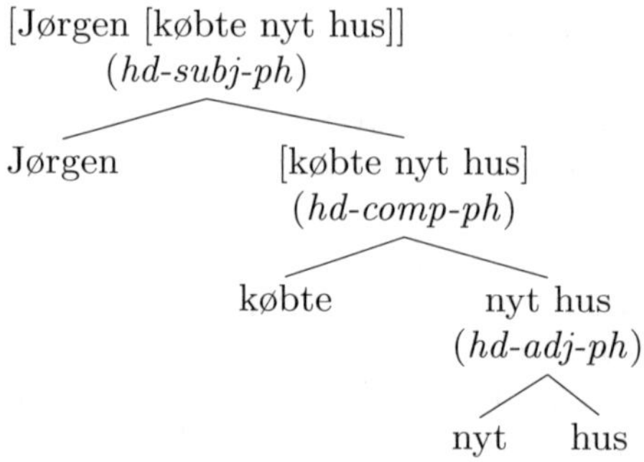

c.

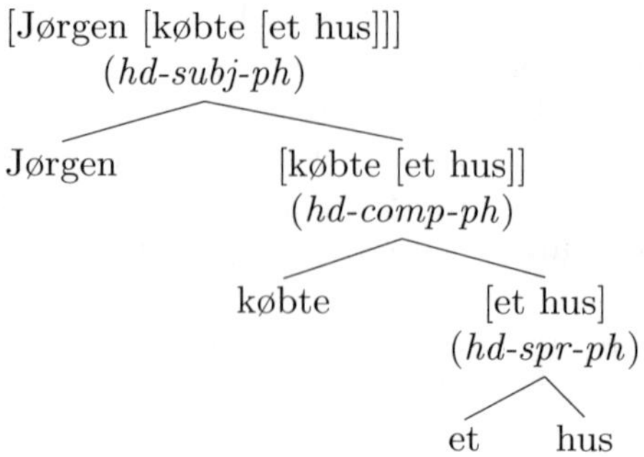

That phrasal types may affect phonological phrasing differently is a hypothesis that is motivated by the SNI data. Ultimately, we hope to find further, independent support for this hypothesis. One important factor that we have not said anything about is the effect of focus, and more generally information structure, on phonological phrasing.

1.5 Conclusion

In this paper, we have presented a formal treatment of grammatical interfaces using description level lexical rules in the lexicon and phonologically augmented constraints on phrasal types in the syntax. The empirical motivation for this analysis came from syntactic noun incorporation in Danish, but we believe the core ideas can be extended to other domains. Throughout, the lexicon and syntax have played a crucial role in tying together the restrictions on SNI in various grammatical domains. The analysis shows how Abeillé and Godard's *lite/nonlite* distinction is relevant for Danish and how cross-classification of types (Flickinger et al., 1985) is necessary to capture the correct restrictions on the nominal elements that may incorporate in Danish (i.e., the incorporated element can be a word or a phrase, as long as it is *lite*).

We have extended the HPSG treatment of phonology to deal with (word) stress and phrasing, though the relationship between the two remains an empirical question and we leave its investigation for future research. Our analysis shows how phonological phrasing can be built up in parallel with syntactic combination. This is in line with recent proposals by Steedman (2000), who argues for a syntax-prosody isomorphism, and Truckenbrodt (1999), who argues for a constraint-governed syntax-prosody mapping.

However, our parallel approach is distinct from both of these other approaches. Unlike Steedman, we do not posit that phonological phrasing is isomorphic to syntactic structure. Although we build up the two in parallel, using the standard combinatorics of HPSG, we allow for other constraints concerning information structure and postlexical accent placement to affect phrasing. The parallel approach is also different from Truckenbrodt's mapping approach, where syntax and phonology are built up independently and are then related in an Optimality Theory constraint interaction.

Our approach to the syntax-prosody interface is compatible with the core HPSG notion of parallelism in information encoding. The bracketing conventions introduced may also serve to state domain restrictions on phonological processes, such as assimilation, deletion, final lengthening, etc.

The representation we use for phonological phrasing has a number of properties that we summarize here. First, we use brackets, rather than boundary symbols, committing us to a constituency rather than boundary segment approach (Hayes, 1989). Second, we allow for recursive phonological structure, since phrasing is built up in parallel with the syntax, which is recursive (see the trees in (21) above). Since our brackets are unlabelled, this does not violate Strict Layering (Selkirk, 1984), which postulates that a phonological constituent cannot contain a phonological constituent of the same kind. We do not have 'kinds' of phonological constituents, so our representations satisfy this requirement vacuously, despite being recursive.

Acknowledgments

We would like to thank Mike Calcagno, Edward Flemming, Paul Kiparsky, Paula Monachesi, Chris Potts, Geoff Pullum, Ivan Sag, Ida Toivonen, two anonymous reviewers, and audiences at Stanford, HPSG-99, and the University of Ottawa for their comments. None of these people should be held responsible for any remaining errors. Asudeh's work is partially funded by SSHRC Doctoral Fellowship 752-98-0424.

References

Abeillé, A. and D. Godard. 2000. French word order and lexical weight. In R. D. Borsley, ed., *The Nature and Function of Syntactic Categories*, pages 325–360. New York: Academic Press.

Asudeh, A. 1999. Intonation as a disambiguation strategy in Danish. Ms., Stanford Linguistics Department.

Basbøll, H. 1995. Degrees of stress in Modern Danish: Primary, secondary and tertiary. In Rischel and Basbøll (1995), pages 21–47.

Bird, S. and E. Klein. 1994. Phonological analysis in typed feature systems. *Computational Linguistics* 20:55–90.

Bittner, M. 1994. *Case, Scope and Binding*. Dordrecht: Kluwer.

Fischer-Jørgensen, E. 1983. The acoustic manifestation of stress in Danish with particular reference to the reduction of stress in compounds. In M. van den Brocke, V. van Heuven, and W. Zonneveld, eds., *Sound Structures. Studies for Antonie Cohen*, pages 81–104. Dordrecht: Foris.

Flickinger, D., C. Pollard, and T. Wasow. 1985. Structure-sharing in lexical representation. In *Proceedings of the 23rd Annual Meeting of the Association for Computational Linguistics*.

Gerdts, D. B. 1998. Incorporation. In A. Spencer and A. Zwicky, eds., *The Handbook of Morphology*, pages 84–100. Oxford: Blackwell.

Hayes, B. 1989. The prosodic hierarchy in meter. In P. Kiparsky and G. Youmans, eds., *Rhythm and Meter*, vol. 1 of *Phonetics and Phonology*. New York: Academic Press.

Hayes, B. 1995. *Metrical Stress Theory: Principles and Case Studies*. Chicago: University of Chicago Press.

Hentze, R. 1996. *Unit Accentuation in a Topological Grammar of Danish: A Constraint-Based Approach*. Master's thesis, University of Copenhagen.

Herslund, M. 1997. The object relation and the notion of incorporation. In L. Schøsler and S. Kirchmeier-Andersen, eds., *Studies in Valency II: The Pronominal Approach Applied to Danish*. Odense: Odense University Press.

Jespersen, O. 1934. *Modermaalets fonetik*. Copenhagen: Nordisk Forlag. Reprinted 1949.

Liberman, M. and A. Prince. 1977. On stress and linguistic rhythm. *Linguistic Inquiry* 8:249–336.

Meurers, W. D. 1995. Towards a semantics for lexical rules as used in HPSG. Revised version of the paper presented at the Conference on Formal Grammar, 1995, Barcelona.

Meurers, W. D. 1999. *Lexical Generalizations in the Syntax of German Non-Finite Constructions*. Ph.D. thesis, Seminar für Sprachwissenschaft, Universität Tübingen, Tübingen, Germany. Volume 145 in Arbeitspapiere des SFB 340.

Mithun, M. 1984. The evolution of noun incorporation. *Language* 60:847–894.

Monachesi, P. 1999. *A Lexical Approach to Italian Cliticization*. Stanford, CA: CSLI Publications.

Nedergaard Thomsen, O. 1992. Unit accentuation as an expression device for predicate formation. The case of syntactic noun incorporation in Danish. In M. Fortescue, P. Harder, and L. Kristoffersen, eds., *Layered Structure and Reference in a Functional Perspective*, pages 173–229. Amsterdam: John Benjamins.

Nedergaard Thomsen, O. 1995. Discourse, grammar, and prosody in a corpus of spoken Danish — a functional pragmatic account. In Rischel and Basbøll (1995), pages 129–213.

Rischel, J. 1983. On unit accentuation in Danish – and the distinction between deep and surface phonology. *Folia Linguistica* 17:51–97.

Rischel, J. and H. Basbøll, eds. 1995. *Aspects of Danish Prosody*. Odense: Odense University Press.

Sag, I. A. 1997. English relative clause constructions. *Journal of Linguistics* 33:431 – 483.

Selkirk, E. 1984. *Phonology and Syntax*. Cambridge, MA: MIT Press.

Steedman, M. 2000. Information structure and the syntax-phonology interface. *Linguistic Inquiry* 31(4).

Truckenbrodt, H. 1999. On the relation between syntactic phrases and phonological phrases. *Linguistic Inquiry* 30(2):219–255.

Van Geenhoven, V. 1998. *Semantic Incorporation and Indefinite Descriptions: Semantic and Syntactic Aspects of Noun Incorporation in West Greenlandic*. Stanford, CA: CSLI Publications.

2

Incorporating Contracted Auxiliaries in English

EMILY M. BENDER AND IVAN A. SAG

2.1 Introduction

Spencer (1991) and Sadler (1997) argue that there are two different phenomena that have been grouped together as 'contracted auxiliaries'. On the one hand are the SYLLABIC reduced auxiliaries that are unselective in what they attach to. On the other hand, there are NONSYLLABIC reduced auxiliaries that exhibit lexical idiosyncrasy, stem allomorphy, and word-internal phonological processes. Sadler (1997:1–2) illustrates the two classes with data like those in (1)–(2):[1]

(1) a. The tree'd */d/, /əd/ been burnt.
  b. Bo's flu'll */l/, /əl/ be gone by tomorrow.
  c. The kid who is laughing'll */l/, /əl/ open the jar.
  d. You and I've */v/, /əv/ tried to help her.

(2) a. He'd /d/, */əd/ been waiting for you.
  b. You'll /l/, */əl/ be able to go home at two o'clock.
  c. I'll /l/, */əl/ be leaving tomorrow.
  d. I've /v/, */əv/ taken several tables.

Spencer and Sadler both propose to treat the syllabic reduced auxiliaries (1) as clitics. Their proposal regarding the nonsyllabic reduced auxiliaries (2), on the other hand, is to treat them as affixes attached to the prior pronominal. Sadler also claims that the syllabic forms are not

[1]Judgments of ungrammaticality reported in this paper are based on intuitions about 'normal' rate speech. In fast speech, some of the examples we starred may well occur. However, we believe that the intuitive contrasts still stand, if only in slower speech, and therefore must be accounted for.

Grammatical Interfaces in HPSG.
Ronnie Cann, Claire Grover and Philip Miller.

available with non-coordinated pronoun subjects, so that in sentences like (2) only the nonsyllabic pronunciation is available.

Thus the syllabic auxiliaries in Sadler's proposal are treated in a standard fashion—in terms of normal auxiliary verbs in the syntax, subject to a post-lexical prosodic process. For the affix-type auxiliaries, however, Sadler presents an analysis in terms of tense marking on the subject pronouns. Barron (1998) independently proposed essentially the same analysis for *have* contraction, in order to show how a lexicalist, movement-free analysis could account for facts that have been argued (Radford 1988) to motivate verb movement. For now, we will concentrate on Sadler's analysis, but we will return to Barron's analysis and the facts Radford cites below.

Taking advantage of the device of inside-out equations in LFG, Sadler writes lexical entries for these words as illustrated in (3) (1997:8):

(3) you'll: D
$(\uparrow \text{PRED}) = \text{`PRO'}$
$(\uparrow \text{PERS}) = 2$
$((\text{SUBJ} \uparrow)\ \text{TENSE}) = \text{FUT}$

The effect of the last equation in (3a) is that when the form *you'll* is used, it carries the information that the superordinate functional structure whose subject requirement it fulfills has the TENSE value FUT (future). This can be seen in the f-structure in (4b). The c-structure is shown in (4a). In this structure, the IP is exocentric. The LFG principle of economy of expression states that all c-structure nodes are optional and are not used unless required for expressivity or completeness. As there is no lexical item I, there is no position I.

(4) a.

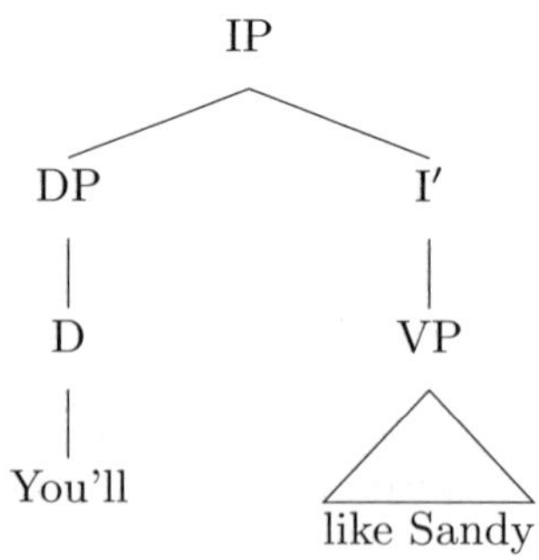

b.

$$\begin{bmatrix} \text{PRED} & \text{`like}\langle\ (\text{SUBJ})\ (\text{OBJ})\ \rangle\text{'} \\ \text{TENSE} & \text{future} \\ \text{OBJ} & \begin{bmatrix}\text{`Sandy'}\end{bmatrix} \\ \text{SUBJ} & \begin{bmatrix} \text{PRED} & \text{`PRO'} \\ \text{PERS} & 2 \end{bmatrix} \end{bmatrix}$$

Sadler, following Spencer, cites various kinds of evidence that the combinations involving the nonsyllabic forms of the auxiliary, e.g., *you'll*, *we'll*, *you've*, *I'm*, *he'll* etc., are a morphological unit, rather than the result of a post-lexical cliticization. The arguments are sketched in (5).

(5) a. The nonsyllabic auxiliary is highly selective about its 'host', attaching only to noncoordinate pronominal subjects.

b. The stem forms exhibit variation that is not predictable on purely phonological grounds, e.g.:

1. we'll: /wɪl/ for /wiːl/,
2. you've: /yʊv/ for /yuːv/,
3. you're: /yəɹ/, /yɔɹ/ for /yuːɹ/,
4. we're: /wəɹ/ for /wiɹ/,
5. they've: /ðɪv/ for /ðeⁱv/,
6. they're: /ðɛɹ/ for /ðeyɹ/,
7. I'm: /am/ for /aⁱm/

c. the nonsyllabic auxiliary fails to take scope over a coordinate subject.

Moreover, Sadler argues that this analysis interacts with the LFG theory of blocking presented by Andrews (1990) to predict the ungrammaticality of the starred forms in (2). According to this theory, since the word *you'll* contains more information (about tense) than the word *you*, structures involving *you'll* will block otherwise equivalent structures involving *you* plus /əl/.

Note first of all that the kind of analysis proposed by Sadler and Barron could be directly incorporated within an HPSG grammar. All that would be required is the supposition of an unheaded clausal construction type similar to those familiar in the GPSG/HPSG literature (for example the one examined by Bender (2001, pp. 95–101)). Thus at the level of HPSG theory, little is at stake in the grammar of English auxiliary contraction. In this paper, however, we propose to replace the Sadler/Barron kind of analysis with a head-driven alternative in which the contracted forms are auxiliaries that have incorporated the subject pronouns. Our approach builds on Sadler and Barron's insight that these forms are best treated as single lexical items, but, as we will argue, it seems to provide a superior account of the relevant English data, once we consider functions of auxiliaries other than tense marking.

2.2 A Broader Perspective on the Data

Before presenting our analysis, we first consider the contraction data in a larger context. Spencer and Sadler present a picture in which the distinction between syllabic and nonsyllabic auxiliaries lines up with the distinction between lexicalized affixes and clitics. However, there are two ways in which things are actually more complicated. The first has to do with /z/ contraction, that is, the contraction of *is* and *has*. Most speakers allow the non-syllabic form with hosts other than subject pronouns (Pullum and Zwicky 1997):

(6) The sky over California's /z/ always blue.

Further, Pullum and Zwicky also find that there is massive variation across speakers with respect to when each auxiliary can contract all the way to its nonsyllabic form.

We take the interesting distinction within the class of contracted auxiliaries to be not syllabicity, but rather the possibility of a specific phonological rule, viz., the rule of laxing of tensed vowels that applies only to the vowels of pronouns in combination with contracted auxiliaries.[2] Thus while we can get the nonsyllabic forms /z/ and /v/ in both the a and b examples of (7) and (8), only the a examples allow laxing of the vowel.[3]

(7) a. What do you mean he's /hi:z/, /hɪz/ already here?
    b. What do you mean B's /bi:z/, */bɪz/ a good grade?

(8) a. I've /a^{i}v/, /av/ already tried to help.
    b. You and I've /a^{i}v/, */av/ already tried to help.

This distinction provides evidence for a lexical treatment of pronoun plus contracted auxiliary combinations, but not for all nonsyllabic contracted auxiliaries.[4]

A second problem with the way Sadler and Spencer present the data has to do with the issue of preemption. As observed throughout a hundred-year old tradition that begins with Sweet (1890) and includes Selkirk (1984), Zwicky, Pullum and others, reduced auxiliary forms do not preempt less reduced forms. Within this tradition, all of the variants in (9) and (10) are presumed to be alternate ways of saying the same thing.

(9) a. They are /ðe^{i} aɹ/ willing to go.
    b. They're /ðeyəɹ/ willing to go.

[2]Given the many kinds of fast speech reductions that are available in English, it is conceivable that a purely phonological treatment could be developed, even for forms like /ðɛɹ/ and /yʊv/. We are not aware of any such proposal, however, and accept Sadler and Simpson's conclusion that such forms are lexicalized.

[3]Note that the contrast involving the pronoun *I* is only interesting in dialects (like ours) that don't generally allow the pronunciation /a/ for this pronoun.

[4]The distribution of nonsyllabic forms beyond those that occur with pronouns is an interesting question. See Pullum and Zwicky 1997 for discussion.

c. They're /ðeⁱɹ/ willing to go.
d. They're /ðɛɹ/ willing to go.

(10) a. They will /ðeⁱ wɪl/ do that.
b. They'll /ðeyəl/ do that.
c. They'll /ðeⁱl/ do that.
d. They'll /ðɛl/ do that.

Sadler and Barron both claim that preemption of syllabic contracted forms such as (9b) and (10b) is a consequence of their analyses. However, it does not follow directly from the inflected-pronoun analysis alone, only from that analysis combined with a theory of blocking. What is required is a system that accounts for the distribution of the non-syllabic forms without necessarily blocking the syllabic forms in the same contexts. For varieties that do have such blocking, a separate mechanism is required. Further, it is not clear how /ðɛl/ could block /ðeyəl/ without also blocking /ðeⁱ wɪl/, as the three variants all have the same semantic content. Thus preemption is neither a desirable feature nor a necessary consequence of the inflected pronoun analysis.

In the following sections, we discuss an alternative to Sadler and Barron's analysis, and argue that it is better suited to the English data.

2.3 Analysis

As noted in the introduction, the kind of analysis suggested by Barron and by Sadler could be directly incorporated into an HPSG grammar of English with no consequences for any of the principles that are fundamental to HPSG's theory of headed constructions, i.e. the Valence Principle and the Head Feature Principle. Moreover HPSG's locality result, i.e. the locality of selection, head-marking agreement, role assignment and case assignment that is a consequence of current HPSG valence theory, would also remain unaffected by the supposition of a headless Sadler-Barron construction.

Consider the examples in (11), where a finite clause would have to consist of a tensed subject and a nonverbal element.

(11) a. [They're [happy]].
b. [I'm [all ears]].
c. [You're [in the way]].

If these finite clauses were verbless, then a zero copula construction would allow a tensed S to be built from a 'tensed' subject and just those elements that are ordinarily selected by the lexeme *be*. But in our view, any analysis formulated along these lines (whether it is cast in HPSG, in LFG or in some other framework) will lead to unnecessary redundancy.

We argue that the lexical idiosyncrasy of nonsyllabic contracted auxiliaries can be accommodated in a way that is entirely consistent with the notion of 'headed construction' in current HPSG theory.

Rather than seeing the auxiliary as a tense affix on the pronoun, we propose to treat the pronoun as an incorporated subject of the auxiliary verb. That is, we posit lexical entries like (13) for *they're* as it occurs in (12):

(12) They're at school.

(13)
$$\begin{bmatrix} \textit{word} & \\ \text{PHON} & /\text{ðɛɹ}/ \\ \text{SYNSEM} & \begin{bmatrix}\text{LOCAL} & \begin{bmatrix}\text{CAT} & \begin{bmatrix}\text{HEAD} & \begin{bmatrix}\textit{verb} & \\ \text{VFORM} & \textit{finite}\end{bmatrix}\\ \text{VAL} & \begin{bmatrix}\text{SUBJ} & \langle\ \rangle \\ \text{COMPS} & \langle\boxed{1}\rangle\end{bmatrix}\end{bmatrix}\end{bmatrix}\end{bmatrix} \\ \text{ARG-ST} & \left\langle \boxed{3}\text{NP}[\textit{3pl}],\ \boxed{1}\begin{bmatrix}\text{PRED} & + \\ \text{SUBJ} & \langle\boxed{3}\rangle\end{bmatrix}\right\rangle \end{bmatrix}$$

The word shown in (13) has two arguments, but it has an empty SUBJ list (we'll come back to this) and a singleton COMPS list—i.e., it is looking to combine with just a predicative complement. It will do this via a head-complement construction, which in this case (as in the case of case-marking prepositions—see Pollard and Sag (1994), ch. 9) builds a saturated phrase (i.e., a saturated clause).[5]

The class of lexical entries that our analysis requires is small, but perhaps the regularity is worthy of a Lexical Rule. The Pronoun Incorporation Lexical Rule presented here takes two lexical entries as input, and provides as output a third entry that combines information from

[5] As Bob Levine points out to us, this kind of lexical entry might also be useful in dealing with the well-known agreement puzzle illustrated in (i)-(ii):

(i) *There is (believed to be) five people in the elevator.

(ii) There's (believed to be) five people in the elevator.

That is, if *there's* is an independent lexical item, it can simply not require the normal number agreement that follows in (i) from the lexical properties of *is*.

both inputs.[6,7]

(14) Pronoun Incorporation LR:

$$\left\langle \begin{bmatrix} \textit{word} & \\ \text{PHON} & \langle \boxed{1} \rangle \\ \text{SS}|\text{LOC} & \boxed{3}\,\textit{pr-local} \end{bmatrix}, \begin{bmatrix} \textit{word} & \\ \text{PHON} & \langle \boxed{2} \rangle \\ \text{HEAD} & \boxed{4}\begin{bmatrix} \textit{verb} & \\ \text{AUX} & + \\ \text{VFORM} & \textit{fin} \end{bmatrix} \\ \text{ARG-ST} & \boxed{5} \end{bmatrix} \right\rangle \Longrightarrow$$

$$\begin{bmatrix} \text{PHON} & \text{F}_{PI}(\boxed{1},\boxed{2}) \\ \text{SUBJ} & \langle\ \rangle \\ \text{HEAD} & \boxed{4} \\ \text{ARG-ST} & \boxed{5}\left\langle \begin{bmatrix} \textit{aff} & \\ \text{LOC} & \boxed{3} \end{bmatrix}, \ldots \right\rangle \end{bmatrix}$$

The LR output describes an auxiliary verb whose SUBJ list is empty, and whose phonological form is determined from the phonological forms of the inputs according to the multi-valued function sketched in (15).

(15)

ϕ_1	ϕ_2	$F_{PI}(\phi_1,\phi_2)$
wiː	wɪl	wɪl
wiː	aɹ	wəɹ
yuː	hæv	yʊv
yuː	aɹ	yəɹ, yɔɹ
ðe^{i}	hæv	ðɪv
ðe^{i}	aɹ	ðɛɹ
a^{i}	æm	am

Finally, this function is simply undefined for any auxiliary verb form lacking a nonsyllabic (or idiosyncratic nonsyllabic) reduced form.

We have represented the phonological facts in terms of a function, but other analyses are compatible with the syntactic aspects of our analysis (viz., the SUBJ, HEAD, and ARG-ST values). In particular, one might consider positing a phonological rule of vowel laxing which applies to this class of words.

In the LR in (14), the first argument of the output has its LOCAL value determined by the pronominal input (*pr-loc* is the type of LOCAL

[6]We thank Arnold Zwicky for suggestions that led us to this analysis.

[7]In order to translate this lexical rule into a purely type-based analysis, some way must be found to have derivational types make reference to two types at the same time.

value assigned to pronominals by Abeillé et al. (1999)), yet that argument is also specified as *aff*, which is a subtype of *noncan(onical)* (in the sense of Miller and Sag (1997)). In this analysis, the incorporated subject is similar to so-called 'clitic' pronouns in French, which Miller and Sag have argued are, in fact, affixal. On our approach, the first argument of the LR output is prevented from appearing on the output's COMPS list by the fact that it is *noncan*. This effect is achieved because the Argument Realization Principle (shown in (16)) allows for *noncan* arguments that appear on the ARG-ST but not the COMPS list, and the SYNSEM values of all signs must be *canon(ical)* (as ensured by (17)):

(16) Argument Realization Principle:

$$\textit{word} \;\Rightarrow\; \begin{bmatrix} \text{SUBJ} & \boxed{1} \\ \text{COMPS} & \boxed{2} \ominus \text{list}(\textit{noncan}) \\ \text{ARG-ST} & \boxed{1} \oplus \boxed{2} \end{bmatrix}$$

(17) Principle of Canonicality:

$$\textit{sign} \;\Rightarrow\; \begin{bmatrix} \text{SYNSEM} & \textit{canon} \end{bmatrix}$$

If we said nothing more, the ARP would allow arguments to be freely instantiated as *aff* as they may be freely instantiated as *gap*, another subtype of *noncan*. One way to avoid this undesirable consequence (free incorporation of any argument) is to posit the subhierarchy in (18), and constrain the argument structures of lexemes as in (19).

(18)

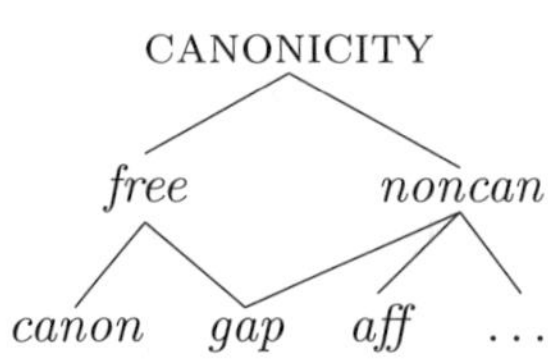

(19) $\textit{lexeme} \Rightarrow \begin{bmatrix} \text{ARG-ST} & / \text{ list}(\textit{free}) \end{bmatrix}$

Thus all of the *synsems* on a lexeme's argument structure are specified to be *free* (*gap* or *canon*) by default. Only when this default is specifically overridden, as in the lexical rule's specifying the first element as *aff*, can they be of another type.[8]

[8]The '...' under *noncan* in (18) signify that there may be other types of non-

The motivation for these concerns about ARGUMENT-STRUCTURE is binding theory. Since the pronominal inputs to the LR all bear agreement information, the first element on the argument structure will also bear this information. This allows binding theory violations like (20) to be ruled out in a systematic fashion.

(20) *I've seen yourself.

If the incorporated subject did not appear on the ARG-ST list, then the analysis would make the wrong predictions about the binding facts.

There are other properties of these auxiliaries that are of interest, for example, their limited participation in Verb Phrase Ellipsis:

(21) a.*They're not tall, but I'm.
b. They're tall, but I'm not.

The same pattern appears with the non-lexicalized contracted auxiliaries (22) and the silent copula in African American Vernacular English (AAVE) (23) (Bender 2001).

(22) a.*Kim isn't coming, but the student I met's.
b. Kim's coming, but the student I met's not.

(23) a.*The say he('s) wild and he ϕ.
b. They say they're best friends and shit but they not.

Bender's account of the AAVE facts involves a constraint on the COMPS value of the silent auxiliary which entails that its complements can be elided only if some complement is canonically expressed. Given our account of contracted forms like *I'm* as verbal, and therefore as selecting their complements, this account can be extended to the lexicalized (as well as non-lexicalized) contracted auxiliary forms.

2.4 Comparison

2.4.1 Similarities

Our account makes many of the same predictions as Sadler's:

- The restricted distribution of idiosyncratic nonsyllabic reduced auxiliaries is accounted for.
- Only the non-idiosyncratic reduced auxiliary occurs with a coordinate subject (this is the phonologically reduced form of the

canonical synsems. In particular, *PRO*, the type assigned to controlled subjects may be of type *noncan* (but not *free*) in English. In a general pro-drop language, *PRO* would be *noncan* and *free*.

auxiliary without incorporation). On our analysis, this is because such forms as (24) would involve the coordination of a noun (*you*) and a verb (*I've*), which is generally disallowed in coordination.

(24)*You and I've /av/ already tried to help Kim.

Our account also makes the same predictions as Barron's with respect to Radford's (1988) putative argument in favor of traces. In brief, Radford's argument runs as follows: *Have* can reduce to /v/ attached to a preceding pronoun as in (25).[9]

(25) You've /yu:v/ won.

However, in cases like (26b) *have* contraction is blocked, presumably because it cannot apply across the gap left by the gapping of *could.*[10]

(26) a. I could have been playing tennis, and *you could have* been playing football.
b. = I could have been playing tennis, and *you* ϕ *have* been playing football.
c. ≠ I could have been playing tennis, and *you've* been playing football.

Similarly, contraction is not possible when the pronoun and *have* have been brought together by inversion:[11]

(27) Would *you have*/**you've* wanted to come with me?

Radford argues that this shows that there is also some empty element between *you* and *have* in (27), presumably the trace left by verb movement. Our account of these facts is essentially the same as Barron's: the contracted form involves finite *have*, and in both (26b) and (27) *have* is non-finite.

Sadler and Barron cite preemption (e.g., blocking of the syllabic form as in (2)) as a further prediction of their analyses. As noted above, this is not in fact a desirable consequence. However, preemption follows not

[9]In fact, this applies only to vowel-final pronouns, as Radford and Barron note.
[10]Examples from Radford 1988:408.
[11]Example from Barron 1998:224.

from the specific analysis of lexical items such as *you've*, but from a theory of blocking that allows such items to preempt phrasal counterparts. That is, the theory of blocking would work in exactly the same way with the lexical entries that we have posited. Thus, rather than differentiating between the two types of lexicalist analysis, this issue poses a problem for Andrews's (1990) theory of blocking (which is criticized on entirely independent grounds by Blevins (1995)).

2.4.2 Differences

We have seen that our analysis makes much the same predictions as Sadler's or Barron's for the data that they consider. The primary difference between the two analyses lies in which element is the head of the sentence. Under the inflected-pronoun analysis, the tense inflection is treated as a morpheme attaching to a noun that does not head the sentence, though the inflection contributes to the outermost level of the sentence's f-structure projection. Under our subject-incorporation analysis (which also rejects the morpheme-based view of morphology assumed by Barron and Sadler), the fused lexical element is a verb that heads its clause. In this section, we will argue that that is the preferable state of affairs for English because English auxiliaries (contracted and non-contracted) are more than just tense/aspect markers.

First we should note that Barron briefly considers the issue of which node in the c-structure the inflected pronouns belong to. She argues that placing them in I would be "tantamount to claiming that this phenomenon of Standard English is an instance of pro-drop" and that "the inflected pronoun and the VP can be interrupted by conventional IP adverbials, such as *probably*, etc." (1998:240) First, no argument is offered for why this phenomenon should not be identified with pro-drop in other languages. Secondly, if *probably* can occur after contracted *have*, it can also appear after full-form *have*, and so has no bearing on the issue.

(28) a. I've probably seen it.
 b. I have probably seen it.

Turning now to the syntactic functions of English auxiliaries, the first piece of evidence for subject incorporation comes from the morphological dependency between auxiliaries and their complement VPs. For example, as is well known, *have* cooccurs with past participles and *will* with base form verbs. The same is true of the contracted forms /v/ and /l/.

(29) a. You have/you've been there.
 b.*You have/you've be there.
 c. You will/you'll go there.

d.*You will/you'll gone there.

That is, in addition to providing tense/aspect information, /v/ and /l/, like *have* and *will*, select complements with a particular morphological form.

Contraction of *be* presents an even more interesting case. *Be*, including contracted forms, can appear in at least the following valence patterns:

(30) a. **As a raising verb with a predicative complement:**
They're doctors/in a meeting/busy all the time.
They're likely to be available.

b. **In existentials of various types:**
There's a unicorn in the garden.
There's no such thing as unicorns.
There're two good reasons to believe that.

c. **In identity sentences:**
You're the one who painted the barn.

d. **In *it*-clefts:**
It's Kim that Sandy saw eat the cake.

e. **In various collocations and idiomatic constructions:**
It's because they refused to do it.
It's just that things won't be the same.

Two things can be concluded from this evidence: First, given that any valence pattern of *be* that can have a pronoun subject is possible with contracted *be*, this regularity should be captured somehow within an adequate grammar.[12] Our lexical rule, which creates incorporated verb forms by fusing pronouns to verb forms, appears to be more natural from the perspective of English grammar, which has a whole class of lexical rules that map auxiliary verbs into other, somewhat modified, auxiliary verbs. The Barron/Sadler alternative would appear to require a lexical rule that creates nominal affixes from inflected verb forms, a type of rule which is otherwise unparalleled in English grammar. Such observations are at best suggestive, however, as both lexical rules are technically feasible.

Second, we conclude that auxiliaries in English serve syntactic functions beyond tense marking. They impose morphological constraints on

[12]Note that even expletive-selecting uses of *be* exhibit irregular forms, e.g., (i).

(i) There're (/ðɛːɹ/) five reasons to be suspicious.

the main verb and in certain cases (notably, the verb *be*) license a range of valence patterns, including patterns with multiple complements.

In HPSG, these properties motivate the treatment of auxiliaries as the head of the sentence. In LFG the notion of head is relativized to the different levels of structure recognized within the framework. At c-structure, the head (if there is one) of a constituent is the element that determines the category of the constituent, according to X-bar theory. At f-structure, the head is the element that contributes the PRED value. The equations that relate c-structures to f-structures generally put the heads in correspondence, but exceptions are possible (e.g., in the case of exocentric c-structure constituents).

The additional level of m-structure proposed by Butt et al. (1996) provides a way of representing morphological dependencies that is independent of other aspects of head-dependent structure. This opens up the possibility that certain elements may place morphological restrictions on other words in the sentence but otherwise show no head-like properties. In fact, this is precisely what Butt et al. claim to be the case for auxiliaries in English, French and German. Their analysis implies a c-structure rule such as the following:

(31) $$\begin{array}{llll} \text{VP} & \rightarrow & \text{AUX} & \text{VP} \\ & & \uparrow=\downarrow & \uparrow=\downarrow \\ & & \mu\ \text{M}^* = \mu\ * & (\mu\ \text{M}^*\ \text{DEP}) = \mu\ * \end{array}$$

The first line of equations establishes that the mother and both daughters correspond to the same f-structure. The second establishes that the mother and the AUX daughter correspond to the same m-structure, in which the m-structure corresponding to the VP daughter is the value of the feature DEP(endent). The auxiliaries are lexically specified so as to contribute TENSE information to f-structure and to select for dependents of the appropriate form in m-structure. Thus, if English auxiliaries only provide tense information and a morphological dependency, there is no requirement that they be c- or f-structure heads.

However, as argued above, auxiliaries do not only impose morphological dependencies on their arguments. In certain cases (existentials, identity sentences, etc.) it is clear that they license the occurrence of those arguments. In LFG terms, this means that the arguments of the auxiliary bear grammatical functions. But grammatical functions can only be licensed by a PRED value. Therefore, auxiliaries, contracted or otherwise, must be able to contribute PRED values, i.e., they must be able to head f-structures.

Now, following the way that Sadler and Barron use Nordlinger's

(1998) Principle of Morphological Composition to enable tense inflection to contribute information to the higher f-structure, one could in principle do the same thing with PRED information. For example, the suffix /z/ on *there's* could have an entry like this:

(32) ((SUBJ ↑) TENSE) = PRES
((SUBJ ↑) PRED) = 'be⟨ XCOMP ⟩(SUBJ)(OBJ)'
(↑FORM) = there
...

Thus it is technically feasible to account for all of the head properties of contracted auxiliaries without assigning them to a head position in c-structure. In the absence of a precise proposal, however, this possible alternative is difficult to evaluate.

2.5 Conclusion

It is not surprising that the idiosyncrasy of the finite auxiliaries *have* and *be* can be handled in more than one way in HPSG. Much the same is true of other frameworks. Indeed the subject-incorporation analysis put forth here could also, as far as we can see, be directly expressed in LFG.

Work in LFG is exploring various hypotheses about headedness, many of which embody a relaxed notion of locality. For example, there is nothing in current LFG theory that prevents one from positing the existence of a lexical item that selects for functional information at a particular arbitrary depth (e.g., verbs specified as in (33)).

(33) a. (↑XCOMP COMP FORM) = fin
b. (↑COMP COMP OBJ CASE) = acc
...

Work in HPSG, on the other hand, has pursued a uniform cross-linguistic conception of valence which, because only *synsem* objects of dependents can be selected, excludes the possibility of such lexical entries. Indeed, the uniform behavior of selection, head-marking agreement, role assignment and case assignment across languages makes it highly desirable to have such a theory of valence—one that predicts the absence of nonlocal selection.

In this paper, we have tried to show that the 'inflected subject' analysis of auxiliary contraction should be replaced by the subject-incorporation analysis we presented in section 2.3. Our account allows the basic insights of Sadler and Barron to be preserved, but it also deals with relevant data that appears problematic for their proposals. Our analysis thus illustrates how contracted auxiliaries in English conform to HPSG's strong assumptions about headedness, locality and the cross-linguistic nature of headed constructions.

Acknowledgments

This research was conducted as part of CSLI's Linguistic Grammars Online (LINGO) project, in conjunction with the Verbmobil project. In that connection, we gratefully acknowledge the support of the Bundesministerium für Bildung, Wissenschaft, Forschung, und Technologie (Project VERBMOBIL) and the National Science Foundation (grant number IRI-9612682). We would like to thank Rachel Nordlinger, Louisa Sadler, Peter Sells and Arnold Zwicky for helpful discussion of the ideas in this paper.

References

Abeillé, A., D. Godard, and I. A. Sag. 1999. French relative clause constructions. Stanford University.

Andrews, A. 1990. Unification and morphological blocking. *Natural Language and Linguistic Theory* 8:507–558.

Barron, J. 1998. *Have* contraction: Explaining "trace effects" in a theory without movement. *Linguistics* 36(2):223–251.

Bender, E. M. 2001. *Syntactic Variation and Linguistic Competence: The Case of AAVE Copula Absence*. Ph.D. thesis, Stanford University.

Blevins, J. P. 1995. Syncretism and paradigmatic opposition. *Linguistics and Philosophy* 18(2):113–152.

Butt, M., M.-E. Niño, and F. Segond. 1996. Multilingual processing of auxiliaries within lfg. In D. Gibbon, ed., *Natural Language Processing and Speech Technology: Results of the 3rd KONVENS Conference*. Berlin: Mouton de Gruyter.

Miller, P. H. and I. A. Sag. 1997. French clitic movment without clitics or movement. *Natural Language and Linguistic Theory* 15:573–639.

Nordlinger, R. 1998. *Constructive Case: Evidence from Australian Languages*. Stanford, CA: CSLI.

Pollard, C. and I. A. Sag. 1994. *Head-driven Phrase Structure Grammar*. Chicago: Chicago University Press.

Pullum, G. K. and A. M. Zwicky. 1997. Licensing of prosodic features by syntactic rules. Paper presented at the 1997 Linguistic Society of America meeting, Chicago.

Radford, A. 1988. *Transformational Grammar: A First Course*. Cambridge: Cambridge University Press.

Sadler, L. 1997. English auxiliaries as tense inflections. Version of November, 1997. To appear in the *Special Issue of Essex Research Reports produced on the occasion of the retirement of Keith Brown.*

Selkirk, E. O. 1984. *Phonology and Syntax: The Relation between Sounds and Structure*. Cambridge, MA: MIT Press.

Spencer, A. 1991. *Morphological Theory*. Oxford: Blackwells.

Sweet, H. 1890. *A Primer of Spoken English*. Oxford: Clarendon Press.

3

Negation in Colloquial Welsh

ROBERT D. BORSLEY AND BOB MORRIS JONES

3.1 Introduction

Welsh negation displays a variety of complexities, especially in the colloquial language. In this paper, we will concentrate on colloquial Welsh and we will restrict our attention to main clauses, ignoring subordinate clauses and especially the very interesting properties of non-finite negation (see Borsley and Jones 2000 for discussion). We will also concentrate on syntax, largely ignoring questions about meaning. Building on the proposals of Borsley and Jones (2000), we will argue that an analysis rather like those proposed by Kim and Sag (1996), Kim (2000) and Warner (2000) for English can accommodate the facts quite satisfactorily.

3.2 Some Data

Like the other Celtic languages, Welsh has VSO order in finite clauses. In literary Welsh, negative sentences involve the preverbal particle *ni* (*nid* before a vowel). They may also contain a post-verbal n-word, but this is not necessary. In colloquial Welsh, *ni* does not normally appear, but many verbs show the mutation traditionally attributed to the particle and some forms of *bod* 'be' show a remnant of the particle in the form of an initial *d*. The following are representative negative sentences:[1]

(1) Does neb yn yr ystafell.
is no one in the room
'There is no one in the room.'

[1]In our examples, some of the spellings are modified to reflect spoken forms (e.g., *llyfre* and *welish* instead of literary *llyfrau* and *welais*).

Grammatical Interfaces in HPSG.
Ronnie Cann, Claire Grover and Philip Miller.

(2) Welish i neb.
saw-1SG I no one
'I saw no one.'

(3) Cha' i ddim sefyll yma.
can I NEG stand here
'I can't stand here.'

(4) Dydy Mair byth yn gweithio.
is Mair never in work
'Mair never works.'

The initial *d* in (1) is a remnant of the preverbal particle, and the verbs in (2) and (3) show the mutation that is traditionally attributed to the particle.[2] All four sentences contain an n-word.[3] The following are related affirmative sentences:

(5) Mae Gwyn yn yr ystafell.
is Gwyn in the room
'Gwyn is in the room.'

(6) Welish i Gwyn.
saw-1SG I Gwyn
'I saw Gwyn.'

(7) Ga' i sefyll yma.
can I stand here
'I can stand here.'

(8) Mae Mair yn gweithio.
is Mair in work
'Mair is working.'

---

[2] *Yn* in (4) is homophonous with a preposition meaning 'in'—hence the gloss—but we assume that it is a member of a class of aspect markers in this use. It does not trigger mutation whereas the preposition triggers so-called nasal mutation, giving, for example, *yn Nolgellau* for 'in Dolgellau' (a Welsh town).

[3] Other n-words are *dim byd* 'nothing/anything' (literally 'no world') and *erioed*, which, like *byth*, translates as 'never/ever'. *Byth* is used in non-perfective contexts, while *erioed* is used in perfective contexts. Both *byth* and *erioed* also occur in positive environments with positive meanings. The following illustrates this for *byth*

(i) Dw i'n aros yma am byth.
am I in stay here for ever
'I am staying here for ever.'

The verbs in (6) and (7) show mutation traditionally attributed to an affirmative particle. As these examples show, some but not all negative sentences contain a distinctive verb form.

As one might expect, the n-words in (1–4) can appear in other positions. The following illustrate:

(9) Dw i ddim wedi gweld neb.
am I NEG after see nobody
'I haven't seen anybody.'

(10) Dydy hi ddim wedi newid dim.
is she NEG after change NEG
'She has not changed at all.'

(11) Dydy Mair ddim yn gweithio byth.
is Mair NEG in work never
'Mair never works.'

In (9), *neb* appears as object of a non-finite verb. In (10), *dim*, the basic unmutated form of *ddim*, follows a non-finite verb. (We will refer to this element as *dim* in subsequent discussion.) In (11), *byth* appears after a non-finite verb. Notice that all these examples contain two n-words, but have just a simple negative interpretation. Thus, like many languages, colloquial Welsh has negative concord.

The final n-words in (9) and (10) can be replaced by non-negative elements with no change in truth conditional content, as in the following:

(12) Dw i ddim wedi gweld unrhyw un.
am I NEG after see anyone
'I haven't seen anybody.'

(13) Dydy hi ddim wedi newid o gwbl.
is she NEG after change at all
'She has not changed at all.'

(9) and (10) are essentially emphatic versions of these examples.

In contrast, it is not possible to replace the n-words in (1–3) by a non-negative element. Thus, the following examples are ungrammatical:

(14) * Does unrhyw un yn yr ystafell.
is anyone in the room

(15) * Welish i unrhyw un.
saw-1SG I anyone

(16) * Cha' i o gwbl sefyll yma.
can I at all stand here

It seems, then, that negative sentences must contain an n-word. This is perhaps not surprising given that the verb in a negative sentence often fails to identify the sentence as negative.

Notice now that it is not possible to omit post-subject *dim* from (9–11).

(17) * Dw i wedi gweld neb.
am I after see nobody

(18) * Dydy hi wedi newid dim.
is she after change NEG

(19) * Dydy Mair yn gweithio byth.
is Mair in work never

It looks, then, as if negative sentences in colloquial Welsh must contain an n-word in close proximity to the verb, more precisely in subject or object position, or as a post-subject adverb.[4]

3.3 Negative Adverbs

We want now to look more closely at negative adverbs, especially the basic negative adverb *dim*. In the examples we have considered, *dim* is followed by what we might call a predicative phrase. One might suppose that it is a premodifier of this phrase. We will argue that this is not the case and that it is in fact a complement of the preceding verb. This is essentially the analysis which Kim and Sag (1996), Kim (2000) and Warner (2000) propose for English *not* where it follows a finite auxiliary and French *pas* where it follows a finite verb.[5]

Evidence that *dim* is not a pre-modifier of a predicative phrase comes from examples like the following:

---

[4]However, subordinate clauses may contain the preverbal negative particle *na(d)* and no other marker of negation. We have examples like the following:

(i) Dw i 'n gwbod [na fydd Mair yna]
am I in know NEG will-be Mair there
'I know Mair won't be there.

[5]It is argued in these references that *not* is also a premodifier of non-finite VPs, and that French *ne-pas* has the same function. Welsh *dim* does not have this function. In Welsh, non-finite negation involves a defective negative verb *peidio*, illustrated in the following (where it is mutated):

(i) Ceisiodd Gwyn beidio (ag) ateb y cwestiwn.
tried Gwyn NEG with answer the question
'Gwyn tried not to answer the question.'

See Borsley and Jones (2000) for discussion.

(20) Aeth Megan ddim i 'r dref.
Went Megan NEG to the town
'Megan didn't go to the town.'

Here, *dim* is followed by an ordinary verbal argument. Thus, it need not be followed by a predicative phrase. Evidence that *dim* is not a premodifier of any kind comes from the following:

(21) Agorodd y drws ddim.
opened the door NEG
'The door didn't open.'

Here nothing follows *dim*. Hence, unless we allow premodifiers of empty elements, it cannot be a premodifier.

Further evidence that *dim* is not a premodifier comes from its restricted distribution. If it were a premodifier of the following phrase, one would expect it to be possible wherever the phrase is possible. This is not what we find. Consider the following data:

(22) Nesh i ddim mynd i Aberystwyth.
did-1SG I NEG go to Aberystwyth
'I did not go to Aberystwyth.'

(23) * Dw i 'n disgwyl i Mair ddim mynd i Aberystwyth.
am I in expect to Mair NEG go to Aberystwyth
'I expect Mair not to go to Aberystwyth.

(24) * Mae Gwyn yn degyg o ddim mynd i Aberystwyth.
is Gwyn in likely of NEG go to Aberystwyth
'Gwyn is likely not to go to Aberystwyth.'

(25) * Mae Gwyn yn awyddus i ddim mynd i Aberystwyth.
is Gwyn in eager to NEG go to Aberystwyth
'Gwyn is eager not to go to Aberystwyth.'

In (22), *dim* appears before a VP which is the complement of a finite verb. In (23–25), it appears before VPs in other positions. Only (22) is grammatical. This suggests not only that post-subject *dim* is not a premodifier but also that it is licensed by the preceding finite verb. Obviously, if it is a complement of the verb, this will be the case.

Some independent evidence that this is the right analysis for *dim* comes from the fact that it is mutated. Borsley (1999) argues that a number of instances of mutation in Welsh are the result of a rule which assigns mutation to a complement immediately preceded by a phrasal sister. This rule will account for the mutation of *dim* provided it is a complement.[6]

We can return now to the semantically more complex negative adverb *byth*. Notice first that the following are ungrammatical:

(26) a. * Dw i ddim byth yn yfed cwrw.
am I NEG ever in drink beer

b. * Dw i byth dim yn yfed cwrw.
am I ever NEG in drink beer
'I never drink beer.'

This suggests that post-subject *byth* occupies the same position as post-subject *dim* and hence that it too is a complement of the preceding finite verb. Consider now the following data:

(27) * Fydd neb ddim yma.
will-be no one NEG here
'No one will be here.'

(28) * Wela' i ddim Gwen eto.
will-see-1SG I NEG Gwen still
'I won't see Gwen again.'

(29) Fydd neb byth yma.
will-be no one never here
'No one will ever be here.'

(30) Wela' i byth Gwen eto.
will-see-1SG I never Gwen still
'I will never see Gwen again.'

Here we see that while *dim* cannot be preceded by a negative subject or be followed by any kind of object, both are possible with *byth*. Thus, although these two elements are quite similar, there are also some important differences between them.

3.4 A Negative Quantifier

The ungrammaticality of (28) raises an obvious question: if *dim* cannot be followed by an object, how can a simple transitive sentence be negated? The answer is that it can be negated with a negative quantifier

[6]There is no mutation after *dim* in (22). This suggests that *dim* is a non-phrasal complement. There is also no mutation after *byth* in (35), presumably for the same reason.

homophonous with the basic negative adverb, which takes a bare indefinite NP or a PP containing *o* 'of' and a definite NP as its complement. The following illustrate:

(31) Welish i ddim dyn.
saw-1SG I NEG man
'I saw no man.'

(32) Welish i ddim o 'r dynion.
saw-1SG I NEG of the men
'I saw none of the men.'

One might suppose that these sentences in fact involve the adverb *dim* and that this requires a definite object to be preceded by *o*. However, it is quite easy to argue against this idea. Some rather simple evidence that we have a different *dim* here comes from the following:

(33) Welodd neb ddim llyfr.
saw no one NEG book
'No one saw any book.'

Here, we see that this *dim*, unlike adverbial *dim*, can be preceded by a negative subject. This is essentially an emphatic form of (34).

(34) Welodd neb lyfr.
saw no one book
'No one saw a book.'.

Further evidence that this *dim* is a different element comes from the following:

(35) Wela' i byth dim o Gwen eto.
will-see-1SG I never NEG of Gwen still
'I will never see Gwen again.'

Here, we see that this *dim*, unlike adverbial *dim*, can be preceded by *byth*. This is an emphatic version of (30).

Evidence that this *dim* forms a constituent with the following NP or PP comes from the fact that *dim* NP and *dim o* NP occur in any NP position within a negative context, for example subject of a finite verb ((36), (37)), object of a non-finite verb ((38), (39)), object of a preposition ((40), (41)), and subject of a non-finite verb ((42), (43)).

(36) Does dim dyn yn yr ystafell.
is NEG man in the room
'There is no man in the room.'

(37) Does dim o 'r dynion yn yr ystafell.
is NEG of the men in the room
'None of the men is in the room.'

(38) Dw i ddim wedi prynu dim llyfr.
am I NEG after buy NEG book
'I haven't bought any book.'

(39) Dw i ddim wedi prynu dim o 'r llyfre.
am I NEG after buy NEG of the books
'I haven't bought any of the books.'

(40) Dydy Sioned ddim yn chwilio am ddim llyfre.
is Sioned NEG in look for NEG books
'Sioned is not looking for any books.'

(41) Dydy Sioned ddim yn chwilio am ddim o 'r llyfre.
is Sioned NEG in look for NEG of the books
'Sioned is not looking for any of the books.'

(42) Dydy Gwyn ddim yn disgwyl i ddim bechgyn fynd adre
is Gwyn NEG in expect for NEG boys go home
'Gwyn doesn't expect any boys to go home.'

(43) Dydy Gwyn ddim yn disgwyl i ddim o 'r bechgyn fynd
is Gwyn NEG in expect for NEG of the boys go
adre.
home
'Gwyn doesn't expect any of the boys to go home.'

Thus, there is quite strong evidence that *dim* NP and *dim o* NP are constituents. Given this, it is natural to assume that *dim* is a quantifier with an NP or PP complement. In other words, it is natural to assume that it is rather like the quantifiers *rhai* and *peth*, both of which can be glossed as 'some', which also take a bare indefinite NP or a PP containing *o* and a definite NP as their complement. We have examples here like the following (in which *rhai* and *peth* are mutated):

(44) a. Gollish i rai llyfre ar y trên.
lost-1SG I some books on the train
'I lost some books on the train.'

b. Gollish i beth siwgr ar y llawr.
lost-1SG I some sugar on the floor
'I spilled some sugar on the floor.'

(45) a. Gollish i rai o 'r llyfre ar y trên.
lost-1SG I some of the books on the train
'I lost some of the books on the train.'

b. Gollish i beth o 'r siwgr ar y llawr.
lost-1SG I some of the sugar on the floor
'I spilled some of the sugar on the floor.'

Thus, the assumption that *dim* is sometimes a negative quantifier with an NP or a PP complement seems quite well motivated. It seems, then, that Welsh has both simple negative NPs containing *neb* and also more complex negative NPs containing the quantifier *dim*.[7]

There is more to be said about negative NPs of the form *dim o* NP. When such phrases appear as the complement of a non-finite verb or as the subject of a finite verb they have a partitive interpretation. This means that they are only acceptable where it is possible for the referent of the NP to be partially involved in the process or state denoted by the verb. There is no problem where the NP is plural or contains a singular mass noun, but there may be where the NP contains a singular count noun. Hence, the following are unacceptable:

(46) * Dw i ddim wedi agor dim o 'r drws.
am I NEG after open NEG of the door
'I haven't opened any of the door.'

(47) * Fydd dim o 'r goriad dan y llechan.
will-be NEG of the key under the slate
'None of the key will be under the slate.'

However, when *dim o* NP appears as the complement of a finite verb, it need not have a partitive interpretation. Hence, any kind of NP is acceptable here. Unlike (46), the following is perfectly acceptable.

[7]Rowlett (1998) argues that French *pas* is also both an adverb and a quantifier. However, it differs from *dim* in a number of ways. First, it always corresponds to logical negation, which is not the case with *dim* given examples like (10) and (38–43). Second, quantifier *pas* is associated with a pseudo-partitive PP, which it need not be adjacent to. Rowlett cites examples like the following here:

(i) Max n' a pas composé de sonatas.
Max ne has pas composed of sonatas
'Max hasn't composed any sonatas.'

In contrast, quantifier *dim* is always adjacent to its complement.

(48) Agoresh i ddim o 'r drws.
opened-1SG I NEG of the door
'I didn't open the door.'

Thus, objects of finite verbs have a special status here.[8]

There is a further point that we should note here. In finite object position, *dim o* can be reduced to *mo*. This is not possible in non-finite object position or in subject position. Thus, we have the following data:

(49) Wela' i mo 'r sêr heno.
will-see-1SG I NEG the stars tonight
'I won't see the stars tonight.'

(50) * Fydd Sioned ddim yn yfed mo 'r gwin.
will-be Sioned NEG in drink NEG the wine
'Sioned won't be drinking any of the wine.'

(51) * Fydd mo 'r gwin yn cal i yfed.
will-be NEG the wine in get 3SGM drink
'None of the wine will be drunk.'

Again, then, objects of finite verbs have a special status.

3.5 An HPSG Analysis

We will now develop an HPSG analysis of the facts that we have set out in the foregoing sections.[9] At the heart of this analysis is the idea that Welsh has a number of types of negative verb, which may or may not have a distinctive form but always have different selectional properties from the related affirmative verbs. This is very similar to the approach to English and French finite negation in Kim and Sag (1996), Kim (2000) and Warner (2000). As we noted at the end of section 3.1, negative sentences in colloquial Welsh must contain an n-word in subject or object position, or as a post-subject adverb. On our analysis this is a result of the selectional properties of negative verbs.

We will assume, as is standard in HPSG, that VSO sentences have a flat structure, with verb, subject, and complements as daughters of S. We will also assume that the verb in a negative sentence is marked [NEG +] and that negative constituents are [NC +] (NC = negative concord). Given these assumptions, (1) and (2) will have structures of the form in

[8] Examples like (47) are grammatical in some Southern dialects but not in the Welsh of North and Mid-Wales.

[9] Rouveret (1994, 2.4.3) sketches an analysis of some aspects of Welsh negation within the Principles-and-Parameters (P&P) framework. It is not clear to us how the full range of facts could be accommodated within P&P.

(52) and (53), respectively, while (3) and (4) will have structures of the form in (54).

(52)

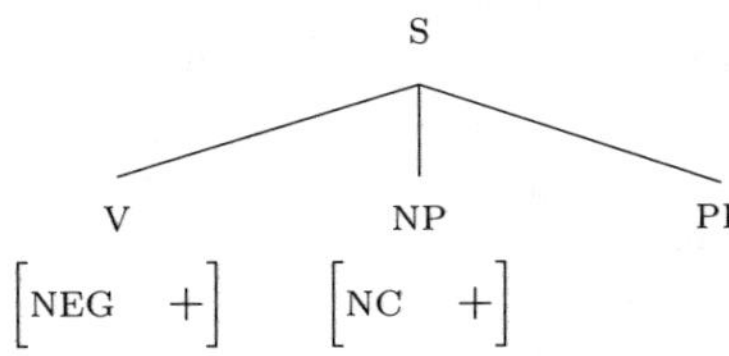

(53)

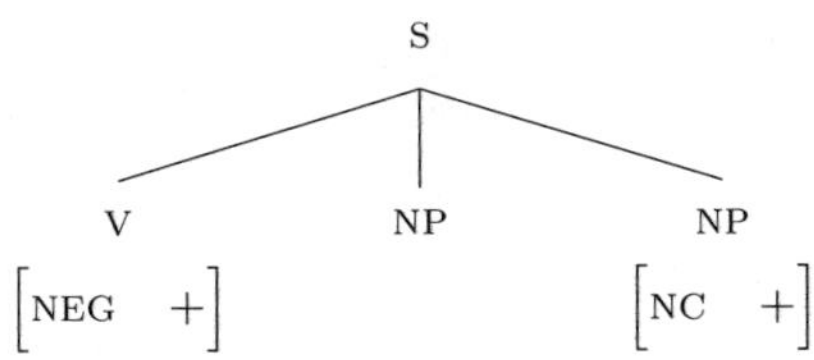

(54)

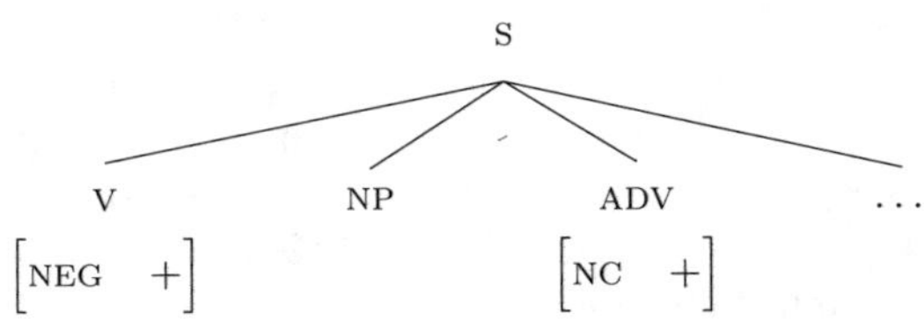

We argued earlier that negative adverbs are extra complements. We will also assume following Borsley (1989) that post-verbal subjects in Welsh are extra complements. To accommodate the full range of facts we need to distinguish between the two negative adverbs. We will do this with a feature ADVFORM, marking *dim* as [ADVFORM *dim*] and *byth* as [ADVFORM *byth*]. It is also necessary to distinguish finite object position from other nominal positions. We will not try to decide how this should be done. Clearly, however, it would be a simple matter to do it with some binary feature.

Before we proceed, we should note that we do not necessarily assume that negative verbs have negation as part of their meaning. This might be the right assumption, but the fact that negative verbs are often formally identical to their affirmative counterparts perhaps casts some doubt on it. One alternative is to assume that negation resides in an n-word. Notice, however, that we cannot assume that n-words are always negative because, as (9–11) and (38–43) show, it is possible to have more than one n-word and a simple negative interpretation. Hence, this approach would entail that n-words are systematically ambiguous with both negative and non-negative meanings.[10] Another alternative is to assume that negation is a property of the construction and does not reside in particular lexical items.[11] We will not try to decide between these approaches.

Given the various assumptions that we have just introduced, we can propose the following category for the verb *does* in (1), (36), (37):[12]

(55)
$$\begin{bmatrix} \text{HEAD} & \textit{verb}\begin{bmatrix}\textit{fin}, \text{NEG} & +\end{bmatrix} \\ \text{COMPS} & \left\langle \text{NP}[\text{NC} \;\; +]\,, \text{PP}\right\rangle \end{bmatrix}$$

Here the first item in the COMPS list corresponds to the subject. Hence, this requires a negative subject. For *welish* in (2), (31) and (32), we can propose the category in (56).

(56)
$$\begin{bmatrix} \text{HEAD} & \textit{verb}\begin{bmatrix}\textit{fin}, \text{NEG} & +\end{bmatrix} \\ \text{COMPS} & \left\langle \text{NP}\,, \text{NP}[\text{NC} \;\; +]\right\rangle \end{bmatrix}$$

This requires a negative object. As noted earlier, we assume that objects of finite verbs are distinguished from other NPs in some way. Given this, it is not too hard to accommodate the distinctive properties of finite object position. We can analyze *mo* as a quantifier which takes a definite NP as its complement and is restricted to finite object position. This will allow (49) while excluding (50) and (51). We can also propose that there are two quantifiers *dim*, one requiring a partitive interpretation and appearing anywhere in a negative context, the other with no partitive requirement and restricted to finite object position. This will allow (48) while excluding (46) and (47). Turning now to *cha'* in (3), we can propose the category in (57).

(57)
$$\begin{bmatrix} \text{HEAD} & \textit{verb}\begin{bmatrix}\textit{fin}, \text{NEG} & +\end{bmatrix} \\ \text{COMPS} & \left\langle \text{NP}\;[\text{NC} \;\; -], \text{ADV}\begin{bmatrix}\text{NC} & + \\ \text{ADVFORM} & \textit{dim}\end{bmatrix}, \text{VP}\right\rangle \end{bmatrix}$$

This requires *dim* as a post-subject adverb. The [NC −] specification on the subject will prevent a negative subject. Finally, for *dydy* in (4), we can propose the following category:

[10] An analysis of French negation in which n-words are systematically ambiguous is developed in Richter and Sailer (1999).

[11] An analysis of this kind is proposed by Przepiórkowski (1999) for Italian, in which a finite clause is negative if it contains a preverbal n-word or the preverbal negative marker *non*.

[12] Here and subsequently, we omit [SUBJ <>] from our categories.

(58)
$$\begin{bmatrix} \text{HEAD} & \textit{verb}\begin{bmatrix}\textit{fin}, \text{NEG} & +\end{bmatrix} \\ \text{COMPS} & \left\langle \text{NP}, \text{ADV}\begin{bmatrix}\text{NC} & + \\ \text{ADVFORM} & \textit{byth}\end{bmatrix}, \text{AspP} \right\rangle \end{bmatrix}$$

We assume that the complement in (4) is an Aspect Phrase (see fn. 3). This category requires *byth* as a post-subject adverb. The subject is not constrained. Hence, a negative subject is not excluded.

We need categories like (55) and (58) for all verbs, categories like (56) for all transitive verbs, and categories like (57) for all intransitive verbs. How should we provide these categories? One possibility is with lexical rules. This is the approach which is taken by Kim and Sag (1996) and Kim (2000). We can provide for categories like (55) and (56) with the following lexical rules:

(59) **Subject negation**

$$\begin{bmatrix} \text{HEAD} & \textit{verb}\begin{bmatrix}\textit{fin}, \text{NEG} & -\end{bmatrix} \\ \text{COMPS} & \left\langle \text{NP}, \ldots \right\rangle \end{bmatrix} \Rightarrow \begin{bmatrix} \text{HEAD} & \textit{verb}\begin{bmatrix}\textit{fin}, \text{NEG} & +\end{bmatrix} \\ \text{COMPS} & \left\langle \text{NP}\,[\text{NC} \;\; +], \ldots \right\rangle \end{bmatrix}$$

(60) **Object negation**

$$\begin{bmatrix} \text{HEAD} & \textit{verb}\begin{bmatrix}\textit{fin}, \text{NEG} & -\end{bmatrix} \\ \text{COMPS} & \left\langle \text{NP}, \text{NP}, \ldots \right\rangle \end{bmatrix} \Rightarrow \begin{bmatrix} \text{HEAD} & \textit{verb}\begin{bmatrix}\textit{fin}, \text{NEG} & +\end{bmatrix} \\ \text{COMPS} & \left\langle \text{NP}, \text{NP}\,[\text{NC} \;\; +], \ldots \right\rangle \end{bmatrix}$$

For categories like (57), we can propose the following lexical rule (where $\oplus$ indicates list concatenation):

(61) **Simple adverbial negation**

$$\begin{bmatrix} \text{HEAD} & \textit{verb}\begin{bmatrix}\textit{fin}, \text{NEG} & -\end{bmatrix} \\ \text{COMPS} & \langle \text{NP} \rangle \oplus \boxed{1} \end{bmatrix} \Longrightarrow$$

$$\begin{bmatrix} \text{HEAD} & \textit{verb}\begin{bmatrix}\textit{fin}, \text{NEG} & +\end{bmatrix} \\ \text{COMPS} & \left\langle \text{NP}\,[\text{NC} \;\; -], \text{ADV}\begin{bmatrix}\text{NC} & + \\ \text{ADVFORM} & \textit{dim}\end{bmatrix} \right\rangle \oplus \boxed{1} \end{bmatrix}$$

$$\neg\,(\,\boxed{1} = \langle\, \text{NP}, \ldots \rangle\,)$$

The condition on the rule will ensure that it only applies to transitive verbs, thus ensuring that only such verbs have a category which requires adverbial *dim* as an extra complement. Finally, for categories like (58), we can propose the following:

(62) **Complex adverbial negation**

$$\begin{bmatrix} \text{HEAD} & verb\begin{bmatrix} fin, \text{ NEG } - \end{bmatrix} \\ \text{COMPS} & \langle \text{ NP}, \ldots \rangle \end{bmatrix} \Longrightarrow$$

$$\begin{bmatrix} \text{HEAD} & verb\begin{bmatrix} fin, \text{ NEG } + \end{bmatrix} \\ \text{COMPS} & \left\langle \text{NP, ADV} \begin{bmatrix} \text{NC} & + \\ \text{ADVFORM} & byth \end{bmatrix}, \ldots \right\rangle \end{bmatrix}$$

Notice that all these rules apply to lexical items which are [NEG −] and produce lexical items which are [NEG +]. This means that none of the rules will be able to apply to its own output or to the output of any other rule.

This approach will give the right results. However, there are some important objections to it. Firstly, a number of HPSG linguists, notably Bouma (1997) and Koenig (1999), have argued against the use of lexical rules to capture relations between lexical items. Secondly, the analysis misses a generalization. There are certain similarities between the four types of negative verb. These similarities are missed by an approach involving four separate lexical rules. Thirdly, the analysis makes the facts look more complex than they really are. We have four different types of negative verb here. However, it does not follow that we need four different grammatical statements. We will argue that in fact just two constraints are necessary.

A more satisfactory approach is possible if we assume that the various negative verb categories are the result of fleshing out certain basic underspecified verbal categories in different ways. An approach of this kind is developed for English in Warner (2000). Warner assumes a complex hierarchy of lexical types with constraints associated with each type. We advocate a similar approach in Borsley and Jones (2000). However, it now seems to us that there is no need for a complex hierarchy of lexical types here.

The most basic feature of negative sentences, highlighted at the end of section 3.2, is that they must contain an n-word in subject or object position or as a post-subject adverb. Within the approach we have developed this means that a [NEG +] finite verb has subject, object, or post-subject adverb which is [NC +]. We propose that this is a result of the following constraint:

(63) $\begin{bmatrix}\text{HEAD} & \textit{verb}\begin{bmatrix}\textit{fin}, \text{NEG} & +\end{bmatrix}\end{bmatrix} \longrightarrow$

$\begin{bmatrix}\text{COMPS} & \left\langle \ldots, [\text{NC} \;\; +], \ldots \right\rangle\end{bmatrix}$

All four types of negative verb conform to this constraint. We need to make certain additional assumptions here. First, we need to assume that all finite verbs optionally allow an adverb as the second member of their COMPS list. Some independent evidence for this assumption comes from the fact that certain adverbs can immediately follow the subject in an affirmative sentence. Consider, for example, (64).

(64) Ga' i wastad sefyll yma.
can I always stand here
'I can always stand here.'

If this option is taken in a negative sentence, an adverb which is [NC +] will be one way of satisfying (63). We will also assume that only NPs and adverbs can be [NC +]. Welsh has no double object verbs, and we assume that adverbials that do not immediately follow the subject such as *ddoe* in (65) are not complements but adjuncts (see Borsley (1999) for some motivation for this assumption).

(65) Esh i yna ddoe.
went I there yesterday
'I went there yesterday.'

It follows that there are just three ways of satisfying (63): with a subject, with an object and with a post-subject adverb. Thus, we can account for the most basic feature of negative sentences with just one constraint and some natural ancillary assumptions.[13] A second important fact about negative sentences, illustrated by (27) and (28), is that adverbial *dim* does not co-occur with a negative subject or any kind of object. We can impose these restrictions with the following constraint:

(66) $\begin{bmatrix}\text{COMPS} & \left\langle \boxed{1}, [\text{ADVFORM} \;\; \textit{dim}\,] \right\rangle \oplus \boxed{2}\end{bmatrix} \longrightarrow$

$\boxed{1} = [\text{NC} \; -] \;\&\; \neg(\boxed{2} = \langle \text{ NP}, \ldots \rangle\,)$

The category in (57) obviously conforms to this constraint since the first member of the COMPS list is [NC −] and *dim* is not followed by an NP.

[13]The fact, noted in footnote 4, that no n-word is required in subordinate clauses, suggests that (63) should be limited to main clause verbs.

The other categories conform to it vacuously since they do not satisfy the antecedent.

This approach is simpler than a lexical rule approach and it captures the similarities between the various types of negative verb which are missed by a lexical rule approach. It seems to us, then, that it is preferable to a lexical rule approach.

The analysis needs some additional elements. Most obviously, we need appropriate categories for the various n-words. As noted earlier, there is an issue about their semantics, whether they are always non-negative or ambiguous with both negative and non-negative meanings. There is also a question about the how the partitive requirement should be imposed on the unrestricted form of the quantifier *dim*. Otherwise, however, things seem quite straightforward. We also need a mechanism to license additional n-words in positions where they are allowed but not required. A detailed HPSG account of the licensing of n-words in Polish and Italian is developed in Przepiórkowski and Kupść (1999). We assume that essentially the same approach can be applied here.

3.6 Concluding Remarks

In this paper, we have identified the main features of Welsh negative sentences and developed an HPSG analysis involving a number of types of negative verb. We have argued that an analysis in which the various negative verbs result from the fleshing out of basic underspecified verbal categories in different ways is preferable to one employing lexical rules. We have not discussed all aspects of Welsh negative sentences. As we noted at the outset, we have limited our attention to main clauses and have ignored non-finite negation.[14] However, we have provided an

[14]We have also ignored the distinctive properties of certain dialects. Some southern dialects have special negative forms of the copula which do not require an accompanying n-word. Thus where most colloquial varieties of Welsh have (i), these dialects have some version of (ii).

(i) Dw i ddim yn gweithio heno.
am I NEG in work tonight
'I am working tonight.'

(ii) Sa/So/Smo i 'n gweithio heno.
NEG+be+PRES I in work tonight
am I NEG in work tonight
'I am working tonight.'

Negation also has distinctive properties in Pembrokeshire Welsh, discussed in Awbery (1990). In particular, the sequence *dim y* N, which does not occur in most varieties of colloquial Welsh, occurs both immediately following the finite verb and immediately following the subject in Pembrokeshire Welsh. Unfortunately, Awbery

account of subject and object negation, which are not discussed in the HPSG literature on English and French. They are more important in Welsh than in English and French (because simple adverbial negation is impossible with transitive verbs) but they are not unimportant in English and French. In fact they are quite important in French, where *pas* cannot co-occur with a negative subject just as adverbial *dim* cannot co-occur with a negative subject in Welsh. The following illustrates:

(67) Personne n' est (* pas) venu.
no-one NEG is NEG come
'No-one has come.'

Also in French as in Welsh, the counterpart of 'never' can co-occur with a negative subject.

(68) Personne ne sera jamais riche.
no-one NEG will-be never rich
'No-one will ever be rich.'

It seems to us, then, that the analysis we have developed for Welsh is potentially relevant to both English and French, and perhaps to other languages as well.

Acknowledgements

Earlier versions of this paper were presented at the University of Manchester Institute of Science and Technology in February 1999 and at the HPSG Conference in Edinburgh in August 1999. The research on which the paper is based was largely carried out at the Grapes Hotel in Maentwrog, Gwynedd, North Wales. We are grateful to Adam Przepiórkowski for typically insightful comments, which led to major improvements in the paper, and also to two anonymous referees for a number of helpful comments. Any remaining imperfections are our responsibility.

References

Awbery, G. 1990. Dialect Syntax: A Neglected Resource for Welsh. In R. Hendrick, ed., *Syntax and Semantics 23: The Syntax of the Modern Celtic Languages*, pages 1–25. San Diego: Academic Press.

Borsley, R. D. 1989. An HPSG Approach to Welsh. *Journal of Linguistics* 25:277–302.

Borsley, R. D. 1999. Mutation and Constituent Structure in Welsh. *Lingua* 109:263–300.

does not provide the kind of data that would enable us to determine whether *dim* in these sequences is the quantifier or the adverb.

Borsley, R. D. and B. M. Jones. 2000. The Syntax of Welsh Negation. *Transactions of the Philological Society* 98:1:15–47.

Bouma, G. 1997. Valency alternations without relations. Rijksuniversiteit Groningen.

Kim, J.-B. 2000. *The Grammar of Negation: A Constraint-Based Approach.* Stanford: CSLI Publications.

Kim, J.-B. and I. A. Sag. 1996. French and English negation: A lexicalist alternative to head-movement. Stanford University.

Koenig, J.-P. 1999. *Lexical Relations*. Stanford: CSLI Publications.

Przepiórkowski, A. 1999. Negative Polarity Questions and Italian Negative Concord. In V. Kordoni, ed., *Tübingen Studies in Head-Driven Phrase Structure Grammar*, pages 353–400.

Przepiórkowski, A. and A. Kupść. 1999. Eventuality Negation and Negative Concord in Polish and Italian. In A. Przepiórkowski and R. D. Borsley, eds., *Slavic in HPSG*. Stanford: CSLI Publications.

Richter, F. and M. Sailer. 1999. A Lexicalist Collocation Analysis of Sentential Negation and Negative Concord in French. In V. Kordoni, ed., *Tübingen Studies in Head-Driven Phrase Structure Grammar*, pages 231–300.

Rouveret, A. 1994. *Syntaxe du Gallois: Principes Généraux et Typologie.* Paris: Editions du CNRS.

Rowlett, P. 1998. *Sentential Negation in French.* Oxford: Oxford University Press.

Warner, A. R. 2000. English Auxiliaries without Lexical Rules. In R. D. Borsley, ed., *The Nature and Function of Syntactic Categories*. New York: Academic Press.

4

Argument Realization and Dutch R-Pronouns: Solving Bech's Problem without Movement or Deletion

GOSSE BOUMA

4.1 Introduction

Extraction out of Dutch prepositional phrases is in general only allowed if the extracted element is a so-called 'R-pronoun' (van Riemsdijk, 1978):

(1) a. **Waar** heb je **aan** gedacht?
Where/What have you on thought
What were you thinking about?

b. **Hier** (* **Deze oplossing**) had Kim niet **aan** gedacht.
Here/this (this solution) had Kim not on thought
Kim had not thought about this (* this solution).

Contrary to ordinary NPs, R-pronouns normally must precede the preposition of which they are an object, and in spite of the fact that adjacent occurrences of an R-pronoun and preposition are written as a single word, the two elements are not inseparable:

(2) a. Kim heeft **eraan/hieraan/daaraan** gedacht
Kim has there+on/here+on/there+on thought
Kim has thought about this.

b. * Kim heeft aan **er/hier/daar** gedacht.

Grammatical Interfaces in HPSG.
Ronnie Cann, Claire Grover and Philip Miller.

c. Kim heeft **er/hier/daar** niet **aan** gedacht
Kim has there/here/there not on thought
Kim has not thought about this.

R-pronouns not only occur as objects of prepositions, but can also be used as locative adverbs. In addition, the pronoun *er* occurs in impersonal passive constructions and in existential constructions as an expletive element filling the subject position:

(3) a. **Er** wordt gepraat
There is talked
One is talking.

b. **Er** heerst onzekerheid over de rente.
There rules uncertainty about the interest
There exists uncertainty about the interest.

One of the puzzling aspects of *er* is that in some cases several functions can be combined:

(4) a. **Er** wordt **over** gepraat
There is about talked
One is talking about it.

b. **Er** heerst onzekerheid **over**.
There rules uncertainty about
There exists uncertainty about it.

Er may only occur sentence-initially if it is used as an expletive subject. In (4) *er* must therefore have a subject function. At the same time, *er* must function as a prepositional object, as prepositions cannot occur without an object. This puzzling phenomenon was first observed in Bech (1952) and is therefore referred to as *'Bech's problem'* in Model (1991).

The distribution of R-pronouns in the Middle Field has been accounted for in transformational grammar (van Riemsdijk, 1978, Model, 1991, chapter 10, Bennis, 1986) by assuming a structurally unique position in phrase structure functioning as a landing site for pronouns or clitics. In addition, Bennis (1986) accounts for function amalgamation by appealing to a deletion rule. In this paper, a constraint-based, non-transformational, alternative, formulated is developed in terms of Head-driven Phrase Structure Grammar (Pollard and Sag, 1994). The core of the analysis is the observation that, except in those cases where there is a clear *filler-gap* relation between a fronted R-pronoun and a preposition, R-pronouns are used adverbially. Adverbs may be freely added to the lexical argument structure of verbs to form an extended argument structure known as *dependency structure* (Bouma et al., 2001). Verbs whose dependency structure contains an R-pronoun have two special properties. They may bind a gap introduced by a preposition, thus allowing an R-pronoun in the Middle Field to be interpreted as the (extracted) argument of a preposition. In impersonal passives and existential constructions, an R-pronoun may fill the syntactic subject position. The combination of these two properties leads to function amalgamation.

4.2 Data Overview

R-pronouns can be used as arguments of prepositions, as locative adverbs and as subjects of impersonal passives and existential constructions. In some cases, several functions of an R-pronoun coincide.[1]

Dutch prepositions take full NPs, anaphoric NPs, as well as most pronouns as argument, but not the impersonal pronouns *het (it), dit (this)* and *dat (that)*:[2]

(5) Kim denkt aan ons/ de kinderen/ *het/ *dit/ *dat
Kim thinks about us/ the children/ it/ this/ that

Instead, in cases where one might expect an impersonal pronoun, an R-pronoun can be used, which precedes rather than follows the preposition:

(6) Kim denkt **eraan/hieraan/daaraan**.
Kim thinks there+on/here+on/there+on about

Kim thinks about it/this/that

Although adjacent combinations of an R-pronoun and preposition are written as a single word, the two can be separated in the Middle Field by other constituents:

(7) a. We offeren **er** geen stukje park **voor** op.
We sacrifice there no patch park for PRT

We do not sacrifice a patch of park for it.

b. Ik sprak **er** overigens met Willemsen **over**.
I talked there by-the-way with Willemsen about.

I happened to talk about it with my friend Willemsen.

As illustrated in example (1) of the introduction, extraction out of PPs is allowed only if the argument is an R-pronoun. Extraction may be

[1] The pronoun *er* also has a quantitative or partitive use (Haeseryn et al., 1997). The latter construction is not taken into consideration in this paper.

[2] See Haeseryn et al. (1997) for a number of exceptions, involving, among others, the preposition *zonder* (*without*) and coordinated pronouns.

long-distance (8a). Also, extraction is not restricted to verbal complements, but may also involve extraction out of APs (8b) and NPs (8c).

(8) a. **Waar** denkt Kim [$_S$ dat Karel **bij** betrokken is]?
Where thinks Kim that Carl with involved is
What does Kim think that Carl is involved in?

b. **Waar** is Kim [$_{AP}$ verliefd **op**]?
Where is Kim in love at
What is Kim in love with?

c. **Waar** schreef Karel [$_{NP}$ een boek **over**]?
Where wrote Carl a book about
What did Carl write a book about?

Most prepositions can take both regular NPs and R-pronouns as argument. However, some prepositions exhibit a form alternation when their argument is an R-pronoun:

(9) a. Kim snijdt het vlees **met een mes**
Kim cuts the meat with a knife

b. Kim snijdt **er** het vlees **mee**
Kim cuts it the meat with
Kim cuts the meat with it

c. Deze beslissing leidt **tot problemen**
This decision leads to problems

d. **Waar** leidt deze beslissing **toe**?
Where leads this decision to
To what does this decision lead?

Note that the alternative form appears both when the R-pronoun appears in the Middle Field and when it is fronted.

R-pronouns not only occur as arguments of prepositions, but can be used as locative adverbs as well:

(10) Laten we **hier/daar/ergens** gaan zitten
Let us here/there/somewhere go sit
Let us sit here/there/somewhere

(11) Maria bleef **er** dertig jaar
Maria stayed there thirty years

Furthermore, R-pronouns can occur as subject in existential constructions and impersonal passives:

(12) a. **Er/Daar** stond een moeder op.
There stood a mother PART.
A mother stood up.

b. **Er/Ergens** werd gebeld.
There/somewhere was called.
The phone rang (somewhere).

The reduced R-pronoun *er* in these examples is often analyzed as an expletive subject. Apart from the fact that its locative interpretation is less strong in these examples, an important reason for distinguishing between the expletive and locative use of *er* is the fact that sentence-initial occurrences of *er* are restricted to existential and impersonal passive constructions:

(13) * **Er** woonde Maria dertig jaar
There lived Maria thirty years

Sentences may contain more than one R-pronoun:

(14) **Er** stond **daar** een groot huis.
there stood there a large house

(15) **Hier** wil de apostel **er** ons de ogen voor openen.
here wants the apostle there us the eyes for open
Here, the apostle want to open our eyes for it.

The pronouns *daar* and *hier* are interpreted as locative in this case, whereas *er* is an expletive subject in (14) and a prepositional object in (15). Two occurrences of the same R-pronoun are generally not allowed. In such cases, the two functions of a pronoun may be fused or amalgamated into a single word. A clear example of this phenomenon is is the combination of expletive and prepositional uses of the R-pronoun *er*:

(16) **Er** wordt **aan een oplossing** gewerkt.
there is on a solution worked.
One works on a solution.

(17) * **Er** wordt **eraan** gewerkt.
there is there+on worked.

(18) **Er** wordt **aan** gewerkt.
there is on worked
One works on it.

(19) **Er** kwam een prins **in het verhaal** voor.
There came a prince in the story PART
A prince figured in the story.

(20) * **Er** kwam een prins **erin** voor
there came a prince there+in PART

(21) **Er** kwam een prins **in** voor.
there came a prince in PART
A prince figured in it.

Example (16) is an impersonal passive containing a PP and an expletive R-pronoun as subject. Replacement of the PP with an R-pronoun + preposition combination leads to ungrammaticality (17). Example (18), on the other hand, which contains only a single *er*, and a preposition without a following object, is grammatical. The same situation also occurs where *er* is the expletive subject of an existential clause (19–21). Expletive *er* is in general optional in impersonal passives if there is another (preferably locative) phrase which can fill the subject position. In sentences with an indefinite subject, the occurrence of *er* is also optional. Note, however, that it is not likely that the *er* in (18) and (21) is only prepositional, as prepositional *er* is normally excluded in sentence-initial position. Therefore, the usual explanation for such examples is that two functions of the R-pronoun *er* are fused into a single word.

4.3 Previous Work

To account for the fact that R-pronouns may occur in positions in the Middle Field where they are non-adjacent to the preposition selecting them, van Riemsdijk (1978) and Model (1991) assume a designated phrase structure position where R-pronouns may be moved to. Van Riemsdijk introduces a phrasal node PRO, which acts as a landing site for pronouns. Model sees *er* as a second position clitic and assumes a clitic movement transformation. Bennis (1986) argues against a designated position for R-pronouns, and accounts for the fact that they can be moved leftward within the Middle Field by appealing to a general tendency for 'light' elements to move leftward.

Bennis also extends the analysis to other uses of R-pronouns. Most importantly, he addresses the question of function-amalgamation. He briefly considers an analysis in which a single R-pronoun could potentially be co-indexed with traces occupying different argument positions, but concludes that such a 'parasitic-gap' analysis raises a number of serious problems. He then opts for a solution in which multiple occurrences of the identical R-pronouns are allowed at S-structure, and proposes a phonological deletion rule to account for the fact that typically only a single R-pronoun is realized.

An analysis of extracted prepositional R-pronouns in terms of HPSG is provided in Rentier (1993, 1994). He accounts for the extraction of the complement of a preposition by means of a lexical rule which creates SLASH*ed* PPs. To account for the distribution of R-pronouns in the Middle Field, Rentier (1994) proposes a HEAD-FILLER-COMPS structure. Apart from introducing a somewhat *ad-hoc* phrase structure schema, the main shortcoming of this proposal is that it fails to provide a solution for cases where various functions of R-pronouns are amalgamated.

4.4 Argument Realization Principles

The introduction of argument structure (ARG-ST) in HPSG as a level of representation independent from valence, has opened up the possibility of accounting for a range of data in terms of dissociations between argument structure and valence. Initially (i.e., in chapter 9 of Pollard and Sag (1994)) ARG-ST was understood as a (slightly redundant) level of representation, introduced mainly to facilitate the formulation of binding theory, and which always consisted of the concatenated values of the valence features SUBJ, SPR and COMPS. In later work, the strict correspondence between valence and ARG-ST is broken, and *argument realization principles* are formulated which allow for different mappings between the two levels.

The treatment of adjuncts as complements generally assumes that COMPS may contain adverbial *synsem*'s which are not part of ARG-ST (see, among others, Miller (1992), van Noord and Bouma (1994), Manning et al. (1999), Przepiórkowski (1999a, 1999b)). In Bouma et al. (2001), this idea is formalized using an auxiliary level of representation, called DEPS (for *dependency structure*), which acts as an intermediary between ARG-ST and valence. The idea is that verbs come with a specific argument structure, that DEPS is essentially argument structure extended with any number of adjuncts, and that the contents of DEPS in turn gets mapped onto the valence lists SUBJ and COMPS and the nonlocal feature SLASH.

Following Bouma et al. (2001), the Verbal Argument Structure Extension Principle given in (22) below defines the relationship between ARG-ST and DEPS for non-passive verbs in Dutch. It differs from the Argument Structure Extension Principle as given in Bouma et al. (2001) in that it is restricted to non-passive verbs and that it allows, in addition to 'regular' adverbial *synsem*'s which are concatenated at the end, an optional 'locative' adverbial to be introduced in the initial DEPS-position. The motivation for these modifications is presented in section 4.10.

(22) **Verbal Argument Structure Extension:**[3]

$$\begin{bmatrix} \textit{word} & \\ \text{SYNSEM} \mid \text{LOC} \mid \text{CAT} \mid \text{HEAD} & \begin{bmatrix} \textit{verb} & \\ \text{VFORM} & \neg\ \textit{pas} \end{bmatrix} \end{bmatrix} \Rightarrow$$

$$\begin{bmatrix} \text{SS}\ \boxed{2} & \begin{bmatrix} \text{L} \mid \text{C} & \begin{bmatrix} \text{DEPS} & \left(\left\langle \begin{bmatrix} \textit{`loc-ss'} \\ \text{MOD}\ \boxed{2} \end{bmatrix} \right\rangle \oplus \right) \boxed{1} \oplus \textit{listof}\left(\begin{bmatrix} \textit{`adv-ss'} \\ \text{MOD}\ \boxed{2} \end{bmatrix}\right) \\ \text{ARG-ST} & \boxed{1} \end{bmatrix} \end{bmatrix} \end{bmatrix}$$

Bouma et al. (2001) propose the following principle for the mapping between DEPS on the one hand and valence and SLASH on the other:

(23) **Argument Realization:**[4]

$$\textit{word} \quad \Rightarrow$$

$$\begin{bmatrix} \text{SYNSEM} \mid \text{LOC} \mid \text{CAT} & \begin{bmatrix} \text{VAL} & \begin{bmatrix} \text{SUBJ} & \boxed{1} \\ \text{COMPS} & \boxed{2} - \textit{listof}(\textit{gap-ss}) \end{bmatrix} \\ \text{DEPS} & \boxed{1} \oplus \boxed{2} \end{bmatrix} \end{bmatrix}$$

The verb *denken* (*to think*) in (24) has an ARG-ST containing two elements. Verbal Argument Structure Extension imposes the constraint that its DEPS-list must contain these two elements and may contain, in addition, an arbitrary number of adverbial *synsem*'s (i.e., *synsem*'s whose MOD value is non-empty and unifiable with that of the *synsem* of the lexical item at hand[5]). Argument Realization states that the elements on DEPS are either present on SUBJ or COMPS or are of type *gap-synsem*, i.e., the type used for gaps in the lexicalist approach to extraction introduced below. The AVM in (24) satisfies both constraints.

(24)
$$\begin{bmatrix} \text{PHON} & \textit{denken} \\ \text{SUBJ} & \langle \boxed{1} \rangle \\ \text{COMPS} & \langle \boxed{2}, \boxed{3} \rangle \\ \text{DEPS} & \langle \boxed{1}, \boxed{2}, \boxed{3}\text{ADV} \rangle \\ \text{ARG-ST} & \langle \boxed{1}\text{NP}[\textit{nom}], \boxed{2}\text{PP}[\textit{aan}] \rangle \end{bmatrix}$$

[3] The $\oplus$ operator denotes the concatenation of two lists.

[4] The $-$ operator denotes the difference of two lists.

[5] Adding the latter constraint to Verbal Argument Structure Extension introduces a circular path equation. This can be avoided by restricting the value of MOD to the features which must be accessed by the modifier (i.e., HEAD and CONT).

Assuming a HEAD-SUBJ-COMPS schema for Dutch main clauses,[6] this allows for the derivation of the example below:

(25) Kim denkt nooit aan dit probleem.
Kim thinks never about this problem.
Kim never thinks about this problem.

(26)

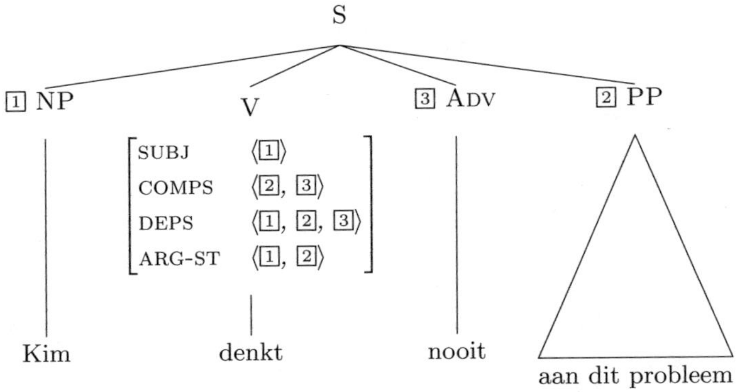

Bouma et al. (2001) argue that Argument Realization allows the lexicalist, traceless, account of complement extraction in Sag (1997) to be extended to subject and adjunct extraction. Instead of positing phonologically empty elements, it is assumed that the type *synsem* has subtypes *canonical-synsem* and *gap-synsem*, where the latter are *synsem*'s whose LOC and SLASH values are reentrant:

(27) $$\textit{gap-synsem} \Rightarrow \begin{bmatrix} \text{LOC} & \boxed{1} \\ \text{SLASH} & \{\boxed{1}\} \end{bmatrix}$$

As a lexical entry will usually only require of its arguments that they must be of type *synsem*, the introduction of *gap-synsem* in general allows any argument to be realized as *gap-synsem* or *canonical-synsem*.

Dependents of type *gap-synsem* do have an effect on the value of SLASH, as a consequence of the Slash Amalgamation (28). It defines the value of SLASH of a given lexical entry as the union of all the SLASH-values of its dependents, minus those elements on SLASH bound by this particular entry. BIND is used to account for so-called *easy*-constructions, where an adjective selects for a complement with a non-empty SLASH-value and 'binds' this element locally. An example derivation is given

[6]This phrase structure schema is used here mainly for presentational convenience. More sophisticated treatments of Germanic main clauses and verb-second can be found in Pollard (1996) and Frank (1994), among others. These proposals are compatible with the analysis of R-pronouns presented here.

in (29). As SLASH-amalgamation collects the SLASH-values of elements on DEPS, instead of just COMPS as in earlier work, it covers subject and adjunct extraction as well.

(28) **Slash Amalgamation:**

word ⇒

$$\left[\text{SYNSEM}\ \left[\begin{array}{ll}\text{LOC}\,|\,\text{CAT}\,|\,\text{DEPS} & \langle[\text{SLASH}\ \boxed{1}], \text{DOTS}, [\text{SLASH}\ \boxed{n}]\rangle\\ \text{SLASH} & (\boxed{1}\cup\ldots\cup\boxed{n}) - \boxed{2}\\ \text{BIND} & \boxed{2}\end{array}\right]\right]$$

(29)

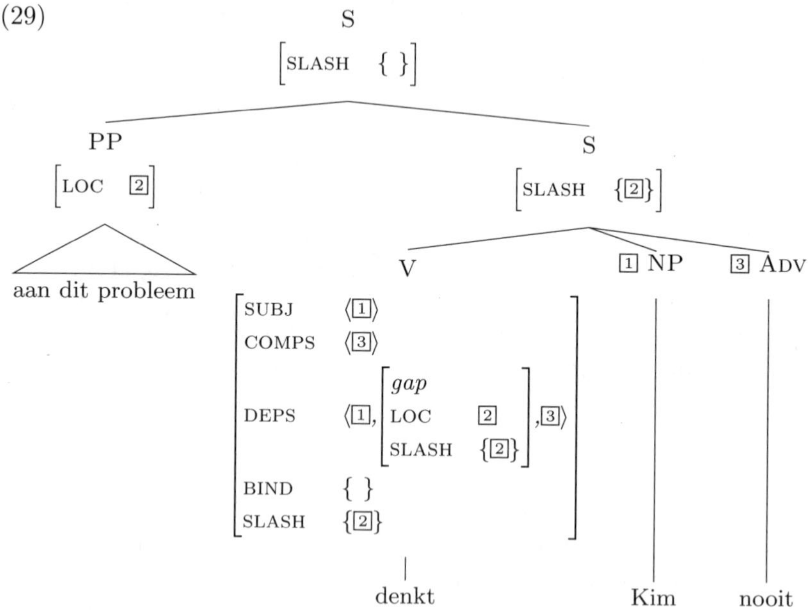

4.5 Lexical Entries for R-Pronouns

The following lexical entries are assumed for the R-pronouns *daar* and *er*:

(30)

$$\left[\begin{array}{ll}\text{PHON} & \textit{daar}\\ \text{SYNSEM}\,|\,\text{LOC} & \left[\begin{array}{ll}\text{CAT} & \left[\begin{array}{ll} \multicolumn{2}{l}{\textit{major}}\\ \text{HEAD} & \left[\begin{array}{ll}\multicolumn{2}{l}{\textit{noun}}\\ \text{MOD} & \textit{verb}\end{array}\right]\end{array}\right]\\ \text{CONT} & \textit{r-pro}\end{array}\right]\end{array}\right]$$

(31)
$$\begin{bmatrix} \text{PHON} & er \\ \text{SYNSEM}\,|\,\text{LOC} & \begin{bmatrix} \text{CAT} & \begin{bmatrix} minor \\ \text{HEAD} & \begin{bmatrix} noun \\ \text{MOD} & verb \end{bmatrix} \end{bmatrix} \\ \text{CONT} & r\text{-}pro \end{bmatrix} \end{bmatrix}$$

R-pronouns are treated as noun phrases, and thus can be selected by prepositions. The 'full' R-pronoun *daar* and the 'reduced' form *er* differ in that the CATEGORY of *daar* is of sort *major*, whereas it is *minor* for *er*. The distinction between major and minor categories is due to van Eynde (1999), and can be used, among others, to account for the fact that *er* cannot be fronted or coordinated.

(32) **Daar/*Er** had ze niet **aan** gedacht.
there had she not of thought
Of that she had not thought.

(33) Wil je liever **hier** of **daar/*er** zitten ?
want you rather here or there sit
Would you rather sit here or there?

R-pronouns can be used adverbially (see section 4.7 below), and thus have a MOD-vlaue compatible with verbal *synsems*.

In Pollard and Sag (1994), the CONTENT value of NPs is of sort *nom-obj*, with subsorts *non-pronoun* and *pronoun*, where *pronoun* has the subsorts *personal pronoun* and *anaphoric pronoun*. To account for the distribution of Dutch R-pronouns, the following refinement of the sort *nom-obj* is required:

(34)

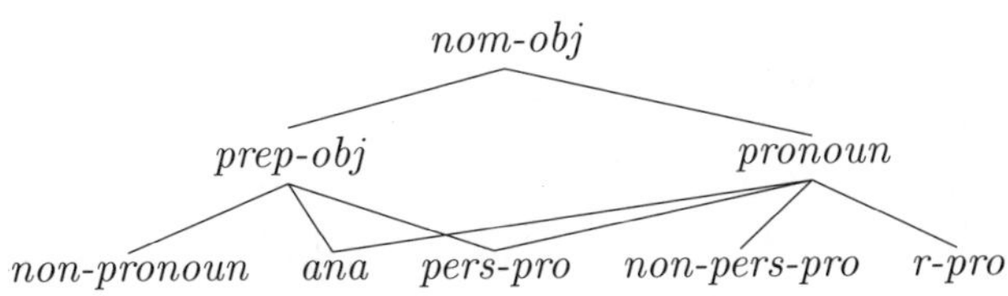

The sort *pronoun* now has subsorts for anaphoric, personal, (non-r) non-personal, and r-pronouns. The sort *prep-obj* picks out exactly those nominal objects which can be the local complement of a preposition (i.e., non-pronominal NPs, anaphoric pronouns, and personal pronouns).

4.6 Argument Realization for Prepositions

A canonical lexical entry for a preposition is given in (35). The preposition *aan* does not impose any requirements on its argument, other than that it must be an accusative NP. The preposition *met* (which does not allow extraction) in (36) requires that its argument must be [CONT *prep-obj*], whereas *mee* (which requires extraction) in (37) selects a [CONT *r-pro*] argument.

(35)
$$\begin{bmatrix} \text{PHON } \textit{aan} \\ \text{SYNSEM} \mid \text{LOC} \mid \text{CAT} & \begin{bmatrix} \text{HEAD} & \textit{prep} \\ \text{ARG-ST} & \left\langle \begin{bmatrix} \text{HEAD} & \textit{noun}[\textit{acc}] \\ \text{CONT} & \textit{nom-obj} \end{bmatrix} \right\rangle \end{bmatrix} \end{bmatrix}$$

(36)
$$\begin{bmatrix} \text{PHON } \textit{met} \\ \text{SYNSEM} \mid \text{LOC} \mid \text{CAT} & \begin{bmatrix} \text{HEAD} & \textit{prep} \\ \text{ARG-ST} & \left\langle \begin{bmatrix} \text{HEAD} & \textit{noun}[\textit{acc}] \\ \text{CONT} & \textit{prep-obj} \end{bmatrix} \right\rangle \end{bmatrix} \end{bmatrix}$$

(37)
$$\begin{bmatrix} \text{PHON } \textit{met} \\ \text{SYNSEM} \mid \text{LOC} \mid \text{CAT} & \begin{bmatrix} \text{HEAD} & \textit{prep} \\ \text{ARG-ST} & \left\langle \begin{bmatrix} \text{HEAD} & \textit{noun}[\textit{acc}] \\ \text{CONT} & \textit{r-pro} \end{bmatrix} \right\rangle \end{bmatrix} \end{bmatrix}$$

For prepositions, the following argument realization principle is assumed:

(38) **Prepositional Argument Realization:**

$$\begin{bmatrix} \textit{word} \\ \text{SYNSEM} \mid \text{LOC} \mid \text{CAT} \mid \text{HEAD} & \textit{prep} \end{bmatrix} \Rightarrow$$

$$\begin{bmatrix} \text{SYNSEM} & \begin{bmatrix} \text{LOC} \mid \text{CAT} & \begin{bmatrix} \text{SUBJ} & \langle\ \rangle \\ \text{COMPS} & \textit{listof}([\text{CONT } \textit{prep-obj}\ ]) \\ \text{DEPS} & \boxed{1} \\ \text{ARG-ST} & \boxed{1} \end{bmatrix} \\ \text{SLASH} & \textit{setof}([\text{CONT } \textit{r-pro}\ ]) \end{bmatrix} \end{bmatrix}$$

This principle captures three properties of prepositions:[7] they do not take a subject, they do not allow adjuncts as dependents (and thus

[7]The value of the valence feature SPR is ignored here. Prepositions heading adverbial PPs sometimes occur with a specifier.

DEPS and ARG-ST are structure shared), and, finally, the CONT-value of (local) complements must be of sort *prep-obj*, whereas that of extracted arguments must be of sort *r-pro*.[8] Note that the value of COMPS and SLASH is further constrained by the general Argument Realization Principle given in (23) and SLASH-amalgamation (28): if the argument of a preposition is realized as a canonical *synsem*, it must appear on COMPS, and if it is realized as a *gap-synsem*, it does not appear on COMPS but the SLASH-value of the gap is amalgamated into the SLASH-value of the preposition. These constraints imply that the entries for *met* and *mee* in (36) and (37) can be expanded as follows:

(39)
$$\begin{bmatrix} \text{PHON} & \textit{met} \\ \text{COMPS} & \langle \boxed{1} \rangle \\ \text{DEPS} & \langle \boxed{1} \rangle \\ \text{ARG-ST} & \left\langle \boxed{1} \begin{bmatrix} \text{HEAD} & \textit{noun}[\textit{acc}] \\ \text{CONT} & \textit{prep-obj} \end{bmatrix} \right\rangle \\ \text{SLASH} & \{\ \} \end{bmatrix}$$

(40)
$$\begin{bmatrix} \text{PHON} & \textit{mee} \\ \text{COMPS} & \langle\ \rangle \\ \text{DEPS} & \langle \boxed{1} \rangle \\ \text{ARG-ST} & \left\langle \boxed{1} \begin{bmatrix} \textit{gap} & \\ \text{LOC} & \boxed{2} \begin{bmatrix} \text{HEAD} & \textit{noun}[\textit{acc}] \\ \text{CONT} & \textit{r-pro} \end{bmatrix} \\ \text{SLASH} & \{\boxed{2}\} \end{bmatrix} \right\rangle \\ \text{SLASH} & \{\boxed{2}\} \end{bmatrix}$$

The lexical entry for *aan* can be expanded into a feature structure similar to (39) or (40).

Prepositional Argument Realization thus accounts for the fact that prepositions take full NPs but not impersonal pronouns as local complements (41a,b), that extraction is only allowed with R-pronouns (41c,d), and that *met* never allows extraction, whereas *mee* requires extraction (41e,f). The derivation of (41c) is given in (42).

[8]In a more exhaustive treatment of lexical categories, both the fact that prepositions do not take subjects as well as the fact that they do not take adjuncts as dependents would probably follow from implicational constraints not restricted to prepositions only.

(41) a. Kim denkt aan de voorstelling.
Kim thinks about the show

b. * Kim denkt aan het
Kim thinks about it

c. **Waar** denkt Kim **aan**?
What thinks Kim about

d. * Wie denkt Kim aan?
Who thinks Kim about

e. Kim snijdt het vlees met(*mee) een mes.
Kim cuts the meat with a knife

f. * **Waar** snijdt Kim het vlees **mee(*met)**?
Where cuts Kim the meat with

(42)

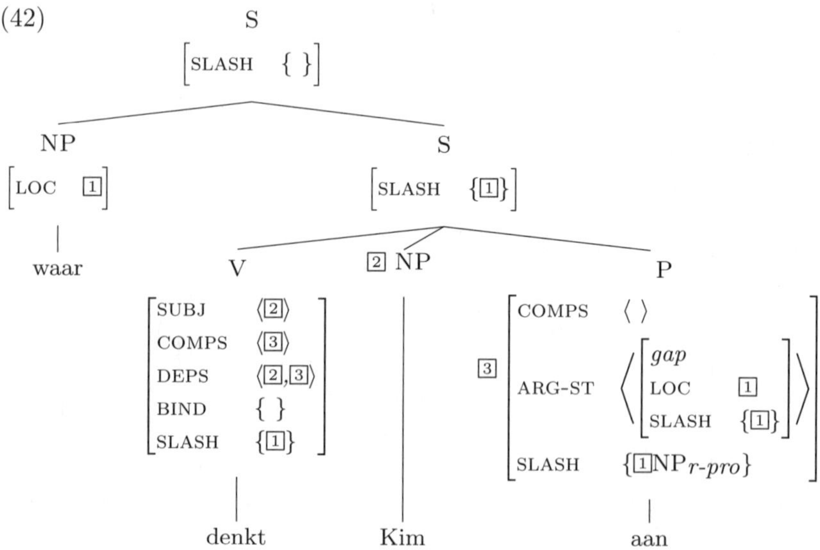

Note finally that an account of R-pronoun extraction in terms of SLASH also covers instances of long-distance extraction and relative clause formation:

(43) a. **Waar** denkt Kim dat Karel zijn boeken **vandaan** haalt?
Where thinks Kim that Carl his books from gets

b. de oplossing **waar** Kim niet **aan** gedacht had
the solution which Kim not about thought had

4.7 Locative R-Pronouns

R-pronouns are assumed to be 'adverbial' and thus carry a [MOD *verb*] specification. They can be introduced on DEPS by means of the Verbal Argument Structure Extension principle given in (22). Thus, given a transitive verb such as *zien*, which has an argument structure with two elements, an enriched feature structure can be obtained with three elements on DEPS, including an R-pronoun:

(44)
$$\begin{bmatrix} \text{PHON} & \textit{zien} \\ \text{SUBJ} & \langle \boxed{1} \rangle \\ \text{COMPS} & \langle \boxed{2}, \boxed{3} \rangle \\ \text{DEPS} & \langle\ \boxed{1}, \boxed{2}, \boxed{3}\text{NP}_{\textit{r-pro}} \rangle \\ \text{ARG-ST} & \langle \boxed{1}\text{NP}[\textit{nom}], \boxed{2}\text{NP}[\textit{acc}] \rangle \end{bmatrix}$$

This allows examples such as (45) to be derived as in (46).

(45) Kim ziet **daar** een fout.
Kim sees there a mistake

(46)

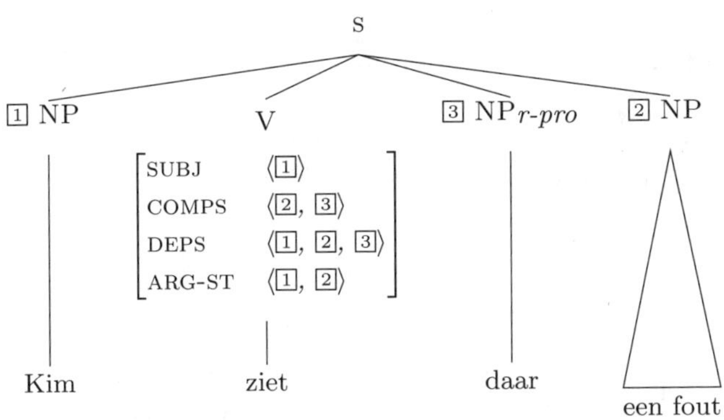

One of the advantages of treating adjuncts as complements is the fact that, in combination with the lexicalist account of extraction developed in Bouma et al. (2001), it predicts that adjuncts can be extracted:

(47) a. **Waar** dacht Kim dat Karel zijn boeken kocht?
where thought Kim that Karel his books bought

b. de enige plaats **waar** Kim nog een fout zag
the only place where Kim still a mistake saw

4.8 Prepositional R-Pronouns in the Middle Field

The account of prepositional R-pronouns in the Middle field presented below builds on the fact that R-pronouns may be introduced lexically on the DEPS-list of a verb. Below, a constraint is proposed which allows a verbal head to bind an R-pronoun on SLASH of one of its dependents, if the R-pronoun is present on DEPS.

Remember that BIND is the feature used in extraction constructions which allows a head to *bind* an element on SLASH of one of its dependents (see Pollard and Sag, 1994, p. 166 ff.). Thus, if a lexical item has a non-empty BIND value, it can select a complement with a non-empty SLASH-set, without amalgamating the element(s) in SLASH of its complement in its own SLASH-set. This feature is used to account for *easy*-constructions such as *Kim is easy to please.* Here, it is assumed that *easy* selects for a slashed VP-complement, but also has a non-empty value for BIND. As a consequence, the AP *easy to please* is not slashed.

The fact that R-pronouns in the Middle Field can be interpreted as arguments of a slashed preposition is a consequence of the following implication:

(48) **Bind R-Pronoun Principle**:

$$\begin{bmatrix} \textit{word} & \\ \text{SYNSEM} \mid \text{LOCA} \mid \text{CAT} \mid \text{HEAD} & \textit{verb} \end{bmatrix} \Rightarrow$$

$$\begin{bmatrix} \text{DEPS} & \left\langle \ldots, \begin{bmatrix} \textit{canon-synsem} \\ \text{LOC } \boxed{1} \begin{bmatrix} \text{CONT } \textit{r-pro} \end{bmatrix} \end{bmatrix}, \ldots \right\rangle \\ \text{BIND} & \{\boxed{1}\} \end{bmatrix} \vee \begin{bmatrix} \text{BIND } \{\ \} \end{bmatrix}$$

The first disjunct allows a verb which has an R-pronoun on its DEPS-list to bind an R-pronoun on SLASH of its dependents. It accounts for examples such as (49) below.

(49)

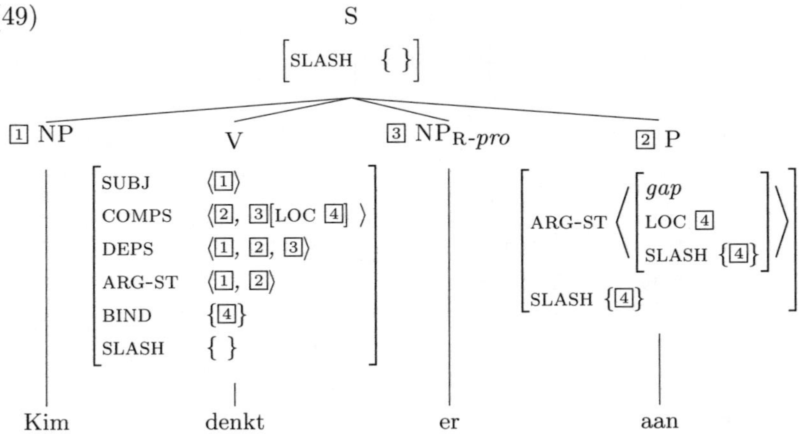

The second disjunct sets the BIND-value of a verb to the empty set. Note that in all cases where DEPS contains no R-pronoun, only the second disjunct applies, and thus examples such as (50) are correctly ruled out.

(50) * Kim denkt aan
Kim thinks about

In (51), on the other hand, no R-pronoun is present on the DEPS-list of the verb *denkt*, hence the element on SLASH of the preposition is amalgamated into the sign for the phrase *denkt Kim aan*, which in turn can combine with *waar* to form a FILLER-HEAD phrase.

(51) **Waar** denkt Kim **aan**.
What thinks Kim about

By using SLASH as a means for connecting the R-pronoun and the preposition, the present account predicts the possibility of extraction from prepositions embedded in another constituent, as in (52):

(52) a. Kim is **er** tevreden **mee**.
Kim is there happy with

b. Maar ik heb **er** wat moeite **mee**.
But I have there some difficulty with

Here, the SLASH-value of the preposition is amalgamated into the SLASH-value of the larger phrase, where it can be bound by the verb:

(53)

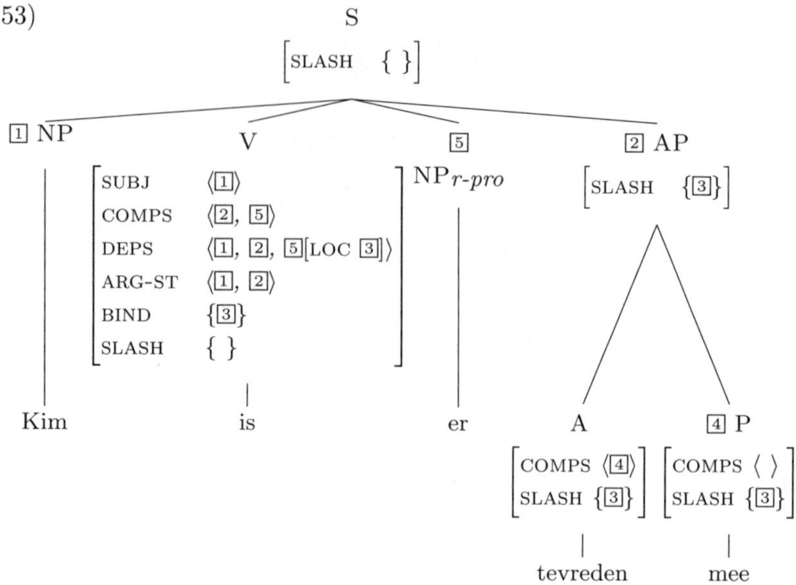

Note, however, that an R-pronoun on DEPS cannot 'bind' an element on SLASH which originates from an embedded clause, as shown in (54). Extraction of R-pronouns out of embedded clauses in general is not excluded, as shown in (43a). One might try to rule out cases such as (54) by introducing a distinction between R-pronouns in the Middle Field and fronted R-pronouns, e.g., -/+ TOPIC, and marking R-pronouns on SLASH of subordinate clauses as [+TOPIC].

(54) * Jan dacht **er** dat iedereen tevreden **mee** was.
John thought there that everybody happy with was

4.9 Slash vs. Argument Inheritance

It is worthwhile to compare this analysis of R-pronouns in the Middle Field with analyses in HPSG of clitic-climbing in the Romance languages such as Miller and Sag (1997) and Monachesi (1995). Although R-pronouns are not treated as clitics or pronominal affixes in this case (but see Model (1991)), there is nevertheless a similarity between the two phenomena in that R-pronouns apparently can be dependents of a higher predicate while being arguments of a lower predicate.

Both Miller and Sag (1997) and Monachesi (1995) take the position that clitic-climbing is a consequence of argument inheritance, i.e., the mechanism which allows arguments of an embedded predicate to be inherited by a higher predicate. Once arguments are 'visible' to the higher predicate in this way, they can be realized as clitics by means of the same mechanism responsible for realizing 'ordinary' arguments as clitics. On the other hand, some instances of clitic-climbing (such as the account of *en*-clitization in Miller and Sag (1997)) have been accounted for by assuming a slashed dependent and a higher predicate which binds the element on SLASH of the dependent by realizing it as a clitic. In particular, Miller and Sag (1997) argue that *en*-clitization is subject to the same constraints as extraction of *de*-phrases from subjects and objects, and thus is best analyzed in terms of SLASH.

The account of prepositional R-pronouns above does not involve argument inheritance, but is formulated solely in terms of SLASH and BIND. Although argument inheritance plays an important role in the syntax of Dutch verb clusters (van Noord and Bouma, 1997; Bouma and van Noord, 1997), an approach based on argument inheritance seems highly unlikely for R-pronouns. First of all, prepositions which do not allow extraction (such as *met*) cannot be associated with an R-pronoun in the Middle field either. If two different mechanisms are used to account for these two phenomena, such generalizations are easily lost. Second, as argument inheritance normally involves the composition of two COMPS-lists, R-pronouns would have to be allowed on COMPS, even though they can, apart from a few exceptional cases, never appear in a position following the preposition. Third, the set of argument inheritance verbs must now not only contain auxiliaries and modals, but all verbs which select a (prepositional) complement. Examples such as (52) introduce further complications for an argument inheritance approach, as it suggests that predicative adjectives and nouns must be argument inheritors as well. Finally, it will be argued below that amalgamation of syntactic functions of *er* follows naturally from the fact that R-pronouns are adjuncts which are introduced independently of the question whether there is a preposition with a non-empty SLASH-value. In an argument inheritance approach, the relationship between valence and syntactically realized arguments has to be one-on-one, and thus there is no room for amalgamation of syntactic functions.

4.10 R-pronouns as Subjects

In existential constructions and impersonal passives, *er* may appear in sentence-initial position:

(55) **Er** liep niemand op straat.
There walked nobody in the street

(56) **Er** wordt gevoetbald.
There is play-soccer

One explanation is that *er* is the subject in these constructions, and thus the examples above do not involve a HEAD-FILLER construction, with *er* as a filler. Bennis (1986, 212 ff.) suggests that this is part of a more general phenomenon which allows locative phrases to fill the subject position in existentials and impersonal passives:

(57) In Amsterdam liep niemand op straat.
In Amsterdam walked nobody in the street

(58) In onze straat wordt gevoetbald.
In our street is play-soccer

In Dutch main clauses, (non-extraposed) syntactic subjects must be adjacent to the finite verb. The fact that in existential sentences the indefinite NP filling the most prominent argument position may appear in positions non-adjacent to the finite verb, is therefore further evidence for an analysis in which the locative phrase fills the syntactic subject position:

(59) **Er** zit plots een man tegenover haar.
there sits suddenly a man opposite her

The interaction with raising verbs such as *schijnen (seem)* and *blijken (appear)* also suggests that locative phrases may fill a subject position:

(60) **Er** scheen plots een man tegenover haar te zitten.
There seemed suddenly a man opposite her to sit

(61) In de tuin blijkt te worden gedanst.
In the garden appeared to be danced

The possibility of inserting a locative in the (syntactic) subject position follows from Verbal Argument Realization as presented in section 4.4. After proposing an account of passive compatible with the architecture introduced so far, a constraint is given which restricts locatives in subject position to existential and passive constructions.

The principle in (62) below is a simple proposal for passive, which leaves the ARG-ST subject unrealized on DEPS. It is related to the proposal in Manning and Sag (1998) in that it recognizes the need to make available both the 'underlying' and actual ordering of arguments within one lexeme. Note that no attempt is made to characterize which verbs can be realized as passive or how the [VFORM *pas*] specification relates to morphological form.

(62) **Passive Argument Structure Extension:**

$$\begin{bmatrix} \textit{word} & \\ \text{SYNSEM}\,|\,\text{LOC}\,|\,\text{CAT}\,|\,\text{HEAD} & \begin{bmatrix}\textit{verb} & \\ \text{VFORM} & \textit{pas}\end{bmatrix}\end{bmatrix} \Rightarrow$$

$$\begin{bmatrix}\text{SS } \boxed{3} \begin{bmatrix}\text{L}\,|\,\text{C} \begin{bmatrix}\text{DEPS} & \left(\left\langle\begin{bmatrix}\textit{`loc-ss'}\\ \text{MOD } \boxed{3}\end{bmatrix}\right\rangle \oplus\right)\boxed{2} \oplus \textit{listof}\left(\begin{bmatrix}\textit{`adv-ss'}\\ \text{MOD } \boxed{3}\end{bmatrix}\right)\\ \text{ARG-ST} & \langle\boxed{1}\rangle \oplus \boxed{2}\end{bmatrix}\end{bmatrix}\end{bmatrix}$$

Passive Argument Structure Extension is like Verbal Argument Structure Extension, except that it leaves the ARG-ST subject unrealized. Impersonal passives result if this principle is applied to intransitive verbs with [VFORM *pas*]. The result will be a sign whose DEPS list contains no elements from ARG-ST.

Existential constructions require an indefinite ARG-ST subject. Locative subjects can therefore be restricted to impersonal passives and existential constructions by means of the following constraint:

(63) **Locative Subject Constraint**:

$$\neg\begin{bmatrix}\textit{word} & \\ \text{SS}\,|\,\text{LOC}\,|\,\text{CAT}\,|\,\text{DEPS} & \langle \textit{`loc'}, \text{NP}[+\textit{def}], \ldots\rangle\end{bmatrix}$$

Passive Argument Structure Extension together with the possibility of filling the syntactic subject position with a locative phrase in cases satisfying the Locative Subject Constraint, accounts for examples (55) and (56):

(64)

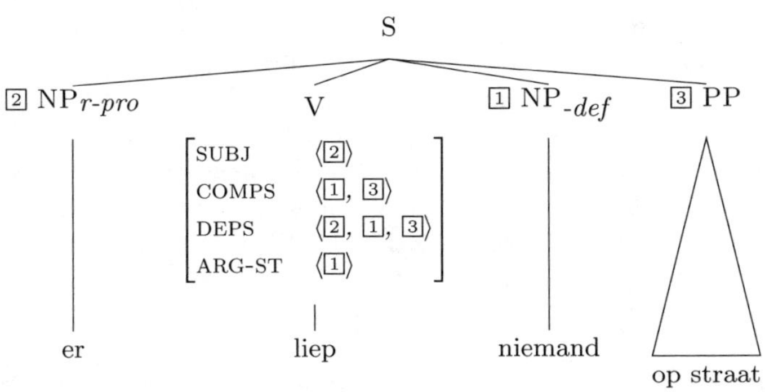

(65)

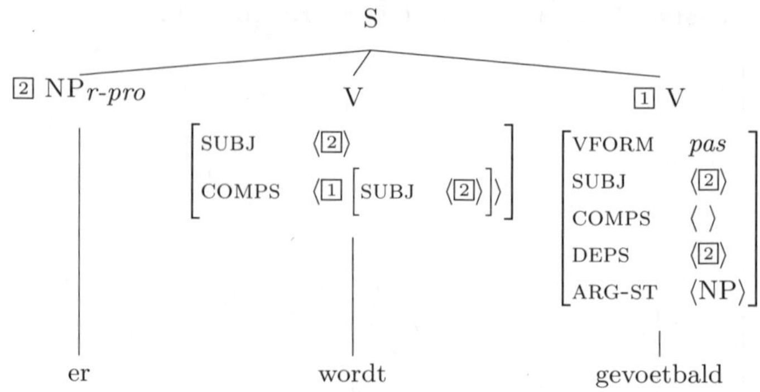

Note that *liep* is an intransitive verb with a single element on ARG-ST. An R-pronoun can appear in the first DEPS-position (and, consequently, in the subject position), as the ARG-ST subject of *liep* is indefinite. The passive participle *gevoetbald* in (65) has an ARG-ST subject which is not realized on DEPS, and a DEPS list containing an initial R-pronoun filling the subject position. The passive auxiliary *werd* is probably best treated as an argument inheritance verb (Bouma and van Noord, 1997). Here it suffices to observe that the auxiliary selects for a passive participle, and that it is a subject-raising verb, i.e., syntax and semantics is shared between the subject of the auxiliary and of the embedded passive participle.

4.11 A Solution for Bech's Problem

Amalgamation of the prepositional syntactic function of R-pronouns with other syntactic functions follows from the analysis introduced above. The account of prepositional R-pronouns in the Middle Field relies on the fact that R-pronouns can be freely added to the DEPS-list of a verb. Therefore, there is no requirement of a one-to-one correspondence between SLASHed preposition and R-pronoun, as would be the case if R-pronouns in the Middle Field would have been analysed as fillers in a regular filler-gap dependency. Consequently, it is possible for an R-pronoun to bind an element on SLASH of the verb, and at the same time to act as subject in an existential or impersonal passive. This situation is illustrated in the analysis of examples (18) and (21) below.[9]

[9] Again, the fact that the passive auxiliary *worden* is an argument inheritance verb, and thus in (66) takes both *aan* and *gewerkt* as complements, is ignored.

(66)

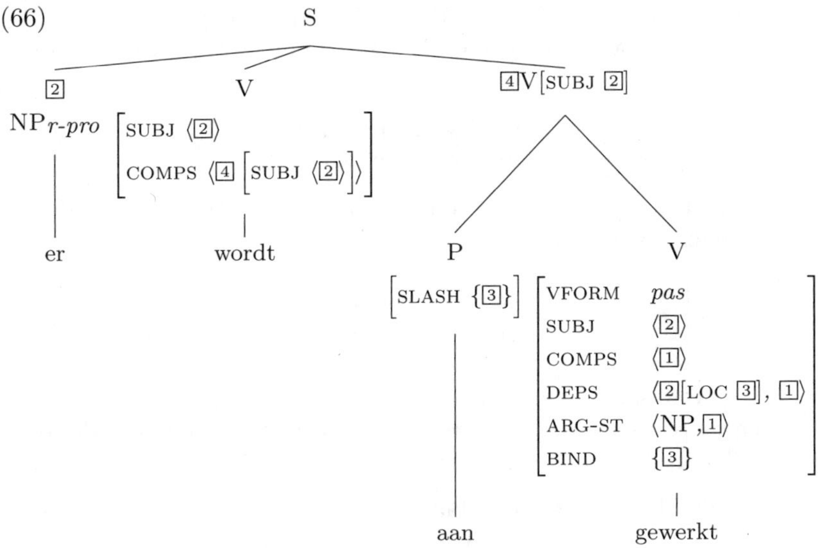

(67)

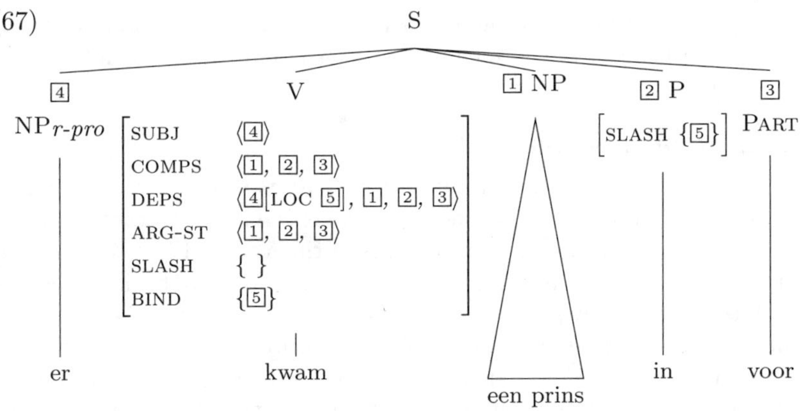

While the present account predicts the possibility of function merger, and thus solves Bech's problem, there is nothing so far that blocks the presence of multiple R-pronouns. In general, this is correct, as different R-pronouns can be combined, as is illustrated in (68) (which is actually ambiguous - the current analysis predicts the two different derivations corresponding to the two readings), and in examples (14) and (15).

(68) **Waar**$_{\text{LOC/P}}$ wordt **hier**$_{\text{LOC/P}}$ aan gewerkt?
where is here on worked
What is being worked on here?
Where is this being worked on?

Multiple occurrences of (non-quantitative) *er* are in general not allowed, however, as shown (69) below, and in examples (17) and (20) of section 4.2.

(69) * **Er** wordt **er** hard aan gewerkt.
There is there hard on worked.

One might account for these data by restricting the number of minor R-pronouns on DEPS to at most one:

(70)
$$\neg \left[\text{DEPS} \left\langle \ldots, \begin{bmatrix} \text{CAT} & \textit{minor} \\ \text{CONT} & \textit{r-pro} \end{bmatrix}, \ldots, \begin{bmatrix} \text{CAT} & \textit{minor} \\ \text{CONT} & \textit{r-pro} \end{bmatrix}, \ldots \right\rangle \right]$$

However, something more general is clearly needed, as other cooccurrences of R-pronouns, as well as some combinations of different R-pronouns lead to poor results as well:

(71) ?* **Hier** wordt **hier/daar** hard aan gewerkt.
Here is here/there hard on worked.

This suggests that an account which takes the locative (and deictic and discourse) aspects of the meaning of R-pronouns into account, is worth pursuing.

4.12 Conclusions

In this paper an analysis of Dutch R-pronouns was presented which accounts for a range of uses of these pronouns (i.e., as extracted arguments of prepositions, as adverbs, as adverbs in the Middle Field binding a gap originating in a PP, and as subject). Furthermore, by taking the adverbial use of R-pronouns as basic, and by treating such adverbs as lexically introduced dependents, an account of function amalgamation was possible. The present analysis appears to be simpler than transformational alternatives, which involve movement and deletion transformations subject to complex constraints on their applicability. Also, it has been argued an account of prepositional R-pronouns in the Middle Field in terms of SLASH seems preferable over a potential alternative analysis using argument inheritance. Given the complexity of the data, it is not surprising that a number of issues were left for further investigation.

References

Bech, G. 1952. Über das niederländische Adverbialpronomen *Er*. *Travaux du Cercle Linguistique de Copenhague* 8.

Bennis, H. 1986. *Gaps and Dummies*. Ph.D. thesis, Katholieke Hogeschool Tilburg.

Bouma, G., R. Malouf, and I. A. Sag. 2001. Satisfying constraints on extraction and adjunction. *Natural Language and Linguistic Theory* 19:1–65.

Bouma, G. and G. van Noord. 1997. Word order constraints on Germanic verb clusters. In E. Hinrichs, T. Nakazawa, and A. Kathol, eds., *Complex Predicates in Nonderivational Syntax*, pages 43–72. New York: Academic Press.

Frank, A. 1994. Verb second by underspecification. In H. Trost, ed., *Konvens 94*, pages 121–130. Vienna.

Haesereyn, W., K. Romijn, G. Geerts, J. De Rooy, and M. Van den Toorn. 1997. *Algemene Nederlandse Spraakkunst*. Martinus Nijhoff Uitgevers Groningen / Wolters Plantyn Deurne. Tweede, geheel herziene druk.

Manning, C., I. Sag, and M. Iida. 1999. The lexical integrity of Japanese causatives. In R. Levine and G. Green, eds., *Readings in HPSG*, pages 39–79. Cambridge: Cambridge University Press.

Manning, C. D. and I. A. Sag. 1998. Argument structure, valence, and binding. *Nordic Journal of Linguistics* 21.

Miller, P. 1992. *Clitics and Constituents in Phrase Structure Grammar*. New York: Garland.

Miller, P. and I. Sag. 1997. French clitic movement without clitics or movement. *Natural Language and Linguistic Theory* 15(3):573–639.

Model, J. 1991. *Grammatische Analyse*. Dordrecht: ICG Publications.

Monachesi, P. 1995. *A Grammar of Italian Clitics*. Ph.D. thesis, Katholieke Universiteit Brabant, Tilburg.

Pollard, C. and I. Sag. 1994. *Head-driven Phrase Structure Grammar*. Center for the Study of Language and Information Stanford.

Pollard, C. J. 1996. On head non-movement. In H. Bunt and A. van Horck, eds., *Discontinuous Constituency*, Natural language processing, pages 279–305. Berlin, New York: Mouton de Gruyter.

Przepiórkowski, A. 1999a. Adjuncts as complements: Evidence from case assignment. In A. Kathol, J.-P. Koenig, and G. Webelhuth, eds., *Lexical and Constructional Aspects of Linguistic Explanation*, pages 231–246. CSLI Publications.

Przepiórkowski, A. 1999b. On complements and adjuncts in Polish. In R. D. Borsley and A. Przepiórkowski, eds., *Slavic in HPSG*, pages 183–210. Stanford: CSLI Publications.

Rentier, G. 1993. Dutch clitic pronouns and preposition stranding. In *Computational Linguistics in the Netherlands, papers from the third CLIN Meeting*, pages 109–120. Tilburg.

Rentier, G. 1994. A lexicalist approach to preposition stranding. In *Konvens 94*, pages 280–289. Berlin: Springer.

Sag, I. 1997. English relative clause constructions. *Journal of Linguistics* 33:431–484.

van Eynde, F. 1999. Major and minor pronouns in Dutch. In G. Bouma, E. W. Hinrichs, G.-J. M. Kruijff, and R. T. Oehrle, eds., *Constraints and Resources in Natural Language Syntax and Semantics*, pages 137–152. Stanford: CSLI Publications.

van Noord, G. and G. Bouma. 1994. Adjuncts and the processing of lexical rules. In *Proceedings of the 15th International Conference on Computational Linguistics (COLING)*, pages 250–256. Kyoto.

van Noord, G. and G. Bouma. 1997. Dutch verb clustering without verb clusters. In P. Blackburn and M. de Rijke, eds., *Specifying Syntactic Structures*, pages 123–153. Stanford: CSLI Publications.

van Riemsdijk, H. 1978. *A Case Study in Syntactic Markedness: The binding nature of prepositional phrases*. Foris Publications, Dordrecht.

5

Syntactic Transparency of Pronominal Affixes

BERTHOLD CRYSMANN

Approaches to bound pronominals in HPSG reflect a strict dichotomy between postlexical clitics and lexical (or phrasal) affixes, a distinction already drawn in cliticisation theories developed by Miller (1992) or Halpern (1995). Motivated by the rigorous application of the diagnostic criteria suggested in Zwicky and Pullum (1983) and Miller (1992), clitics in Romance languages are treated as lexical afixes, whose morphological and morphosyntactic properties are derived entirely within the lexicon (Miller and Sag, 1997; Monachesi, 1999). Weak pronominals in Polish (Kupść, 1999) and second position clitics in Serbo-Croat (Penn, 1999), however, enjoy a much higher degree of syntactic transparency, favouring an analysis in terms of linearisation approaches. In this paper, I will suggest that European Portuguese (EP) represents a transitional type, where clitics have already acquired the morphological properties of lexical affixes, yet, "the rules governing clitic placement seem to relate more to syntax than to prosody or morphology" (Spencer, 1991, p. 365). I will argue that the distinction between constituent structure and order domains, as drawn in linearisation-based variants of HPSG, provides the necessary tools to model the syntax of transparent affixes, relating EP clitics to both their Romance and Slavic counterparts.

5.1 Lexical Properties of European Portuguese Clitics

Weak pronominals in EP, similar to their French and Italian counterparts, display a number of properties characteristic of lexical affixes. With the exception of Zwicky and Pullum's (1983) CRITERIA A and E (=promiscuity and syntactic opacity) and Miller's (1992) COORDI-

Grammatical Interfaces in HPSG.
Ronnie Cann, Claire Grover and Philip Miller.

nation Criterion, all other diagnostic criteria argue in favour of a morphological treatment of these elements, some of which will be briefly discussed below (see Crysmann 2000a for details).

Arbitrary Gaps (Criterion B) The set of combinations attested for EP clitics display some arbitrary gaps, a property much more typical of inflectional paradigms than of cliticisation. Thus, EP bound pronominals fail to attach to participles, although participles can be combined with ordinary NP objects.

(1) a. Lidos os livros às crianças, vamos passear.
read the books to.the children go walk
'Having read the books to the children, we go out for a walk.' (Duarte et al., 1995)

b. * Lidos-lhes os livros, vamos passear.
read-to.them the books go walk
(Duarte et al., 1995)

Within the clitic cluster itself, dative reflexive clitics do not combine with third person accusative clitics, though no such restriction holds between each of the clitics and full NP arguments (Crysmann, 1997).

(2) a. Eu ofereci-me um bolo.
I offered-to.me a biscuit
'I offered myself a biscuit.'

b. * Eu ofereci-mo.
I offered-me.it

c. Ele ofereceu-mo.
he offered-me.it
'He offered it to me.'

d. Eu ofereci-o a mim.
I offered-it to me
'I offered-it to myself.'

Morphological Idiosyncrasies (Criterion C) With third person accusative clitics (*o/a/os/as*), a preceding /s/, /z/, or /r/ obligatorily neutralises to [l], affecting affixes (3a), stems (3b), and other clitics (3c) alike.

(3) a. fazer + -o → fazê-lo
do.INF it to do-it

b. far- + -o + ía → fá-lo-ía
do.STEM it would (s)he would do it

c. dar + nos + o → dar-no-lo
give.INF us it to give it to us

This process is highly idiosyncratic, as it cannot be attested anywhere else in the grammar of EP, neither with the homophonous definite article (*todos os rapazes* 'all the boys' vs. **todo[l] os rapazes*) nor with the equally homophonous participial agreement markers (*preso* 'arrested' vs. **pre[l]o*.

Mesoclisis (Criterion F) Probably the most compelling piece of evidence in favour of affixal status is provided by *mesoclisis*. In the future and conditional tenses, the pronominal clitics may appear infixed between the tense/agreement marker and the verbal stem.

(4) Mostrar -no -los -á.
show -us- them -FUT.3S

'He will show them to us.' (Spencer, 1991, p. 366)

The future and conditional morphemes themselves are indubitably affixes: first, except pronominal clitics, no other material can appear between these affixes and the stem; second, they can trigger allomorphy on the verbal stem, and, third, their position with respect to the verbal head reflects the canonical position of affixes, whereas it contradicts the canonical position of syntactic heads in this SVO language. If, however, the future/conditional markers are affixes, the pronominals infixed between these affixes and the stem are most likely to be affixes as well, rather than postlexical clitics.

Thus, as far as morphological and lexical properties are concerned, we have good reason to believe that EP clitics are derived in the lexical component, on a par with other inflectional affixes.

5.2 Placement Properties of EP Lexical Clitics

It has repeatly been observed in the literature (Duarte, 1983; Spencer, 1991, among others) that EP cliticisation displays an alternation between a prefixed (proclitic) and a suffixed (enclitic) realisation which, unlike other Romance languages, is not attributable to morphological properties of the clitic host alone. In this respect, EP contrasts quite sharply with e.g., Italian where a mere finiteness distinction captures the basic facts of clitic placement with respect to its host (cf. Monachesi, 1999). Rather, the presence of certain elements (proclisis triggers) in a specific syntactic domain preceding the verbal complex determines the order in which the clitic and its host surface. When realised in preverbal position, complementisers (5a,b), wh-expressions (5c,d), negation, quantified NPs, as well as temporal adverbials, enforce proclisis. Absence of a trigger in this domain makes enclisis (or mesoclisis) obligatory (6).

(5) a. que os amigos lhes deram livros
that the friends to them gave books
'that the friends gave them books'

b. * que os amigos deram-lhes livros

c. Que mentira lhe contaste?
Which lie him you told
'Which lie did you tell him?'

d. * que mentira contaste-lhe? (Duarte, 1983)

(6) a. * Os amigos lhes deram livros

b. Os amigos deram-lhes livros
the friends gave-to.them books
'The friends gave them books'

5.2.1 Quantifiers

Among the elements which trigger preposing of the clitic, nominal and adverbial quantifiers constitute a major class. However, the set of quantifiers licensing EP proclisis is only a proper subset of the natural language quantifiers identified in Generalised Quantifier Theory (GQT) (e.g., Barwise and Cooper, 1981; Bach et al., 1995). While both positive and negative universals, as well as non-classical quantifiers like *poucos* force the clitic to precede its host (7), some others do not: in addition to definite descriptions, proper names, and ordinary indefinites, there are also true quantifiers like *muitos* 'many' and *alguns* 'some' which do not exhibit the relevant syntactic effect (8).

(7) a. {Todos os, Poucos, Nenhuns} alunos lhe telefonaram.
{All, Few, No} students him phoned
'{All, Few, No} students phoned him.'

b. * {Todos os, Poucos, Nenhuns} alunos telefonaram-lhe.

(8) a. * {Muitos, Alguns} alunos lhe telefonaram.

b. {Muitos, Alguns} alunos telefonaram -lhe.
{many, some} students phoned him
'{Many, Some} students phoned him.'

A crucial observation regarding the partitioning of quantifiers into triggers and non-triggers is that it generalises from quantification over properties of individuals (D-quantifiers) to quantification over events (A-quantifiers): while the adverbial counterparts of (7) again enforce proclisis (9), no such effect can be observed with the correlates of (8), as illustrated in (10).

(9) a. O João {sempre, poucas vezes, nunca} me dá razão.
John {always, seldom, never} me gives reason
'John {always, seldom, never} agrees with me.'

b. * O João {sempre, poucas vezes, nunca} dá-me razão.

(10) a. * O João {muitas vezes, às vezes} me dá razão.

b. O João {muitas vezes, às vezes} dá-me razão.
John {often, sometimes} gives me reason
'John {often, sometimes} agrees with me.'

The parallelism between these two classes of quantifiers suggests that we are actually dealing with a systematic grammatical phenomenon, rather than just arbitrary properties of individual lexical items. I have argued in previous work (Crysmann, 1999a) that neither determiner strength nor appeal to the distinction between cardinal/proportional quantifiers, as suggested by Martins (1994), will perform a proper partitioning into triggers and non-triggers. Instead, the set of quantifiers licensing proclisis should be characterised as exactly those quantifiers which are downward monotone in either their restrictor (↓MON) or domain argument (MON↓).[1] It is of note that this very class of quantifiers also plays a crucial role in the syntax of EP negation, being banned from occuring in a position linearly preceding the negative marker *não* 'not' (Branco and Crysmann, 1999).

We have already mentioned in passing that proclisis is only enforced by triggers which linearly precede the clitic in the clause. As illustrated by the data in (11a-d), neither inverted subjects, nor postverbal adverbials can license preposing of the clitic. Similarly, postverbal floating quantifiers equally fail to trigger proclisis, although they unambiguously quantify over the preverbal subject (11e,f).

[1] It may appear puzzling that left monotone quantifiers apparently license proclisis in the wrong argument. In the domain of NPI licensing, however, this phenomenon is not unheard of: Horn (1996, p. 27–30) notes that the MON↓ quantifiers like *only*, *not all*, and *not everyone* can license weak NPIs such as *any* or *ever* in their upwards entailing restrictor argument.

Q		↓MON	MON↓	Proclisis
todos	'all'	+	−	+
cada	'every'	+	−	+
nem todos	'not all'	−	+	+
nenhun	'no'	+	+	+
poucos	'few'	−	+	+
no máximo n	'at most *n*'	+	+	+
a maioria	'most'	−	−	−
pelo menos n	'at least *n*'	−	−	−
muitos	'many'	−	−	−
alguns	'some'	−	−	−
n	*n*	−	−	−
o/a	'the'	−	−	−

TABLE 1 Downward monotonicity and proclisis licensing

(11) a. Ontem, telefonaram -lhe todos os alunos.
yesterday phoned to him all the students
'Yesterday, all friends phoned him.'

b. * Ontem, lhe telefonaram todos os alunos.

c. Os alunos telefonaram -lhe (poucas vezes).
the students phoned to him (seldom)
'The students phoned him (seldom).'

d. * Os alunos lhe telefonaram (poucas vezes).

e. Os alunos leram -no todos.
the students read it all
'All the students read it.'

f. * Os estudantes o leram todos

One might wonder, whether the linear position of subjects or floating quantifiers in (11) is related to a difference in interpretation, yielding only a narrow scope, collective interpretation when used postverbally. However, this does not seem to be the case: while, in general, postverbal quantifiers are ambiguous between a wide scope and a narrow scope reading, in (12) world knowledge only permits an interpretation where the universal quantifier outscopes the indefinite.

(12) a. Falaram com um Papa todos os reis portugueses.
spoke with a pope all the kings Portuguese
'All Portuguese kings talked to a pope.'

b. Os reis Egípcios envenenaram todos um competitor.
the kings Egyptian poisened all a rival
'All Egyptian kings poisened a rival.'

Similarly, postverbal subject quantifiers may also take wide scope with respect to preverbal negation (Branco and Crysmann, 1999). Given the apparent irrelevance of scope properties and the insensitivity to the argument status of the trigger, we are left with surface order as the only remaining generalisation providing a unified characterisation of the distribution of triggers. I therefore conclude that clitic placement in EP should best be regarded as a linearisation phenomenon.

We have already established that the placement of EP clitics is conditioned by factors other than the morphological properties of its host. In fact, the same alternation we observed with finite verbs can equally be attested in infinitives. Moreover, infinitival constructions provide a good testing ground to establish the clause-boundedness of the phenomenon.

(13) a. Eles lamentaram poucos guardas os terem matado.
they regretted few guards them have.3p killed
'They regret that few guards have killed them.'

b. * Eles lamentaram poucos guardas terem-nos matado.

c. Poucos guardas lamentaram eles terem-nos matado
few guards regretted they have.3p-them killed
'Few guards regretted that they have killed them.'

d. * Poucos guardas lamentaram eles os terem matado.

In (13a,b), the subject of the inflected infinitive is a monotone decreasing quantifier, requiring the clitic to precede its host. In the examples in (13c,d), however, no proclisis licensor is present in the infinitival clause, making enclitic realisation obligatory. The downward monotone matrix subject apparently fails to license proclisis in the embedded clause.

(14) a. Eles lamentaram não {os ter / *tê-los} matado
they regretted not {them have / have-them} killed
'They regretted not having killed them.'

b. Eles não lamentaram {*os ter / tê-los} matado.
they not regretted {them have / have-them} killed
'They didn't regret having killed them.'

c. Eles lamentaram [poucas vezes os ter matado].
they regretted seldom them have killed
'They regretted having rarely killed them.'

d. Eles lamentaram {*os ter / tê-los} matado
they regretted {them have / have-them} killed
poucas vezes.
seldom

e. Eles lamentaram poucas vezes [tê-los matado].
they regretted seldom have-them killed

'They seldom regretted having killed them.'

A similar observation can be made regarding uninflected infinitives: while negated infinitives do not allow enclisis (14a), matrix negation fails to trigger proclisis in the infinitive (14b). Likewise, downward monotone A-quantifiers in infinitives only license preposing of the clitic, if they precede the infinitive within the embedded clause (14c). Neither postverbal modifiers (14d), nor matrix modification (14e) will cause the relevant syntactic effect. Under the assumption that linearisation is a clause-bound phenomenon, the placement properties of the clitic cluster in finite and non-finite clauses are amenable to a unified treatment.

5.2.2 Wh-Questions

The second major class of proclisis triggers I will address is formed by wh-expressions: if the wh-phrase precedes the clitic in a matrix clause, proclisis is obligatory (5c,d), if, however, it follows the clitic-verb complex, enclisis must be used (cf. e.g., Duarte 1983):

(15) a. * O João lhe contou que mentira?

b. O João contou-lhe que mentira?
the João told-him which lie

'John told him which lie?'

Although the pattern observed here is clearly parallel to the case of quantifiers and negation, one could object that the relevant difference would rather lie in the fact that (5c,d) constitutes a UDC, while *in situ* wh-questions like (15) do not. The choice between these two alternatives has direct repercussions for the theoretical status of EP clitics: if linear position of the wh-phrase is the relevant concept, we have additional support that the clitic cluster participates in syntactic ordering, if, however, the distinction between non-local wh-constructions and wh-*in situ* proves to be correct, clitic placement in wh-questions may be analysed without reference to syntax at all, because, in current traceless theories of extraction (e.g., Sag, 1997), all the necessary information will be readily available to the lexical component.

(16) a. O que lamentaram eles terem-lhe lido?
what regret they have.3P-to.him read
'What do they regret having read to him?'

b. * O que lamentaram eles lhe terem lido.

c. Quantos livros lamentaram eles ter-lhe lido?
how.many books regret they have-to.him read
'How many books do they regret having read to him?'

d. * Quantos livros lamentaram eles lhe ter lido.

Considering long-distance extraction from both inflected (16a,b) and uninflected (16c,d) infinitives, we find that proclisis is illicit in the absence of a clause-local trigger. In embedded infinitival wh-questions (17), such a locally preceding trigger is provided and proclisis is possible, if not strongly preferred.

(17) a. Perguntei-me o que lhe ler?
asked-me what to him read
'I wondered what to read to him?'

b. ?? Perguntei-me o que ler-lhe?

Thus, the rules determining clitic placement are not just sensitive to the mere existence of a non-local wh-dependency; rather, it depends on where exactly, in terms of linear structure, this dependency is bound off.

5.2.3 Interpolation

So far, we have argued that placement of the clitic cluster w.r.t. the host should be regarded as a word order phenomenon, requiring a separate syntactically transparent representation of the cluster. In principle, it should then be possible for other syntactic material to intervene between the clitic and its host.

(18) O Carlos disse que me não podia ir buscar.
the Carlos said that me not could go pick up
'Carlos said that it would not be possible to pick me up.'

In fact, when the clitics are realised in preverbal position, the negative marker *não* 'not' may be positioned between the clitic and the verb.[2] In EP, the negative marker is clearly a syntactic word: it can be used in isolation, it can appear in constructions with verb ellipsis (19a), and it combines with syntactic material other than verbs (19b).

[2]In Northern varieties of Portuguese (Barbosa, 1996), interpolation is far less restricted: besides the negative marker, adverbs and even subject pronouns may separate the proclitics and the verb:

(19) a. Electricidade é um meio, não um fim.
electricity is a means, not a goal

'Electricity is a means, not a goal.'

b. Não muitos estudantes viram o Pedro.
not many students saw the Pedro

'Not many students saw Peter.'

Thus, the syntactic separability of preverbal clitics and the verb lends additional support to a syntactic linearisation approach of EP clitic placement.

5.3 Analysis

As a first step towards an analysis of clitic placement we need to address the lexical representation of clitic-verb complexes in this language and how this representation interfaces with the word order component. As far as morphological properties are concerned (cf. section 5.1), EP clitics very much resemble their French and Italian counterparts. I will follow the proposals by Miller and Sag (1997) and Monachesi (1999) regarding French and Italian pronominal affixes, and assume that clitics in EP are argument markers as well, lexically saturating a valence of the verb. This view is further supported by the existence of inherent clitics, i.e., clitics whose semantic contribution cannot easily be determined on compositional grounds.

As depicted in (20) below, the lexical representation of the clitic-verb complex specifies a subject, a direct object, and an indirect object in the argument structure (ARG-ST), where the indices of the morphologically saturated objects are restricted to appropriate values. As the subcategorisation requirement for the objects is already satisfied by the pronominal affixes, the cliticised verb in (20) specifies an empty COMPS list. Thus, the only argument this cliticised verb may combine with in syntax is the third person singular subject. As far as the tectogrammatical side is concerned, clitic-verb complexes in EP do not differ in any significant respect from the representations suggested for French (Miller

i. O Carlos pediu para o nós irmos buscar.
the Carlos asked for him we go-INF.1PL pick up

'Carlos asked for us to pick him up.'

ii. O Carlos disse que me já não podia ir buscar.
the Carlos said that me already not could go pick up

'Carlos said that it would not yet be possible to pick me up.

and Sag, 1997) or Italian (Monachesi, 1999). In particular, I also adopt the constraint-based theory of valence alternation advanced by Miller and Sag (1997).

(20)

$$\begin{bmatrix} \textit{word} & \\ \text{DOM} & \left\langle \begin{bmatrix}\text{PH} & \langle\text{mostrar}\rangle\\ \text{HD} & \boxed{1}\\ \text{TOPO} & \textit{vc}\end{bmatrix}, \begin{bmatrix}\text{PH} & \langle\text{-no-los-á}\rangle\\ \text{HD} & \textit{noun}\\ \text{TOPO} & \textit{vc}\end{bmatrix}\right\rangle \vee \\ & \left\langle \begin{bmatrix}\text{PH} & \langle\text{no-los}\rangle\\ \text{HD} & \textit{noun}\\ \text{TOPO} & \textit{vc}\end{bmatrix}, \begin{bmatrix}\text{PH} & \langle\text{mostrará}\rangle\\ \text{HD} & \boxed{1}\\ \text{TOPO} & \textit{vc}\end{bmatrix}\right\rangle \\ \text{CAT} & \begin{bmatrix} \text{HD} & \boxed{1}\textit{verb}\\ \text{SUBJ} & \langle \boxed{2}\rangle \\ \text{COMPS} & \langle\rangle \\ \text{ARG-ST} & \left\langle \boxed{2}\begin{bmatrix}\textit{canon-ss} & \\ \text{HD } \textit{noun} & \\ \text{IND} & \begin{bmatrix}\textit{nom-obj} & \\ \text{PER} & 3\\ \text{NUM} & \textit{sg}\end{bmatrix}\end{bmatrix}, \begin{bmatrix}\textit{aff-ss} & \\ \text{HD } \textit{noun} & \\ \text{IND} & \begin{bmatrix}\textit{ppro} & \\ \text{PER} & 3\\ \text{NUM} & \textit{pl}\end{bmatrix}\end{bmatrix}, \begin{bmatrix}\textit{aff-ss} & \\ \text{HD } \textit{noun} & \\ \text{IND} & \begin{bmatrix}\textit{pron} & \\ \text{PER} & 1\\ \text{NUM} & \textit{pl}\end{bmatrix}\end{bmatrix} \right\rangle\end{bmatrix}\end{bmatrix}$$

The major difference between the syntactically opaque French and Italian pronominal affixes and the more transparent EP clitics, however, lies in the place where the order between the clitic cluster and the host is constrained: in French and in Italian, positioning of the cluster with respect to the host is an entirely morphological matter. In Portuguese, clitic placement depends on the linear precedence of other syntactic material and should therefore be dealt with in the word order component.

To achieve this, I follow proposals by Kathol (1995) and Crysmann (1999b) who argue that a word-level sign can specify more than one domain object on its DOM list. In the case of EP clitic-verb complexes, one of the two domain objects corresponds to the verbal head, structure-sharing its categorial information with that of the entire verbal sign, whereas the other domain object will host the clitic cluster, the latter being assigned the HEAD value *noun*. Furthermore, both domain objects are restricted to the verbal cluster ([TOPO *vc*]), reflecting the limited degree of separability (see section 5.3.2 below).

The phonological contribution of the stem and the affixes is distributed over the PHON lists of the two domain objects according to morphological constraints. These constraints specify, inter alia, the introduction of morphological material corresponding to syntactically unexpressed valencies, the mapping of morphological formatives onto domain objects (including morphotactics), and morphophonological alternations.

Morphological material expressing features of syntactically unexpressed arguments (*aff-ss*) are introduced on a word's M(ORPH) list by means of implicational constraints. Members of M(ORPH) are elements of type *morph*, with subtypes *stem* and *affix*, where affixes only carry a PH(ON) feature. Subtyping of affixes and stems can be further used to single out partitions of morphs which share certain morphotactic and/or morphophonological properties (see below).

(21) $$\begin{bmatrix} \textit{word} & \\ \text{ARG-ST} & \left\langle [\,], \begin{bmatrix} \textit{aff-ss} & \\ \text{PER} & \textit{3} \\ \text{NUM} & \textit{pl} \\ \text{GEND} & \textit{m} \end{bmatrix} \right\rangle \oplus \textit{list} \end{bmatrix} \rightarrow \begin{bmatrix} \text{M} & \left\langle \begin{bmatrix} \textit{3rd-acc-aff} & \\ \text{PH} & \left\langle \begin{bmatrix} \text{SURF} & \boxed{1}\text{o} \\ \text{LEX} & \boxed{1} \end{bmatrix}, \begin{bmatrix} \text{SURF} & \boxed{2}\text{s} \\ \text{LEX} & \boxed{2} \end{bmatrix} \right\rangle \end{bmatrix} \right\rangle \bigcirc \textit{list} \end{bmatrix}$$

As for the morphophonological machinery, I follow Koenig (1999) in adopting the feature-based formulation of two-level morphology proposed by Krieger et al. (1993). In their approach, PHON values are essentially lists of pairs, each specifying a LEX and a SURF value. The correspondence between these values is captured by two-level constraints.

In a morphological derivation, the sequence of LEX values of the complex expression is typically a concatenation of the SURF values of its parts. To facilitate the mapping between these values, I introduce a function map, which is informally defined in (22).

(22) $$\mathsf{map}\left(\left\langle \begin{bmatrix}\text{SURF} & \boxed{1}\end{bmatrix}, \ldots, \begin{bmatrix}\text{SURF} & \boxed{n}\end{bmatrix} \right\rangle\right) = \left\langle \begin{bmatrix}\text{LEX} & \boxed{1}\end{bmatrix}, \ldots, \begin{bmatrix}\text{LEX} & \boxed{n}\end{bmatrix} \right\rangle$$

The morphotactics of EP inflectional affixes can now be captured as mappings of MORPH members onto the word's DOM list.

(23) $$\begin{bmatrix} \textit{word} & \\ \text{M} & \left\langle \begin{bmatrix} \textit{1-obj-aff} \\ \text{PH}\ \boxed{1} \end{bmatrix} \right\rangle \bigcirc\ \textit{list} \end{bmatrix} \rightarrow \begin{bmatrix} \text{DOM} & \left\langle \begin{bmatrix} \text{PH} & \mathsf{map}(\boxed{1}) \oplus\ \textit{list} \\ \text{HEAD} & \textit{noun} \\ \text{TOPO} & \textit{vc} \end{bmatrix} \right\rangle \bigcirc \\ & \left\langle \begin{bmatrix} \text{HEAD} & \textit{verb} \\ \text{TOPO} & \textit{vc} \end{bmatrix} \right\rangle \end{bmatrix}$$

(24) $$\begin{bmatrix} \textit{word} & \\ \text{M} & \left\langle \begin{bmatrix} \textit{3-acc-aff} & \\ \text{PH} & \boxed{1} \end{bmatrix} \right\rangle \bigcirc\ \textit{list} \end{bmatrix} \rightarrow \begin{bmatrix} \text{DOM} & \left\langle \begin{bmatrix} \text{PH} & \textit{list} \oplus \mathsf{map}(\boxed{1}) \oplus\ \textit{list} \\ \text{HEAD} & \textit{noun} \\ \text{TOPO} & \textit{vc} \end{bmatrix} \right\rangle \bigcirc \\ & \left\langle \begin{bmatrix} \text{HEAD} & \textit{verb} \\ \text{TOPO} & \textit{vc} \end{bmatrix} \right\rangle \end{bmatrix}$$

As illustrated in (23), affixes of type *1-obj-aff* (e.g., *nos*) must appear first on some nominal domain object, without specifying, however, how this domain object is ordered with respect to the verb. Third person accusative affixes are likewise constrained to map onto a nominal domain object in the verbal cluster, but they are less constrained regarding the alignment of their phonological contribution (cf. 24).

(25) $$\begin{bmatrix} \textit{word} \\ \text{M} \quad \left\langle \begin{bmatrix} \textit{fut-agr-aff} \\ \text{PH } \boxed{1} \end{bmatrix} \right\rangle \end{bmatrix} \rightarrow \begin{bmatrix} \text{DOM} \quad \textit{list} \oplus \left\langle \begin{bmatrix} \text{PH} \quad \textit{list} \oplus \mathsf{map}\left(\boxed{1}\right) \end{bmatrix} \right\rangle \end{bmatrix}$$

The future tense-agreement affixes, by contrast, are completely unselective as to the domain object they map to, provided they appear in right-most position (25): if the pronominal affixes appear before the verb, the future markers attach to the verbal stem, if, however, the pronominal affixes are enclitic to the verb, the future marker attaches to the clitic cluster, giving rise to *mesoclisis*.[3] Unification of these morphotactic constraints yields the two linearisations depicted in (20) above.

Using morphological type information, idiosyncratic morphophonological alternations can straightforwardly be integrated with a two-level approach to allomorphy.

(26) $$\begin{bmatrix} \textit{word} \\ \text{DOM} \quad \left\langle \begin{bmatrix} \text{PH } \textit{list} \oplus \left\langle \boxed{1}\begin{bmatrix} \text{LEX } \{\text{r,z,s}\} \end{bmatrix} \right\rangle \oplus \mathsf{map}\left(\boxed{2}\right) \oplus \textit{list} \end{bmatrix} \right\rangle \bigcirc \textit{ list} \\ \text{M} \quad \left\langle \begin{bmatrix} \textit{3-acc-aff} \\ \text{PH} \quad \boxed{2} \end{bmatrix} \right\rangle \bigcirc \textit{ list} \end{bmatrix}$$

$$\rightarrow \begin{bmatrix} \text{DOM} \quad \left\langle \begin{bmatrix} \text{PH } \textit{list} \oplus \left\langle \boxed{1}\begin{bmatrix} \text{SURF l} \end{bmatrix} \right\rangle \oplus \textit{list} \end{bmatrix} \right\rangle \bigcirc \textit{ list} \end{bmatrix}$$

(27) $$\begin{bmatrix} \textit{word} \\ \text{DOM} \quad \left\langle \begin{bmatrix} \text{PH } \textit{list} \oplus \left\langle \boxed{1}\begin{bmatrix} \text{LEX } \{\text{r,s,z}\} \end{bmatrix} \right\rangle \end{bmatrix} \right\rangle \oplus \left\langle \begin{bmatrix} \text{PH } \mathsf{map}\left(\boxed{2}\right) \oplus \textit{list} \end{bmatrix} \right\rangle \\ \text{M} \quad \left\langle \begin{bmatrix} \textit{3-acc-aff} \\ \text{PH} \quad \boxed{2} \end{bmatrix} \right\rangle \bigcirc \textit{ list} \end{bmatrix}$$

$$\rightarrow \begin{bmatrix} \text{DOM} \quad \left\langle \begin{bmatrix} \text{PH } \textit{list} \oplus \left\langle \boxed{1}\begin{bmatrix} \text{SURF l} \end{bmatrix} \right\rangle \end{bmatrix} \right\rangle \oplus \textit{list} \end{bmatrix}$$

As sketched by the two constraints above, lexical /r/, /s/, and /z/ correspond to surface [l], if they immediately precede a third person accusative pronominal within some domain object (26), or, if they immediately precede it at the junction between two lexical domain objects (27). Having morphophonology expressed as a two-level correspondence on

[3]The treatment of the future marker as an edge-oriented affix is actually very similar to the analysis of Fox inflectional prefixes given in Crysmann (1999b).

the morphological complex, together with type information on morphs, greatly facilitates the separation of morphotactic and morphophonological aspects and enables us to express unselective, yet idiosyncratic neutralisations with a certain degree of generality.

The morphological constraints outlined provide a representation of EP clitic-verb complexes in terms of partially specified DOM lists. Similar to Kathol's (1995) treatment of German separable prefix verbs, the order of the two domain objects contributed by the clitic-verb complex is crucially underspecified for linear order. Thus, all truely morphological aspects are entirely captured in the lexical component, while the linearisation component will only decide on the preverbal or postverbal position of the cluster. It is of note that almost all internal morphological information is effectively hidden from the syntactic component: in a sense, the mapping of MORPH elements onto domain objects is our direct analogue to the concept of bracket erasure as employed in Lexical Phonology and Morphology.

5.3.1 Modelling Monotonicity

In their analysis of EP negative concord, Branco and Crysmann (1999) have proposed a formal representation of monotonicity properties in Minimal Recursion Semantics (MRS) (Copestake et al., 1998).

(28)
$$
\left[\text{SS}\,|\,\text{LOC}\,|\,\text{CONT}\,|\,\text{LISZT}\left\langle \begin{bmatrix} \textit{every-rel} & \\ \text{HANDEL} & \boxed{0}\ \textit{handle} \\ \text{BV} & \boxed{2}\ \textit{ref-ind} \\ \text{REST} & \boxed{1}\ \textit{handle} \\ \text{SCOPE} & \textit{handle} \end{bmatrix}, \begin{bmatrix} \textit{man-rel} & \\ \text{HANDEL} & \boxed{1} \\ \text{INST} & \boxed{2} \end{bmatrix} \right\rangle \right]
$$

Meaning composition in MRS is performed by collecting the semantic contribution of individual signs on a flat, unordered list (LISZT). The elements on this list are feature structures of type *mrs*, introducing a HANDEL feature: Hierarchical relations, such as quantifier scope, can be expressed by means of coindexing an argument feature of the functor, e.g., REST, with the value of the argument's HANDEL, cf. (28). The value of these structure-sharings is constrained to be of type *handle*. Other than restricting the range of possible coindexations, the type *handle* does not encode any further meaningful information. Branco and Crysmann (1999) therefore suggest, that this type can be augmented with a type hierarchy to express the monotonicity contexts introduced by quantifiers:

(29)
$$
\textit{mon-context} \equiv \textit{i-mon-conx} \vee \textit{d-mon-conx} \vee \textit{non-mon-conx}
$$

(30)
$$\begin{bmatrix} \textit{scope-rel} \\ \text{ARGS nelist}(\textit{mon-context}) \end{bmatrix}$$
$$\begin{bmatrix} \textit{unary-scope-rel} \\ \text{ARGS } \langle \textit{mon-context} \rangle \end{bmatrix} \quad \begin{bmatrix} \textit{binary-scope-rel} \\ \text{ARGS } \langle \textit{mon-context}, \textit{mon-context} \rangle \end{bmatrix}$$

Furthermore, they argue for a list-valued representation for the arguments of scope-taking functors, facilitating generalisations across unary and binary functors (30). By convention, the scope argument is encoded as the first element on the list. Consequently, the example given in (28) will now be represented as follows (31):

(31)
$$\begin{bmatrix} \text{LISZT} & \left\langle \begin{bmatrix} \textit{every-rel} & \\ \text{HANDEL} & \boxed{0}\ \textit{mon-context} \\ \text{BV} & \boxed{2}\ \textit{ref-ind} \\ \text{ARGS} & \langle \textit{i-mon-conx}, \boxed{1}\ \textit{d-mon-conx} \rangle \end{bmatrix}, \begin{bmatrix} \textit{man-rel} & \\ \text{HANDEL} & \boxed{1} \\ \text{INST} & \boxed{2} \end{bmatrix} \right\rangle \end{bmatrix}$$

For purposes of semantic selection, MRS introduces a feature KEY which points to the *mrs* contributed by the semantic head of the phrase. In the case of NPs, Copestake et al. (1998) take this to be the head noun. For the treatment of monotonicity-sensitive phenomena (e.g., NPI licensing and negative concord), however, it would be advantageous, if the KEY referenced the determiner instead. I therefore follow the position standardly assumed in GQT and Montagovian Semantics in taking the determiner as the semantic head. In addition to monotonicity properties, such a move will also facilitate the description of definiteness effects, including the restriction of *there*-contexts to weak determiners. Semantic selection of noun properties can still be achieved straightforwardly by having the subcategorising head contribute an *mrs* whose INST value is structure-shared with the BV value of the head determiner. The effect of semantic selection is then obtained by intersecting all *mrs* whose INST values are token-identical, including of course, the head noun. Note that this is identical to the treatment of intersecting modification in MRS.

Given a convenient representation for monotonicity information, we can now define the class of left or right monotone decreasing functors as in (32).

(32)
$$\textit{d-mon-func} \rightarrow \begin{bmatrix} \text{KEY } \boxed{1} \\ \text{LISZT} \left\langle \ldots \boxed{1} \begin{bmatrix} \text{ARGS} \left\langle \ldots \textit{d-mon-conx} \ldots \right\rangle \end{bmatrix} \ldots \right\rangle \end{bmatrix}$$

In essence, the class of $\downarrow$MON $\cup$ MON$\downarrow$ functors will be exactly those domain objects whose semantic head creates a downward monotone context in at least one argument; including two-place quantifiers as well as one-place functors like negation.

5.3.2 Clitic Placement

Having laid out the fundamental lexical and semantic representations, I will now present an analysis of EP clitic placement in terms of word order variation. Despite the relatively free word order where, e.g., complements and adjuncts can be easily interspersed, Portuguese sentence topology observes quite a strict dichotomy between preverbal and postverbal positions. This dichotomy is manifest not only in the strong restriction of complements to postverbal position, it can also be observed in the domain of negative concord (Crysmann, 1999a; Branco and Crysmann, 1999), an observation familiar from other Romance languages, such as Italian (cf. e.g., Ladusaw, 1992). Under a field-based theory of linearisation such as Kathol's (1995), this can be captured by assigning subjects and objects appropriate TOPO values (*pre* ∨ *post* and *post*, resp.) and constraining the linearisation of fields as in (33) below.

(33) $\begin{bmatrix}\text{TOPO}\ \mathit{pre}\end{bmatrix} < \begin{bmatrix}\text{TOPO}\ \mathit{vc}\end{bmatrix} < \begin{bmatrix}\text{TOPO}\ \mathit{post}\end{bmatrix}$

Modifiers, by contrast can appear quite freely; preceding the subject, intervening between subject and verb, as well as between the complements and the verb. The only field which is highly restricted as to the elements it may contain is the verbal cluster, where only the verb, negation, the clitic cluster, and a few adverbs can appear. Thus, it seems quite natural to describe linearisation in the Portuguese clause by means of complex order domains. Assigning negation and the clitic cluster to the same topological field will ensure that these items can in principle flip position, while at the same time, it bans intervention by most other syntactic material.

Following Kathol (1995), complex order domains are built up by shuffling the domain objects contributed by the head with the domain objects contributed by the non-head daughter. In HEAD-COMPLEMENT structures, cf. (34), the domain list of the non-head daughter is *compacted* (Kathol, 1995) into a single domain object, in order to ensure that material contributed by different complements cannot be interleaved.

(34)
$$\begin{bmatrix}\text{DOM} & \boxed{4} \bigcirc \left\langle \begin{bmatrix}\text{PH} & \boxed{i_1} \oplus \ldots \oplus \boxed{i_n} \\ \text{SS} & \boxed{2} \\ \text{TOPO} & \mathit{post}\end{bmatrix} \right\rangle \\ \text{SS}\,|\,\text{L}\,|\,\text{CAT} & \begin{bmatrix}\text{HEAD} & \boxed{1} \\ \text{COMPS} & \boxed{3}\end{bmatrix}\end{bmatrix}$$

$$\begin{bmatrix}\text{DOM} & \boxed{4} \\ \text{SS}\,|\,\text{L}\,|\,\text{CAT} & \begin{bmatrix}\text{HEAD} & \boxed{1} \\ \text{COMPS} & \left\langle \boxed{2} \right\rangle \oplus \boxed{3}\end{bmatrix}\end{bmatrix} \qquad \begin{bmatrix}\text{DOM} & \left\langle \begin{bmatrix}\text{PH} & \boxed{i_1}\end{bmatrix}, \ldots, \begin{bmatrix}\text{PH} & \boxed{i_n}\end{bmatrix} \right\rangle \\ \text{SS} & \boxed{2}\end{bmatrix}$$

In Portuguese, the same will be true for all the other ID schemata, which can be defined in an analogous way. As a consequence, a flat representation of all major constituents in the clause is built up, including the complementiser, the filler, and of course the domain objects contributed by the lexical head: the clitic cluster and the verb. The placement properties of EP clitics can then be captured by the following implicational constraints.

(35)
$$\begin{bmatrix} \textit{phrase} \\ \text{DOM} \left\langle \ldots \begin{bmatrix} \text{INH}\,|\,\text{QUE} & \textit{neset} \\ \text{TOPO} & \textit{pre} \end{bmatrix} \ldots \right\rangle \end{bmatrix} \rightarrow \begin{bmatrix} \text{HD } \textit{noun} \\ \text{TOPO } \textit{vc} \end{bmatrix} < \begin{bmatrix} \text{HD } \textit{verb} \\ \text{TOPO } \textit{vc} \end{bmatrix}$$

(36)
$$\begin{bmatrix} \textit{phrase} \\ \text{DOM} \left\langle \ldots \begin{bmatrix} \text{CONT} & \textit{d-mon-func} \\ \text{TOPO} & \textit{pre} \vee \textit{vc} \end{bmatrix} \ldots \right\rangle \end{bmatrix} \rightarrow \begin{bmatrix} \text{HD } \textit{noun} \\ \text{TOPO } \textit{vc} \end{bmatrix} < \begin{bmatrix} \text{HD } \textit{verb} \\ \text{TOPO } \textit{vc} \end{bmatrix}$$

(37)
$$\begin{bmatrix} \textit{phrase} \\ \text{DOM} \left\langle \ldots \begin{bmatrix} \text{HD} & \textit{mark} \vee \textit{prep} \\ \text{LEX} & + \\ \text{TOPO} & \textit{pre} \end{bmatrix} \ldots \right\rangle \end{bmatrix} \rightarrow \begin{bmatrix} \text{HD } \textit{noun} \\ \text{TOPO } \textit{vc} \end{bmatrix} < \begin{bmatrix} \text{HD } \textit{verb} \\ \text{TOPO } \textit{vc} \end{bmatrix}$$

The definition of complex domain formation, as specified by the HEAD-COMPLEMENT schema in (34), immediately captures the clause-boundedness observed with proclisis licensing: Whenever a clause, be it finite or non-finite, combines with the head that subcategorises for it, the DOM list of the embedded clause is compacted into a single, clausal domain object, rendering its internal linear structure opaque to ordering in the higher domain. Thus, clause-external triggers will never be represented on the same DOM list as the embedded clitic.

(38)
$$\begin{bmatrix} \text{DOM} \left\langle \boxed{1} \begin{bmatrix} \text{V} & \\ \text{PH} & \langle \text{perguntei} \rangle \\ \text{TOPO} & \textit{vc} \end{bmatrix}, \boxed{2} \begin{bmatrix} \text{N} & \\ \text{PH} & \langle \text{me} \rangle \\ \text{TOPO} & \textit{vc} \end{bmatrix}, \begin{bmatrix} \text{S} & \\ \text{PH} & \langle \text{o que lhe ler} \rangle \\ \text{TOPO} & \textit{post} \end{bmatrix} \right\rangle \end{bmatrix}$$

$$\begin{bmatrix} \text{DOM } \boxed{1} \bigcirc \boxed{2} \end{bmatrix} \qquad \begin{bmatrix} \text{DOM} \left\langle \begin{bmatrix} \text{NP} & \\ \text{PH} & \langle \text{o que} \rangle \\ \text{TOPO} & \textit{pre} \end{bmatrix}, \begin{bmatrix} \text{N} & \\ \text{PH} & \langle \text{lhe} \rangle \\ \text{TOPO} & \textit{vc} \end{bmatrix}, \begin{bmatrix} \text{V} & \\ \text{PH} & \langle \text{ler} \rangle \\ \text{TOPO} & \textit{vc} \end{bmatrix} \right\rangle \end{bmatrix}$$

For illustration, consider the embedded interrogative in (38) above: a locally realised wh-phrase precedes the clitic and the verb in the order domain of the embedded clause. According to (35), the presence of a wh-phrase in the preverbal field requires the clitic cluster to appear to the left of the verb.

(39)
$$\begin{bmatrix} \text{DOM} \left\langle \begin{bmatrix} \text{NP} \\ \text{PH } \langle \text{o que} \rangle \\ \text{TOPO } \textit{pre} \end{bmatrix}, \begin{bmatrix} \text{V} \\ \text{PH } \langle \text{lamentaram} \rangle \\ \text{TOPO } \textit{vc} \end{bmatrix}, \begin{bmatrix} \text{NP} \\ \text{PH } \langle \text{eles} \rangle \\ \text{TOPO } \textit{post} \end{bmatrix}, \begin{bmatrix} \text{S} \\ \text{PH } \langle \text{ter-lhe lido} \rangle \\ \text{TOPO } \textit{post} \end{bmatrix} \right\rangle \end{bmatrix}$$

In (39), however, no trigger is present in the order domain of the embedded clause. When the embedded clause combines with the matrix verb, its order domain compacts into a single domain object, rendering its internal structure opaque. Thus, the presence of a trigger in the matrix clause cannot affect ordering of the embedded clitic anymore.

5.4 Conclusion

I have argued in this paper that an account of clitic placement in European Portuguese (EP) requires a certain degree of syntactic transparency for bound pronominals, which are morphologically clearly affixes. As far as the diagnostic criteria advanced by Zwicky & Pullum are concerned, we are thus faced with a dilemma: while almost all morphological criteria positively suggest a lexical treatment, the syntactic criterion E strongly militates in favour of a linearisation analysis. Recognising the value of theory-independent criteria as guidelines for linguistic analysis, I argue, however, that multi-dimensional grammatical frameworks, such as HPSG, allow us to draw more fine-grained distinctions than a strict affix/clitic dichotomy would permit. Following previous work in linearisation-based HPSG (Kathol, 1995; Crysmann, 1999b), a lexical representation of clitic-verb complexes has been proposed which introduces the clitic cluster and the verbal host as separate domain objects, providing the technical basis for a linearisation-based analysis. While at first sight, this move may appear to violate the letter of the Lexical Integrity Hypothesis, it still effectively encapsulates the internal morphological structure in the lexical component, providing the word-order component with a limited and entirely syntactic representation of the clitic cluster suitable for linearisation.

The approach adopted here has also been fruitfully applied to morpho-syntactic mismatch in Fox complex predicates (Crysmann, 1999b) and Udi subject agreement (Crysmann, 2000b). In the present analysis, it has further been shown that clitic placement in infinitives and in finite clauses can be modelled by the same set of order constraints. Locality effects have been derived from independently motivated principles of complex domain formation. Finally, the set of syntactic items conditioning clitic placement has been reduced to three natural classes: wh-phrases, embedding complementisers and prepositions, and left or right downward entailing functors.

References

Bach, E., E. Jelinek, A. Kratzer, and B. Partee, eds. 1995. *Quantification in Natural Language*, Studies in Linguistics and Philosophy, Dordrecht. Kluwer Academic Publishers.

Barbosa, P. 1996. Clitic placement in European Portuguese and the position of subjects. In A. L. Halpern and A. M. Zwicky, eds., *Approching Second. Second Position and Related Phenomena*, no. 61 in CSLI Lecture Notes, pages 1–40. CSLI Publications.

Barwise, J. and R. Cooper. 1981. Generalized quantifiers and natural language. *Linguistics and Philosophy* 4:159–218.

Branco, A. H. and B. Crysmann. 1999. Negative concord and linear constraints on quantification. In Y. d'Hulst, J. Rooryck, and J. Schroten, eds., *Selected Papers from Going Romance '99* (Working Title). John Benjamins.

Copestake, A., D. Flickinger, and I. Sag. 1998. Minimal recursion semantics. An introduction. Proceedings of ESSLLI 10, Saarbrücken.

Crysmann, B. 1997. Cliticization in European Portuguese using parallel morpho–syntactic constraints. In M. Butt and T. H. King, eds., *Proceedings of the LFG97 Conference*. Stanford: CSLI Publications.

Crysmann, B. 1999a. Licensing proclisis in European Portuguese. In F. Corblin, C. Dobrovie-Sorin, and J.-M. Marandin, eds., *Empirical Issues in Formal Syntax and Semantics. Selected papers from the Colloque de Syntaxe et de Sémantique de Paris (CSSP 1997)*, pages 255–276. The Hague: Thesus.

Crysmann, B. 1999b. Morphosyntactic paradoxa in Fox. In G. Bouma, E. Hinrichs, G.-J. Kruiff, and R. Oehrle, eds., *Constraints and Resources in Natural Language Syntax and Semantics*, Studies in Constraint-Based Lexicalism, pages 41–61. Stanford: CSLI publications.

Crysmann, B. 2000a. Clitics and coordination in linear structure. In B. Gerlach and J. Grijzenhout, eds., *Clitics in Phonology, Morphology and Syntax*, vol. 36 of *Linguistik Aktuell/Linguistics Today*. John Benjamins.

Crysmann, B. 2000b. On the placement and morphology of Udi subject agreement. Paper presented at the 7th International Conference on Head-driven Phrase Structure Grammar, Berkeley.

Duarte, I. 1983. Variação paramétrica e ordem dos clíticos. *Revista de Faculdade de Letras* 4:158–178.

Duarte, I., G. Matos, and I. Faria. 1995. Specificity of European Portuguese clitics in Romance. In I. H. Faria and M. J. Freitas, eds., *Studies on the Acquisition of Portuguese*. Lisboa: Edições Colibri.

Halpern, A. 1995. *On the Placement and Morphology of Clitics*. Dissertations in Linguistics. Stanford: CSLI Publications.

Horn, L. R. 1996. Exclusive company: *Only* and the dynamics of vertical inference. *Journal of Semantics* 13:1–40.

Kathol, A. 1995. *Linearization-Based German Syntax*. Ph.D. thesis, Ohio State University.

Koenig, J.-P. 1999. *Lexical Relations*. Stanford: CSLI publications.

Krieger, H.-U., J. Nerbonne, and H. Pirker. 1993. Feature-based allomorphy. In *Proceedings of the Thirty-First Annual Meeting of the ACL*, pages 140–147. Association for Computational Linguistics, Columbus. Also published as Report RR-93-28, DFKI, Saarbrücken.

Kupść, A. 1999. Haplology of the Polish reflexive marker. In R. D. Borsley and A. Przepiórkowski, eds., *Slavic in Head-Driven Phrase Structure Grammar*, Studies in Constraint-Based Lexicalism, chap. 4, pages 91–124. Stanford: CSLI.

Ladusaw, W. A. 1992. Expressing negation. In C. Barker and D. Dowty, eds., *SALT II: Proceedings of the Second Conference on Semantics and Linguistic Theory*, vol. 40 of *Ohio State University Working Papers in Linguistics (OSU WPL)*. Columbus: Ohio State University.

Martins, A. M. 1994. *Clíticos na história do Português*. Ph.D. thesis, Universidade de Lisboa.

Miller, P. and I. A. Sag. 1997. French clitic movement without clitics or movement. *Natural Language and Linguistic Theory* 15(3):573–639.

Miller, P. H. 1992. *Clitics and Constituents in Phrase Structure Grammar*. Outstanding Dissertations in Linguistics. New York: Garland.

Monachesi, P. 1999. *A Lexical Approach to Italian Cliticization*. CSLI Publications.

Penn, G. 1999. Linearization and *WH*-extraction: Evidence from Serbo-Croatian. In R. D. Borsley and A. Przepiórkowski, eds., *Slavic in Head-Driven Phrase Structure Grammar*, Studies in Constraint-Based Lexicalism, chap. 6, pages 149–182. Stanford: CSLI.

Peres, J. 1997. Extending the notion of negative concord. In D. Forget, P. Hirschbühler, F. Martineau, and M.-L. Rivero, eds., *Negation and Polarity*, vol. 155 of *Current Issues in Linguistic Theory*, pages 289–310. Amsterdam: Benjamins.

Sag, I. A. 1997. English relative clause constructions. *Journal of Linguistics* 33(2):431–484.

Spencer, A. 1991. *Morphological Theory. An Introduction to Word Structure in Generative Grammar*. No. 2 in Blackwell Textbooks in Linguistics. Oxford: Blackwell.

Zwicky, A. and G. K. Pullum. 1983. Cliticization vs. inflection: English *n't*. *Language* 59:502–513.

6

From Argument Raising to Dependent Raising

KORDULA DE KUTHY AND W. DETMAR MEURERS

6.1 The Empirical Issue

An extensive literature on partial constituent fronting in German deals with examples in which partial constituents have been fronted, leaving behind one or more *arguments*:[1]

(1) a. [Verkaufen] will er *das Pferd.*
sell wants-to he the horse
'He wants sell the horse.'

b. [Stolz] ist er *auf seine Kinder* gewesen.
proud is he of his children been
'He was proud of his children.'

c. [Ein Buch] hat Hans *über Syntax* ausgeliehen.
a book has Hans on syntax borrowed
'Hans borrowed a book on syntax.'

In (1a), the transitive verb *verkaufen* has been fronted, leaving its complement, the NP *das Pferd*, behind. In (1b), the AP *stolz* is topicalized without its PP argument *auf seine Kinder.* And in (1c), the NP *ein Buch* has been fronted, leaving its PP complement *über Syntax* behind. In De Kuthy and Meurers (1998, to appear) we showed that such cases of partial constituent fronting can successfully be analyzed by generalizing the argument-raising approach to partial VP fronting proposed in

[1]See, for example, Thiersch (1985), Webelhuth and Besten (1987), G. Müller (1996), Hinrichs and Nakazawa (1994), and the HPSG argument-raising proposals mentioned below.

Grammatical Interfaces in HPSG.
Ronnie Cann, Claire Grover and Philip Miller.

HPSG.[2] to complements of different categories.[3]

Interestingly, there is a second kind of partial constituent phenomenon not discussed in most of these publications, namely examples where the partiality of the fronted constituent results from leaving behind an *adjunct* modifying the fronted head. The following sentences illustrate this possibility with adjuncts of fronted verbal, adjectival, and nominal heads.

(2) a. [Frieren] müssen sie deshalb aber *in der nächsten Woche* nicht.
freeze have to they therefore but in the next week not
'But they will not have to freeze next week because of this.'

b. [Interessiert] ist er *sehr* an den Umständen des Diebstahls.
interested is he very in the circumstances of the theft
'He is very interested in the circumstances of the theft.'

c. [Nur zwei Gemälde] werden *aus seinem Spätwerk* gezeigt.
only two paintings are from his late works shown
'Only two paintings were shown from the end of his career.'

In (2a) the partially fronted VP *frieren* leaves behind the temporal adjunct PP *in der nächsten Woche.* In (2b) the fronted AP *interessiert* is separated from its intensifying adverb *sehr.* Finally, in (2c) the adjunct PP *aus seinem Spätwerk* is not included in the fronted NP *nur zwei Gemälde.* Note that in all three cases the adjunct in the Mittelfeld is interpreted as modifying the head of the fronted constituent and not the finite verbs *müssen, ist,* or *werden* in verb-second position.

In this paper we want to take a closer look at this second partial constituent phenomenon. Starting out with a discussion of the head movement analysis of S. Müller (1999), the only approach to the phenomenon we are aware of, we argue that it is attractive to explore an alternative approach which captures the parallel character of the two kinds of partial constituent phenomena. We investigate whether the argument-raising approach to partial constituents missing arguments of the kind we saw in (1) can be generalized to the cases involving partial constituents lacking adjuncts as illustrated in (2). We show that extending the notion of argument raising to a concept we will call *dependent raising* properly accounts for both kinds of partial constituent phenomena as well as their interaction.

[2]See, in particular, Pollard (1996), Nerbonne (1994), Kathol (1995, sec. 7.7), S. Müller (1997), Meurers (1999a), and Bouma and van Noord (1998, sec. 3.4)

[3]De Kuthy (2000) argues, however, that PPs such as those in (1c) should be analyzed as adjuncts, not complements.

6.2 A Head Movement Analysis and its Problems

In his discussion of the partial constituent phenomenon, S. Müller (1999, pp. 360ff) also covers the example (3) involving an adjunct which has not been included in the fronted constituent.

(3) [Vortragen] wird er es *morgen*.
present will he it tomorrow
'He will present it tomorrow.'

He proposes to license the fronted verbal head *vortragen* as an extraction of the head of a head-adjunct structure, leaving the temporal adjunct *morgen* behind. He illustrates this with the tree in figure 1.[4]

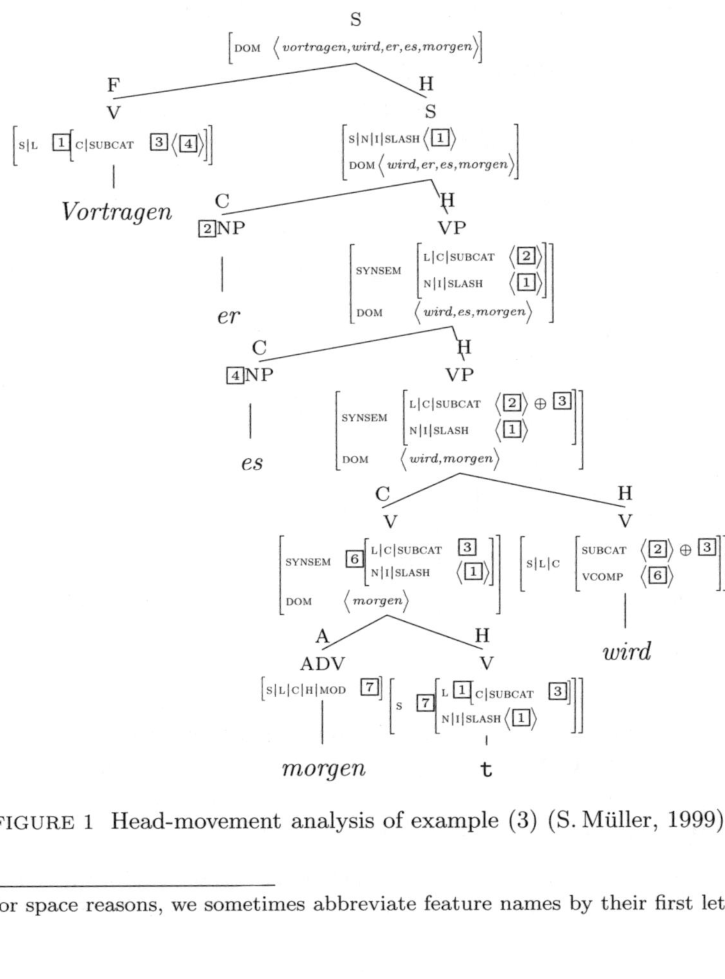

FIGURE 1 Head-movement analysis of example (3) (S. Müller, 1999)

[4]For space reasons, we sometimes abbreviate feature names by their first letter.

Note that S. Müller (1999) uses a linearization approach with word order domains (DOM) that are larger than local trees. In figure 1, the linear occurrence of the finite verb in verb-second position is a result of such linearization. In our context we are mainly interested in the fronted verb *vortragen*. The trace of this verb and the adverb *morgen* modifying this verb are realized in a head adjunct structure which functions as the verbal complement of the finite verb *wird*.

Introducing traces as head daughters in this way opens up a hornet's nest of problems, though, since it entails the elimination of a central restriction on the occurrence of empty elements. In traditional HPSG, for example, this restriction is expressed by the Trace Principle: "Every trace must be subcategorized by a substantive head." (Pollard and Sag, 1994, p. 172). Since eliminating this restriction to allow head traces would lead to severe overgeneration, S. Müller (1999) decides against introducing traces altogether and instead defines special immediate dominance schemata tailored to the specific extraction phenomena. The sentence (3), for example, under his analysis is licensed on the basis of the *PVP-Slash-Introduction Schema (Adjunct)* shown in figure 2.

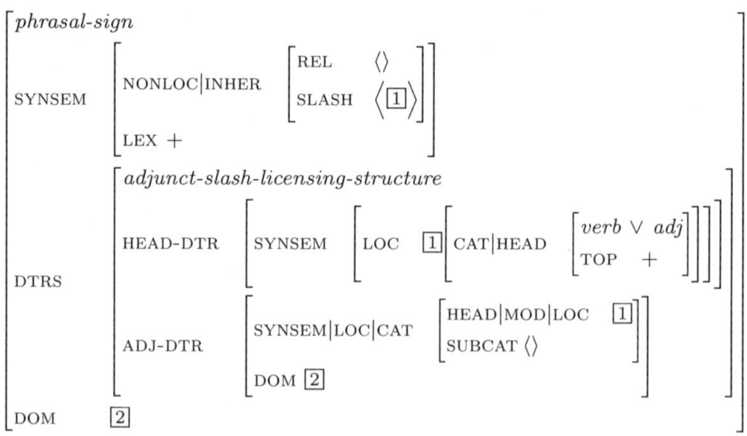

FIGURE 2 PVP-Slash-Introduction Schema (Adjunct) (S. Müller, 1999)

Note that the mother introduces a non-empty slash value which is specified to be identical to the (local value of the) head daughter. Since the head daughter represents the extracted element, it does not contribute its phonology to the order domain DOM of the mother.[5] The

[5]The reason that S. Müller (1999) specifies such a *adjunct-slash-licensing-structure* to have a HEAD-DTR at all is related to processing considerations. One could eliminate

head daughter is further restricted to be an adjective or a verb.

The specialized immediate dominance schema of figure 2, together with a second one licensing the extraction of partial *complements* from head cluster structures, successfully accounts for the envisaged partial fronting constructions. The solution in essence consists of encoding each case as a special construction instead of trying to derive both kinds of partial fronting phenomena as the effect of a more general grammar mechanism. In the following, we investigate an alternative to head movement with specialized constructions.

6.3 From Argument Raising to Dependent Raising

In the introductory section we discussed basic data highlighting the parallel character of the partial fronting cases involving adjuncts and the more widely studied partial fronting phenomenon where a complement is left behind. Additional empirical support for a uniform treatment of the two classes of examples can be derived from the fact that the two kind of partial fronting phenomena can interact. In example (4a), the verb *verkaufen* has been fronted, leaving behind both its nominal complement *das Pferd* and the temporal adjunct PP *im Herbst* modifying the fronted verb. And in (4b), the verb *verkaufen* forms a constituent with the modal verb *wollen* so that the nominal complement and the temporal adjunct PP must have been raised twice.

(4) a. [Verkaufen] will er *das Pferd im Herbst.*
sell wants he the horse in the autumn

'He wants to sell the horse in autumn.'

b. [Verkaufen wollen] wird er *das Pferd im Herbst.*
sell want will he the horse in the autumn

'He will want to sell the horse in autumn.'

Such interaction between the two kind of partial constituent phenomena is to be expected if both phenomena are licensed by the same underlying mechanism.

To investigate whether the argument-raising analysis we proposed for constituents missing complements can be generalized to include raising of adjuncts, we first need to review the essential ingredients of our argument-raising analysis.

---

this attribute and state the restrictions on the head daughter on the SLASH value of the mother instead.

6.3.1 The Starting Point

The heart of our proposal to partial constituents missing complements in De Kuthy and Meurers (1998, to appear) (henceforth: DKM) is the *Lexical Argument-Raising Principle (LARP)* shown in figure 3. The

$$\begin{bmatrix} \textit{word} \\ \textsc{s}|\textsc{l}|\textsc{c}|\textsc{head} \;\; \boxed{4}\begin{bmatrix} \textit{verb} \\ \textsc{vform} & \textit{bse} \end{bmatrix} \end{bmatrix} \rightarrow \begin{bmatrix} \textsc{s}|\textsc{l}|\textsc{c}|\textsc{v} & \begin{bmatrix} \textsc{subj} & \boxed{1} \\ \textsc{comps} & \textit{raised}\left(\boxed{3}\right) \oplus \boxed{2} \end{bmatrix} \\ \textsc{arg-st} & \textit{distrib-args}\left(\boxed{4},\boxed{1},\boxed{2}\right) \wedge \left(\boxed{3} \bigcirc \textit{indep}\right) \end{bmatrix}$$

FIGURE 3 The Lexical Argument-Raising Principle (LARP)

essential part of the principle is that the value of the valence attribute COMPS is defined to consist of the non-subject[6] elements of the argument structure ($\boxed{2}$) plus (potentially) some elements raised from $\boxed{3}$.[7] What exactly can be raised and whether there are additional restrictions empirically depends on the category of the argument-raising source, i.e., the element from which an argument is raised. This is captured by the definition of the relation *raised* in figure 4.

$$\begin{aligned} &\textit{raised}\left(\langle\rangle\right) := \langle\rangle. \\ &\textit{raised}\left(\left\langle \begin{bmatrix} \textsc{lex} & + \\ \textsc{l}|\textsc{c} & \begin{bmatrix} \textsc{head} & \textit{verb} \vee \textit{adj} \\ \textsc{v}|\textsc{comps} & \boxed{1} \end{bmatrix} \end{bmatrix} \right\rangle\right) := \boxed{1}\ \textit{lex-minus-list}. \\ &\textit{raised}\left(\left\langle \begin{bmatrix} \textsc{l}|\textsc{c} & \begin{bmatrix} \textsc{head} & \textit{noun} \\ \textsc{v}|\textsc{comps} & \boxed{1} \end{bmatrix} \end{bmatrix} \right\rangle\right) := \boxed{1}\ \textit{prep-list}. \end{aligned}$$

FIGURE 4 Definition of possible argument-raising sources

If there is no argument-raising source, no arguments can be raised. For

[6] Which of the arguments, if any, fills the subject valence is specified by the relation *distrib(ute)-arg(ument)s* defined below—a task which requires special attention to subjectless and raising verbs, which here are assumed to be recognizable by their head subtype:

$$\begin{aligned} &\textit{distrib-args}\left(\textit{subj-less-verb}, \langle\rangle, \boxed{2}\right) && := && \boxed{2} \\ &\textit{distrib-args}\left(\textit{subj-raising-verb}, \boxed{1}, \boxed{2}\right) && := && \boxed{2}\left\langle\left[\textsc{l}|\textsc{c}|\textsc{v}|\textsc{subj} \;\; \boxed{1}\right]\right\rangle \\ &\textit{distrib-args}\left(\textit{subj-verb}, \left\langle\boxed{1}\right\rangle, \boxed{2}\right) && := && \left\langle\boxed{1} | \boxed{2}\right\rangle \end{aligned}$$

[7] All arguments not belonging to the list of argument-raising sources $\boxed{3}$ are required to be *indep(endent)*. This notion defined below encodes that these arguments have realized their own complements and are not part of a lexical head cluster:

$$\begin{aligned} &\textit{indep} := \langle\rangle. \\ &\textit{indep} := \left\langle \begin{bmatrix} \textsc{l}|\textsc{c}|\textsc{v}|\textsc{comps} & \langle\rangle \\ \textsc{lex} & - \end{bmatrix} \middle| \ \textit{indep} \right\rangle. \end{aligned}$$

verbal and adjectival raising sources all non-lexical cluster elements can be raised, whereas for nominal raising sources raising is restricted to prepositions.

For a simple example sentence with a partial topicalized VP lacking an argument, such as the sentence we saw in (1a), the generalized argument-raising approach sketched above results in the analysis in figure 5.

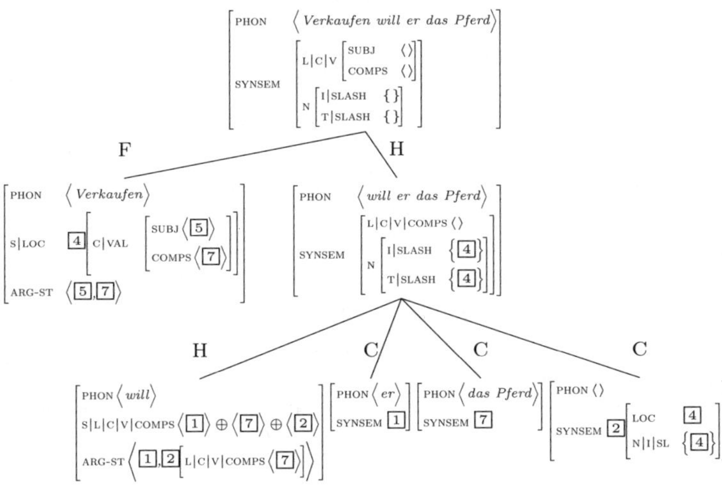

FIGURE 5 Sketch of an argument-raising analysis of partial fronting

In order to make this example tree comprehensible, we briefly have to mention two further aspects of the theory provided in De Kuthy and Meurers (to appear). While the Lexical Argument-Raising Principle applies to base form verbs, finite verbs are derived from these base forms by a lexical rule which among other things removes the subject from SUBJ and encodes it together with the complements on COMPS in the tradition of Pollard (1996). In the same tradition, the Head-Complement Immediate Dominance Schema licenses flat finite verbal structures so that the verb-second position of the finite verb can be obtained by linearization in this local tree.

Returning to the central aspect of argument raising in the analysis sketched in figure 5, the Lexical Argument-Raising Principle has the effect that the finite verb *will* raises the NP complements *das Pferd* ([7]) of (the trace of) its verbal complement *verkaufen* ([2]) onto its own COMPS list. *Verkaufen* can then be realized in the fronted position independently of its complement *das Pferd*, while *will* combines with its subject *er*, the raised NP *das Pferd*, and the trace of the fronted verbal argument in a head-complement structure.

6.3.2 Adjuncts as Dependents

Turning to the question how the sketched argument-raising approach to partial constituents could be generalized to include partial constituents missing adjuncts, the key problem to resolve is that in the traditional HPSG framework (Pollard and Sag, 1994) on which our argument-raising analysis is built, adjuncts are not represented lexically but inserted syntactically in head-adjunct structures. The lexical head therefore does not represent whether its projection includes a modifier or not, which is incompatible with the lexical encoding of argument raising which we adopted from Hinrichs and Nakazawa (1989). If we want adjuncts to undergo such raising, we thus need to ensure that the selection of adjuncts is lexically represented.

The idea of lexicalizing the selection of adjuncts has been argued for in a line of work in HPSG going back at least to Miller (1992) and Van Noord and Bouma (1994). In the most recent incarnation of the idea, Bouma, Malouf, and Sag (to appear) (henceforth: BMS) specify a lexical principle which maps the elements of the argument structure and a list of adjuncts of unspecified length onto a so-called dependents list. The definition of this *Argument Structure Extension* is shown in figure 6.

$$
\textit{verb} \;\longrightarrow\; \left[\textsc{s}|\textsc{loc}\ \left[\begin{array}{ll}\textsc{cat} & \left[\begin{array}{ll}\textsc{head} & \boxed{3}\\ \textsc{deps} & \boxed{1} \oplus \textit{list}\left(\left[\textsc{l}|\textsc{c}|\textsc{h}|\textsc{mod}|\textsc{loc}\ \left[\begin{array}{ll}\textsc{cat}|\textsc{head} & \boxed{3}\\ \textsc{cont}|\textsc{key} & \boxed{2}\end{array}\right]\right]\right)\\ \textsc{arg-st} & \boxed{1}\end{array}\right]\\ \textsc{cont} & \left[\textsc{key}\ \boxed{2}\right]\end{array}\right]\right]
$$

FIGURE 6 Argument Structure Extension of BMS[8]

A second principle entitled *Argument Realization* maps the arguments and adjuncts collected on DEPS onto the valence attributes SUBJ

[8]We show the principles of BMS including the full feature paths according to the feature geometry BMS provide in their figure (17). Note that the type *verb* in figure 6 represents a subtype of *word* instead of the usual subtype of *head*, and ARG-ST is shown as appropriate for *category* objects while usually ARG-ST is defined for objects of type *word*. Since we are not aware of arguments for these changes, our own proposal below is based on the traditional HPSG feature geometry.

and COMPS. The combined effect of these two principles is that selection of adjuncts and complements is lexically represented as part of the head, and both kind of dependents can be realized as part of ordinary head-complement structures.

The BMS proposal includes a traceless analysis of argument and adjunct extraction. Extracted elements, which are marked by a subtype of *synsem*, are represented on DEPS but not mapped onto COMPS. For presentation reasons, the argument raising approach in De Kuthy and Meurers (to appear) includes the basic trace-based extraction theory of Pollard and Sag (1994) and so does the generalization of that approach presented in the following.[9] Our dependent-raising approach could also be integrated with a traceless analysis, but as discussed in De Kuthy and Meurers (1999) the traceless variant differs from the trace-based one in a relevant aspect: Under the traceless approach, extracted elements can never undergo dependent raising since they are not represented on COMPS. Under the trace-based analysis, on the other hand, an element can be extracted from a higher COMPS list to which it has been raised—which makes it more similar to the structures licensed by a reanalysis approach to partial constituents we argue for in De Kuthy and Meurers (to appear).

6.3.3 A Theory for Dependent Raising

With a proposal for lexicalizing adjunct selection at hand, the task of this section is to integrate such lexicalized adjunct selection into our general argument-raising theory in order to arrive at a uniform treatment of both kind of partial constituent phenomena.

A straightforward way of performing this integration is to take the specification of the list of adjunct requirements from the Argument Structure Extension principle of BMS (figure 6) and insert it into the Lexical Argument-Raising Principle of figure 3. The Lexical Dependent-Raising Principle (LDRP) resulting from this integration is shown in figure 7.

The central change in this principle compared to the Lexical Argument-Raising Principle is the addition of a list of adjuncts requirements which is shuffled (◯) into the list of complements. In addition, the LDRP has a more general antecedent than the LARP. This is necessary to introduce adjuncts as dependents of heads of different categories in order to license the different categories of partially fronted constituents we saw in (2).[10]

[9]The DEPS attribute used by BMS to collect all elements which can be extracted thus is not be needed in our approach.

[10]While the data presented in section 6.1 shows that at least some adjuncts of non-verbal heads should be treated as dependents, this clearly is not the case for all

$$
\textit{lexeme} \rightarrow
\begin{bmatrix}
\text{S|LOC} & \begin{bmatrix}
\text{CAT} & \begin{bmatrix}
\text{HEAD} & \boxed{4} \\
\text{VAL} & \begin{bmatrix}
\text{SUBJ} & \boxed{1} \\
\text{COMPS} & \left(\textit{raised}\left(\boxed{4},\boxed{3}\right) \oplus \boxed{2}\right) \bigcirc \\
 & \textit{list}\left(\begin{bmatrix}\text{L|C|H|MOD|LOC} & \begin{bmatrix}\text{CAT|HEAD} & \boxed{4} \\ \text{CONT|KEY} & \boxed{5}\end{bmatrix}\end{bmatrix}\right)
\end{bmatrix}
\end{bmatrix} \\
\text{CONT|KEY} & \boxed{5}
\end{bmatrix} \\
\text{ARG-ST} & \textit{distrib-args}\left(\boxed{4},\boxed{1},\boxed{2}\right) \wedge \left(\boxed{3} \bigcirc \textit{indep}\right)
\end{bmatrix}
$$

FIGURE 7 The Lexical Dependent-Raising Principle (LDRP)

And parallel to the LARP, the LDRP should define the mapping only for base forms to be compatible with the sentence structure setup following Pollard (1996). We therefore introduce a type *lexeme* as subtype of *sign* and redefine the inflectional lexical rules such as the finitivization lexical rule as lexeme to word mappings.[11]

To be compatible with the more general antecedent of the LDRP, the relation *raised* has to be modified so that it takes the category of the head into account. The otherwise unchanged definition is shown in figure 8.

$$
\textit{raised}\left(\textit{head}, \langle\rangle\right) := \langle\rangle.
$$

$$
\textit{raised}\left(\textit{verb}, \left\langle \begin{bmatrix} \text{LEX} & + \\ \text{L|C} & \begin{bmatrix} \text{HEAD} & \textit{verb} \vee \textit{adj} \\ \text{V|COMPS} & \boxed{1} \end{bmatrix} \end{bmatrix} \right\rangle\right) := \boxed{1}\ \textit{lex-minus-list}.
$$

$$
\textit{raised}\left(\textit{verb}, \left\langle \begin{bmatrix} \text{L|C} & \begin{bmatrix} \text{HEAD} & \textit{noun} \\ \text{V|COMPS} & \boxed{1} \end{bmatrix} \end{bmatrix} \right\rangle\right) := \boxed{1}\ \textit{prep-list}.
$$

FIGURE 8 Definition of possible argument-raising sources

At first sight, the fact that the new argument for the head category of all argument-raising sources is specified to be verbal seems to suggest that the additional argument is essentially a complication forced upon us by the need to generalize the antecedent for the adjunct treatment.

kinds of adjuncts. A more elaborate theory of adjunct realization will have to restrict the subclass of adjuncts which are intended to construct as dependents and which are not.

[11]The description level formalization of lexical rules provided in Meurers (1995, 1999b) readily supports such a revision.

Askedal (1989) shows, however, that in addition to the verbal heads generally discussed, certain adjectival elements can also occur as heads in a head cluster.[12] To extend the coverage of our generalized argument-raising approach to such adjectival heads, it is sufficient to add a clause to the definition of the *raised* relation in figure 8 specifying *adjective* as the first argument. The possibility of having argument-raising sources of different categories thus is also empirically motivated.

Returning to our general task of extending the argument-raising approach to general dependent raising, the essential new aspect of the Lexical Dependent-Raising Principle replacing the Lexical Argument-Raising Principle is that adjuncts are now also represented on the COMPS list. Since the *raised* relation permits verbal, adjectival or nominal complements of verbal heads to be partial if their remaining COMPS elements are raised, the adjuncts represented on COMPS lists can now also be subject to such raising. We thus obtain the intended result that partial constituents can result from raising of adjuncts.

To get a better understanding of how such partial constituents missing adjuncts are licensed, let us take a look at two concrete examples.

6.3.4 Examples

We start with the discussion of the simple example (5) involving raising of an adjunct from a verbal complement.

(5) [Zurückkehren] wollen sie *im nächsten Frühjahr.*
return want to they in the next spring

'They want to return next spring.'

A sketch of the analysis for this example resulting from our theory is shown in figure 9. The partially fronted constituent *zurückkehren* is licensed in the following way: The verb *zurückkehren* in the example tree has one argument on its ARG-ST list, its own subject [5]. As an effect of the LDRP of figure 7 the verb has two elements on its valence lists, its subject [5] on SUBJ and the PP adjunct *im nächsten Frühjahr* ([3]) on COMPS.

[12] Askedal (1989, p. 103) shows this on the basis of examples such as the following one from Thomas Mann's *Der Zauberberg.*

(i) da man Eiweiß auf Gift nicht mehr zu reimen gewohnt war.
because $one_{N'}$ *white of* $egg_{A''}$ *on* $poison_{P''}$ $not_{Neg'}$ *anymore to* $rhyme_{V''}$ *used to* $was_{V'}$

'Because one was no longer used to rhyme white of egg with poison.'

The negation *nicht* is interpreted as belonging to the outer predicate *gewohnt sein.* But it intervenes between the inner predicate *zu reimen* and its complements *Eiweiß* and *auf Gift.* The possibility of performing such permutations of elements belonging to different heads is one of the tests of Bech (1955) for the formation of a head cluster. See Meurers (1999b, ch. 9.7.2) for a discussion.

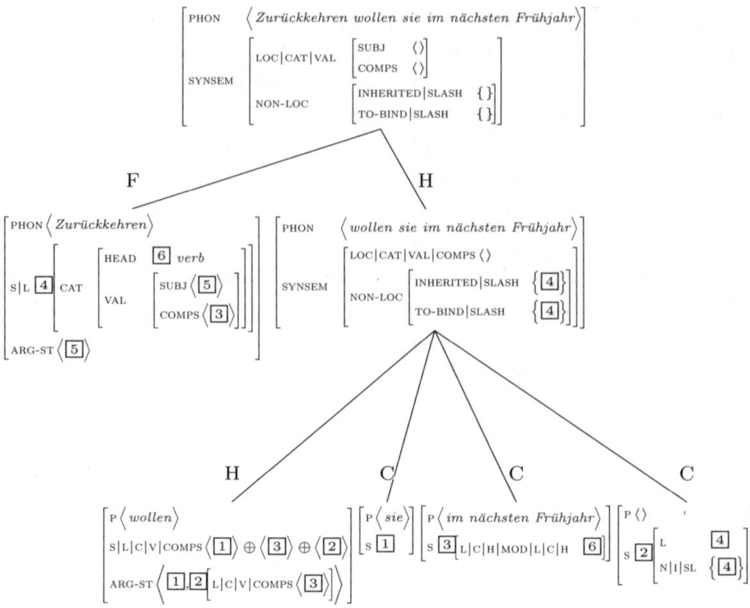

FIGURE 9 An adjunct-raising analysis

The finite verb *wollen* in figure 9 has two elements on its ARG-ST list, the subject NP [1] and a verbal complement [2]. According to the LDRP it raises the COMPS element [3] of this verbal argument onto its own COMPS list. The occurrence of *wollen* in the tree thus has three elements on its COMPS list, its own two arguments, and the dependent [3] raised from the verbal argument *zurückkehren.* The subject NP *sie*, the PP adjunct *im nächsten Frühjahr* and the trace of the topicalized verbal complement *zurückkehren* are then all realized in a head-complement structure.

Interaction of Argument and Adjunct Raising Returning to the more complex example (4a) involving raising of both an argument and an adjunct. We see the sketch of an analysis tree for this example in figure 10. The occurrence of the transitive verb *verkaufen* in the tree has two elements on its ARG-ST list, its subject [5] and the object NP *das Pferd* ([7]). The LDRP maps these two arguments onto the valence members SUBJ and COMPS and additionally introduces the modifying PP [3]. Similar to the example tree in figure 9 the finite verb *will* in this tree has two elements on its ARG-ST list, its subject and a verbal complement. The LDRP maps these two elements onto the COMPS list. In addition the two complements of the verbal complement are raised

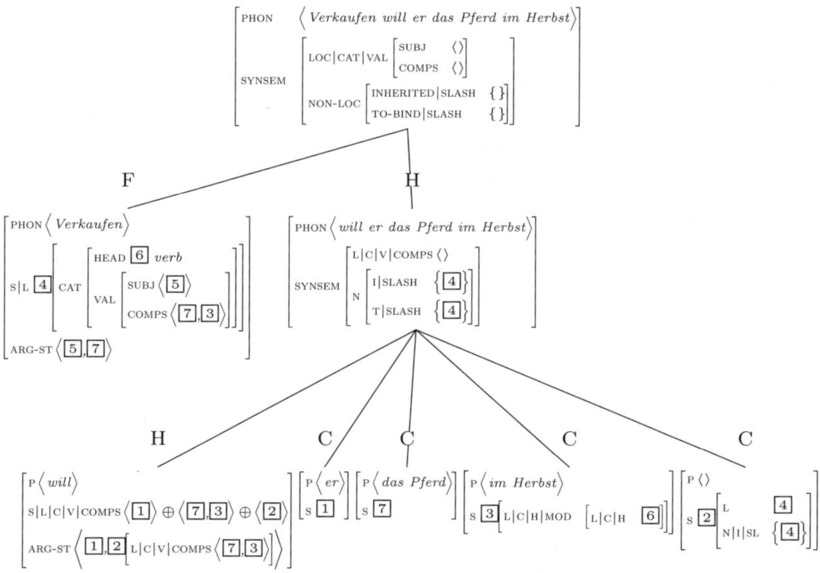

FIGURE 10 Interaction of argument and adjunct raising

onto this list and the finite verb *will* then realizes the trace of the fronted verbal complement, the raised modifying PP and the raised complement and its own subject in a flat head-complement structure.

6.4 Conclusion

This paper addresses an empirical aspect of the partial constituent phenomenon in German which has generally been neglected in the literature: the possibility of fronting constituents which are partial due to missing adjuncts.

We argued that a head-movement analysis of these data such as the one proposed by S. Müller (1999) fails to take into account the parallel character of the partial fronting cases involving adjuncts and the more widely studied partial fronting phenomenon where a complement is left behind. Furthermore, such head movement has to be attached to very specific constructions in order to avoid serious overgeneration.

Taking the parallel character of the two partial constituent phenomena seriously, we proposed to derive both from the same underlying mechanism. We showed that such a mechanism can be obtained by generalizing the lexical argument-raising principle we proposed in De Kuthy and Meurers (to appear) to a mechanism licensing raising of dependents in general. Formally, this generalization consists of integrating a lexicalized selection of adjuncts as proposed in the adjuncts-as-dependents tradition of HPSG (Miller, 1992; Van Noord and Bouma, 1994; Bouma, Malouf, and Sag, to appear) into our lexical argument-raising principle.

The resulting theory thus has two interesting aspects: On the empirical side, it extends the empirical coverage of previous HPSG proposals in a way providing a uniform analysis of both kinds of partial constituent phenomena. On the theoretical side, it shows how argument raising and adjuncts-as-dependents as two widely applied HPSG mechanisms can be integrated.

Acknowledgments

We would like to thank Stefan Müller, Jürgen Pafel, the anonymous reviewers, and the participants of the HPSG-99 conference in Edinburgh for comments and discussion.

References

Askedal, J. O. 1989. über den infinitiv ohne bzw. mit "zu" im heutigen deutsch: Klassenbildung regierender lexeme und hauptzüge der distribution (i). *Deutsch als Fremdsprache* 26:2–7.

Bech, G. 1955. *Studien über das deutsche verbum infinitum*. Historisk-filologiske Meddelelser udgivet af Det Kongelige Danske Videnskabernes Selskab. Bind 35, no. 2, 1955; Bind 36, no. 6, 1957; Kopenhagen. Reprinted 1983, Tübingen: Max Niemeyer Verlag.

Bouma, G., R. Malouf, and I. A. Sag. 2001. Satisfying constraints on extraction and adjunction. *Natural Language and Linguistic Theory* 19:1–65.

Bouma, G. and G. van Noord. 1998. Word order constraints on verb clusters in German and dutch. In E. W. Hinrichs, A. Kathol, and T. Nakazawa, eds., *Complex Predicates in Non-derivational Syntax*, vol. 30 of *Syntax and Semantics*. New York, et al.: Academic Press.

De Kuthy, K. 2000. *Discontinuous NPs in German — A Case Study of the Interaction of Syntax, Semantics and Pragmatics*. Phil. diss., Universität des Saarlandes, Saarbrücken.

De Kuthy, K. and W. D. Meurers. 1998. Towards a general theory of partial constituent fronting in German. In G. Bouma, G.-J. Kruijff, and R. Oehrle, eds., *Proceedings of the Joint Conference on Formal Grammar, Head-driven Phrase Structure Grammar, and Categorial Grammar (FHCG-98)*, pages 113–124. Saarbrücken: Universität des Saarlandes.

De Kuthy, K. and W. D. Meurers. 1999. Argument raising meets adjuncts-as-dependents and traceless extraction. In *Proceedings of the Sixth Int. Conference on HPSG*, pages 45–50. Edinburgh: University of Edinburgh.

De Kuthy, K. and W. D. Meurers. To appear. On partial constituent fronting in German. *Journal of Comparative Germanic Linguistics*.

Hinrichs, E. W. and T. Nakazawa. 1989. Flipped out: Aux in German. In *Papers from the 25th Regional Meeting of the Chicago Linguistic Society*, pages 193–202. Chicago, IL.

Hinrichs, E. W. and T. Nakazawa. 1994. Partial-VP and Split-NP topicalization in German – an HPSG analysis. In E. W. Hinrichs, W. D. Meurers, and T. Nakazawa, eds., *Partial-VP and Split-NP Topicalization in German – An HPSG Analysis and its Implementation*, Arbeitspapiere des SFB 340 Nr. 58, pages 1–46. Tübingen: Universität Tübingen.

Kathol, A. 1995. *Linearization-Based German Syntax*. Ph.D. thesis, Ohio State University, Columbus, OH.

Meurers, W. D. 1995. Towards a semantics for lexical rules as used in HPSG. In *Proceedings of the ACQUILEX II Workshop on the Formalisation and Use of Lexical Rules*, pages 1–20. Cambridge, UK. Also presented at the First Conference on Formal Grammar, Barcelona, 1995.

Meurers, W. D. 1999a. German partial-VP topicalization revisited. In G. Webelhuth, J.-P. Koenig, and A. Kathol, eds., *Lexical and Constructional Aspects of Linguistic Explanation*, Studies in Constraint-Based Lexicalism, pages 129–144. Stanford, CA: CSLI Publications. Published version of a paper presented at the 3rd Int. Conference on HPSG, May 1996, Marseille.

Meurers, W. D. 1999b. *Lexical Generalizations in the Syntax of German Non-Finite Constructions*. Ph.D. thesis, Seminar für Sprachwissenschaft, Universität Tübingen, Tübingen. Available as Volume 145 in Arbeitspapiere des SFB 340, 2000.

Miller, P. H. 1992. *Clitics and Constituents in Phrase Structure Grammar*. New York, NY: Garland. Published version of 1991 Ph. D. thesis, University of Utrecht, Utrecht.

Müller, G. 1996. *Incomplete Category Fronting*. Habilitationsschrift, Universität Tübingen, Tübingen. Published as SfS-Report 01–96.

Müller, S. 1997. Yet another paper about partial verb phrase fronting in German. Research Report RR–97–07, DFKI, Saarbrücken. A shorter version appeared in *Proceedings of the 16th Conference on Computational Linguistics (COLING-96)*.

Müller, S. 1999. *Deutsche Syntax deklarativ. Head-Driven Phrase Structure Grammar für das Deutsche*. No. 394 in Linguistische Arbeiten. Tübingen: Max Niemeyer Verlag.

Nerbonne, J. 1994. Partial verb phrases and spurious ambiguities. In J. Nerbonne, K. Netter, and C. Pollard, eds., *German in Head-Driven Phrase Structure Grammar*, no. 46 in CSLI Lecture Notes, pages 109–150. Stanford, CA: CSLI Publications.

Pollard, C. 1996. On head non-movement. In H. Bunt and A. van Horck, eds., *Discontinuous Constituency*, vol. 6 of *Natural Language Processing*, pages 279–305. Berlin and New York, NY: Mouton de Gruyter. Published version of a Ms. dated January 1990.

Pollard, C. and I. A. Sag. 1994. *Head-Driven Phrase Structure Grammar*. Chicago, IL: University of Chicago Press.

Thiersch, C. 1985. VP and scrambling in the German Mittelfeld. Ms., dated 22. April 1985, Universität Köln, Köln and University of Conneticut, Storrs, CT.

Van Noord, G. and G. Bouma. 1994. The scope of adjuncts and the processing of lexical rules. In *Proceedings of the 15th Conference on Computational Linguistics (COLING-94)*, pages 250–256. Kyoto.

Webelhuth, G. and H. d. Besten. 1987. Remnant topicalization and the constituent structure of VP in the Germanic SOV languages (abstract for the 10th GLOW colloquium). In H. Bennis and J. Koster, eds., *GLOW Newsletter Nr. 18*, pages 15–16. Dordrecht: Foris Publications.

7

The Nature of Pragmatic Information

Georgia M. Green

7.1 Introduction

One of the defining aspects of HPSG as explicated in Pollard & Sag (1987, 1994) is that information of disparate types, including semantic and pragmatic information as well as syntactic, is essential for the description of licensed expressions in a language. The main point of this paper is that the pragmatic information available from the use of linguistic signs has a very different character from the more specifically linguistic information carried by signs. When this is clearly understood, representing background information accurately requires considerably more analysis and elaboration than is apparent from most published discussion. At the same time, it reveals that the inheritance of contextual (including presuppositional) information is not the problematic matter it has long been understood to be: the avoidance (or acceptance) of top-level contradictions in contextual information is a problem that speakers have to deal with in understanding the world around them, not in understanding language that they hear. One consequence of this is that unless their goal is to model interactants' beliefs about the mental states of their interlocutors, natural language implementations with HPSG backbones are not burdened with the extremely difficult problem of requiring consistency in the unconstrained domain of world knowledge.

Bar-Hillel discussed the character of pragmatic information 45 years ago (1954), but because it took me so long to reach my present understanding of what he wrote, I believe it is useful to look at the issues from the perspective of today's generative grammars. Briefly, pragmatic in-

Grammatical Interfaces in HPSG.
Ronnie Cann, Claire Grover and Philip Miller.

formation, even including indexical information (i.e., indices for speaker, hearer, time and location of the act of uttering something that the sign represents), is not so much information about the sign as it is about the relation between the user of the sign and the **act** of using the sign. First and foremost, pragmatic information is information about mental models: speaker's and addressee's mental models of each other. Linguistic pragmatics irreducibly involves the speaker's model of the addressee, and the hearer's model of the speaker (potentially recursively). For George to understand Martha's utterance of "X" to him, he must not only recognize (speech perception, parsing) that she has said "X," he must have beliefs about her which allow him to infer what her purpose was in uttering "X," which means that he has beliefs about her model of him, including her model of his model of her, and so on.

And any of these beliefs is liable to be incorrect at one level of detail or another. (That is why, in the illustration, we see that George's image of Martha, and his of her, as well as his belief about what she meant, are not quite accurate.) Since acts are interpreted at multiple levels of granularity, this holds for acts involved in choosing words and construction types, as well as for acts of uttering sentences containing or instantiating them. From this it follows that the distinction between pragmatic effects called "intrusive pragmatics" (Levinson, 2000) or explicature (Sperber & Wilson 1986) and those described as implicature proper has little necessary significance for an information-based account of language structure. Because the computation of pragmatic effects (by whatever name) involves analysis of what is underspecified by what is actually uttered, and how what is uttered compares to what might reasonably have been expected, it involves importing propositions, a process beyond the bounds of computation within a finite domain, even if supplemented by a finite set of functions. These points will be demonstrated in discussion of the quintessentially pragmatic problems raised by sentence-final particles, discourse markers, illocutionary forces, and honorifics.

7.2 Pragmatics

7.2.1 Indexicals

Pragmatics is not just about the interpretation of indexicals—linguistic elements whose interpretation is bound to the circumstances of their utterance, like *I, here, now, this* as in (1).

(1) I'm on 27th Street at Fifth Avenue now.

There are several classes of expressions whose interpretation is directly bound to the interpretation of such "primary indexicals"; pragmatics necessarily extends to both deictic and anaphoric pronominals generally, tenses (Kiparsky 1968, McCawley 1971), covert pronominals like *local, enemy* (Partee 1989) as in (2), and to sentence initial use of logical connectives like *And, So, But, Now* as in (3) (see Section 5 below).

(2) a. (pointing) That's the kind of hat he wore!
 b. Dan Rather went to a local bar. [local relative to his characteristic location? to his location at speech-time? to the location of the speaker at speech time? to the characteristic location of the speaker?]

(3) But that doesn't mean there is nothing we can do!

7.2.2 Descriptions: Secondary Indexicals

In addition, as has long been acknowledged in references to "the universe of discourse," interpretation of the definite article invokes indexical reference; the uniqueness presupposition associated with use of the definite article amounts to a belief by the speaker that the anchor of the index of the definite NP is salient to the addressee. Indeed, insofar as the interpretation of ordinary kind names varies with the expectations about the universe of discourse that the speaker imputes to the addressee (Nunberg 1978), this larger class of indexicals encompasses the immense class of descriptive terms, including *cat, mat, window, hamburger, red,* and the like as in (4).

(4) a. The blond hamburger spilled her coffee.
    b. The cat shattered next to the mat.

The important point here is that with these secondary indexicals (and in fact, even with the so-called primary indexicals (Nunberg 1993)), interpretation is not a simple matter of observing properties of the speech situation (source of the speech sound, calendric time, etc.), but involves making judgements about possible mappings from signal to referent (anchor).[1] Bar-Hillel (1954) and Morgan (1978) pointed out that the interpretation of demonstratives involves choosing from among many (perhaps indefinitely many) objects the speaker may have been pointing at, as well as what distinct class or individual the speaker may have intended to refer to by indicating that object (as pointed out by Nunberg (1978)). Thus, the interpretation of indexicals involves choices from the elements of a set (possibly an infinite set) that is limited differently in each speech situation.

7.3 Background

As illustrated in Green (1994), representing relevant beliefs and intentions of a speaker in CONTEXT values on signs results in surprisingly complex constraints. The structural complexity of the detailed representations derives from the fact that distinct references to mutual belief and reflexive intentions appear to be necessary. The reason for this is that sometimes one is invoked and sometimes the other; particular kinds of intentions are part of the description of particular illocutionary forces and intended perlocutionary effects of a manner of speaking, but the description of constraints on the use of lexical elements and constructions involves invoking mutual beliefs of speaker and addressee. This means that it will not be sufficient to characterize the feature CONTEXT as representing some 'proposition(s) that the speaker believes or intends,' precisely because it is necessary to distinguish beliefs from intentions. Insofar as interpretation of what are called "contextual factors" involves the interpretation of acts, a theory of the projection of background propositions of words and phrases must be just the linguistic subcase of a more general theory of the interpretation of events of human behavior, not something specifically linguistic. As even Grice

[1] Indeed, I have argued (Green 1995) that the inferential processes in interpretation and disambiguation are essentially the same.

(1975) described it, conversational implicature is a function of a general theory of action, in particular, a certain kind of intentional action and its interpretation. Therefore, I believe it is useful to reframe the Cooperative Principle and the maxims so they do not look like imperatives for language use,[2] but rather represent the outlines of a theory of joint action (Cohen & Levesque, 1991):

(5) **The Cooperative Principle:**
Individuals act in accordance with their goals.

(6) **Grice's "Maxims"** (recast):

a. QUANTITY:
   I. An agent will do as much as is required for the achievement of the current goal.
   II. An agent will not do more than is required.

b. QUALITY: Agents will not deceive co-agents. Consequently, an agent will try to make any assertion one that is true.
   I. Agents will not say what they believe to be false.
   II. Agents will not say that for which they lack adequate evidence.

c. RELATION: An agent's action will be relevant to and relative to an intention of the agent.

d. MANNER: Agents will make their actions perspicuous to others who share a joint intention.
   I. Agents will not disguise actions from co-agents. Consequently, agents will not speak obscurely in attempting to communicate.
   II. Agents will act so that intentions they intend to communicate are unambiguously reconstructible.
   III. Agents will spend no more energy on actions than is necessary.
   IV. Agents will execute sub-parts of a plan in an order that will maximize the perceived likelihood of achieving the goal.

In addition, it is important to make a clear distinction between the circumstances under which something is conventionally uttered, and the content, if any, of that utterance. The sign *Hello!*, for example, does not **mean** 'speaker greets addressee,' although it is conventionally uttered to achieve that effect (Morgan 1978). The following sections demonstrate how in general, BACKGROUND propositions are not directly observable

[2]See Green 1990 for discussion of the consequences of this.

"facts," but rather attitudes toward propositions of the sort 'the speaker believes that ... ' or 'it is normally believed that ... '.

7.4 Sentence Final Particles

Sentence-final particles (SFPs) are morphemes (typically monosyllables) in languages like Chinese (Lu 1995) and Japanese (Suzuki 1997) that go at the very end of a sentence and indicate something about how the speaker's saying what she has just said relates (in her view) to the addressee's beliefs. The syntax of the attachment of these morphemes is unclear, and possibly irrelevant. Their use conveys such nuances of communication as:

(7) a. I believe you should already know this. (Cf. English *That's your brother, y'know/for Pete's sake!*)

b. I believe this contradicts your current attitude. (Cf. English *It really is your brother.*)

c. I am not sure this is correct. (Cf. English *That's your brother, isn't it?*)

d. I am confident of the correctness of this. (Cf. English *Hey! That's your brother.*)

The closest English equivalents to Chinese and Japanese sentence-final particles are often various parentheticals, "particles," or interjections like *I suppose, well, hey!, y'know* and similar fixed expressions like *don't ya think.*[3] The syntax of many of these English elements is equally unclear, and likely beyond the reach of most current theories. Of course, all of these particles have many uses, and any given Chinese or Japanese SFP will not always have the same English counterpart. This is not suprising, because the English expressions do not reference exactly the same attitudes as the Chinese and Japanese particles. Lu and Suzuki show that the basic content of the Chinese and Japanese particles entails that use of a particular particle with a particular sentence will in some circumstances will be polite or deferential, and in other circumstances, rude or insulting.

This means that politeness or deference cannot be part of the meaning, or even the [BACKGROUND] of a particle, although deference or concern may be implied by what they invoke, given certain mutual assumptions of speaker and addressee. The larger problem that they pose is that in relating to "what has just been said," like metalinguistic negation (Horn 1985), they refer to any aspect of the content OR the form

[3]Sometimes, however, the closest translation is a truth-conditional adverbial like *really* or *perhaps*.

of the utterance to which they attach, exactly as Grice's explication of the implications of the Cooperative Principle predicts. What it will take to represent in feature-structures and AVMs the BACKGROUND proposition that the speaker has a certain propositional attitude towards the utterance to which the sentence-final particle attaches will have to be worked out by linguists cleverer than me, but that is what it will take to represent the contextual contribution of sentence-final particles.

7.5 Discourse Markers

Sentence-initial discourse markers like *OK, Now, But, Yet, And, Therefore* and their ilk are used to enable the addressee to infer something about how what is about to be said relates to what has already been said. The use of sentence-initial connective particles such as *now, so, yet, but*, and *thus* reflects how the speaker wants the addressee to understand the relation between what will be said and what has been said, usually something along the lines of the sentiments expressed in (8).

(8) a. We're done with the topic we were just discussing. Now I'm going back to where we were before.

b. The point I am about to make contrasts with the point I have just made.

c. The point I am about to make is a consequence of the fact I have just established.

They present all of the same problems as SFPs, with the added wrinkle that exactly what bit of discourse they refer to is not specified. Markers like *OK, Now* and *And* may do little more than indicate that discussion of the immediately preceding issue is, in the speaker's mind, complete, and the speaker is moving on to a previously implicated or projected next step in her exposition. The markers *But* and *Yet* close the discussion of the previous issue, and announce that what immediately follows contrasts with a point that has just been made. In both cases, the hearer is left to infer exactly what the issue or point in question is; it might be a sentence-worth, or a whole seven-paragraph section's-worth.

Discourse markers are not vague about whether they refer to the form or the content of what has just been said, but they are vague about what boundaries *just* refers to. Again, even if some clever linguist can figure out how to represent this situation, it will not enable a mechanical determination of what discourse unit has just been sewed up: imagine trying to write a LISP or PROLOG editor that reconstructed bracketing when you indicated that a certain right bracket was an end, but not necessarily the end of either the smallest or the largest open expression.

Importantly, both sentence-final particles (and their counterparts in other languages[4]) and discourse markers provide an example of how the intention to produce a perlocutionary effect that is intended to be recognized as intended figures in conditions on the use of linguistic signs.

7.6 Illocutionary Intentions

7.6.1 The Representation of Illocutionary Force

Some years ago, it was commonly accepted that 1) illocutionary force was represented overtly by performative verbs (Austin 1962) or other Illocutionary-Force-Indicating-Devices (IFIDs, Stampe 1975) such as intonation or "markers" like preverbal *please*), and that 2) where illocutionary force was ambiguous or unclear, that was because the performative clause prefixed to the sentence (Lakoff 1968, Ross 1970, Fraser 1974, Sadock 1974) was "abstract" and invisible. Linguists have been pretty silent on this issue for the last 25 years, and I am inclined to accept Dennis Stampe's (1975) conclusion that so-called performative verbs are really constative, and that the appearance of performativity is an inference from the ACT of utterance. This makes performativity more a matter of the illocutionary intentions of the speaker than of the classification of visible or invisible "markers" of illocutionary force. By "illocutionary intentions" I mean to include the relatively large but limited set of illocutionary forces described and classified by Austin (1962) and Searle (1969) and many others (stating, requesting, promising and the like). So, expositives are utterances which a speaker (S) makes with the intention that the addressee (A) recognize S's intention that A believe that S believes their content. Promises are made with the intention that A recognize S's intention that A believe that S will be responsible for making their content true. Interrogatives are uttered with the belief that A will recognize S's intention that A provide information which S indicates.

But as far as I can tell, from the hearer's point of view such illocutionary intentions are not significantly different from intentions about the essentially unlimited class of possible perlocutionary effects that a speaker might intend an addressee to recognize as intended on an occasion of use. So, reminders are expositives uttered with the intention that A will recognize that S believes A has believed what S wants A to

[4]I have in mind elements like *well* and *why* in English, whose use also reflects how the speaker wants the addressee to take the fact that she has said what she has said as reflecting her beliefs about the addressee's beliefs about her beliefs and intentions (Lakoff 1973, Schourup 1982).

believe. Warnings are utterances the uttering of which is intended to be recognized as intended to inform A that some imminent or contingent state of affairs will be bad for A. An insult is uttered with the intention that A recognize S's intent to convey S's view of A as having properties normally believed to be bad.

Both kinds of intentions figure in conditions on the use of linguistic expressions of various sorts. For example, the [VFORM *base*] verb *beware* appears to occur only in utterances intended to be understood as warnings (9), or in references to warnings (10), or at least situations which the speaker believes are potentially dangerous to the subject of *beware*, as in (11).

(9) a. Beware of the bandersnatch!
b. I want you to beware of the bandersnatch.
c. You better beware of the bandersnatch.
d. Do you promise you'll beware of the bandersnatch?

(10) a. I told them to beware of the bandersnatch.
b. No one will have to tell them to beware of the bandersnatch.

(11) a. They'll have to beware of the bandersnatch.
b. I hope they have the sense to beware of the bandersnatch.

When it is difficult to construe the uttering of a *beware* sentence as being or relating to a warning, its acceptability is diminished, as illustrated in (12).

(12) a. ??Do you suppose you will beware of the bandersnatch?
b. ??I'm confident they'll beware of the bandersnatch.
c. *I'm confident I'll beware of the bandersnatch.

Similarly, there are a whole host of of phrasal verbs[5] such as *butt out*, that can be described as directive-polarity expressions (instantiating, reporting, or evoking directives), as illustrated in (13).

(13) a. Butt out!
b. *They may butt out.
c. *Why do they butt out?
d. They were asked to butt out.
e. They refused to butt out.
f. Why don't you butt out?

[5]Many meaning roughly 'go away'.

Just as there are expressions like *beware* and *butt out* that depend on a particular illocutionary force, there are expressions whose distribution depends on other mental states of the speaker concerning the addressee. Often it is an intention to produce a particular perlocutionary effect, as with threat-polarity expressions like *Or else!*, exemplified in (14).

(14) a. Get out, or else!
b. *I want to get out, or else!
c. *Who's on first, or else?
d. They said we had to get out, or else.
e. They knew they had to get out, or else.
f. *They were surprised that we had to get out, or else.

Sometimes, however, the relevant mental state of the speaker does not involve intentions at all. This is the case with ignorance-polarity constructions and idioms (*WH-the hell* (Horn 1972, 1978), sluicing (Green 1981)) which are acceptable only in contexts where a relevant being (typically the speaker) is ignorant of the answer to an indicated question, as in (15) and (16).

(15) a. Where the hell is it?
b. I couldn't figure out where the hell it was.
c. *We went back to the place where the hell we left it.
d. *I knew where the hell it would be found.

(16) a. Dale broke something—guess what.
b. Dale broke something, but it's not clear what.
c. *Sandy bought something, and it's clear what.
d. *Sandy bought something, and I washed what.

Now, it is possible to represent this kind of selection in HPSG feature-structure descriptions (if you can do it in first-order predicate calculus, you can do it in HPSG). Insofar as speaker intentions and speaker and addressee beliefs about intentions, actions, existence, knowledge and values can be represented in terms of conjoined and/or nested propositions, they can be represented as members of a sign's CONTEXT|BACKGROUND set. Thus, the illocutionary force of promising some state of affairs could be represented as in (17), with a CONTEXT|BACKGROUND value somewhat reminiscent of Generative Semantic lexical decompositions.

(17) A feature structure for the illocutionary force of promising

$$\begin{bmatrix} \text{CXT} & \begin{bmatrix} \text{C-INDS} & \begin{bmatrix}\text{SPKR} & \boxed{1}\\ \text{ADDR} & \boxed{2}\end{bmatrix} \\ \text{BKD} & \left\{ \begin{bmatrix} \textit{intend} & \\ \text{EXPR} & \boxed{1} \\ \text{SOA} & \begin{bmatrix} \textit{recognize} & \\ \text{EXPR} & \boxed{2} \\ \text{SOA} & \begin{bmatrix} \textit{intend} & \\ \text{EXPR} & \boxed{1} \\ \text{SOA} & \begin{bmatrix}\textit{believe} & \\ \text{EXPR} & \boxed{2}\\ \text{SOA} & \begin{bmatrix}\textit{commit} & \\ \text{AGT} & \boxed{1}\\ \text{SOA} & \begin{bmatrix}\textit{responsible} & \\ \text{THEME} & \boxed{1}\\ \text{SOA} & \textit{psoa}\end{bmatrix}\end{bmatrix}\end{bmatrix}\end{bmatrix}\end{bmatrix}\end{bmatrix} \right\} \end{bmatrix}\end{bmatrix}$$

To the extent that the reflexive intention about a proposition (the speaker's intention that the addressee recognize the speaker's intention that the addressee believe that proposition) is a universal aspect of intentional utterance, most of the exterior structure in (17) could be reduced to a single relation of reflexive intention (defined as the intend-recognize-intend-believe structure in (17)), simplifying representation to (18).

(18) A feature structure for the illocutionary force of promising, simplified

$$\begin{bmatrix} \text{CXT} & \begin{bmatrix} \text{C-INDS} & \begin{bmatrix}\text{SPKR} & \boxed{1}\\ \text{ADDR} & \boxed{2}\end{bmatrix} \\ \text{BKD} & \left\{ \begin{bmatrix} \textit{refl-intend} & \\ \text{EXPR} & \boxed{1} \\ \text{THEME} & \boxed{2} \\ \text{SOA} & \begin{bmatrix}\textit{commit} & \\ \text{AGT} & \boxed{1}\\ \text{SOA} & \begin{bmatrix}\textit{responsible} & \\ \text{THEME} & \boxed{1}\\ \text{SOA} & \textit{psoa}\end{bmatrix}\end{bmatrix}\end{bmatrix} \right\} \end{bmatrix}\end{bmatrix}$$

7.6.2 Inference of Illocutionary Intentions

Of course, it is not the sign which is the indicator of illocutionary intentions, but the act of uttering it. An utterance is a warning just in case S intends A to recognize THE UTTERING OF IT as intended to cause A to recognize that some situation may result in a state which A would consider bad. Syntacticians need to be concerned with such things because the character of illocutionary intentions impacts the description of the distribution of forms: the [VFORM *base*] verb *beware* occurs where the speaker believes that the subject of *beware* would be endangered. To the extent that the HPSG system for grammatical descriptions allows the conditions that characterize a warning to be described within the same framework as that used to describe grammatical properties of linguistic expressions, those conditions could be referenced as constraints in the lexical entries for restricted forms like *beware*. Such an illocutionary force and a restricted item that depends on it are sketched in (19) and (20), respectively.

(19) The illocutionary force of warning, represented in a feature structure description

$$\begin{bmatrix} \text{PHON} & \boxed{3} \\ \text{CXT} & \begin{bmatrix} \text{C-INDS} & \begin{bmatrix}\text{SPKR} & \boxed{1}\\ \text{ADDR} & \boxed{2}\end{bmatrix} \\ \text{BKD} & \left\{ \begin{bmatrix} \textit{refl-intend} & \\ \text{EXPR} & \boxed{1} \\ \text{STD} & \boxed{2} \\ \text{SOA} & \begin{bmatrix} \textit{cause} & \\ \text{CAUSE} & \begin{bmatrix} \textit{utter} & \\ \text{AGENT} & \boxed{1} \\ \text{GOAL} & \boxed{2} \\ \text{UTTERANCE} & \boxed{3}\end{bmatrix} \\ \text{EFFECT} & \begin{bmatrix} \textit{realize} & \\ \text{EXPR} & \boxed{2} \\ \text{SOA} & \begin{bmatrix} \textit{endanger} & \\ \text{THEME} & \textit{index} \\ \text{EXPR} & \boxed{2}\end{bmatrix}\end{bmatrix}\end{bmatrix}\end{bmatrix} \right\} \end{bmatrix}\end{bmatrix}$$

(20) Partial lexical entry for a restricted form

$$\begin{bmatrix} \text{PHON} & \boxed{3}\ \langle \text{biwer} \rangle \\ \text{CAT} & \begin{bmatrix} \text{HEAD} & \begin{bmatrix} \text{VFORM} & \textit{base} \end{bmatrix} \\ \text{ARG-ST} & \langle\ NP_{\boxed{1}},\ PP\text{-}of_{\boxed{2}}\ \rangle \end{bmatrix} \\ \text{CONTENT} & \begin{bmatrix} \textit{watch-out-for} \\ \text{AGENT}\ \boxed{1} \\ \text{THEME}\ \boxed{2} \end{bmatrix} \\ \text{CONTEXT} & \begin{bmatrix} \text{BKD} & \left\{ \begin{bmatrix} \textit{believe} \\ \text{EXPR}\ \textit{ref} \\ \text{SOA} \begin{bmatrix} \textit{endanger} \\ \text{EXPR}\ \boxed{1} \\ \text{THEME}\ \boxed{2} \end{bmatrix} \end{bmatrix} \right\} \end{bmatrix} \end{bmatrix}$$

The speaker and addressee of the actual utterance containing *beware* are not specified in (20), since utterances containing *beware* might not make reference to any actual warning utterance (cf. (10b), (11)). Similarly, a threat-polarity item like *or else!* presupposes a warning context, with the additional information that the speaker intends the addressee to recognize (that the speaker intends the addressee to recognize) that some individual or situation will be responsible for some state of affairs that endangers the referent of the subject of the clause to which *or else* is appended.

As far as I can tell, reflexive intentions like this are the minimum of what has to be represented if illocutionary forces and other mental states of speakers that are intended to be communicated through utterance are considered part of the CONTEXT-value of a sign. I have not said anything up to this point about how the CONTEXT constraints on individual lexical signs get projected between lexical signs and the phrases they are a part of. I will return to this issue shortly.

7.7 Honorifics

The constraints on honorifics differ from other pragmatic constraints only in the particular relations invoked. Honorifics are often described (misleadingly, I think) as "expressing" the speaker's attitude, and for a long time were treated as contributing to a kind of ungrammaticality when the attitude reflected by one form in a sentence was inconsistent with an attitude reflected by some other form in that sentence. I could illustrate, as I did with illocutionary forces, what a more formal and explicit representation of the constraints on the use of honorifics would be, but I think it will suffice to describe the nature of the problem in plain language. Suppose that the condition on the use of honorifics is something like 'the anchor of this index is honorable' (or respectable, or owed deference—what the correct predicate is is beyond my expertise, and may well vary from language to language (or culture to culture)). Whatever the details, the issue is not a linguistic one, because honorifics are not lexically selected by words. They are selected by utterers (by act of will), to categorize intended referents of those words in accordance with particular social goals. Reflecting disrespect does not make a sentence ungrammatical, although uttering such a sentence might be imprudent. Being inconsistent in displaying respect does not make sentences ungrammatical, although it might prompt hearers to wonder about the beliefs and attitudes of the speaker.

At any rate, the condition is not specifically that the speaker respect the anchor of the honorificked index. Respect is shown through a CONVERSATIONAL implicature of saying something, the saying of which presupposes that the speaker believes the referenced individual deserves respect.[6] Thus, that the speaker respect the referent is not actually a linguistic usage condition. Rather, as with the conditions on content terms generally (see Appendix), for Gricean reasons a speaker who uses an honorific communicates that it is normally believed that the referent is honorable. The normal belief that the referent of the honorific deserves respect is all that needs to be specified for the use of the honorific to invite the inference that the speaker respects the referent (cf. Green 1992). This analysis predicts that out of deference to their addressees, speakers will avoid using an honorific with reference to an individual whom the speaker knows the addressee has no respect for, even if the speaker respects this person. Similar principles constrain the use of second person pronouns in various European languages.

In this kind of analysis, information about attitudes is referenced only in the CONTEXT attribute of lexical items—honorifics do not involve any type of subcategorization or agreement. Merely uttering a form with a background restriction implies belief in the factuality of the content of

[6]For this reason, it is a mistake to assume that the use of forms which reflect conflicting assumptions necessarily results in a defective utterance (called "infelicitous" rather than "ungrammatical" because the "violation" is pragmatic rather than a matter of grammar). As often as not, when language users hear IN CONTEXT an utterance which would seem to require mutually inconsistent background assumptions, they will attribute to the speaker ADDITIONAL beliefs which eliminate the inconsistency. For example: given the propositions that the Speaker respects Y and that the Speaker does not respect Y, they may add domains or reasons for each proposition and be content to assume that the Speaker respects Y in some role, but does not respect Y in some other role.

that restriction, by familiar Gricean principles. No special features or new principles are needed. Beliefs about the relations of participants are represented as just that. Certainly, it is not necessary to represent the speaker's intent that uttering the form will cause the addressee to believe that the speaker intends the addressee to believe the propositions in the form's BACKGROUND value; the Cooperative Principle guarantees that on hearing the speaker utter some expression, the addressee will attribute intentions to the speaker in doing so, and they will include the intention to represent herself as believing the propositions required for the felicitous utterance of that expression.

Again, because the use of such forms reflects beliefs about the speaker's association with participants which the speaker believes to be mutual beliefs, it will induce inferences when those beliefs are not in fact mutually held. For example, if someone speaking Japanese were to use an honorific in reference to a member of a despised category, such as shoemakers, as in (21), hearers would assume that the speaker held shoemakers, or at least this person she identified as a shoemaker, in very high regard.

(21)	Kutsuya-san	wa	kore	o	oyomi-ni-natta
	shoemaker-HON	TOP	this	OBJ	read-HON-PAST
	'The shoemaker read this.'				

This would be an inference, in particular, a conversational implicature (possibly short-circuited; cf. Morgan 1978) from the manner of expression.

All that is conventional about negative judgements regarding this example is the value system that is implicit in the ranking of occupations, and the custom of acknowledging shared evaluations as affirming group membership. We might or might not infer that the speaker assumed everyone else shared her evaluation of her referent or his occupation. Indeterminacy of this sort is one of the properties that distinguishes conversational implicature from conventional implicature and entailment.

7.8 The Projection of Contextual Information

Is presupposition the characteristic example of a background proposition associated with the utterance of a linguistic sign? Maybe not. An addressee does not have to believe every background proposition of an uttered sentence to consider the sentence to be felicitous or evaluatable as true or false. She only has to be willing to infer that the speaker believes that proposition, and expects that the addressee can reasonably infer that he does. This is why sentences like (22a) are commonly understood as intended to convey to the addressee that her slip is showing, why the threat to face inherent in asserting the object complement of (22b) is reduced by the implication, when it is embedded this way, that the audience is assumed to be among those who realize the enormity of the danger mentioned, and why someone to whom (22c) is addressed may be annoyed if she believes that the speaker could not have waded in a frozen creek. In all cases, the explanation is that the speaker is treating the proposition in the presupposition construction as noncontroversial, even though it may, in fact, be controversial and not taken for granted by the addressee.

(22) a. Do you realize that your slip is showing?

b. Not everyone realizes that the passage of Senator Eks' amendment would seriously jeopardize currently protected First Amendment rights.

c. Although the temperature never went above 15 degrees Fahrenheit, we didn't regret wading in the creek.

Pollard and Sag (1994: 332–335) represent the projection of BACKGROUND values from lexical items to ever-larger phrases as a problem for the theory still to resolve. Morgan (1973) showed that neither the problem nor the solution is strictly linguistic, but depends instead on beliefs attributed to the anchors of relevant indices (e.g., the speaker, and agents and experiencers of propositional attitude verbs). Morgan's account, and Gazdar's (1979) formalization of it, show that the presuppositions associated with lexical items are filtered in being projected as presuppositions of the sentence of which they form a part, by conversational implicature, among other things. Conversational implicature, of course, is a function of a theory of human behavior generally, not something specifically linguistic,[7] because it is based on inference of intentions for actions generally, not on properties of the artifacts that are the result of linguistic actions. Conversational implicatures arise from the assumption that it is reasonable (under the particular circumstances of the speech event in question) to expect A to infer that S intended A to recognize S's intention from the fact that S uttered whatever S uttered. Thus, it would be naive to anticipate that the filtering in the projection of presuppositions COULD be represented as a constraint or set of constraints on values of the BACKGROUND feature, and therefore as of the same character as, say, the Valence Principle, precisely because conversational implicature is inherently indeterminate (Grice 1975, Morgan 1973, Gazdar 1979).

[7]See Green 1993.

7.9 A CONTEXT Inheritance Principle

This does not necessarily mean that a CONTEXT Inheritance Principle is logically impossible. In fact, if the representation of lexical presuppositions is distinguished from the representation of background propositions that relate directly to speaker attitudes,[8] [9] then perhaps their projection can be computed in interaction with the very simple CONTEXT Inheritance Principle that Pollard & Sag proposed (1994: 333). That principle said simply that the BACKGROUND value of a phrase is the union of the BACKGROUND values of the daughters.

(23)
$$\begin{bmatrix} \textit{phrase} \\ \text{LOCAL}|\text{CONTEXT}|\text{BKD } \boxed{1} \cup \boxed{2} \cup \ldots \cup \boxed{n} \\ \text{HD-DTR}|\text{LOC}|\text{CXT}|\text{BKD } \boxed{1} \\ \text{NON-HD-DTRS } \left\langle \begin{bmatrix}\text{LOC}|\text{CXT}|\text{BKD } \boxed{2}\end{bmatrix}, \ldots, \begin{bmatrix}\text{LOC}|\text{CXT}|\text{BKD } \boxed{n}\end{bmatrix} \right\rangle \end{bmatrix}$$

This sort of CONTEXT Inheritance Principle would be completely consistent with the inherently indeterminate character of Gricean conversational implicature. If the phrase's CONTEXT value should happen to contain inconsistent predications, or predications that are inconsistent with situations that are asserted to hold, that does not pose a logical problem, or a problem for the formal theory. Indeed, it is not a linguistic problem at all. It **is** a problem for a human being who wants to construe the speaker's behavior in uttering the sentence as rational. Doing that will have to utilize knowledge of principles of sense and/or reference transfer, and lexical rules, as well as beliefs about what is sensible, and what is goofy, but the resolution of such contradictions is precisely what the Cooperative Principle was invented for (Grice 1975, Green 1995)), and what the computation of implicatures is about, as Morgan and Gazdar demonstrated.

7.10 Conclusion

Pragmatic information is information about the speaker's mental models (including her model of the addressee, and her model of the addressee's model of her, and so on). This is evident for discourse particles and discourse markers, and on reflection, true also for illocutionary intentions

[8] For example, lexical presuppositions might be represented as some kind of second-order proposition derived through meaning postulates of the sort described in Lappin & Pollard (1999) that would represent them in lexical entries as a relation between CONTENT values and CONTEXT|BACKGROUND values.

[9] Or maybe even if it isn't. One way of resolving a conflict involving lexical presuppositions would be to interpret them as intended in a figurative mode, so that the supposedly inconsistent propositions can be regarded as all true.

that govern the distribution of a variety of forms, including honorific signs. Representations which ignore this fact do so at peril of

- precluding explanatory analyses of particles and markers
- precluding a common account of selection for particular illocutionary forces and particular intended perlocutionary effects
- unnecessarily complicating the projection and interpretation of contextual information from lexical and constructional signs

The understanding that pragmatic information is information about the speaker's mental models enables an account of the fact that words and constructions are constrainted in terms of standard illocutionary forces and to intended perlocutionary effects in exactly the same way. The Gricean approach to illocutionary force that it offers may simplify the semantics by making it unnecessary to represent illocutionary force there.

Acknowledgments

This is a revised version of a paper presented at HPSG-99, in Edinburgh. The present version owes a lot to Jerry Morgan, and to comments from participants at the conference. This work was supported in part by the Beckman Institute for Advanced Science and Technology at the University of Illinois at Urbana-Champaign.

Appendix: Are CONTENT Values Fixed?

The HPSG ontology of types makes it appear as if words have contents inherently associated with them, down to the level of what relations among events or objects they describe. Either this is an oversimplification, or the lexicon is massively polysemous. A more explanatory understanding, due to Geoff Nunberg (1978), sees the conventions of word meanings as cultural, and culturally or situationally relative, rather than strictly linguistic. According to Nunberg, even so-called literal meanings have an indexical character in depending on the speaker's ability to infer correctly what an addressee will assume a term is intended to refer to on an occasion of use. Even the sense or CONTENT of a predicative lexical item in an utterance is not fixed by or in a linguistic system, but can only be deduced in connection with assumptions about the speaker's beliefs about the knowledge and expectations of the addressee.

One consideration behind this conclusion is that practically any word can be used to denote an almost limitless variety of kinds of objects or functions (Ruhl 1989, Green 1998). For example, *program* unremarkably refers to a goal, a schedule, a curriculum or course of study, a list of instructions for a computational device, a written representation of any of these, a show broadcast on radio or TV, and potentially to a person responsible (in any relevant sense) for any of these.

(24) a. The program of this group is to subvert the youth of America.
b. Their program calls for 10 pushups three times a day.
c. She entered the program in 1977.
d. We're expanding our program with the addition of two new faculty members, and six new courses.
e. The program would not execute.
f. The programs are all smudged.
g. If you have a VCR you can tape your programs while you're at work or asleep.
h. The program just called and said she'd be late.

Doesn't Interpretation in a "Null" Context Allow "Core Lexical Meanings" to be Defined?

The standard strategy of trying to infer a "core literal meaning" from interpretation in a "null" context is an impossible task. Impossible not in just a Sisyphean sense, but in the sense of an M.C. Escher drawing. There are no null contexts where speaker and hearer make no assumptions about each other in which utterances could be interpreted. As Crain and Steedman put it (1985: 338), the so-called null context is no more than an unknown and uncontrolled context. When we are asked to act as informants, and make judgements about expressions or their meanings "out of context" or "in a null context," we cannot help but imagine SOME context consisting of a speaker directing that expression as an utterance to some audience. We differ, as individuals, and on occasions, in how much context we import into the judgement task, and in what we are willing to imagine when we try to construe the expression as a sensible thing to utter on an occasion of the sort we assume.[10] Consequently, if we abstract away from systems of normal beliefs that inhere in all the various possible groups of users of a language (for example, English), we do not arrive at anything that looks much like what we imagine for a notion of either "normal English user" or "normal English." The usage of such a "normal user", depending on whether we abstract by intersecting or by unioning the memberships of all the groups, would either be that of a person who belonged to no subgroups within the English-speaking world (imagine it—a person with no family, no country, no religion, no occupation, no avocations, no ethnic background—such a person would be the epitome of a social misfit,

[10]Cf. Schmerling 1978, Green 1995, 1998.

and we would be saying they represented a normal user), or it would be a person who was a member of every subgroup (a Welsh Singaporean Catholic Jewish evangelical Christian Muslim Hindu (etc.) needleworker professor accountant clerical worker multi-sport athlete insurance salesman) and his[11] usage would reflect the sum of all possible usages, and the Hydra of unlimited polysemy would be staring us in the face again.

If Words Have "Normal" Meanings, it is Only Relative to an Assumed Speech Community

When it comes to using words to refer to things, properties, and events, what it is considered normal to use a word to refer to—say *tack* or *host* or *rock* or *metal*—varies with the community (sailors, strategists, horsemen, religious folk, historians, archaeologists, aficionados of popular music, etc.). Such details are social facts, facts about societies, and only incidentally and contingently and secondarily facts about words. More precisely, they are facts about what speakers believe other speakers believe about conventions for using words.

Despite Indeterminacy, Plausible Candidates for the Intended Reference of a Word in a Given Context are Limited

Although the interpretation that a word COULD have in context are virtually unlimited, rationality severely limits what a speaker is likely to use a term to refer to in a given context. Rational speakers consider how likely it is that their intended audience will be able to correctly identify their intended referent from the use of a candidate expression. It would be highly irrational to use a word to refer to anything except what we estimate our addressee is likely to take it to refer to; it would be self-defeating.

Expectation of Speaker's Intention is Key to Understanding

In general, we are able to understand each other as well as we do (which is not near as well as we think we do) because we all use language in accordance with the Cooperative Principle. This entails (cf. Grice 1957) that we will only use a referential term x when we believe that our addressee will be able to identify our intended referent FROM the reference to it by that term in that context, and will believe that we intended him to do so. But the bottom line is that whether there is massive polysemy, or massive underspecification, or some scheme amounting to both,[12] the task of the addressee is the same—to deduce what sense the speaker

[11] Or her, if you like; the mind boggles at imagining the sex and gender of such an individual.

[12] Cf. Nunberg 1978, Green 1998.

most likely intended, and he will use all available clues to do so, without regard to whether they come from within or outside the immediate sentence or bit of discourse at hand.

References

Austin, J. L. 1962. *How To Do Things With Words*. Cambridge, MA: Harvard University Press.

Bar-Hillel, Y. 1954. Indexical Expressions. *Mind* 63:359–379.

Cohen, P. R. and H. J. Levesque. 1991. Teamwork. *Nous* 25:487–512.

Crain, S. and M. Steedman. 1985. On not being led up the garden path: the use of context by the psychological parser. In D. Dowty, L. Karttunen and A. Zwicky, eds., *Natural Language Parsing: Psychological, Computational, and Theoretical Perspectives*, pages 320–358. Cambridge: Cambridge University Press.

Fraser, B. 1974. An examination of the performative analysis. *Papers in Linguistics* 7:1–40.

Gazdar, G. 1979. *Pragmatics, Implicature, Presupposition, and Logical Form*. New York: Academic Press.

Green, G. M. 1981. Pragmatics and syntactic description. *Studies in the Linguistic Sciences* 11(1):27–38. Urbana, IL: Department of Linguistics, University of Illinois.

Green, G. M. 1990. On the universality of Gricean interpretation. In K. Hall, J-P. Koenig, M. Meacham, S. Reinman and L. Sutton, eds., *Proceedings of the 16th Annual Meeting of the Berkeley Linguistics Society*, pages 411–428. Berkeley, CA: Berkeley Linguistics Society.

Green, G. M. 1992. The cooperative principle, rationality, and the nature of politeness. Ms.

Green, G. M. 1993. Rationality and Gricean inference. Cognitive Science Technical Report UIUC-BI-CS-93-09. Urbana, IL: University of Illinois at Urbana-Champaign.

Green, G. M. 1994. The structure of CONTEXT; the representation of pragmatic restrictions in HPSG. In J. H. Yoon, ed., *Proceedings of the Fifth Annual Conference of the Formal Linguistics Society of Mid-America*, Studies in the Linguistic Sciences 24:215–232. Urbana, IL: Department of Linguistics, University of Illinois.

Green, G. M. 1995. Ambiguity resolution and discourse interpretation. In K. van Deemter and S. Peters, eds., *Semantic Ambiguity and Underspecification*. Stanford, CA: CSLI Publications.

Green, G. M. 1996. *Pragmatics and Natural Language Understanding*, second edition. Hillsdale, NJ: Lawrence Erlbaum Associates.

Green, G. M. 1998. Natural kind terms and a theory of the lexicon. Studies in the Linguistic Sciences 28(1):1–26. Urbana, IL: Department of Linguistics, University of Illinois.

Green, G. M. and J. L. Morgan. 1976. Notes toward an understanding of rule government. Studies in the Linguistic Sciences 6(1):152–169. Urbana, IL: Department of Linguistics, University of Illinois.

Green, G. M. and J. L. Morgan. 1980. Pragmatics and reading comprehension. In R. Spiro, B. C. Bruce and W. Brewer, eds., *Theoretical Issues in Reading Comprehension*, pages 113–140. Hillsdale, NJ: Lawrence Erlbaum Associates.

Grice, H. P. 1957. Meaning. *Philosophical Review* 66:377–388.

Grice, H. P. 1975. Logic and conversation. In P. Cole and J. L. Morgan, eds., *Syntax and Semantics 3: Speech Acts*, pages 41–58. New York: Academic Press.

Horn, L. 1972. *On the Semantic Properties of Logical Operators in English.* Ph.D. thesis, University of California at Los Angeles. (Distributed by Indiana University Linguistics Club, 1976)

Horn, L. 1978. Some aspects of negation. In J. Greenberg, C. Ferguson and E. Moravcsik, eds., *Universals of Human Language 4: Syntax*, pages 127–210. Stanford, CA: Stanford University Press.

Horn, L. 1985. Metalinguistic negation and pragmatic ambiguity. *Language* 61:121–174.

Kiparsky, P. 1968. Tense and mood in Indo-European syntax. *Foundations of Language* 4:30–57.

Lakoff, R. L. 1968. *Abstract Syntax and Latin Complementation.* Cambridge, MA: MIT Press.

Lakoff, R. L. 1973. Questionable answers and answerable questions. In B. B. Kachru, R. B. Lees, Y. Malkiel, A. Pietrangeli and S. Saporta, eds., *Issues in Linguistics: Papers in Honor of Henry and Renee Kahane*, pages 453–567. Urbana, IL: University of Illinois Press.

Lappin, S. and C. Pollard. 1999. A hyperintensional theory of natural language interpretation without indices or situations. Ms.

Levinson, S. C. 2000. *Presumptive Meanings: The Theory of Generalized Conversational Implicature.* Cambridge, MA: MIT Press.

Lu, W-Y. 1995. *A Pragmatic Study of Sentence-Final Particles as Attitude Markers in Modern Mandarin Chinese.* Ph.D. thesis, University of Illinois.

McCawley, J. D. 1971. Tense and time reference in English. In C. Fillmore and D. T. Langendoen, eds., *Studies in Linguistic Semantics*, pages 97–113. New York: Holt, Rinehart and Winston.

Morgan, J. L. 1973. *Presupposition and the Representation of Meaning: Prolegomena.* Ph.D. thesis, University of Chicago.

Morgan, J. L. 1978. Two types of convention in indirect speech acts. In P. Cole, ed., *Syntax and Semantics 9: Pragmatics*, pages 261–280. New York: Academic Press.

Nunberg, G. 1978. *The Pragmatics of Reference.* Ph.D. thesis, CUNY. Bloomington, IN: Indiana University Linguistics Club. (Also published by Garland Publishing, Inc.)

Nunberg, G. 1993 Indexicality and deixis. *Linguistics and Philosophy* 16:1–44.

Partee, B. 1989. Binding implicit variables in quantified contexts. In *Papers from the 25th Regional Meeting of the Chicago Linguistic Society*. Chicago IL: Chicago Linguistic Society.

Pollard, C. and I. Sag. 1987. *Information-Based Syntax and Semantics, Volume 1: Fundamentals*. Stanford, CA: CSLI Publications.

Pollard, C. and I. Sag. 1994. *Head-Driven Phrase Structure Grammar*. University of Chicago Press and CSLI Publications.

Ross, J. R. 1970. On declarative sentences. In R. A. Jacobs and P. S. Rosenbaum, eds., *Readings in English Transformational Grammar*, pages 222–272. Waltham, MA: Ginn.

Ruhl, C. 1989. *On Monosemy; a Study in Linguistic Semantics*. Albany: State University of New York Press.

Sadock, J. M. 1974. *Toward a Linguistic Theory of Speech Acts*. New York: Academic Press.

Schmerling, S. F. 1978. Synonymy judgements as syntactic evidence. In P. Cole, ed., *Syntax and Semantics 9: Pragmatics*, pages 299–314. New York: Academic Press.

Schourup, L. 1982. *Common Discourse Particles in English Conversation*. Ph.D. thesis, Ohio State University. (Published 1985 by Garland Publishing, Inc.)

Searle, J. 1969. *Speech Acts*. Cambridge: Cambridge University Press.

Sperber, D. and D. Wilson. 1986. *Relevance; Communication and Cognition*. Cambridge, MA: Harvard University Press.

Stampe, D. 1975. Meaning and truth in the theory of speech acts. In P. Cole and J. L. Morgan, eds., *Syntax and Semantics 3: Speech Acts*, pages 1–40. New York: Academic Press.

Suzuki, Y. 1997. *The Pragmatics of Japanese Sentence-Final Particles*. Ph.D. thesis, University of Illinois.

8

The Morphosyntax of Lai Relative Clauses

ANDREAS KATHOL

8.1 Introduction

This paper presents an analysis of relative clauses in Lai (Hakha Chin), a Tibeto-Burman language spoken in Western Burma (Chin State) with predominant SOV order. Relative clauses in this language are formed by means of an invariant relative marker such as *mii*, following the verb (and arguably not part of the verbal morphology). As is typical for a head-final language, the relative clause precedes the modified head. The example in (1) illustrates the case of a subject relative clause modifying the noun *lawthlawpaa* ('farmer').

(1) [[Vok rool ʔa pee] mii **lawthlawpaa**] ka m̥uʔ.
pig food 3S.SBJ give REL farmer 1S.SBJ see
'I saw the farmer who gave food to the pig.'

The marker *mii* also allows for relativization of a nonsubject. In the case of ditransitive verbs two relative clause variants are possible, one for each complement, as shown in (2a,b):[1]

(2) a. [[Lawthlawpaa rool ʔa peek] mii **vok**] ka m̥uʔ.
farmer food 3S.SBJ give REL pig 1S.SBJ see
'I saw the pig which the farmer gave food to.'

[1] Apart from the difference in relativized grammatical function, the sentences in (2) also display a different verbal morphology (*peek* vs. *pee*). This alternation plays a significant role for relativization possibilities. However, for expository purposes, I postpone discussion until section 8.7 below.

Grammatical Interfaces in HPSG.
Ronnie Cann, Claire Grover and Philip Miller.

b. [[Lawthlawpaa vok ʔa peek] mii **rool**] ka m̥uʔ.
farmer pig 3S.SBJ give REL food 1S.SBJ see
'I saw the food which the farmer gave to the pig.'

The modified head noun is understood as referentially linked to a constituent left unexpressed within the preceding relative clause. Such constructions therefore bear a superficial resemblance to relative clauses in languages like English in that the dependent to be relativized must not be given overtly, cf. the ungrammatical example in (3):

(3)*[**Lawthlawpaa** vok rool ʔa pee] mii **upa** ka m̥uʔ.
farmer pig food 3S.SBJ give REL elder 1S.SBJ see
(Intended: 'I saw the **elder**$_i$ such that **that farmer**$_i$ gave food to the pig.')

In analogy with the analysis of English one might assume a long-distance treatment for Lai as well, in particular in terms of threading SLASH information. However, a number of facts argue against such an analysis.

8.2 The Nature of the Missing Element(s)

First, the relation between the external head and the occurrence of a missing constituent has to be strictly local. The head cannot be linked to a missing constituent within a more deeply embedded clause—contrary to what we should expect on the basis of an unbounded dependency-based approach. Concomitantly, we do not have independent evidence for unbounded dependencies of the filler–gap kind elsewhere in the grammar of Lai. In particular, there is no equivalent of topicalization out of clausal structures or *wh*-dislocation from embedded clauses.

Second, a filler–gap-based strategy would fail to extend to other cases of missing syntactic arguments. In particular, Lai exhibits a productive pattern of argument drop in which every syntactic argument can be missing, provided it can be recovered from context. This is exemplified by the question–answer pairs in (4–6):

(4) a. Lawthlawpa zaydaʔ ʔa tuaʔ?
farmer what 3S.SBJ do
'What is the farmer doing?'

b. Vok rool ʔa pee.
pig food 3S.SBJ give
'[He] is feeding the pig.'

(5) a. Vok zaydaʔ ʔa tsaŋ?
pig what 3S.SBJ become
'What is happening to the pig?'

b. Lawthlawpaa niʔ rool ʔa peek.
farmer ERG food 3S.SBJ give
'The farmer is feeding [it].'

(6) a. Rool taʔʔ
food also
'How about the food?'

b. Lawthlawpaa niʔ vok ʔa peek.
farmer ERG pig 3S.SBJ give
'The farmer is feeding [it] to the pig'

I propose to analyze the missing elements in relative clauses in precisely the same terms, that is, as instances of null anaphora, (cf. Cole 1987 for a very similar idea). While null anaphora has often been treated by means of phonologically empty pronouns, no such devices will be required here. Following recent work in HPSG on argument structure (in particular Manning and Sag 1999), I treat unrealized syntactic arguments in terms of a mismatch between the argument structure (ARG-ST) and the valence (SUBJ/COMPS) of a lexical predicator.[2] In (7a), for instance, all arguments are realized, whereas (7b) and (7c) illustrate missing subject and object constructions, respectively.

(7) a.
$$\begin{bmatrix} \text{ARG-ST} & \langle \boxed{1}\text{NP}, \boxed{2}\text{NP}, \boxed{3}\text{NP} \rangle \\ \text{SUBJ} & \langle \boxed{1}\text{NP} \rangle \\ \text{COMPS} & \langle \boxed{2}\text{NP}, \boxed{3}\text{NP} \rangle \end{bmatrix}$$

b.
$$\begin{bmatrix} \text{ARG-ST} & \langle \boxed{1}\text{NP:}\textit{c-ppro}, \boxed{2}\text{NP}, \boxed{3}\text{NP} \rangle \\ \text{SUBJ} & \langle \rangle \\ \text{COMPS} & \langle \boxed{2}\text{NP}, \boxed{3}\text{NP} \rangle \end{bmatrix}$$

c.
$$\begin{bmatrix} \text{ARG-ST} & \langle \boxed{1}\text{NP}, \boxed{2}\text{NP:}\textit{c-ppro}, \boxed{3}\text{NP} \rangle \\ \text{SUBJ} & \langle \boxed{1}\text{NP} \rangle \\ \text{COMPS} & \langle \boxed{3}\text{NP} \rangle \end{bmatrix}$$

Thus, unrealized arguments are still represented in the ARG-ST list, albeit not in any of the valence lists. To ensure that such arguments receive anaphoric interpretation, I assume that the CONTENT of unrealized arguments has to be typed as *c-ppro* (for *covert personal pronoun*), which I take to be a new subtype of *nom-obj*.[3]

[2] I remain uncommitted here as to whether the two lists should be mediated by means of a lexical rule or in some other fashion such as type constraints.

[3] I assume that the semantic interpretation of *c-ppro* arguments is similar to, yet not necessarily identical with, that of overt personal pronouns (*ppro*). One question that will have to await further research is whether unrealized arguments in Lai correspond more to definite or indefinite ellipsis cases in English.

8.3 An HPSG Analysis

Given this analysis, the "function" of the relative marker is to mediate structure sharing between the index of the modified noun and the index of the (unexpressed) relativized phrase. In turn this means that the requirement for nonovert realization corresponds to the constraint that the provider of the relative index within the relative clause be an unrealized pronoun. This idea can be straightforwardly accommodated if we make the value of the REL attribute sets of elements of type *nom-obj*, that is an index with its restriction, rather than simply *index*. This allows us to retain within the REL set information about the phrases that provide the relative index, in particular whether it is provided by an unrealized pronoun (*c-ppro*) or some other expression. If the value of REL simply consisted of a set of indices then specifics of syntactic realization (i.e., whether covert or overt) could not be deduced from the relative index, resulting in the false prediction that (3) should be grammatical.

However, argument drop is not the only way in which a modified noun can be linked to a phrase within the relative clause. There also exist cases in which the nominal head cooccurs with a coreferential **overt** expression inside the relative clause in the form of a possessive such as in (8):

(8) [**ʔan**$_i$ pa ʔa thii] mii ʔin-tshung-khar$_i$ ka m̥uʔ
3PL.POS father 3S.SBJ die REL family 1SG.SUBJ see
(n̥a).
PL.OBJ

'I saw the family whose father died.'

If we group together null anaphora and possessive pronouns under a common supertype as "relativizable pronominals" (*rel-pro*), we arrive at the preliminary lexical description for the relativizer *mii* provided in (9):

(9)
$$\begin{bmatrix} \text{HEAD} \begin{bmatrix} \textit{noun} \\ \text{MOD NP}_i \end{bmatrix} \\ \text{COMPS} \left\langle \text{S}\left[\text{REL} \left\{ \textit{rel-pro}_i \right\} \right] \right\rangle \\ \text{CONTENT} \mid \text{INDEX } i \end{bmatrix}$$

Assuming that the relative index within a clause is passed to the relative clause (whether by head-driven feature amalgamation or some other means), the subject relativization in (1) receives the structural analysis given in (10):

(10)

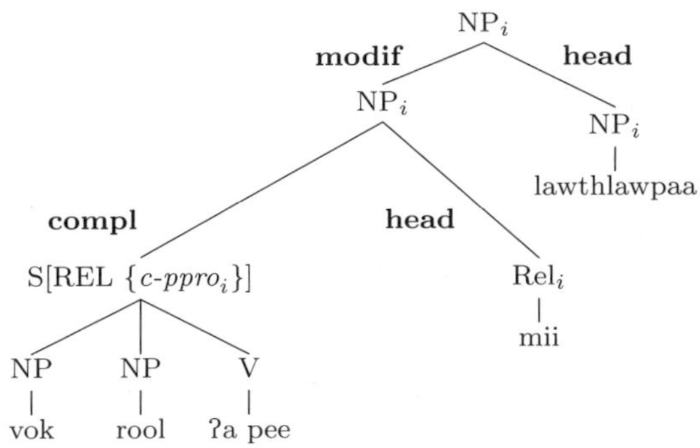

Note that in (9) the relative marker is categorized as *noun*. The motivation for this choice becomes apparent once we consider another type of relative clause environment in which *mii* can occur.

8.4 Internally Headed Relative Clauses

Like many other SOV languages Lai also allows for what are known as *internally headed relative clauses* (IHRC). These contrast with the externally headed relative clauses (EHRC) discussed so far. IHRC are constituents with NP status in which the (head) nominal contributing the referent of the whole NP occurs **inside** the relative clause, rather than outside of it. For instance in (11), the noun *lawthlawpaa* ('farmer') occurs as the subject of a finite (relative) clause. At the same time, the referent of that noun is also understood as the patient of the verb *m̥uʔ* ('see') occurring in the matrix clause.

(11) [**Lawthlawpaa** vok rool ʔa pee] mii ka m̥uʔ.
farmer pig food 3S.SBJ give REL 1S.SBJ see
'I saw the **farmer** [who gave food to the pig].'

Since the element that has been relativized is distinguished neither by morphology nor by word order, a ditransitive predicator such as *pee(k)* ('give') in (12) gives rise to an ambiguity as to which of the nonsubject arguments provides the relative index:

(12) [Lawthlawpaa vok rool ʔa peek] mii ka m̥uʔ.
farmer pig food 3S.SBJ give REL 1S.SBJ see
'I saw the pig which the farmer gave food to.'
'I saw the food which the farmer gave to the pig.'

I propose to treat *mii* as a subtype of *noun* which takes the preceding clause as a complement. As the head of the IHRC, the relative marker automatically ensures that the IHRC has the syntactic status of a noun.

We then obtain (13) as the structural analysis for (11):

(13)

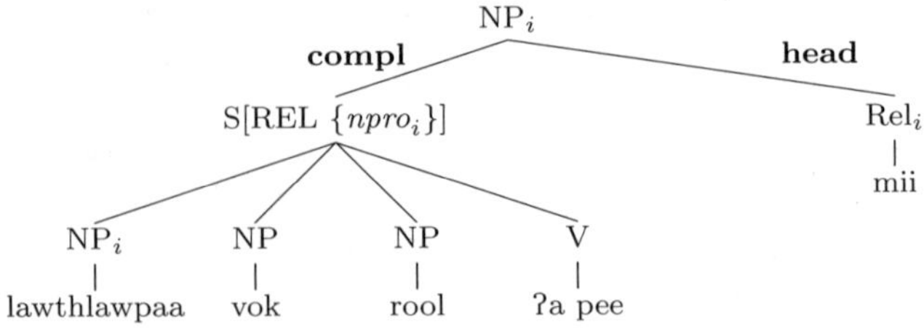

Such structures are licensed by the IHRC variant of *mii*, given in (14).

(14) $\begin{bmatrix} \text{HEAD } \textit{noun} \\ \text{COMPS } \left\langle \text{S}\left[\text{REL } \{\textit{nom-obj}_i\}\right]\right\rangle \\ \text{CONTENT} \mid \text{INDEX } i \end{bmatrix}$

This variant of the relative marker not only lacks any modificational properties, but also does not impose any further constraints on the kind of nominal that provides the relative index. Therefore, the relative index can be provided by an overt nominal such as *lawthlawpaa.* Alternatively, it can be provided by an unexpressed argument. In other words, our account correctly predicts that IHRC and null anaphora can interact. For instance in (15), the subject has been relativized and, at the same time, occurs as an unrealized pronoun.

(15) [Vok rool ʔa pee] mii ka m̥uʔ.
pig food 3S.SBJ give REL 1S.SBJ see
'I saw the one who gave food to the pig.'

Unrealized pronouns lack instantiation only at the level of valence, but not argument structure, where they can be specified as providing a relative index.

Thus, the proper understanding of the designation as "internally headed" is as absence of an external head, rather than requiring the overt presence of the phrase providing the relative index within the relative clause.

8.5 Comparison with Culy 1990

I follow earlier HPSG-based analyses of IHRC in avoiding empty heads of the kind proposed for instance in Cole 1987 (see below). However, I reject the idea of extending to Lai the particular analysis of IHRCs proposed by Culy (1990) (and adopted by Pollard and Sag 1994:234) for languages such as Donno Sɔ. Applied to Lai, such an analysis would involve an exocentric structure in which the relative clause is recategorized as a nominal. In addition, the relative marker would be classified as a determiner that combines with the relative clause N′ to form an NP which would produce the structure in (16) for the example in (11) above.

(16)

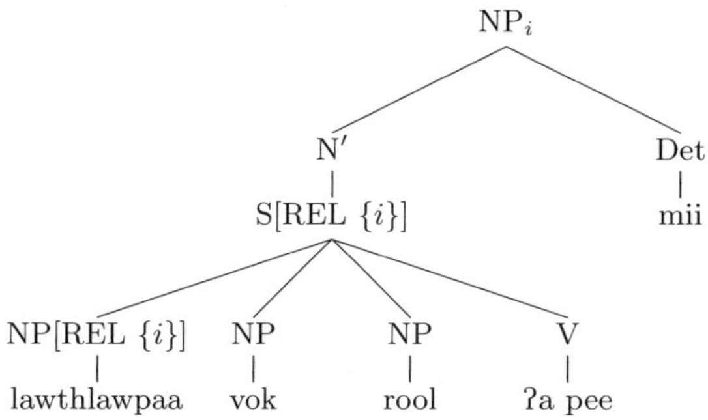

This approach would predict that the relative marker *mii* is able to combine with nominals quite generally to form NPs (or DPs for that matter). However, this is not what we find. While relative markers such as *mii* tend to have uses outside of relativization, free combination with nominals is not possible, arguing strongly against their classification as determiners.

Moreover, and more significantly, *mii* in IHRCs can cooccur with demonstratives such as *kha* ('that'), as is illustrated in (17):[4]

(17) a. [Tsoo ʔa that *(mii) **kha**] ka m̥uʔ.
cow 3S.SBJ kill-I REL DEM 1S.SBJ see.
'I saw that one who killed the cow.'

b. [Tsoo ʔa thaʔ *(mii) **kha**] ka m̥uʔ.
cow 3S.SBJ kill-II REL DEM 1S.SBJ see.
'I saw the cow that he killed.'

On the standard classification of demonstratives as determiners, the cooccurrence with the relative marker would be rather unexpected. Note also that the relative marker *mii* in (17) is obligatory. This is significant because it shows that the relative clause itself without the marker has no nominal status. Otherwise we would expect the demonstrative to be in free variation with the relative marker.

Futher suggestive evidence for the nominal status of the relativizer comes from the fact that *mii* is historically related to a homophonous form meaning 'person', occurring for instance as the subject in examples such as (18) or in with attributive adjectives in (19):

[4]While demonstratives commonly precede the noun, special uses are possible in which they follow.

(18) **Mii** ʔan raa.
person 3P.SBJ come
'People are coming.'

(19) a. **mii** nung
person living
'a living person'

b. **mii** thii
person dead
'a dead person'

Thus, there is considerable evidence for treating *mii* as a noun categorially, which in turn obviates any need for an exocentric analysis of IHRC.

8.6 The Relative Marker *tuu*

In addition to *mii*, Lai possesses the relative marker *tuu*, which has a somewhat more limited range of occurrence.[5] Thus, *tuu* licenses EHRC, as is shown in (20):

(20) [[Vok rool ʔa pee] **tuu** lawthlawpaa] ka m̥uʔ.
pig food 3S.SBJ give REL farmer 1S.SBJ see
'I saw the farmer who gave food to the pig.'

However, *tuu* does not permit the relativization of any nonsubject dependent. Therefore both (21a) and (21b) are ungrammatical.

(21) a.*[[Lawthlawpaa rool ʔa peek] **tuu vok**] ka m̥uʔ.
farmer food 3S.SBJ give REL pig 1S.SBJ see
(Intended: 'I saw the pig which the farmer gave food to.')

b.*[[Lawthlawpaa vok ʔa peek] **tuu rool**] ka m̥uʔ.
farmer pig 3S.SBJ give REL food 1S.SBJ see
(Intended: 'I saw the food which the farmer gave to the pig.')

Like *mii*, *tuu* also occurs in IHRCs as is shown in (22). The same restriction against relativization of nonsubjects applies, as is illustrated in (23):

(22) [Lawthlawpaa vok rool ʔa pee] **tuu** ka m̥uʔ.
farmer pig food 3S.SBJ give REL 1S.SBJ see
'I saw the farmer who gave food to the pig.'

[5] In addition, there also exists a relative marker for instrumental and locative arguments, *naak*, which I will not discuss here (cf. Peterson 1998:119.)

(23)*[Lawthlawpaa vok rool ʔa peek] **tuu** ka m̥uʔ.
farmer pig food 3S.SBJ give REL 1S.SBJ see
(Intended: 'I saw the pig which the farmer gave food to.'
or: 'I saw the food which the farmer gave to the pig.')

As an additional complication, *tuu* can only relativize the subject of a transitive predicate, both in IHRC and EHRC constructions:

(24) a. [T̥uaŋ ʔaʔ lawthlawpaa ʔa ʔit] ***tuu/mii** ka m̥uʔ.
floor LOC farmer 3S.SBJ sleep REL 1S.SBJ see
'I saw the farmer who slept on the floor.'

b. [T̥uaŋ ʔaʔ ʔa ʔit] ***tuu/mii** lawthlawpaa ka m̥uʔ.
floor LOC 3S.SBJ sleep REL farmer 1S.SBJ see
'I saw the farmer who slept on the floor.'

Thus, *tuu* appears to be sensitive to whether or not there exists an *ergative* subject within the relative clause. The notion of ergativity in Lai is independently warranted in that only ergative subjects are eligible to occur with the marker *niʔ*, cf. (25a,b):

(25) a. Maŋkio (*niʔ) ʔa ʔit.
Maŋkio ERG 3S.SBJ sleep
'Mangkio slept.'

b. Maŋkio (niʔ) epal pakhat ʔa ʔei.
Maŋkio ERG apple 3S.SBJ eat
'Mangkio ate an apple.'

To correctly capture the dependence between *tuu* and the ergative status of the relativized dependent, I propose ERG as a list-valued head feature that has as its value a list containing an ergative subject, if there is one, and is empty otherwise.[6] Accordingly, the EHRC variant of *tuu* can be given the lexical description stated in (26)

(26)
$$\begin{bmatrix} \text{HEAD} & \begin{bmatrix} \textit{noun} \\ \text{MOD NP}_i \end{bmatrix} \\ \text{COMPS} & \left\langle \text{S} \begin{bmatrix} \text{ERG} & \langle \text{XP}_i \rangle \\ \text{REL} & \{\textit{rel-pro}_i\} \end{bmatrix} \right\rangle \\ \text{CONTENT} & | \text{ INDEX } i \end{bmatrix}$$

[6]It is similar to the feature ERG of Kathol 1991 and Pollard 1994:280. The intent of this feature is not to express valence, but rather to identify which element among the head's dependents has certain properties. In particular, ERG in the works just cited is used to pick out theme arguments (subjects of unaccusative verbs and objects of transitive verbs) and thus would have more appropriately been called ABS. In contrast, the feature ERG as it is used here is directly linked to the ERGATIVE dependent in languages with an ergative pattern of case marking and/or agreement.

Thus, the description in (26) correctly expresses the intuition that *tuu* requires of its clause that it contain an ergative dependent and that the latter be construed as the relativized phrase.[7]

8.7 Relativization and Verbal Morphology

The discussion so far has conveniently ignored a morphological distinction that plays an important role in further constraining relativization possibilities. Lai verbs typically exhibit two different morphological forms, which I will call "form I" and "form II" here (cf. Melnik 1997). For instance, the Lai equivalent of English 'give' is *pee* (form I) or *peek* (form II), respectively. This distinction is correlated with a number of differences of syntactic distribution (cf. Peterson 1998:89 for some initial observations and Kathol and VanBik 2000 for more extensive discussion). The one that is of crucial interest here is that only verbs with form I morphology allow for relativized subjects. This fact holds regardless of the choice of relative marker and regardless of the IHRC/EHRC distinction as is demonstrated in (27):

(27) a. [[Vok rool ʔa **pee/*peek**] mii/tuu lawthlawpaa] ka
pig food 3S.SBJ give-I/give-II REL farmer 1S.SBJ
m̥uʔ.
see
'I saw the farmer who gave food to the pig.'

b. [Lawthlawpaa vok rool ʔa **pee/*peek**] mii/tuu ka
farmer pig food 3S.SBJ give-I/give-II REL 1S.SBJ
m̥uʔ.
see
'I saw the farmer who gave food to the pig.'

Conversely, nonsubjects may be relativized only if the verb exhibits form II morphology, as is demonstrated in (28–29). Again, the IHRC/EHRC distinction does not play a role.

(28) a. [[Lawthlawpaa rool ʔa ***pee/peek**] mii vok] ka
farmer food 3S.SBJ give-I/give-II REL pig 1S.SBJ
m̥uʔ.
see
'I saw the pig which the farmer gave food to.'

[7] There are, of course, alternative ways of making this intuition explicit. For instance, the elements of REL-sets (*rel-pro*) could further be subtyped so as to reflect grammatical function. I leave discussion of the relative merits of these possibilities for further research.

b. [[Lawthlawpaa vok ʔa ***pee/peek**] mii rool] ka
farmer pig 3S.SBJ give-I/give-II REL food 1S.SBJ
m̥uʔ.
see
'I saw the food which the farmer gave to the pig.'

(29) [Lawthlawpaa vok rool ʔa ***pee/peek**] mii ka m̥uʔ.
farmer pig food 3S.SBJ give-I/give-II REL 1S.SBJ see
'I saw the pig which the farmer gave food to.'
'I saw the food which the farmer gave to the pig.'

These facts suggest that the prohibition against relativization of nonsubjects with *tuu* can be seen in terms of the linking of two dependencies. The first dependency is between morphological expression (form I vs. II) and status of the relativized phrase (subject vs. nonsubject). In the absence of any special morphology, the status of a constituent as a relative phrase simply reduces to whether that phrase has a nonempty value for REL. The grammatical function of a relative phrase can be directly read off by considering the ARG-ST list of the verb of which the relative phrase is a dependent. If the relative phrase is a subject, then the index singleton set of the REL feature is the same as the index of the first element on the verb's ARG-ST list. If this situation holds, the verbal morphology has to be form I, cf. (30a). The converse is not true because, as I mentioned earlier, the same verbal forms are also used to signal other syntactic contrasts outside of relative clauses. Note that in the formulation of this constraint we refer to the subject as the first element on the argument structure list ARG-ST, rather than valence proper (SUBJ). As we have seen above, this makes the right predictions with respect to the interaction of IHRC and null anaphora.

Conversely, in (30b), any nonsubject argument that contributes the relative index requires form II morphology.[8]

(30) a. *Morphological constraint on subject relativization*

$$\begin{bmatrix} \text{HEAD } \textit{verb} \\ \text{ARG-ST } \langle \text{NP}_i, \ldots \rangle \\ \text{REL } \{\textit{rel-pro}_i\} \end{bmatrix} \rightarrow \begin{bmatrix} \text{HEAD } \begin{bmatrix} \text{VFORM I} \end{bmatrix} \end{bmatrix}$$

b. *Morphological constraint on nonsubject relativization*

$$\begin{bmatrix} \text{HEAD } \textit{verb} \\ \text{ARG-ST } \langle \text{NP}_i, \ldots \rangle \\ \text{REL } \{\textit{rel-pro}_j\} \\ i \neq j \end{bmatrix} \rightarrow \begin{bmatrix} \text{HEAD } \begin{bmatrix} \text{VFORM II} \end{bmatrix} \end{bmatrix}$$

[8] I presuppose that an independent constraint rules out the possibility of relative indices that are not linked to any argument of the verb.

We thus have an explanation why the example in (12) above is only two-way ambiguous, rather than allowing three readings. This is a direct consequence of the fact that the constraints in (30) establish a correlation between verbal morphology and relativizable grammatical function.

If we follow standard practice and treat the form I/II distinction as a head feature (VFORM), then the second dependency, i.e., the correlation between verbal morphology and choice of relative marker, can be straightforwardly expressed along the lines given in (31), which lists the EHRC variants of the relative markers:[9]

(31) a. *tuu*

$$\begin{bmatrix} \text{HEAD} & \begin{bmatrix} \textit{noun} \\ \text{MOD NP}_i \end{bmatrix} \\ \text{COMPS} & \left\langle \text{S} \begin{bmatrix} \text{VFORM I} \\ \text{ERG } \langle \text{XP}_i \rangle \\ \text{REL } \{\textit{rel-pro}_i\} \end{bmatrix} \right\rangle \end{bmatrix}$$

b. *mii*

$$\begin{bmatrix} \text{HEAD} & \begin{bmatrix} \textit{noun} \\ \text{MOD NP}_i \end{bmatrix} \\ \text{COMPS} & \langle \text{S}[\text{REL } \{\textit{rel-pro}_i\}] \rangle \end{bmatrix}$$

In the descriptions in (31), both relative markers are treated as subinstances of nouns, on a par with the IHRC version in (14). This may at first seem like a questionable claim given that these would be nominal structures modifying other nouns. However, this assumption is rather natural in light of the nature of attribute modification in Lai in general. N–N compounds are strictly head-final. At the same time, however, attributive adjectives have to follow the modified noun, which is illustrated in the examples in (32).

(32) a. [khua upa] fiim
village elder wise
'wise village elder'

b. [tlaaŋ thiŋ n̥aʔ] r̥iŋ
hill wood leaf green
'green tree leaf'

These facts strongly suggest that only nominal categories can be involved in prenominal modification. Adjectives or locational modifiers can occur prenominally only predicatively, that is embedded in relative clauses. This is demonstrated in (33):

[9]These descriptions are simplified in that they do not take into account the complications arising with relativized possessives as in (8).

(33) a. [ʔa fiim *(mii)] khua upa
3S.SBJ wise REL village elder
'wise village elders'

b. [tupi ʔaʔ ʔaʔum *(mii)] thing
forest LOC be REL tree
'a tree in the forest'

8.8 Comparison with Cole 1987

The current analysis proposes to treat IHRC and EHRC as closely related, albeit separate construction types. The two are crucially distinguished in terms of whether there exists an external head that the relative clause modifies. In this we differ from Cole (1987), who treats both construction types as externally headed. In the IHRC case the head position is instantiated by a null pronoun that is coindexed with an NP within the relative clause, as is shown in (34a). Cole proposes that IHRCs are derivationally linked to EHRC. In particular, the lexical NP moves to the position of the empty element at Logical Form, as is illustrated in (34b):

(34) a. S-structure:

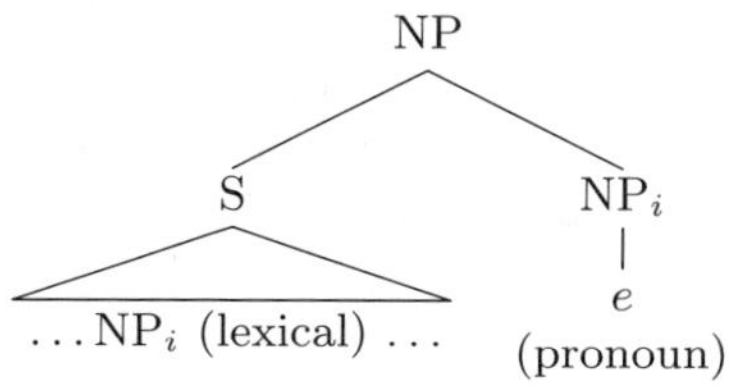

b. Logical Form:

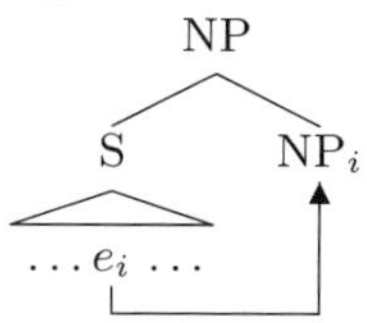

While I agree that a proliferation of disparate structures is in general to be avoided, I doubt that Cole's approach is applicable in the Lai case. Since null pronouns are generally simply silent versions of pronominal elements, we have the immediate prediction that Lai should also permit EHRC structures in which the external head is lexically realized by means of an overt pronoun. Yet, as the example in (35) shows, the result with the pronoun *amaʔ* is ungrammatical.

(35)*[[Vok rool ʔa pee] mii/tuu **amaʔ**] ka m̥uʔ.
pig food 3S.SBJ give REL he 1S.SBJ see
(Intended: 'I saw he/him who fed the pig.')

Analyses of the kind given in (34) are therefore undesirable. In fact, in the approach advocated here Cole's empty head analysis is not even available because the treatment of null anaphora in terms of unrealized arguments only affects members of the verbal argument structure. External heads of relative clauses are licensed as modifiees, hence the kind of variation seen in (7) does not extend to them.

8.9 Conclusion

To conclude, I hope to have shown that the lexicalist analysis advocated here provides the basis for a rather fine-grained description which helps to elucidate the similarities and differences between EHRC and IHRC in terms of lexical variation between different variants of the relative marker. At the same time, there are generalizations about the relationship between verbal morphology and relativized grammatical function for both construction types. Since ARG-ST is a level of representation which is invariant with respect to the syntactic environment in which the relativized phrase occurs, it is arguably the proper level at which these generalizations need to be stated. In addition, if the present analysis is on the right track, it shows that in a language without overt extraction phenomena, the passing of REL information alone may be sufficient to produce structures that superficially resemble English-type nonlocal dependencies.

In the process, the data from Lai cast considerable doubt on any attempt to derive one relative clause type from the other by means of a derivational relationship. This finding is not surprising given that HPSG and related frameworks have long argued that movement operations or their nonderivational equivalents are in many cases inappropriate tools for describing commonalities within constructional families.

A final word may be in order on how the current proposal is related to recent developments in the analysis of relative clauses (Sag 1997). Sag's work makes crucial reference to the notion of "grammatical construction". The fact that there is no need to appeal to that notion as a primitive element in the analysis for the Lai cases should not be taken as an endorsement of a construction-less approach of English relative clauses (of the kind proposed, for instance, in Pollard and Sag 1994). The reason is quite straightforward. Unlike Lai, English has no designated (overt) marker for relative clauses. Rather, it utilizes a filler–gap strategy which lacks a designated lexical exponent and moreover is shared by other syntactic contexts (topicalization, interrogative constructions). Whether Lai relative clauses also possess properties that cannot (plausibly) be attributed to the relative marker remains a question that I leave for further research.

Acknowledgement

I would like to express my gratitude towards Ken VanBik, my consultant for the Lai data and collaborator on an earlier version of this paper Kathol and VanBik (1999). I also benefited from the comments of two anonymous reviewers. All remaining errors are mine.

References

Cole, P. 1987. The structure of internally headed relative clauses. *Natural Language and Linguistic Theory* 5:277–302.

Culy, C. 1990. *The syntax of internally headed relative clauses*. Ph.D. thesis, Stanford University.

Kathol, A. 1991. Verbal and adjectival passives in German. In J. Bobaljik and A. Bures, eds., *Papers from the Third Student Conference in Linguistics*, no. 15 in MIT Working Papers in Linguistics, pages 115–130. Cambridge, MA: MIT.

Kathol, A. and K. VanBik. 1999. Morphology-syntax interface in Lai relative clauses. In P. Tamanji, M. Hirotami, and N. Hall, eds., *Proceedings of the 29th Annual Meeting of the North Eastern Linguistic Society*, pages 427–441. University of Massachusetts, Amherst: GLSA.

Kathol, A. and K. VanBik. 2000. Lexical constraints and constructional overrides: on the syntax of verbal form alternations in Lai. Unpubl. ms., UC Berkeley.

Manning, C. D. and I. A. Sag. 1999. Dissociations between argument structure and grammatical relations. In G. Webelhuth, J.-P. Koenig, and A. Kathol, eds., *Lexical and Constructional Aspects of Linguistic Explanation*, pages 63–78. Stanford: CSLI Publications.

Melnik, N. 1997. Verbal alternations in Lai. In J. Matisoff, ed., *Linguistics of the Tibeto-Burman Area*, vol. 20.2, pages 163–172. Berkeley, CA: University of California, Berkeley.

Peterson, D. 1998. The morphosyntax of transitivization in Lai. In J. Matisoff, ed., *Linguistics of the Tibeto-Burman Area*, vol. 21.1, pages 87–153. Berkeley, CA: University of California, Berkeley.

Pollard, C. J. 1994. Toward a unified account of passive in German. In J. Nerbonne, K. Netter, and C. J. Pollard, eds., *German in Head-Driven Phrase Structure Grammar*, pages 273–296. Stanford: CSLI Publications.

Pollard, C. J. and I. A. Sag. 1994. *Head-Driven Phrase Structure Grammar*. Chicago: University of Chicago Press and Stanford: CSLI Publications.

Sag, I. A. 1997. English relative clause constructions. *Journal of Linguistics* 33(2):431–484.

9

Grammatical Interfaces in Korean Relatives

JONG-BOK KIM AND BYUNG-SOO PARK

9.1 Introduction

The Korean relative clause constructions (RCCs) are often characterized by flexible application of the relative morphology, the lack of relative pronouns and the ommissibility of complements as well as the subject in relative clauses. These characteristics contribute to the overall structural complexity of the RCCs in Korean (and in Japanese). Consider the following two RCCs:

(1) a. [mek-nun] mwul
   eat-REL water
   'water that one drinks'

   b. [John-i mek-un] ceckalak
   John-NOM eat-REL chopsticks

These examples illustrate that the interpretation of relative clauses is in part dependent upon world knowledge or contexts.[1] The natural reading of (1a) is obtained from the relativization of the direct object with the subject *pro*. It would be rather difficult to have the reading of the subject relativization with the object *pro* since 'water' cannot eat/drink anything. The RC (1b) could be ambiguous: the most natural reading is 'the chopsticks that John ate with'. In context, this NP could also mean 'the chopsticks that John ate,' where the direct object is relativized.

Further complications relating to Korean RCCs also could be found in examples like (2) which seem to violate the canonical, syntactic island

[1]See Matsumoto 1990 for the discussion of various contextual factors determining the interpretation of Japanese relative clauses.

Grammatical Interfaces in HPSG.
Ronnie Cann, Claire Grover and Philip Miller.

constraints:

(2) a. [$_{NP}$[$_S$[__ $_i$ __ $_j$ tha-ko tani-nun] **cha$_j$-ka**] mesci-n]
ride drive-REL car-NOM stylish-REL
sinsa$_i$
man
'(lit.) man$_i$ who the car$_j$ that [he$_i$] is driving is stylish'

b. [$_{NP}$[$_S$[__ $_i$ __ $_j$ kacko iss-nun] **khemphwute$_j$-ka**]
in.possession-REL computer-NOM
MAC-i-n] **kyoswu$_i$**
MAC-COP-REL professor
'(lit.) professor$_i$ who the computer$_j$ that [he$_i$] has is MAC'

In (2), the relative heads *sinsa* 'gentleman' and *kyoswu* 'professor' have been relativized out of the more deeply embedded relative clause, violating the Complex Noun Phrase Constraint (CNPC). To our knowledge, no persuasive analysis has yet been provided for such island violating relatives (cf. Kim 1998).

Such context-dependent and island violating RCCs have implied that a single grammatical component such as syntax alone is not enough to deal with Korean relatives. In this paper, we will show that the most feasible approach to Korean relatives is the one that allows grammatical interfaces among morphology, syntax, semantics, and even pragmatics. The tight interface analysis we present here will also provide a streamlined way of solving further properties of Korean relatives. For example, within our interface analysis, we can explain the alleged peculiarity of island-violating relativization in terms of independently motivated properties of the so-called multiple nominative constructions.

9.2 Morphology of Korean Relatives

The starting point of Korean relatives is their morphology. The predicate of a relative clause preceding the head noun is marked with a morphological marker that varies with tense.[2]

(3) a. [Tom-i __ $_i$ ilk-nun] chayk$_i$
Tom-NOM read-PRES.REL book
'the book that Tom reads'

[2]Like mood suffixes, the prenominal relative clause markers map stems into words. These three basic kinds of tense-sensitive markers can be also extended to denote aspects when combined with tense suffixes. Thus the other possible prenominal verb forms of the lexeme *ilk-* 'read' are *ilk-ten* 'read-progressive', *ilk-essten* 'read-past progressive', *ilk-essul* 'read-past conjecture', *ilk-essessul* 'read-past perfective conjecture', *ilk-ko issten* 'read-past perfective progressive'. See Kim 1998 for further discussion.

b. [Tom-i $\_\_{}_i$ ilk-un] chayk$_i$
Tom-NOM read-PST.REL book
'the book that Tom read'

c. [Tom-i $\_\_{}_i$ ilk-ul] chayk
Tom$_i$ read-FUT.REL book
'the book that Tom will read'

Even in complex sentences, the prenominal morphological marker appears on the highest verb:

(4) [motwu-ka [Tom-i $\_\_{}_i$ **ilk-ess-ta-ko**]
everyone-NOM Tom-NOM read-PAST-DECL-COMP
sayngkakha-nun] chayk$_i$
think-REL book
'the book that everyone thinks Tom read'

One simple analysis of these facts involves assuming that the highest verb serves as the head of the relative clause, rather than as the complement of a null relativizer or operator (cf. Kang 1988, Han 1992). Interpreted in HPSG, this assumption leads us to assign the head feature MODIFIER (MOD) specification to the highest verb, as represented in the following structure for the sentence (4):

(5)
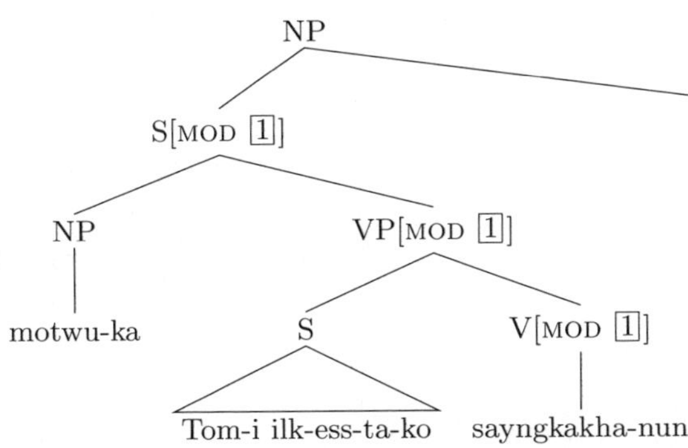

On this view, the verbal form marks the realization of relative clauses. In the constraint-based theory of HPSG (cf. Sag 1997 and Kim 1998), the REL suffixed verbal elements are thus subject to the following constraint:

(6) $$\textit{v-mod-word} \rightarrow \begin{bmatrix} \text{HEAD} & \textit{verb}\begin{bmatrix}\text{MOD } \textit{nominal}\end{bmatrix} \end{bmatrix}$$

The function of the REL marker is thus to add the modification information to its stem. By placing the modification information on the verbal morphology, we thus take a Korean relative clause to be a projection of the highest verb within that clause.

9.3 The Syntax of Korean Relative Clauses

9.3.1 Relativization of an Argument

Most of the syntactic properties of a relative clause is already determined by the morphology of its main verb. Korean relative clauses, one of whose distinctive properties is the absence of any English-like pronoun, allows the relativization of subject as well as complements:

(7) a. [__ Mary-eykey chayk-ul cwu-n] John (Subject Relative)
Mary-DAT book-ACC give-REL John
'John who gave the book to Mary'

b. [John-i __ Mary-eykey cwu-n] chayk (Object Relative)
John-NOM Mary-DAT give-REL book
'the book that John gave Mary'

c. [John-i chayk-ul __ cwu-n] Mary (IO Relative)
John-NOM book-ACC give-REL Mary
'Mary to whom John gave the book'

Adopting Bouma et. al's (1998) analysis, we allow one or more *gap-ss* elements to be present on DEPS, rather than on COMPS:[3]

(8) Argument Realization:

$$\text{VERB} \Rightarrow \begin{bmatrix} \text{SUBJ } \boxed{1} \\ \text{COMPS } \boxed{2} \ominus \text{LIST}(\textit{gap-ss}) \\ \text{DEPS } \boxed{1} \oplus \boxed{2} \end{bmatrix}$$

This Argument Realization constraint opens up the possibility of realizing a non-subject dependent either as a complement or as a gap. For example, the lexeme (9a) can be realized as a *v-mod word* with a gap in (9b).

(9) a. mek-ta 'eat-DECL' b. mek-un 'eat-REL'

$$\begin{bmatrix} \text{HEAD} & \textit{verb} \\ \text{SUBJ} & \langle \boxed{1}\text{NP}[\textit{nom}] \rangle \\ \text{COMPS} & \langle \boxed{2}\text{NP}[\textit{acc}] \rangle \\ \text{DEPS} & \langle \boxed{1}, \boxed{2} \rangle \end{bmatrix} \qquad \begin{bmatrix} \text{HEAD} & \textit{verb}\begin{bmatrix}\text{MOD } \textit{nominal}\end{bmatrix} \\ \text{SUBJ} & \langle \boxed{1}\text{NP}[\textit{nom}] \rangle \\ \text{COMPS} & \langle \; \rangle \\ \text{DEPS} & \left\langle \boxed{1}, \boxed{2}\begin{bmatrix} \textit{gap-ss} \\ \text{LOC } \boxed{3} \\ \text{SLASH } \left\{\boxed{3}\right\} \end{bmatrix} \right\rangle \\ \text{SLASH} & \left\{\boxed{3}\right\} \end{bmatrix}$$

[3]Following Sag (1997), we assume *gap-ss* as a new subtype of *synsem*.

In the feature structure (9b), the second dependent (argument) NP of the verb fails to be realized on COMPS but contributes an element to the verb's SLASH value by SLASH amalgamation (see Sag 1997). This is the kind of feature structure that occurs in relative clauses like (10).

(10) [John-i __ mek-un] sakwa
John __ eat-REL apple
'the apple John ate'

The verb *mek-un* 'eat-REL' whose lexical entry is given in (9b) bears the MOD specification. This head feature value is percolated up to the top of the relative clause by the Head Feature Principle. The verb also carries the SLASH feature amalgamated from one of its arguments according to the SLASH Amalgamation Constraint (see Sag 1997). This amalgamated SLASH value will pass up to the node, S, via the SLASH inheritance constraint. This lexical entry, combined with other principles, generates the structure in (11) for (10).[4]

(11)

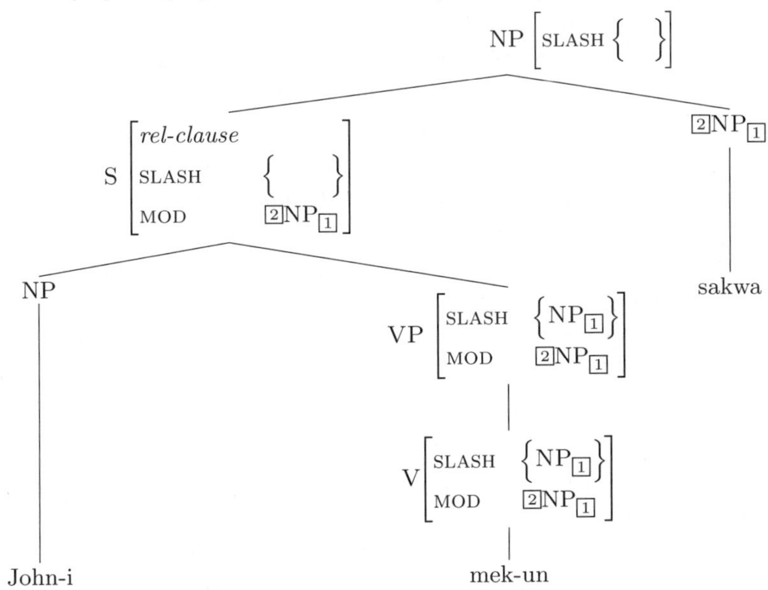

Each sub-structure of the tree in (11) satisfies all the general constraints that the grammar imposes on well-formed structures. Also note that the clause projected from the *v-mod-verb* is a Korean relative clause which is subject to the constructional constraint in (12).

[4]Following Kim (1998), the analysis given here is a traceless theory that posits no invisible element. See Kim 1998 for the details of this analysis and Sag and Fodor (1994) that reexamine the motivations for empty categories.

(12)
$$\textit{rel-cl} \rightarrow \begin{bmatrix} \text{HEAD} & \begin{bmatrix} \textit{verb} \\ \text{MOD } \textit{nominal}_{\boxed{1}} \end{bmatrix} \\ \text{SLASH} & \{\ \} \\ \text{HD-DTR} & \begin{bmatrix} \text{SLASH } \{\text{XP}_{\boxed{1}}\} \end{bmatrix} \end{bmatrix}$$

The constraint in (12) requires that a relative clause modify a nominal element coindexed with the referential parameter of the SLASH value in the head-daughter (cf. Sag 1997 for English relatives). This constraint guarantees that the SLASH value in (11) whose index value is identical with that of the NP head *sakwa* 'apple' is bound off at the S node. Korean relative clauses are thus treated in terms of coindexation between the referential parameter of the modified head noun and that of the SLASHed element—the *gap-ss* argument of the verb within the relative clause whose argument is extracted.

This constraint-based analysis has a number of welcome consequences. For example, by requiring the MOD value to be a nominal element, a relative clause can combine with either N, or N′, or NP:

(13) John-i ilk-un chayk/say chayk/ku say chayk
John-NOM read-REL book/new book/the new book
'book/new book/the new book that John read'

The constraint in (12) further guarantees that all relative clauses must 'bind off' the SLASH value of the head daughter, whose only member is an XP coindexed with the phrase's MOD value. (12) thus ensures that the slashed element is coindexed with the nominal head that the relative clause modifies, eventually blocking cases like the following:

(14) *[[John-i $\_\_{}_i$ ilk-ko iss-nun] haksayng-i_j]
John-NOM read-COMP is-REL student-NOM

The constraint also guarantees that the head daughter of a relative clause (the VP) bears a nonempty SLASH value. This will ensure that the grammar does not generate completely saturated modifying clauses.

(15) *[haksayng-tul-i kapang-ey chayk-ul neh-un] sangca
student-PL-NOM bag-LOC book-ACC put-REL box
'(lit.) the box where the student put the book in the bag'

Note that the analysis presented here also provides a natural account of subject extraction. We have seen that a verb always has one element on its SUBJ list and that its SLASH value is defined as the union of its dependents' SLASH values by the Amalgamation Constraint. Thus, the first member of a verb's DEPS is the same as the single member of its

SUBJ. But there is no constraint blocking this SUBJ element from being of type *gap-ss*. For example, the lexemic information of *mek-un* 'eat-REL' could be realized as the one in (16).

(16)
$$\begin{bmatrix} \textit{v-mod-word} & \\ \text{HEAD} & \begin{bmatrix}\text{MOD } \textit{nominal}\end{bmatrix} \\ \text{SUBJ} & \left\langle \boxed{1}\begin{bmatrix}\textit{gap-ss}\\ \text{LOC } \boxed{4} \\ \text{SLASH } \left\{\boxed{4}\right\}\end{bmatrix}\right\rangle \\ \text{COMPS} & \langle \boxed{2}\text{NP} \rangle \\ \text{DEPS} & \langle \boxed{1}, \boxed{2} \rangle \\ \text{SLASH} & \left\{\boxed{4}\right\} \end{bmatrix}$$

The lexical information in (16) may project the structure like the following:

(17)

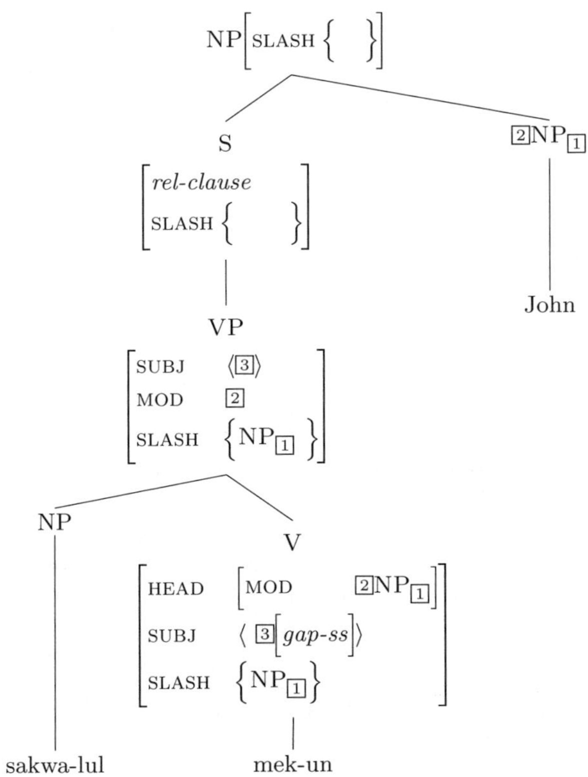

9.3.2 Relativization of an Adverbial

In terms of relativization, there is no distinction between complements and adjuncts. In addition to source or instrument arguments (e.g., (1b)), adverbials such as time, place, manner, degree, process, and reason can be easily relativized as shown in (18).

(18) a. [ku haksayng-i __ nolay-lul pwulu-n] sikan
the student-NOM song-ACC sing-REL time
'the time when the student sang a song '

b. [ku haksayng-i __ nolay-lul pwulu-n] cangso
the student-NOM song-ACC sing-REL place
'the place where the student sang a song'

c. [ku haksayng-i __ nolay-lul pwulu-n] iyu
the student-NOM song-ACC sing-REL reason
'the reason why the student sang a song'

There thus exists no difference between arguments and adjuncts with respect to the relative marking on the highest verb. To capture this parallelism, we adopt the constraint, Argument Structure Extension, from Bouma et al. (1998):[5]

(19) Argument Structure Extension:

$$verb \rightarrow \begin{bmatrix} \text{HEAD } \boxed{3} \\ \text{ARG-ST } \boxed{a} \\ \text{DEPS } \boxed{a} \oplus \text{LIST}\left(\begin{bmatrix} \textit{adverbial} \\ \text{MOD } \begin{bmatrix} \text{HEAD } \boxed{3} \\ \text{KEY } \boxed{2} \end{bmatrix} \end{bmatrix}\right) \\ \text{CONT} \mid \text{KEY } \boxed{2} \end{bmatrix}$$

This constraint brings two main effects. First, it allows a verb's DEPS list to contain any number of adverbials in addition to the verb's arguments.[6] Second, the semantics of the MOD value (the argument) of this adverbial element is identified with that of the verb. This has the effect of making the verb as the semantic argument of the adverbial. For example, the transitive relative verb *pwulu-n* 'sing-REL' can be extended to the verb in (20a) containing an adverbial element in its DEPS list, and this adverbial element then can be realized as a *gap-synsem* as in (20b):

[5] A boxed letter means a list and '⊕' denotes the list concatenation operation.

[6] In Korean, this treatment is motivated from the fact that case marking exhibits patters that apply uniformly to selected complements and the adverbials illustrated above. See See Wechsler and Lee 1996 and Bouma et al. 1998.

(20) Dependent Realization:

a. pwulu-n 'sing-REL'

$$\begin{bmatrix} \textit{v-mod-word} & \\ \text{HEAD} & \begin{bmatrix}\text{MOD } \textit{nominal}\end{bmatrix} \\ \text{SUBJ} & \langle \boxed{1}\text{NP}[\textit{nom}] \rangle \\ \text{COMPS} & \langle \boxed{2}\text{NP}, \boxed{4} \rangle \\ \text{DEPS} & \left\langle \boxed{1}, \boxed{2}, \boxed{4}\begin{bmatrix}\text{HEAD} & \textit{adv} \\ \text{CONT} & \boxed{3}\end{bmatrix} \right\rangle \\ \text{CONT} & \boxed{3} \end{bmatrix}$$

b. pwulu-n 'sing-REL'

$$\begin{bmatrix} \textit{v-mod-word} & \\ \text{HEAD} & \begin{bmatrix}\text{MOD } \textit{nominal}\end{bmatrix} \\ \text{SUBJ} & \langle \boxed{1}\text{NP}[\textit{nom}] \rangle \\ \text{COMPS} & \langle \boxed{2}\text{NP} \rangle \\ \text{DEPS} & \left\langle \boxed{1}, \boxed{2}, \begin{bmatrix}\textit{gap-ss} & \\ \text{LOC} & \boxed{4} \\ \text{SLASH} & \left\{\boxed{4}\right\}\end{bmatrix} \right\rangle \\ \text{SLASH} & \left\{\boxed{4}\right\} \end{bmatrix}$$

Once we posit this DEPS level with relevant constraints, we may appeal to it to account for adjunct extraction. We obtain the lexical structure for *pwulu-n* 'sing' in (20b) by assuming that (a) an adverbial is instantiated as a singleton list, (b) the Dependent Realization Principle instantiates this element as a gap, and (c) the SLASH value of the gap is incorporated into the SLASH value of the verb by the SLASH amalgamation constraint. This lexical structure gives us the following structure for (18a).[7]

(21)

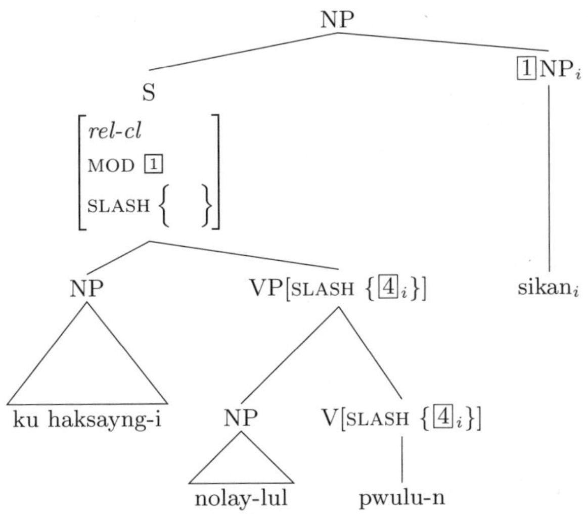

The system we have elaborated so far thus provides a uniform account of both complement and adjunct extraction.

[7] We assume that an adverbial element can also bear such a locative or temporal index. For the properties of such an index, we admit that a finer theory needs to be developed.

9.4 The Roles of Semantics and Pragmatics in Korean Relative Clauses

9.4.1 Relativization of a Specifier

One peculiar type of relative clause in Korean is the relativization of a specifier, as noted in Kim (1998) and Park (1999):

(22) a. [$_{NP}$[__$_i$ apeci-ka] tayhak-ey tani-nun] ai$_i$
father-NOM college-LOC go-REL boy
'boy whose father goes to college'

b. [$_{NP}$[__$_i$ chinkwu-ka] mikwuk-ey iminka-n] salam$_i$
friend-NOM America-LOC immigrated-REL person
'person whose friend immigrated to America'

The unexpressed specifier of the subject NP in the RC is always understood as identical to the head noun that the RC modifies.

Unlike previous approaches that relate such relative clauses to genitive clauses, we argue that these RCs are closely related to double nominative constructions. The evidence comes from case alternations like the following.

(23) a. ai-ka/uy apeci-ka tayhak-ey tani-n-ta
child-NOM father-NOM college-LOC go-PRES-DECL
'The boy's father goes to college.'

b. yangccok-*i/uy pwulsin-i i sathay-lul cholayhayssta
both.sides-NOM mistrust-NOM this state-ACC caused
'The mistrust between the two sides caused this state.'

We claim that Korean allows the relativization of the first nominative subject in the double nominative constructions, but not the genitive specifier. We thus could relativize the subject of *ai-ka* in (23a) but not the gentivie element *yangccok* in (23b), predicting the ungrammaticality of the one in (24).

(24) *[[__ pwulsin-i] i sathay-lul cholayha-n] yangccok
mistrust-NOM this state-ACC cause-REL both sides
'both sides whose mistrust caused this state'

Within this line of reasoning, we must explicate the grammatical role of the first nominative element in examples like (23a), where the main predicate does not obviously select two nominative complements. As suggested by Park (1999) and further justified by Kim (2000), various pieces of evidence lead us to take the first (*i/ka*) nominative-marked nominal in double nominative constructions not as a second subject but as a focused phrase. We assume that Korean employs a base-generated gapless topic/focus construction. More specifically, we take (25) to be a schema that characterizes a type of well-formed phrases in Korea.

(25) Head-Focus Schema:

$$\text{S}\left[\text{INFO-STR} \mid \text{FOC } \langle \boxed{1} \rangle\right] \rightarrow \boxed{1}\text{NP}\left[\text{MRK I/KA}\right], \quad \text{S}\left[\text{SPR}\langle \boxed{1} \rangle\right]$$

The schema simply says that a focused phrase with the focus particle *i/ka* and a sentence looking for a specifier form a well-formed sentence. In fact, the selected specifier will correspond to the specifier of the subject within the S. We thus suppose that unlike English but similar to Catalan, Korean informational interpretation such as focus is signaled by syntactic position as well as by the focus particle *-i/ka*. To integrate this focus information into grammar, we adopt Engdahl and Vallduvi's (1996) idea that the feature attribute INFO-STR(UCTURE)|FOC(US) controls the information structure of a given sentence and its structural realization, together with the assumption that verb lexemes could be realized as those in (26) (either thru a lexical rule or by a constructional constraint).[8]

(26)
$$\begin{bmatrix} \textit{v-word} \\ \text{SPR } \langle \boxed{1}_i [\text{MRK I/KA}] \rangle \\ \text{SUBJ}\langle \text{NP}_j \left[\text{SPR } \langle \boxed{1} \rangle\right] \rangle \\ \text{INFO-STR} \mid \text{FOC } \langle \boxed{1} \rangle \\ \text{CONT} \mid \text{RESTR}\left\langle \ldots, \begin{bmatrix} \text{RELN } \textit{subordinate} \\ \text{ARG1 } i \\ \text{ARG2 } j \end{bmatrix}, \ldots \right\rangle \end{bmatrix}$$

The effect of such realization is simple: It first allows a verb taking an unsaturated nominal subject to have a specifier which is identified with the subject's specifier. This constraint in a sense promotes the subject's specifier to an informational focus in a given sentence. In addition, (26) specifies that the subject and its unsaturated specifier be in a 'subordinate' relation.[9] This semantic constraint prevents examples like (27b), which is otherwise similar to the one in (24).

[8]For constructions with more than three *-i/ka* marked elements, we need an additional constraint on nouns. See Kim 2000 for details.

[9]The term 'subordinate' is borrowed from Na and Huck (1993): "X is thematically subordinate to an entity Y iff Y's having the properties it does entails that X has the properties it does." Under their analysis the subordinate relation is classified into five types: part-whole, quality-to entity, conventional, hierarchical, and taxonomic. See Na and Huck (1993) for further details.

(27) a. kumli-uy halak-i cwusik sicang-ul towassta
interest-GEN dicrease-NOM stock.market-ACC helped
'The decrease in (bank) interests helped the stock market.'

b. *[[__ halak-i] cwusik sicang-ul towu-n] kumli
dicrease-NOM stock.market-ACC boost-REL interest

There exists no subordinate relation between *halak* 'decrease' and *kumli* 'interest'. However, it is not difficult to find a subordinate relation between *father* and *child* as in (23a). The verb *tani-ta* 'work.at-DECL' thus could be realized as the one in (28) with the indicated focus information.

(28)
$$\begin{bmatrix} \text{HEAD } \textit{verb} \\ \text{SPR } \langle \boxed{1}[\text{MRK I/KA}] \rangle \\ \text{SUBJ } \langle \text{NP}\begin{bmatrix}\text{SPR } \langle \boxed{1} \rangle\end{bmatrix} \rangle \\ \text{COMPS } \langle \text{PP}[\text{EY}] \rangle \\ \text{INFO-STR} \mid \text{FOC } \langle \boxed{1} \rangle \end{bmatrix}$$

Our analysis then allows this focused specifier to be relativized.[10] Like the treatment of subject relatives we have seen earlier, the grammar allows this specifier value to be realized as a *gap-synsem*. The examples in (22) are instances of this relativization process.

Support for our analysis also comes from the fact that it is only the subject's unexpressed specifier that the head noun can be coindexed with. No other complement can participate in this coindexing relationship, as illustrated in (29).

(29) a. *[taythonglyeng-i [__ kyoswu-lul] cangkwan-ulo
president-NOM professor-ACC minister-INST
immyengha-n] tayhak
nominate-REL university
'(int.) the university whose professor the president nominated as minister'

b. *[John-i [__ kyoswu-eykey] senmwul-ul cwu-n] tayhak
John-NOM professor-DAT present-ACC give-REL univ.
'(int.) the university whose professor Tom gave a present to'

This prediction is a natural consequence of our approach where the interactions of semantic and pragmatic constraints play a crucial role in the grammar of the so-called specifier relatives: our analysis accords a special status to subject arguments.

[10] Traditionally (cf. Kuno 1973), the relativized element in Japanese and Korean is claimed to be a topic. For the *i/ka* marked focused phrase in question to be a topic, it needs to be topicalized. Such a view requires the focused phrase, like other unfocused phrases, to be vacuously or obligatorily topicalized before the relativization.

9.4.2 Double Relative Clauses and Multiple Nominative Constructions

As noted in the Introduction, the examples in (30) are typical cases where the 'gap' with which the head noun is coindexed has been claimed to be within an embedded relative clause (cf. Kang 1988 and Yang 1989):

(30) a. [[[__ $_i$ __ $_j$ ipko iss-nun] os$_j$-i] mesci-n] sinsa$_i$
wearing is-REL clothes-NOM stylish-REL man
' (lit.) man$_i$ who the clothes that [e$_i$] is wearing are stylish'

b. [[[__ $_i$ __ $_j$ ssu-n] sosel-i] inki-ka iss-nun] cakka
write-REL novel-NOM fame-ACC exist-REL writer
'writer$_i$ who the novel that e$_i$ wrote was popular'

These examples, in which the relative heads *sinsa* 'gentleman' and *cakka* 'writer' appear to be relativized out of the inner relative clause, have cast a serious doubt on the validity of island constraints (such as the CNPC). Such island violations have been the main reason for accepting the assumption that Korean relativization does not involve Move-α, motivating for the base-generated analysis of Han 1992 or the genitive analysis of Kang 1988.[11]

Under our analysis, seemlingly nonlocal relatives like (30) are all local as argued by Kim (1999). These involve focused specifiers originating from double nominative constructions, as proposed in the previous section. When we look into the data that allow relativization from a relative clause, we can notice that the highest verb is the one that allows a multiple nominative NP construction. For example, the verbs of the highest relative clause in (30) all allow the following sentences:

(31) a. ku sinsa-ka os-i **mesci-ta**
the man-NOM clothes-NOM stylish
'The man's clothes is stylish.'

b. ku cakka-ka sosel-i **inki-ka** **iss-ta**
the writer-NOM novel-NOM popularaity-NOM exist
'The writer's novel is popular.'

We thus maintain that the relative clauses in (30) are closely related to those in (31) and that it is the focused subject that is relativized in these examples:

[11]Realizing the problems of such purely syntax-based approaches, Na and Huck (1993) recapture such properties as subjacency violations through the application of the Argument Condition to the semantic/pragmatic interpretation of the constructions. See Na and Huck for details and Kim (1998) and Park (1999) for criticisms of their analysis.

(32) a. **sinsa-ka** [[*pro* ipko iss-nun] os-i] mesci-ta
gentleman-NOM wearing is-REL clothes-NOM stylish-REL
'(literally) It is the gentleman whose clothes he is wearing is stylish.'

b. **cakka-ka** [[*pro* ssu-n] sosel-i] inki-ka iss-ta
writer-NOM write-REL novel-NOM fame-ACC exist-REL
'(literally) It is the writer whose novel he wrote is popular.'

A major difference between our analysis and previous ones (including Na and Huck 1993) is that the subject of the lower relative clause is a *pro* element which is most naturally interpreted as identical to the subject *sinsa* or *cakka.*[12] One piece of evidence for assuming *pro* rather than a variable trace here comes from the possibility of replacing this position with an overt pronominal or reflexive that can occupy the subject position of an independent clause in Korean.

(33) [__ $_i$ [[**caki-ka/ku-ka** __ $_j$ ssu-n] sosel$_j$-i] manh-un]
self/he-NOM write-REL novel-NOM many-REL
cakka$_i$
writer
'(lit.) writer who the novels that [himself] wrote are many.'

One natural interpretive constraint that exists is the coindexing relation between *caki* (or *pro*) in (33) and the relative head. It is difficult to have a context violating this coindexing relation.[13] But if given a suitable context, it is in fact possible to violate this constraint: the example in (34) illustrates that this subject position in the embedded clause can be occupied by a free pronominal:

(34) [__ $_i$ [[**John-i** __ $_j$ pillyekass-ten] (casin-uy) os$_j$-i]
John-NOM borrow.away-REL (self-GEN) clothes-NOM
cciceci-n] sinsa$_i$
torn.up gentleman
'(lit.) the gentleman who the clothes John borrowed from him were torn up'

One consequence of this analysis is that it predicts the asymmetry (subject vs. object) in (35a) and (35b).

(35) a. [[__ $_i$] [[*pro*$_i$ __ $_j$ ssu-n] **sosel$_j$-i**] cal phali-nun] cakka$_i$
write-REL novel-NOM well sell.out-REL writer
'the writer whose novels that (he) wrote sell well'

[12]See Han 1992 for a similar analysis and Hasegawa 1984 for the distributional properties of Japanese *pro*.

[13]We claim that this pragmatic constraint is one of the main constraints in Korean double nominative constructions.

b. *[[[__ $_i$ __ $_j$ ssun-n] **sosel$_j$-ul**] John-i ilk-un]
write-REL novel-ACC John-NOM read-REL

cakka$_i$
writer
'(lit.) the writer who the novels that [he] wrote that John read'

The example (35b) is unacceptable simply because it violates the CNPC or subjacency constraint: *cakka* 'writer' cannot be relativized from a complex noun phrase as can be seen from its source sentence given in (36).

(36) $_{NP}$[$_S$[**cakka-ka** __ $_j$ ssu-n] sosel$_j$-ul] John-i ilkessta.
writer write-REL novel-ACC John-NOM read
'John read the novels that the writer wrote.'

9.5 Conclusion

The highly flexible behavior of Korean relatives poses many puzzles. But once we pin down the role that each grammatical component plays in the formation of relative clauses, we provide a clean analysis of complicated Korean relative clause constructions, as we have shown.

As noted, the morphological information encoded in the highest predicate in the relative clause is a starting point for the analysis. This MOD information is distributed in sentences in accordance with syntactic constraints that also regulate the possibility of argument/adjunct realization. This constraint interacts with lexical, semantic and pragmatic factors, allowing us to treat the so called nonlocal relatives as local relatives. With the introduction of information structure (FOCUS), we have been able to provide a clean analysis of specifier relatives as well as double relatives. This interactive system makes it unnecessary to posit further subconstructions for Korean relative clauses or special selectional restrictions such as those in Na and Huck (1993). The result is a simpler grammar of Korean.

Acknowledgments

An earlier version of this paper was presented at the HPSG-99 conference. Thanks go to the audiences of the conference for criticisms and suggestions. We are also grateful for invaluable suggestions and comments from Chan Chung, Ivan Sag, Peter Sells, and two anonymous reviewers.

References

Bouma, G., R. Malouf, and I. A. Sag. 1998. A unified theory of complement, adjunct and subject extraction. *Proceedings of the FHCG–98*, pages 83–97.

Engdahl, E. and E. Vallduví. 1996. Information packaging in HPSG. In C. Grover and E. Vallduví, eds., *Studies in HPSG*, Edinburgh Working Papers in Cognitive Science, vol. 12, pages 1–31.

Han, J-I. 1992. Syntactic movement analysis of Korean relativization. *Language Research* 28.2:335-357.

Hasegawa, N. 1984. On the so-called 'zero-pronouns' in Japanese. *The Linguistic Review* 4:289–341.

Hukari, T. E. and R. D. Levine. 1995. Adjunct Extraction. *Journal of Linguistics* 31(2):195–226.

Kang, M-Y. 1988. Syntactic movement in Korean relativization. In *Linguistics in the Morning Calm II*. Seoul: Hanshin Publishing.

Kim, J-B. 1998. A head-driven and constraint-based analysis of Korean relative clause constructions. *Language Research* 34(4):767–808.

Kim, J-B. 1999. A local treatment of nonlocal relativization in Korean. To appear in the *Proceedings of the 25th Berkeley Linguistic Society.*

Kim, J-B. 2000. A constraint-based approach to some multiple nominative constructions in Korean. In A. Ikeya and M. Kawamori, eds., *Proceedings of the 14th Pacific Conference on Language, Information and Computation*, pages 165–176.

Kuno, S. 1973. *The Structure of the Japanese Language*. Cambridge, MA: MIT Press.

Matsumoto Y. 1990. The role of pragmatics in Japanese relative clause constructions. *Lingua* 82:111–129.

Na, Y. and G. Huck. 1993. On the state of certain island violations in Korean. *Linguistics and Philosophy* 16:181–229.

Park, B-S. 1999. Relative clause constructions with possessive specifier gaps: a constraint-based approach. In *Proceedings of the 13th Pacific Asia Conference on Language, Information, and Computation*, pages 143–152.

Sag, I. 1997. English relative clause constructions. *Journal of Linguistics* 33:431–484.

Sag, I. and J. D. Fodor. 1994. Extraction without traces. In R. Aranovich et al., eds., *Proceedings of the West Coast Conference on Formal Linguistics 13*, pages 365–384. Stanford: CSLI Publications.

Wechsler, S. and Y-S. Lee. 1996. The domain of direct case assignment. *Natural Language and Linguistic Theory* 14(3):629–664.

Yang, D-W. 1989. *The Basis of the Government and Binding Theory* (in Korean.) Seoul: Sinasa

10

Prosodic Constituency in HPSG

EWAN KLEIN

10.1 Introduction

It is widely assumed that prosodic structure is related in some way to syntactic structure, yet there is little agreement about what the nature of that relation might be. We might take the null-hypothesis to be the following:

Prosodic Isomorphism Hypothesis:

Prosodic constituency is isomorphic to 'conventional' constituent structure.

Although prosodic constituency is clearly informed by syntactic constituency of the standard sort, isomorphism seems to be too strong in general. As an example, consider example (10.1), discussed by Gee and Grosjean (1983), where square brackets are used to indicate prosodic boundaries:

(10.1) [By making his plan known][he brought out][the objections of everyone].

The boundary between *known* and *he* is unsurprising, since it coincides with a syntactic boundary between a preposed adverbial phrase and the main clause. By contrast, the second prosodic constituent, *he brought out* departs dramatically from standard syntactic constituency; for the subject *he* has a tighter juncture with the following main verb (plus particle) than the latter does with its noun phrase object, *the objections of everyone.*

One possible response to this kind of datum is to abandon conventional notions of surface syntactic constituency. This is the approach to prosodic constituency advocated by Steedman (1991), where the availability of function composition and type-raising in a combinatory catego-

Grammatical Interfaces in HPSG.
Ronnie Cann, Claire Grover and Philip Miller.

rial grammar allows subjects and main verbs to combine as constituents. An alternative, due to Abney (1989, 1991), proposes a multistep model of grammatical analysis whose first stage involves the identification of syntactic 'chunks'—roughly, just that part of a conventional constituent up to and including the lexical head. Although this provides an attractive basis for the identification of prosodic constituents, it requires a radically different account of the semantics of complementation to that typically assumed in current grammatical frameworks.

By contrast, I will explore how prosodic constituency might be articulated within recent versions of HPSG (e.g., Sag, 1997). This will be closer to Selkirk's (1984) approach (discussed below), insofar as a fairly traditional notion of syntactic constituency is maintained. However, it differs in that prosodic constituents will be built recursively, in parallel with the recursive definition of syntactic phrases by the grammar. I will not attempt to deal with issues of accent placement, focus and information structure, nor with the possible meanings of intonational tunes. I shall also restrict attention to 'core' syntactic constructions, including transitive and ditransitives VPs, modals, nominal complements, pronominal subjects; other constructions will be largely ignored.

From the perspective of the practising theoretical linguist, prosodic phonology has the disadvantage that relying on one's own or others' intuitions about well-formedness is even more fraught with danger than in the case of syntax. In order to mitigate this problem, I have drawn most of the data used in this paper from the SOLE spoken corpus (Hitzeman et al., 1998).[1] The corpus was based on recordings of one speaker reading around 40 short descriptive texts concerning jewelry, and has sufficient syntactic complexity (unlike typical spoken corpora consisting of spontaneous utterances (Croft, 1995)) to exhibit the kind of phenomena that I am interested in.

Before turning to the treatment of prosodic constituents in HPSG, I will first briefly review some of the main approaches that have been taken in the literature, and then summarise the key areas where syntax and prosody seem to diverge.

10.2 Prosodic Preliminaries

10.2.1 The Prosodic Hierarchy

Much of the work on English prosodic structure above the foot adopts a model that was first published in Selkirk 1981. Prosodic constituents at one level are assembled into those of a higher level:

[1] The task of recovering relevant examples from the SOLE corpus was considerably aided by the Gsearch corpus query system (Corley et al., 2000).

> ...we will see that prosodic words first group in phonological phrases (ϕ), that the phonological phrases are grouped into intonational phrases (I), and finally, that the intonational phrases make up the utterance (υ).

This notion of a prosodic *hierarchy* has been expanded and varied in the subsequent literature; cf. Beckman and Pierrehumbert 1986; Hayes 1989; Nespor and Vogel 1986; Pierrehumbert and Beckman 1988; Selkirk 1984, 1986, 1996. As pointed out by Shattuck-Hufnagel and Turk (1996, p207), there is a fair degree of agreement about the top of the hierarchy (the levels of Utterance and Intonational Phrase), and at the bottom (the levels of Foot, Syllable and Mora), but substantive and terminological disagreement about the midlevels.

According to the widely-accepted Strict Layer Hypothesis (Selkirk, 1984, p26), the hierarchy is non-recursive: a category of level i in the hierarchy can be exhaustively decomposed into a sequence of categories of level $i-1$. Selkirk (1986, p384) notes that "cases of languages where all layers are instantiated are rare".

Intonational Phrases (IPs) are phonologically defined as units which are associated with a characteristic intonational contour; in particular, an IP is marked by the presence of a major pitch accent. The boundary of an IP is canonically manifested as a perceptible pause, accompanied by a local fall or rise in F_0 (fundamental frequency); it can also be marked by constituent-final syllable lengthening, and stronger articulation of constituent-initial consonants. Nevertheless, the phonetic cues to a postulated IP boundary may be considerably weaker than suggested by the canonical case.[2] Selkirk (1984) claims that a sequence of words will belong to a given IP only if they constitute a 'sense unit'; that is, the well-formedness of a given decomposition into IPs is constrained by some notion of semantic coherence. However, this claim has recently been challenged by Taglicht (1998).

The characterization of Phonological Phrases, as a prosodic level lying between Intonational Phrases and Prosodic Words, has been the subject of some debate. Selkirk (1984, p29) denies that they exist in English; however, they have been taken as demarcating the domain for phonological phenomena in several other languages; cf. (Chen, 1997; Nespor and Vogel, 1986; Selkirk, 1986).[3]

In this paper, I will not make a great deal of use of the Prosodic Hierarchy. Most of the phenomena that I wish to deal with lie in the blurry

[2]See (Ladd, 1996) for discussion of this issue.

[3]Interestingly, Chen (1997) claims that, *contra* the Strict Layer Hypothesis, Phonological Phrases in Xiamen cross-cut Intonational Phrase boundaries.

region between the Phonological Word and the Intonational Phrase, and I will just refer to 'prosodic constituents' without committing myself to a specific set of labels. I will not adopt the Strict Layer Hypothesis, which has in any case been significantly weakened in Selkirk (1996). However, it is important to note that every IP will be a prosodic constituent, in my sense. Moreover every such prosodic constituent is *potentially* an IP, though in practise the kinds of prosodic utterances to be considered in this paper will have several prosodic constituents which are not actually IPs.

10.2.2 Metrical Trees

The Prosodic Isomorphism Hypothesis is the starting point for the construction of metrical trees proposed by Liberman and Prince (1977). Thus consider the syntactic analysis in (10.2):

(10.2)

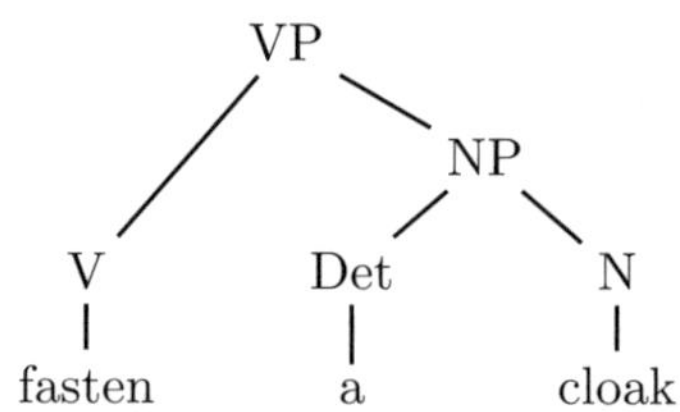

On the approach of Liberman and Prince (1977, p257), syntactic constituents are assigned relative prosodic weight according to the following rule:

(10.3) *NSR*: In a configuration $[_C$ A B$]$, if C is a phrasal category, B is strong.

Prominence is taken to be a relational notion: a constituent labelled 's' is stronger than its sister. Consequently, if B in (10.3) is strong, then A must be weak.

In the case of a tree like (10.2) above, Liberman and Prince's (10.3) yields a binary-branching structure of the following sort (where the root of the tree is unlabeled):

(10.4)

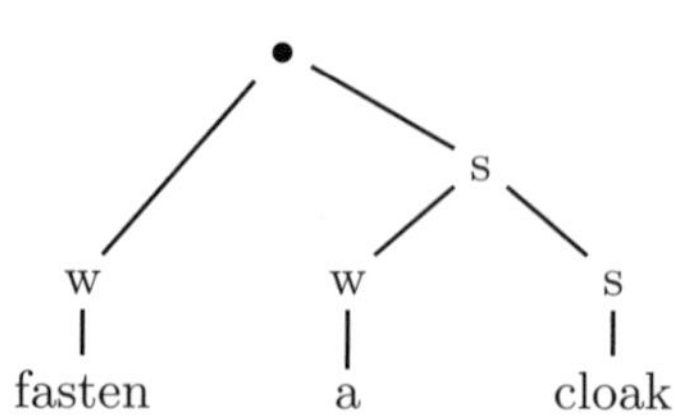

For any given constituent analysed by a metrical tree t, the location of its main stress can be found by tracing a path from the root of t to a terminal element α such that all nodes on that path are labelled 's'. Thus the main stress in (10.4) is located on the element *cloak*. In general, the most prominent element, defined in this way, is called the *Designated Terminal Element* (DTE) (Liberman and Prince, 1977). Note that (10.3) is the metrical version of Chomsky and Halle's 1968 Nuclear Stress Rule (NSR), and encodes the same claim, namely that in the default case, main stress falls on the last constituent in a given phrase. Of course, it has often been argued that the notion of 'default prominence' is flawed, since it supposes that the acceptability of utterances can be judged in a null context. Nevertheless, there is an alternative conception: the predictions of the NSR correctly describe the prominence patterns when the whole proposition expressed by the clause in question receives broad focus (cf. Ladd, 1996). This is the view that I will adopt. Although I will concentrate in the rest of the paper on the broad focus pattern of intonation, the approach I develop is intended to link up eventually with pragmatic information about the location of narrow focus.

In the formulation above, (10.3) only applies to binary-branching constituents, and the question arises how non-binary branching constituent structures, such as (10.5), should be treated:

(10.5)

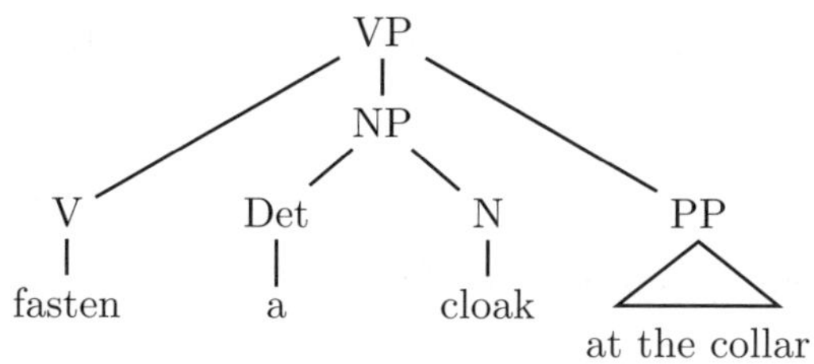

One solution, proposed by Hogg and McCully (1987), is to build a new prosodic node, in a right-to-left mapping from the syntax tree. This allows us to replace the ternary branching VP in (10.5) by a binary right-branching metrical structure. An alternative, advocated by Beckman (1986); Pierrehumbert and Beckman (1988); Nespor and Vogel (1986) would be to drop the restriction that metrical trees are binary, allowing structures such as (10.6).

(10.6)

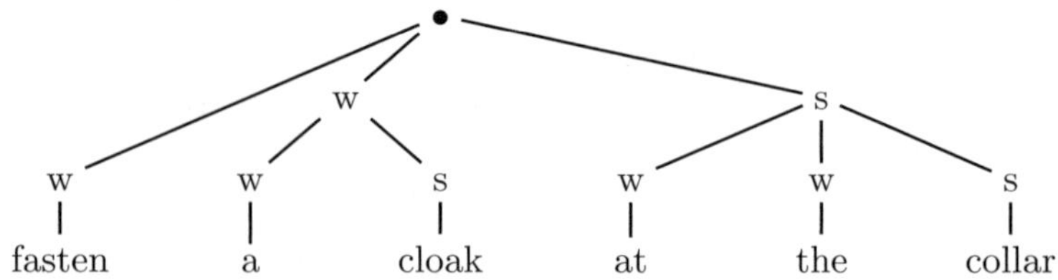

One of the arguments put forward by Pierrehumbert and Beckman (1988, p142) in favour of n-ary metrical tree concerns the phonetic interpretation of such structures.[4] As emphasised by Liberman and Prince (1977), a purely relational representation of prominence provides a phonological constraint on accentual patterns, but does not determine them: a given metrical tree will correspond to numerous pronunciations. Beckman and Pierrehumbert argue that phonetic realization is best handled by assigning absolute values for stress subordination to elements of relatively flat trees, rather than to arbitrarily deep binary-branching trees. In the interests of avoiding unnecessary structure, I will adopt n-ary metrical trees for the rest of this paper.

10.2.3 Juncture

At this point, it will be useful to be more explicit about the intended interpretion of constituent boundaries within metrical trees. That is, I want to clarify how a metrical tree encodes a notion of *juncture*. Borrowing from Gee and Grosjean (1983), let us adopt the the following definition:

Definition 1 (Juncture Value) Let J be the lowest node to dominate two adjacent words in the frontier of a metrical tree. Then the *tightness* of the juncture between those two words corresponds to the number n of branching nodes dominated by J (taking dominance to be reflexive, we include J itself in the count). 1 represents the tightest juncture, and tightness decreases in proportion to n.

To illustrate, let us look at the metrical tree in (10.7):

[4]A second argument is that n-ary metrical trees lend themselves better to headless prosodic constituents, which are claimed to be appropriate for Tokyo Japanese.

(10.7)

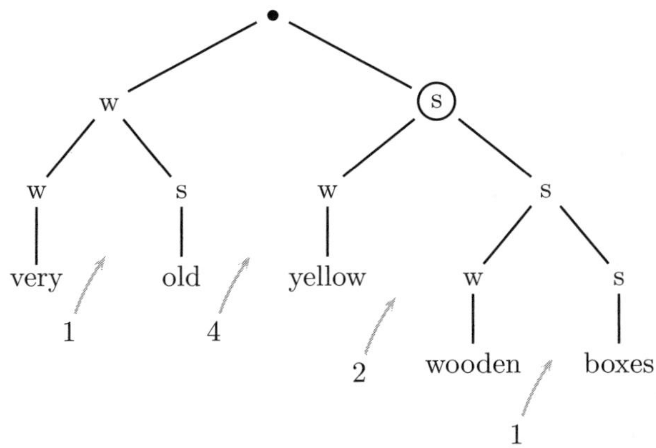

The grey arrows below the tree indicate the value of the relevant juncture, as determined by the definition above. For example, the juncture value between *yellow* and *wooden* is 2 because the relevant node, i.e., the circled 's' node which exhaustively dominates *yellow* and *wooden boxes*, dominates both itself and another one branching node. In Gee and Grosjean (1983), weak monosyllabic function words attach with a degree of juncture that is tighter than 1; I will return to this issue in Section 10.2.5 below.

I will not make any formal use of the notion of juncture value in what follows. However, I will adopt the view that juncture, as defined over metrical trees, is adequate to capture the intuitive notion of 'breaks' between prosodic constituents.

10.2.4 Phonological Phrases

It is argued by Selkirk (1981, 1986), Selkirk and Shen (1990) and Nespor and Vogel (1986) that Phonological Phrases are determined by syntactic structure. In an early presentation (Selkirk, 1981, p126), the mapping is determined in the following manner:

(i) An item which is the specifier of a syntactic phrase joins in with the head of the phrase.[5]

(ii) An item belonging to a non-lexical category, such as Det, Prep, Comp, Verb_{aux}, Conjunction, joins with its sister constituent.

More recently, Selkirk (1986, p385) has reformulated this claim as follows:

> the relation between syntactic structure and prosodic structure above the foot and below the intonational phrase is de-

[5] The term 'specifier' here encompasses pre-head adjectives and adverbs.

> fined in terms of the *ends* of syntactic constituents of designated types. ... a unit of phonological structure, a derived domain, will have as its terminal string the stretch of the surface syntactic structure that is demarcated by the right or left ends of selected constituents ....

Although, as pointed out earlier, the existence of Phonological Phrases in English has been controversial, the end-based approach just sketched appears to certainly capture prosodic properties of headed phrases in English, particularly those headed by nouns.

10.2.5 Function Words

Zwicky (1982, p5) introduces a class of words called *leaners*: these "form a rhythmic unit with the neighbouring material, are normally unstressed with respect to this material, and do not bear the intonational peak of the unit. English articles, coordinating conjunctions, complementizers, relative markers, and subject and object pronouns are all leaners in this sense". Zwicky takes pains to differentiate between leaners and *clitics*; the former combine with neighbours to form Phonological Phrases (with juncture characterized by external sandhi), whereas clitics combine with their hosts to form Phonological Words (where juncture is characterized by internal sandhi).[6] This sharp distinction between leaners (word external) and clitics (word internal) is disputed by Nespor and Vogel (1986) on the basis of data involving Italian clitic pronouns. An alternative approach, advocated by Selkirk (1996), is to classify clitics into distinct subgroups; her *free* clitics seem to correspond best to Zwicky's leaners.

Despite these substantive and terminological divergences, there are good reasons to assign a special prosodic status to the units in question, and I will call them *leaner groups*. I will assume that they consist of a sequence of one or more leaners followed by a single Phonological Word; that is, the stress-bearing element is alway rightmost in the unit. We can represent such a unit within a metrical tree as follows, where x stands for 'w' or 's', and *lnr-grp* is a type annotation of the metrical tree:

(10.8)

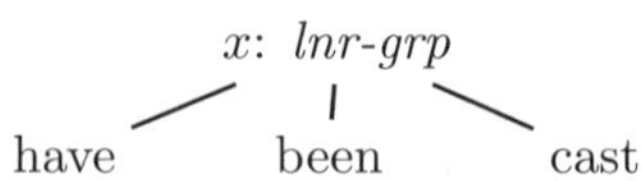

In such a metrical tree, the juncture between elements is intended to be tighter than the 1 value given by Definition 1 of Juncture Value.

[6] Zwicky also points out that some morphemes, such as infinitival *to*, which are ordinarily leaners can also contract with selected verbs to form Phonological Words (e.g., *wanna, hafta*).

10.3 Prosody-Syntax Mismatches

I have already alluded to some cases where syntax and prosody appear to diverge. In this section I want to look in more detail at two classes of constructions which support such a claim.[7]

Prosodic Flattening

As noted in Section 10.2.2, it has been suggested that prosodic structure is flatter than syntactic structure. Schematically we have the pattern shown in Fig. 1.

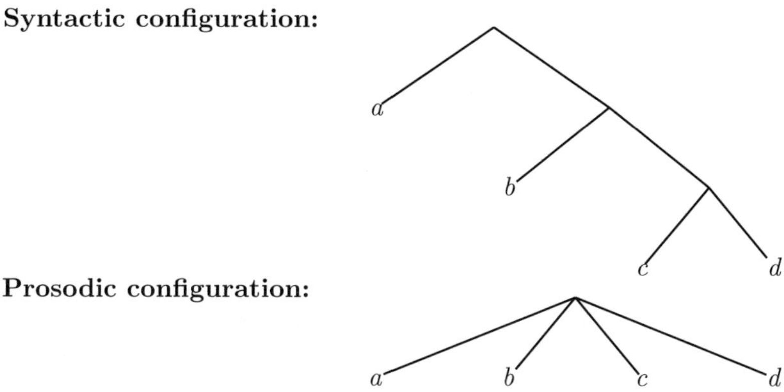

FIGURE 1 Prosodic Flattening

A particularly clear example of where the Prosodic Isomorphism Hypothesis makes the wrong predictions concerns constituent structures with deeply embedded right-branching structure. The paired syntactic and metrical trees in Fig. 2 illustrate this point (assuming a GPSG-style (Gazdar et al., 1985) treatment of modal and auxiliary verbs).

Discussing an example similar to the second tree in Fig. 2, Selkirk (1984, p164) remarks:

> Such a tree is both too rich and too impoverished as a representation of phrasal prominence—too rich because it in principle allows for all the distinctions in level (degree) of stress found in the standard [i.e., SPE] description, too impoverished because it does not represent the patterns of recurrent

[7] I am indebted to Butt and King (1998) for the idea of presenting syntax-prosody mismatches in this format. The notion and terminology of *flattening* is identical to theirs, but I have not adopted the patterns of *heightening* and *regrouping*, which they employ in an analysis of Bengali. It is probably premature to attempt to identify a set of language-universal constraints on syntax-prosody mappings.

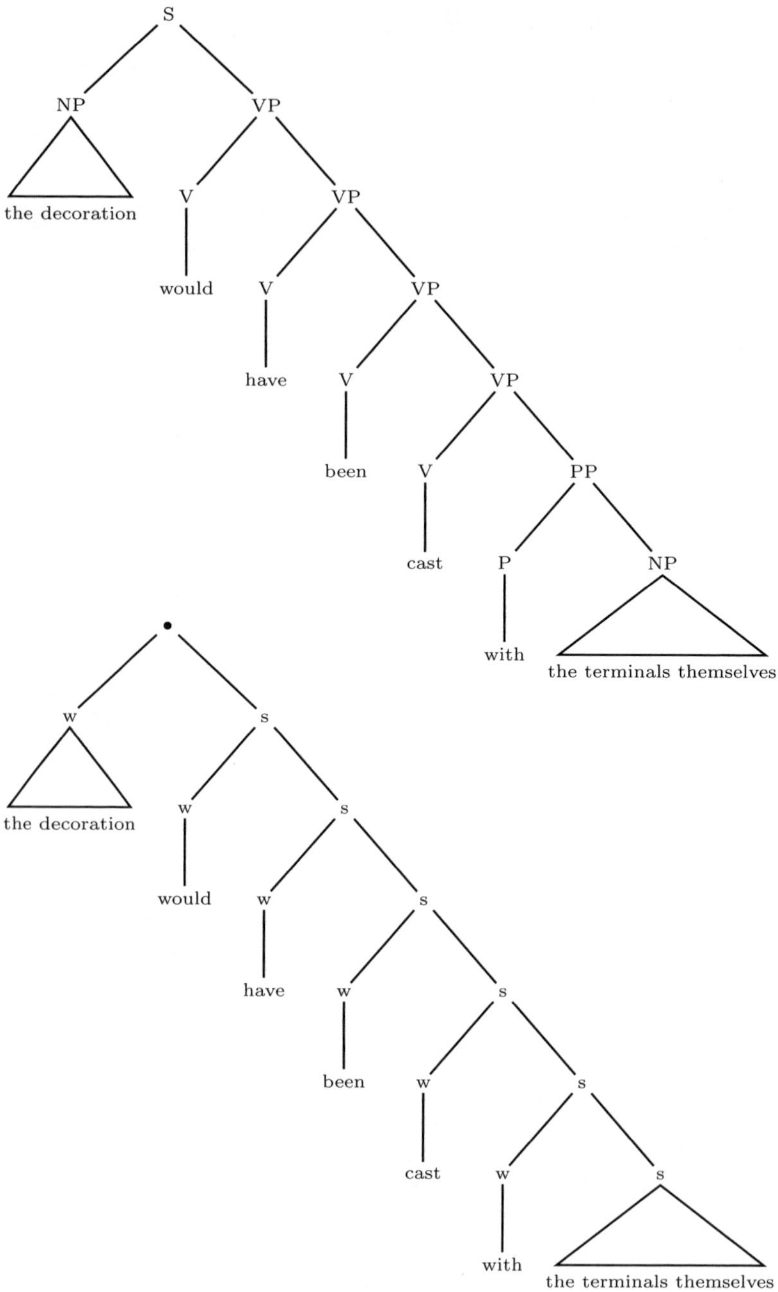

FIGURE 2 Syntactic and Prosodic Structure of Nested Auxiliaries

alternating prominence within the sentence.

There are two considerations which allow us to replace Fig. 2 with a more empirically sound analysis. First, as we saw above, unstressed auxiliaries such as *have* and *been* come into the category of prosodic leaners, and combine with their host to form a function-word group.

Second, n-ary metrical trees provide an appropriately flat structure for the attachment of modals with their complements. This is illustrated in (10.9).

(10.9)

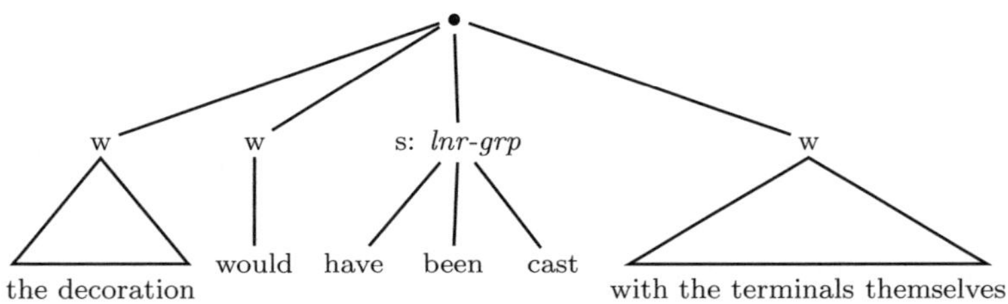

It should be noted, in passing, that although patterns such as (10.9) are quite common, modal verbs often receive prominence by virtue of their informational status, as indicated in the next example, where *may* receives narrow focus.

(10.10) The function of this unique object is unclear, but it MAY have been designed to fasten a turban.

Prosodic Promotion

The next type of mismatch is similar, and occurs when the complement or postmodifier of a syntactic head is 'promoted' to the level of sister of the constituent in which the head occurs; this creates a disjuncture between the lexical head and whatever follows. The pattern is schematized in Fig. 3, where ϕ_{Spec} represents the prosodic contribution of Spec, and similarly for ϕ_{X}.

(10.11) gives a typical example of this phenomenon, where the noun *possession* is followed by a prepositional complement, while (10.12) represents the attested prosodic constituency.

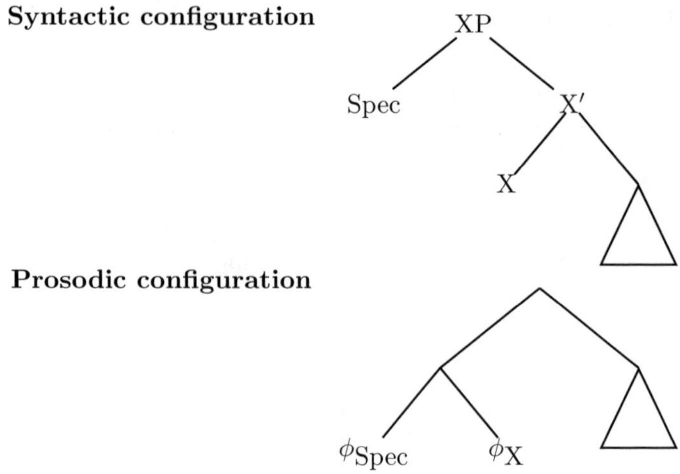

FIGURE 3 Prosodic Promotion of Posthead Material

(10.11)

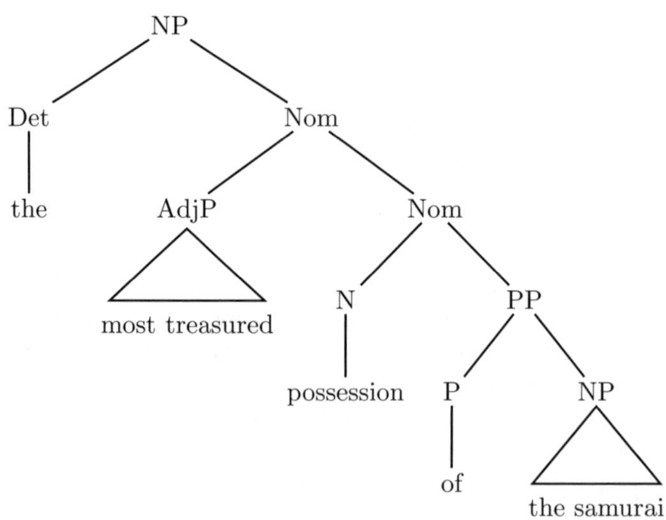

(10.12)

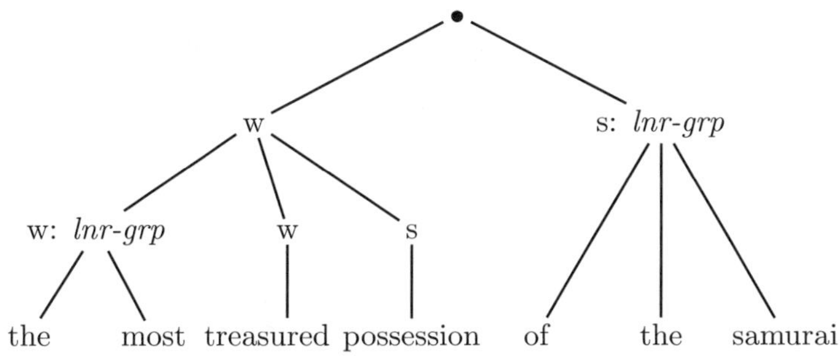

Note that this is not simply another example of Prosodic Flattening, since *of the samurai* belongs to a different prosodic constituent than the one which immediately dominates *the most treasured possession.*

Other noun phrases from the corpus exhibit a similar prosodic structure:

(10.13) [an extraordinary range of accessories][which people have used to decorate themselves]

(10.14) [an explosion][of new materials for art construction and design]

(10.15) [one of a set of vessels of different shapes][for use in a ceremonial banquet]

(10.16) [gilded with a thin layer of gold leaf][applied to the heated bronze surface]

It should be emphasised that the possibility of introducting a prosodic break between a head and its complement or postmodifier does *not* mean that a break will always occur at such a position. This is clearly illustrated in the data above; for example, in (10.14), there could have been a disjuncture immediately after *vessels.*

The grammar only places boundary conditions on which strings are well-formed prosodic consituents (relative to a given rhetorical purpose or information packaging). But performance factors, especially those involving formality and speech rate, will determine where prosodic breaks *actually occur* in a given utterance. There is also an oft-noted tendency for the prosodic constituents in an utterance to be of roughly equal length; I am also regarding this as a performance issue.[8]

Finally, we consider an example similar to the one cited at the beginning of this paper, which falls into a class of cases involving leaner

[8] A relatively simple performance model of this behaviour consists in terminating an IP as soon as possible (i.e., as allowed by grammatical constraints) once the number of syllables already uttered in that IP has reached a certain (parametric) threshold. For some discussion of such algorithms, see Gee and Grosjean 1983; Bachenko and Fitzpatrick 1990; Atterer 2000.

groups. That is, the unaccented pronoun *he* forms a tight unit with the following verb, cutting across the syntactic boundary between subject and verb phrase. This is illustrated below.

(10.17)

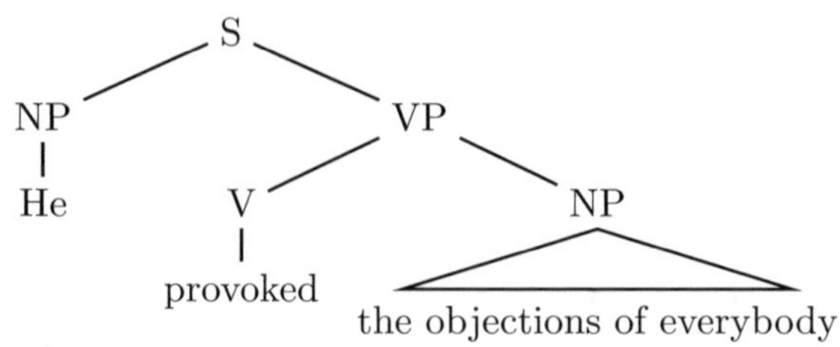

(10.18)

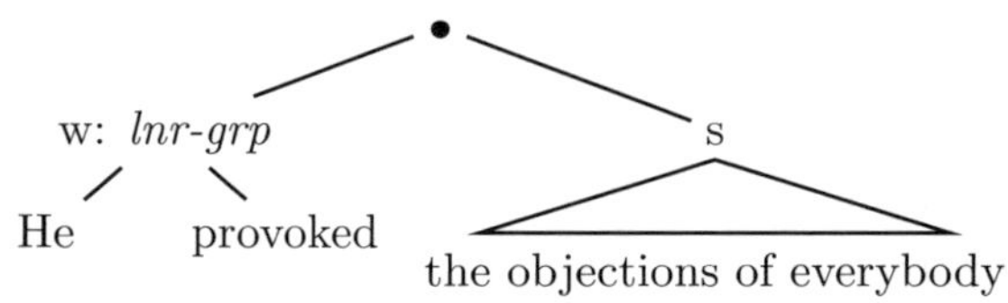

10.4 An HPSG Analysis

10.4.1 Unstructured Phonology

Before examining how to build prosodic structures, it will be useful to look at the standard HPSG approach to phonology. However, I will follow recent steps (Sag, 1999; Donohue and Sag, 1999) which reinstate the distinction between 'categories' and 'rules', now construed as *signs* versus *constructions*.

Signs retain the usual attributes PHON and SYNSEM, but no longer have attributes for daughters. Instead, phrase structure configurations are defined in constructions, a distinct type of feature structure belonging to a distinct hierarchy (see also Sag, 1997). For example, a headed construction, *hd-cx*, will have attributes MOTHER, HD-DTR and NON-HD-DTRS. Phonology values are taken to be lists, where the PHON value of the mother of a construction is built from the list concatenation of the PHON values of its daughters. If we assume that the order of the mother's PHON simply corresponds to the order resulting from prepending the head-daughter to the list of non-head daughters, we arrive at the following constraint:

$$(10.19)\quad hd\text{-}cx \rightarrow \begin{bmatrix} \text{MOTHER} & \begin{bmatrix}\text{PHON} & \phi_0 \oplus \ldots \oplus \phi_n\end{bmatrix} \\ \text{HD-DTR} & \begin{bmatrix}\text{PHON} & \phi_0\end{bmatrix} \\ \text{NON-HD-DTRS} & \left\langle \begin{bmatrix}\text{PHON} & \phi_1\end{bmatrix}, \ldots \begin{bmatrix}\text{PHON} & \phi_n\end{bmatrix} \right\rangle \end{bmatrix}$$

Here, $\oplus$ denotes the standard append operation on lists. The workings of (10.19) are illustrated in Fig. 4.

The PHON value of the VP mother in Fig. 4 is arrived at by virtue of the following identity:

$$(10.20)\quad \langle \textit{fasten} \rangle \oplus \langle \textit{a, cloak} \rangle \oplus \langle \textit{at, the, collar} \rangle = \langle \textit{fasten, a, cloak, at, the, collar} \rangle$$

Note in particular that there is no internal structure here; phonology is taken to be a flat list.

When I come to discuss prosodic constraints in more detail later on, it turns out to be more convenient to abstract away from the conventional division of daughters into a head and a list of non-heads. Instead, I shall use an equivalent notation, shown in (10.21).

$$(10.21)\quad \begin{bmatrix} \text{MOTHER} & \begin{bmatrix}\text{PHON} & \phi_0 \oplus \ldots \oplus \phi_n\end{bmatrix} \\ \text{HD-DTR} & \boxed{0} \\ \text{DTRS} & \left\langle \boxed{0}\begin{bmatrix}\text{PHON} & \phi_0\end{bmatrix}, \begin{bmatrix}\text{PHON} & \phi_1\end{bmatrix}, \ldots \begin{bmatrix}\text{PHON} & \phi_n\end{bmatrix} \right\rangle \end{bmatrix}$$

That is, the value of the attribute DTRS is equal to the concatenation of the values of HD-DTR and NON-HD-DTRS.

In the remainder of this section, I will examine ways of modifying the phonology attribute of signs so that prosodic structure can be handled. The task can be broken into three subtasks:

(i) *representing* prosodic structure in a feature structure;
(ii) defining a prosodic *relation* between phononology values and metrical trees; and
(iii) incorporating the relation into *prosodic constraints* within a constructional hierarchy.

Subtask (i) is concerned with elaborating the value of the PHON attribute in constructions such as Fig. 4. In particular, it requires a choice of representation for metrical trees. Subtask (ii) addresses the ways in which the PHON values of daughters in such a construction can combine to form a PHON value for the mother. Subtask (iii) has two aspects: defining prosodic constraints in terms of the relation provided by (ii); and

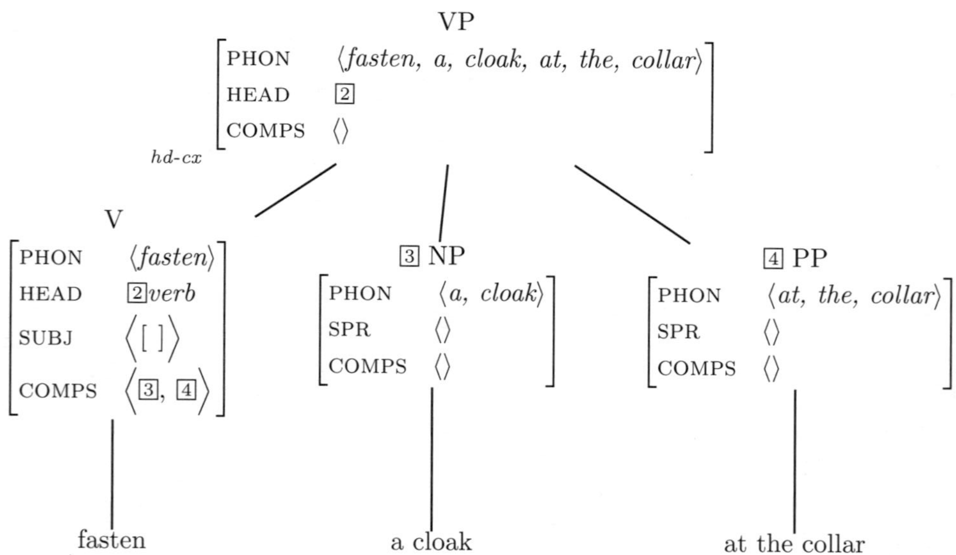

FIGURE 4 Deriving unstructured phonology

showing how prosodic constraints interact with syntactic constructions.

As I mentioned at the outset, the goal of the analysis is to induce prosodic structures in parallel with syntactic phrases. The induction is driven, as might be expected, by HPSG's rules for combining heads with complements, modifiers and specifiers. In this respect, my approach will be analogous to that of Steedman (1991), who builds intonational representations in parallel with combinatory categories for strings; and differs from many approaches (primarily in the transformational grammar paradigm) (Butt and King, 1998; Nespor and Vogel, 1986; Selkirk, 1984, 1986) which map from complete surface structure trees into prosodic representations. I also depart in this respect from Taglicht (1998), who despite using an HPSG framework, does not provide an inductive construction of prosodic constraints.

10.4.2 Representing Prosodic Structure

It is easy to devise ways of encoding metrical trees in a constraint-based grammar framework; unfortunately, it is not so easy to come up with reasons for preferring one over another. The approach I shall propose here is correspondingly tentative, and is perhaps best regarded as a representative of a class of encodings.

Working outside-in from signs, we have the following appropriateness conditions for signs:

$$(10.22) \quad \textit{sign} \rightarrow \begin{bmatrix} \text{PHON} & \textit{pros} \\ \text{SYNSEM} & \textit{synsem} \end{bmatrix}$$

Informally, the type *pros* will have two subtypes: word-forms (the default phonology value for words) and metrical trees. For present purposes, I am not going to decompose words into smaller prosodic elements such as syllables. However, it will be useful to draw a further distinction within the class of word-forms, namely between full lexical items (of type *p-wrd*) and weak function words (of type *lnr*).

Let us turn now to metrical trees. The minimum requirements are that we have, first, a way of representing nested prosodic domains, and second, a way of marking the most prominent element in a given domain. Consequently we postulate a parametrised type $mtr(\tau)$ of metrical tree which introduces two features: DOM (prosodic domain), whose value is a list $list(\tau)$ of prosodic elements, and DTE, whose value is a prosodic element of type *full*. We impose the condition that τ's value is one of the subtypes that are *covered* by *pros*, notated $\tau \lessdot$ *pros*, i.e., that it is a subtype s of *pros*, and there is no x such that $s < x <$ *pros*. As we will see shortly, this limits possible values of τ to *lnr* and *full*.

(10.23) $$mtr(\tau \lessdot pros) \rightarrow \begin{bmatrix} \textsc{dom} & list(\tau) \bigcirc \langle \boxed{1} \rangle \\ \textsc{dte} & \boxed{1}\ full \end{bmatrix}$$

Three points of clarification about (10.23) should be made. First, the parameter $\tau \lessdot$ *pros* in (10.23) is intended to act as a bound variable, in the sense that any instantiation of τ by a subtype in *mtr*($\tau \lessdot$ *pros*) is paralled by the same instantion in *list*(τ). Second, $\bigcirc$ is the domain union relation of Reape (1994); Kathol (1995); that is, the DOM value is a list of *pros* values with an object of type *full* intercalated somewhere within. By default, I will take the DTE to be the final element of the list, but the above constraint does not restrict the location of the DTE. Third, items of type *full* in the DOM value of a *mtr(full)* can be word-forms or metrical trees. This means that the DOM value in a *mtr* can, in principle, be a list whose elements range from simple *p-wrds* to metrical trees of any depth. One way of interpreting this is to say that DOM values fail to obey the Strict Layer Hypothesis (briefly discussed in Section 10.2.1).

To illustrate the feature encoding of metrical trees, the phonology value of sign which corresponded to the metrical tree (10.24) (where the word *this* receives narrow focus) would look like (10.25).

(10.24)

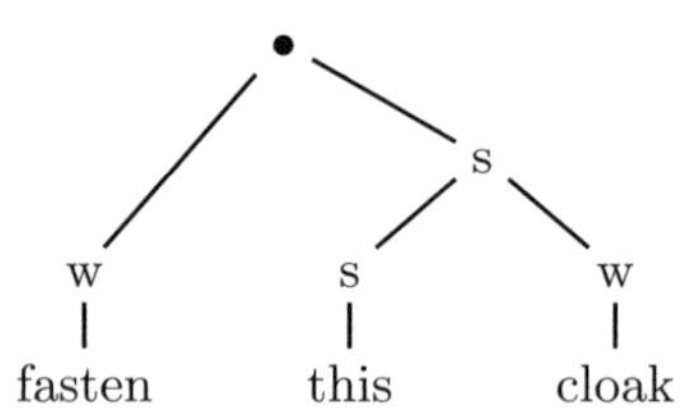

(10.25) $$\begin{bmatrix} sign & \\ \textsc{phon} & \begin{bmatrix} full\text{-}mtr & \\ \textsc{dom} & \left\langle fasten,\ \boxed{1} \begin{bmatrix} full\text{-}mtr & \\ \textsc{dom} & \left\langle \boxed{2} this,\ cloak \right\rangle \\ \textsc{dte} & \boxed{2} \end{bmatrix} \right\rangle \\ \textsc{dte} & \boxed{1} \end{bmatrix} \end{bmatrix}$$

Let us now consider those prosodic groupings where one or more weak monosyllabic function words attach to a stress-bearing host. As hinted above, I will treat these as a subtype *mtr(lnr)* of *mtr*(τ), and hence the DOM value will be of type *list(lnr)*. However, the prosodic host in *mtr(lnr)* will always be of type *p-wrd*, and since it will be the most prominent element in the metrical tree, it will also be the value of DTE. This is imposed by the following type constraint.

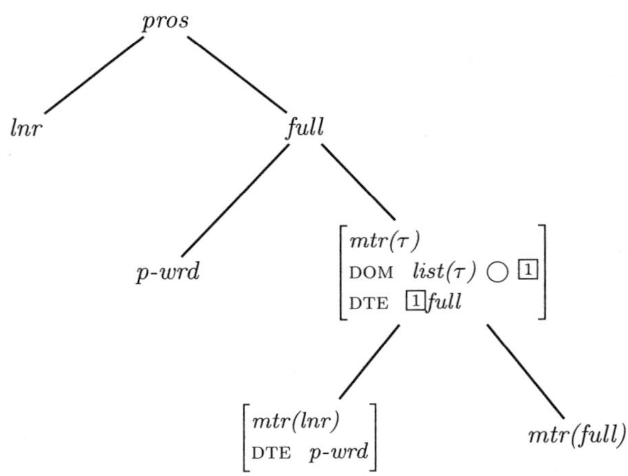

FIGURE 5 Hierarchy of Prosodic Types

$$\text{(10.26)}\quad \textit{mtr(lnr)} \rightarrow \begin{bmatrix}\text{DTE} & \boxed{1}\textit{p-wrd}\end{bmatrix}$$

By inheritance, then, a *mtr(lnr)* has the following characteristics.

$$\text{(10.27)}\quad \begin{bmatrix}\textit{mtr(lnr)} & \\ \text{DOM} & \textit{list(lnr)} \bigcirc \langle\boxed{1}\rangle \\ \text{DTE} & \boxed{1}\ \textit{p-wrd}\end{bmatrix}$$

As we observed earlier, *p-wrd*s and metrical trees pattern together in being possible daughters within a *mtr(full)*, and consequently they are grouped together as subtypes of *full*. This leads us to the hierarchy of prosodic types shown in Fig. 5.

10.4.3 The mkMtr Relation

Now that we have defined some prosodic structures, it is time to consider ways in which such structures are built. As pointed out in Section 10.4.1 above, the prosodic operations will be incorporated into prosodic constructions, which themselves will have to dovetail with syntactic constructions such as the *head-comp-cx* and *head-spr-cx*.

I shall introduce one basic relation for building metrical trees, called mkMtr. This combines a list of prosodic elements (word-forms or metrical trees) into a metrical tree whose right branch is strong. The relation mkMtr is polymorphic in that it applies to a list of objects of any of the subtypes of *pros*.[9] For example, the nodes of the resulting tree could be labelled by elements of type *p-wrd*, or they could be the roots of metrical

[9]This is termed *inclusion polymorphism* by Cardelli and Wegner (1985).

subtrees. Moreover, the relation is parametrised with a type variable, as we saw earlier for the type *mtr(τ⋖ pros)*. To reduce notational clutter, I shall usually write mkMtr^{τ} in place of $\mathsf{mkMtr}^{\tau \lessdot pros}$, and I shall omit angle brackets around its argument list wherever there is no risk of confusion.

Definition 2 $\mathsf{mkMtr}^{\tau \lessdot pros}$: *list(pros)* $\mapsto$ *mtr(τ)*

(M1) $\mathsf{mkMtr}^{\tau}(\boxed{1}pros) = \boxed{1}$

(M2) $$\mathsf{mkMtr}^{\tau}(\boxed{1}, \boxed{2}, \ldots, \boxed{n}) = \begin{bmatrix} mtr(\tau) & \\ \text{DOM} & \langle \boxed{1}, \boxed{2}, \ldots \boxed{n} \rangle \\ \text{DTE} & \boxed{n} \end{bmatrix}$$

(M1) accounts for the case where mkMtr^{τ} has only one prosodic element in its argument list; since a metrical tree must contain at least two daughters, mkMtr^{τ} returns its input element. If there are at least two elements in the argument list, (M2) builds a metrical tree in the standard way. The fact that mkMtr^{τ} assigns rightmost prominence is intended as a default rule of English prosody. The assignment of prominence as a result of narrow focus would override this default. (10.28) illustrates (M2); mkMtr^{full} builds a constituent of type *mtr(full)*, while mkMtr^{lnr} builds one of type *mtr(lnr)*.

(10.28) a. $$\mathsf{mkMtr}^{full}(different,\ shapes) = \begin{bmatrix} mtr(full) & \\ \text{DOM} & \left\langle different,\ \boxed{2}shapes \right\rangle \\ \text{DTE} & \boxed{2} \end{bmatrix}$$

b. $$\mathsf{mkMtr}^{full}\left(Mary, \begin{bmatrix} mtr(full) & \\ \text{DOM} & \left\langle prefers,\ \boxed{1}corduroy \right\rangle \\ \text{DTE} & \boxed{1} \end{bmatrix}\right) =$$

$$\begin{bmatrix} mtr(full) & \\ \text{DOM} & \left\langle Mary,\ \boxed{2}\begin{bmatrix} mtr(full) & \\ \text{DOM} & \left\langle prefers,\ \boxed{1}corduroy \right\rangle \\ \text{DTE} & \boxed{1} \end{bmatrix} \right\rangle \\ \text{DTE} & \boxed{2} \end{bmatrix}$$

c. $$\mathsf{mkMtr}^{lnr}(a,\ cloak) = \begin{bmatrix} mtr(lnr) & \\ \text{DOM} & \left\langle a,\ \boxed{2}cloak \right\rangle \\ \text{DTE} & \boxed{2} \end{bmatrix}$$

It will be useful to have a more succinct notation for prosodic constituents than that illustrated in (10.28). I will use square brackets to indicate constituents of type *mtr(full)* and parentheses for constituents of type *mtr(lnr)*. Thus, the right-hand sides of the equations in (10.28) will have the following abbreviated counterparts.

(10.29) a. [*differentshapes*]
b. [*Mary* [*prefers corduroy*]]
c. (*a cloak*)

As we will see later on, there are cases where the potential input to $\mathsf{mkMtr}^{\mathcal{T}}$ cannot be exhaustively and exclusively interpreted as being either of type *mtr(full)* or of *mtr(lnr)*. An example is shown in (10.30).

(10.30) shŏuld hăve béen thóroughly révised

Given the type constraint declared in (10.27), the whole string cannot be treated as a *mtr(lnr)* (i.e., as in (10.31a)), because it contains more than one element of type *p-wrd*; given (10.23), it cannot be treated as *mtr(full)* (i.e., as in (10.31b)), since it contains elements which are not of type *full*. However, (10.31c) *is* a legitimate prosodic analysis of the string.

(10.31) a. *(shŏuld hăve béen thóroughly révised)
b. *[shŏuld hăve béen thóroughly révised]
c. [(shŏuld hăve béen) thóroughly révised]

Procedurally, we can think of the problem as trying to find the longest prefix of the input string which can be analysed as a *mtr(lnr)*, and then taking the resulting subtree together with the remaining elements of the string as the components of a *mtr(full)*. This approach is incorporated in the following definition, which depends on non-deterministically decomposing a list of prosodic elements into inputs for mkMtr^{lnr} and mkMtr^{full}.

Definition 3 mkMtr: *list(pros)* $\mapsto$ *mtr(pros)*

$$\mathsf{mkMtr}(\boxed{1} \oplus \boxed{2}) = \mathsf{mkMtr}^{full}(\mathsf{mkMtr}^{lnr}(\boxed{1}) \oplus \boxed{2})$$

The definition is illustrated in the next example.

(10.32) mkMtr(⟨should, have, been⟩ ⊕ ⟨thoroughly, revised⟩) =

$\mathsf{mkMtr}^{full}(\mathsf{mkMtr}^{lnr}$(should, have, been), thoroughly, revised) =

[(should have been) thoroughly revised]

To round off this section, I want to consider the problem posed by the following two analyses, where an unaccented preposition combines with a complement NP.

(10.33) a.

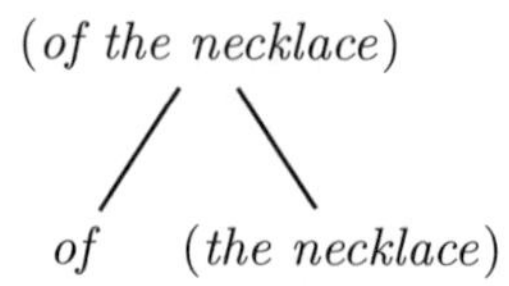

b.

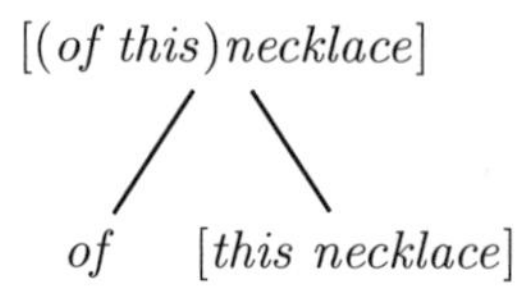

In (10.33a), the complement's PHON value is of type *mtr(lnr)*, as is that of the mother. By contrast, in (10.33a) the complement's PHON value is of type *mtr(full)*, and the leaner combines with the first *p-wrd* of this *mtr(full)* to form a subtree of type *mtr(lnr)*. So far, nothing licenses the combination of a leaner and metrical tree, and consequently the definition of mkMtr^{lnr} needs to be augmented with a further clause.

Definition 4

$$\mathsf{mkMtr}^{lnr}(\boxed{1}\ lnr, \begin{bmatrix}\text{DOM} & \boxed{2}\end{bmatrix}) = \mathsf{mkMtr}(\langle\boxed{1}\rangle \oplus \boxed{2})$$

Informally, this clause says that when a leaner is adjacent to a metrical tree, the mkMtr relation is invoked on the leaner and the daughters of that metrical tree. More informally still, this can be thought of as 'erasing the brackets' around the leaner's complement's prosody. There is a presupposition built into the definition that the metrical tree representing the complement's prosody is of depth one; so far, I have not come up with examples where this restriction is violated.

To summarise, $\mathsf{mkMtr}^{\mathcal{T}}$ is the basic (parametrised) relation, building a metrical tree and assigning a DTE. mkMtr acts as a kind of wrapper for $\mathsf{mkMtr}^{\mathcal{T}}$, and allows any leaners at the beginning of a sequence of words to be assembled into a *mtr(lnr)*. If there are no leaners, then mkMtr reduces to mkMtr^{full}; if there is no prosodic elements beyond what is required to build a *mtr(lnr)*, then mkMtr reduces to mkMtr^{lnr}. Finally, as we have just seen, mkMtr^{lnr} requires an extra clause which allows leaners to associate directly with the daughter nodes of a following metrical tree.

10.4.4 Prosodic Constraints

In this section, I will concentrate on the prosody of headed constructions. The crucial factor here seems to be not the dependency status of the non-head daughters—that is, whether they are complements, modifiers or specifiers—but whether they follow or precede the head.

Following Sag (1997); Koenig (1999), I adopt a cross-classification of constructions in which the dimensions of clausality and headedness are augmented by the dimension of prosody. Tentatively, I propose that the types of prosodic constructions enter into the multiple inheritance hierarchy shown in Fig. 6. There are only two prosodic constraints

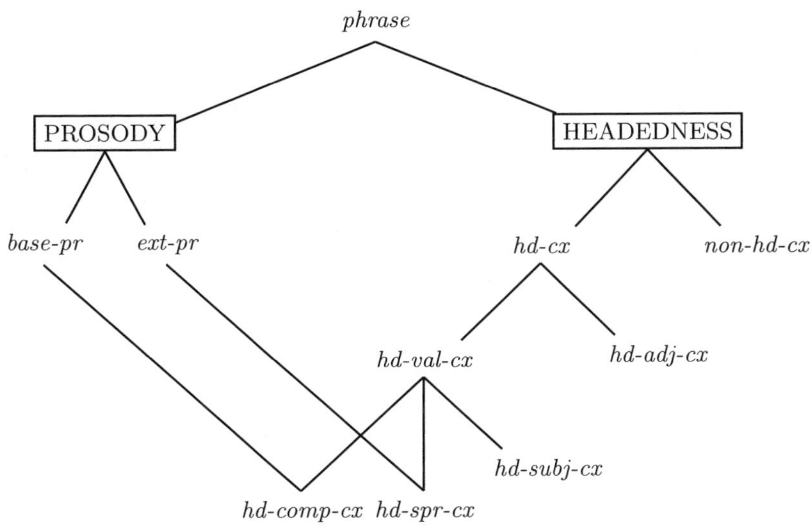

FIGURE 6 Prosody and Headedness

proposed here: *base-pr* (basic prosody) and *ext-pr* (extending prosody). Constructions of type *hd-comp-cx* only inherit from the former, while those of type *hd-spr-cx* only inherit from the latter. *hd-subj-cx* is allowed to inherit from both. The absence of additional information about head-adjunct phrases and non-headed phrases in Fig. 6 reflects the fact that I have not been able to give them sufficient consideration as yet.

Head-Initial Constructions

To begin with, we consider the combination of a head with daughters that follow it. I am following the standard assumption, made in HPSG and other frameworks, that heads combine first with their complements, and only subsequently with specifiers. I am also going to assume (Miller,

1992; Bouma et al., 2001) that posthead modifiers appear on the dependents list of lexical heads, together with complements and specifiers. By and large, the prosody of head-complement contructions obeys the Prosodic Isomorphism Hypothesis.

The type constraint *base-pr* (basic prosody) in (10.34) straightforwardly uses mkMtr to relate the daughters' PHON values to that of the mother.

(10.34) *base-pr* →

$$\begin{bmatrix} \text{MOTHER} \mid \text{PHON} & \mathsf{mkMtr}(\boxed{1}, \ldots, \boxed{n}) \\ \text{DTRS} & \left\langle \begin{bmatrix} \text{PHON} & \boxed{1} \end{bmatrix}, \ldots, \begin{bmatrix} \text{PHON} & \boxed{n} \end{bmatrix} \right\rangle \end{bmatrix}$$

An example of the phonology constructed by this constraint is illustrated in (10.35), which should be compared with the mother node in Fig. 4. Unlike the latter, the revised approach preserves the prosodic structure of the daughter nodes.[10] Note that I use (*a cloak*) to abbreviate the AVM representation of the metrical tree for *a cloak*, and similarly for (*at the collar*).

(10.35)

$$\begin{bmatrix} \textit{hd-comp-cx} \wedge \textit{base-pr} & \\ \text{MTHR} \mid \text{PHON} & \begin{bmatrix} \textit{mtr(full)} & \\ \text{DOM} & \left\langle \boxed{1}\textit{fasten}, \boxed{2}(\textit{a cloak}), \boxed{3}(\textit{at the collar}) \right\rangle \\ \text{DTE} & \boxed{3} \end{bmatrix} \\ \text{DTRS} & \left\langle \boxed{0}\begin{bmatrix} \text{PHON} & \boxed{1} \end{bmatrix}, \begin{bmatrix} \text{PHON} & \boxed{2} \end{bmatrix}, \begin{bmatrix} \text{PHON} & \boxed{3} \end{bmatrix} \right\rangle \\ \text{HEAD-DTR} & \boxed{0} \end{bmatrix}$$

The second instance of *base-pr* illustrates a nominal head combining with its complement.

(10.36)

$$\begin{bmatrix} \textit{mtr(full)} & \\ \text{DOM} & \left\langle \textit{possession}, \boxed{1}[\textit{of the samurai}] \right\rangle \\ \text{DTE} & \boxed{1} \end{bmatrix}$$

What happens when a lexical head combines with a weak pronominal object, as in (10.37)?

(10.37)
a. fasten ĭt
b. fasten ĭt at the collar
c. gave hĭm ĭt

---

[10]See Asudeh and Mikkelsen (2000) for a segment-based approach to achieving this result.

Since unaccented *it* is of type *lnr*, it cannot participate in a *mtr(full)*, since this requires all its daughters to be of type *full*. However, the definition of mkMtr provided earlier deals successfully with such cases, yielding the following structures.

(10.38) a. (fasten it)
b. [(fasten it) (at the collar)]
c. (gave him it)

Recall that mkMtr can only assemble a *mtr(lnr)* if the required constituents are initial in the input list. Consequently, when (10.34) and *hd-comp-cx* are combines, they require any leaner non-head daughters to be adjacent to the head. Where this restriction is not met, as in (10.39), no prosodic structure will be assigned.[11]

(10.39) *We told Kim ĭt.

Head-Final Constructions

I shall take *head-spr-cx* as representative of head-final constructions. One of the phenomena to be captured is illustrated in the following trees.

(10.40) a. [*this treasured possession*]

this [*treasured possession*]

b. [*this possession*(*of the samurai*)]

this [*possession* (*of the samurai*)]

The generalisation seems to be that the specifier 'extends' an existing metrical tree by adding a new prosodic element to the beginning. However, it would also be desirable to capture the structure that was dubbed *prosodic promotion* in Section 10.3. This can be viewed as the result of grouping a prehead element with the head, as in (10.41).

(10.41) [[*this possession*](*of the samurai*)]

this [*possession* (*of the samurai*)]

[11] For more discussion of this constraint, see Zwicky 1986.

In order to accommodate both of these patterns, I propose a minor generalisation of mkMtr, called $\mathsf{mkMtr}^{\mathrm{LA}}$, which allows a *p-wrd* as well as a leaner to left-associate with a following prosodic element.

Definition 5 $\mathsf{mkMtr}^{\mathrm{LA}}$: *list(pros)* $\mapsto$ *mtr(pros)*

$$\mathsf{mkMtr}^{\mathrm{LA}}(\boxed{1} \oplus \boxed{2}) = \mathsf{mkMtr}^{full}(\mathsf{mkMtr}^{\mathcal{T}}(\boxed{1}) \oplus \boxed{2})$$

$\mathsf{mkMtr}^{\mathrm{LA}}$ is now invoked by *ext-pr* (extend prosody), the main prosodic constraint to govern head-final constructions:

(10.42) *ext-pr* $\rightarrow$

$$\begin{bmatrix} \text{MOTHER} \mid \text{PHON} & \begin{bmatrix} \mathit{mtr(pros)} \\ \text{DOM} & \langle \mathsf{mkMtr}^{\mathrm{LA}}(\langle\boxed{1}\rangle \oplus \boxed{2}) \rangle \\ \text{DTE} & \boxed{3} \end{bmatrix} \\ \text{DTRS} & \left\langle \begin{bmatrix} \text{PHON} & \boxed{1} \end{bmatrix}, \begin{bmatrix} \text{PHON} & \begin{bmatrix} \text{DOM} & \boxed{2} \\ \text{DTE} & \boxed{3} \end{bmatrix} \end{bmatrix} \right\rangle \end{bmatrix}$$

It will be helpful to look at a promotion analysis in more detail. (10.43) illustrates the schematic tree structure, while (10.44) spells out how the mother node's prosodic constituency is computed.

(10.43)

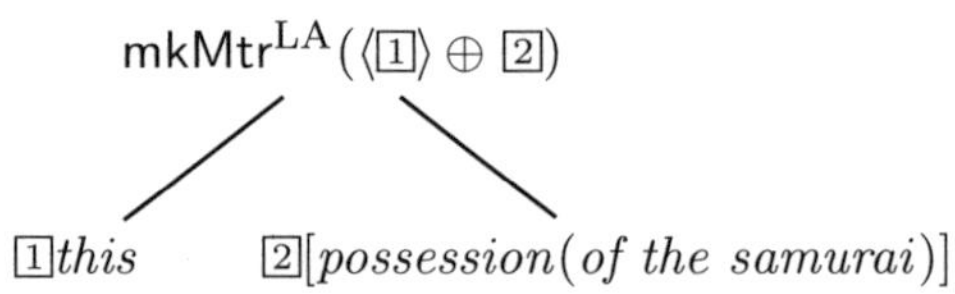

(10.44) $\mathsf{mkMtr}^{\mathrm{LA}}$(*this*, *possession*, (*of the samurai*)) =

mkMtr^{full}(mkMtr^{full}(*this*, *possession*) (*of the samurai*)) =

[[*this*, *possession*] (*of the samurai*)]

Since the definition of $\mathsf{mkMtr}^{\mathrm{LA}}$ has mkMtr as a special instance, left-association of weak determiners follows straightforwardly:

(10.45) a.

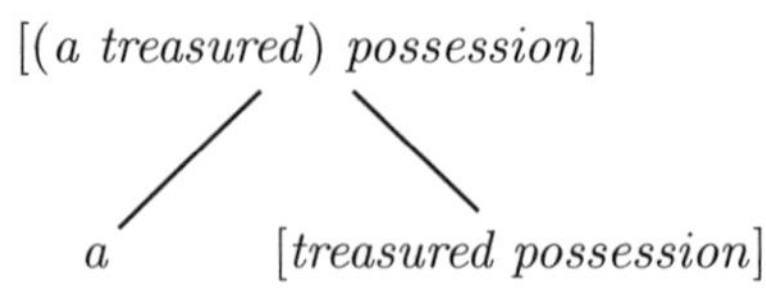

b. [(*the possession*)(*of the samurai*)]

the [*possession* (*of the samurai*)]

Unfortunately, $\mathsf{mkMtr}^{\mathrm{LA}}$ overgenerates, allowing structures such as that shown in (10.46).

(10.46) [[*this treasured*] *possession* (*of the samurai*)]

this [*treasured possession* (*of the samurai*)]

Rather than trying to remedy this directly, I suggest that there is a constraint on headed constructions which forbids metrical trees in which a lexical head is immediately preceded by a subtree of type *mtr(full)*. In order to state the constraint, I will assume that phrases like *treasured possession* are of type *hd-pre-adj-ph*, i.e., a phrase which results from modification by a pre-head adjunct.

(10.47) Lexical Head Association Constraint:

$$hd\text{-}cx \rightarrow \neg \begin{bmatrix} \text{MOTHER} \mid \text{PHON} \mid \text{DOM} & \left\langle \begin{bmatrix} mtr(full) \\ \text{DOM} \quad ne\_list \oplus \boxed{1} \end{bmatrix} \right\rangle \oplus \boxed{2} \\ \text{HD-DTR} & \begin{bmatrix} hd\text{-}pre\text{-}adj\text{-}ph \\ \text{PHON} \mid \text{DOM}\ \boxed{1} \oplus \boxed{2}\ ne\_list \end{bmatrix} \end{bmatrix}$$

Informally, (10.47) prohibits headed constructions from building a PHON value for the mother where (i) the head daughter has undergone pre-head modification, and (ii) a proper subpart (i.e., $\boxed{1}$) of the head's prosodic structure is left-associated with some material which precedes the head and its modifiers. In other words, if some element left-associates with material preceding a head, then it must include the head itself in the grouping. This constraint can be seen as a partial implementation of Selkirk's 1986; 1996 notion of end-based mappings between syntax and phonology.

I will now turn briefly to two kinds of construction which are related to what has gone before, but merit special attention: subject-VP constructions and auxiliary-VP constructions.

Subjects As one might expect, subjects can pattern prosodically like specifiers. This is illustrated in (10.48). The first two examples parallel (10.40a) in extending their head's metrical tree.

(10.48) *hd-subj-cx* ∧ *ext-pr*

a. [[*this piece*] *works equally well*]

[*this piece*] [*works equally well*]

b. [*Mary prefers corduroy*]

Mary [*prefers corduroy*]

The next two are cases of left-association; (10.48a) supplies one of the prosodic bracketings for the example (10.28b), discussed by (Selkirk, 1984, p290–291) and Steedman (1991).

(10.49) *hd-subj-cx* ∧ *ext-pr*

a. [*Mary prefers*] *corduroy*]

Mary [*prefers corduroy*]

b. [(*he found it*) [*behind the shed*]]

he [(*found it*) [*behind the shed*]

(10.48b) (which is also accommodated by *base-pr*), represents an interesting departure from the tendency noted by Gee and Grosjean (1983); Bachenko and Fitzpatrick (1990) for verbs to group either with clausal material either to the left or the right.

Notice that the Lexical Head Association Constraint will prevent a subject from left-associating with a pre-head adverbial modifier.

(10.50) *[[Mary usually] prefers corduroy]

As well as acting prosodically like specifiers, subjects can also combine with VPs according to the pattern which was identified for head-initial constructions. In this case, a new metrical tree is constructed, with the subject's and VP's prosodies embedded as subtrees.

(10.51) *hd-subj-cx* ∧ *base-pr*:

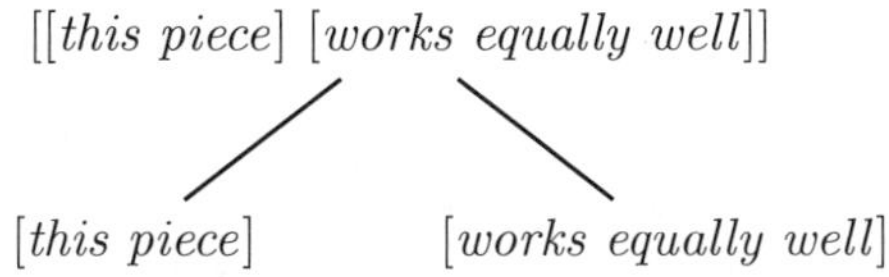

These two possibilities are allowed by the cross-classification of constraints presented earlier in Fig. 6.

Auxiliaries The cross-classification framework allows us to deal with an interesting case which departs from the general correlation between prosodic structure and head-position, namely *hd-comp-cx* constructions where the head is a auxiliary verb. Unlike the case of VPs headed by lexical verbs, (accented) auxiliaries *extend* the prosody of their complements, rather than building a new metrical tree:

(10.52) *aux-hd-comp-cx* ∧ *ext-pr*:

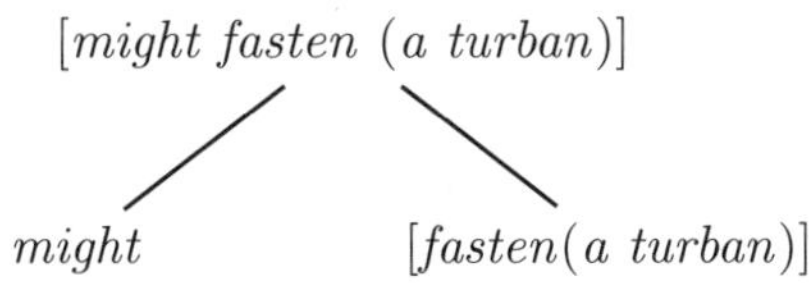

10.5 Conclusion

I hope to have shown that HPSG allows us to express some degree of syntax-prosody mismatch in a succinct and natural manner. The key formal mechanism required is the mkMtr relation, which allows prehead material to combine directly with the phonology of a lexical head, rather than with the phonology of that head's phrasal counterpart. There is little doubt that other frameworks could make appeal to analogous formal mechanisms. Nevertheless, the fact that HPSG adopts a rather conventional approach to phrase structure is highly desirable for my purposes, since it reveals quite clearly just where the tension lies between syntactic and prosodic constituency. Finally, the cross-classification framework of Sag (1997) offers the distinct advantage of allowing prosodic constraints to be defined independently of syntactic constructions, yet related to them by means of multiple inheritance.

Acknowledgements

I am grateful to Paul Taylor for encouraging me to explore this topic. Thanks are also due for helpful discussion and comments from Ash Asudeh, Paola Monachesi, Mike Reape, Ivan Sag and Alice Turk, and from the audiences of HPSG'99, Edinburgh and of

DGfS/Computerlinguistik 99, Saarbrücken.

References

Abney, S. P. 1989. A computational model of human parsing. *Journal of Psycholinguistic Research* 18:129–144.

Abney, S. P. 1991. Parsing by chunks. In R. C. Berwick, S. P. Abney, and C. Tenny, eds., *Principle-Based Parsing: Computation and Psycholinguistics*, vol. 44 of *Studies in Linguistics and Philosophy*. Kluwer.

Asudeh, A. and L. H. Mikkelsen. 2000. Incorporation in Danish: Implications for interfaces. In this volume. CSLI Publications.

Atterer, M. 2000. *Assigning Prosodic Structure for Speech Synthesis via Syntax-Prosody Mapping*. Master's thesis, School of Cognitive Science, Division of Informatics, University of Edinburgh.

Bachenko, J. and E. Fitzpatrick. 1990. A computational grammar of discourse-neutral prosodic phrasing in English. *Computational Linguistics* 16(3):155–170.

Beckman, M. E. 1986. *Stress and Non-Stress Accent*. Dordrecht, Holland: Foris.

Beckman, M. E. and J. B. Pierrehumbert. 1986. Intonational structure in English and Japanese. *Phonology Yearbook* 3:255–310.

Bouma, G., R. Malouf, and I. A. Sag. 2001. Satisfying constraints on extraction and adjunction. *Natural Language and Linguistic Theory* 19:1–65.

Butt, M. and T. H. King. 1998. Interfacing phonology with LFG. In M. Butt and T. H. King, eds., *The Proceedings of the LFG '98 Conference*, CSLI Proceedings On-Line. University of Queensland, Brisbane, Stanford: CSLI Publications.

Cardelli, L. and P. Wegner. 1985. On understanding types, data abstraction, and polymorphism. *Computing Surveys* 17(4):471–522.

Chen, M. Y. 1997. The syntax of Xiamen tone sandhi. *Phonology Yearbook* 4:109–149.

Chomsky, N. and M. Halle. 1968. *The Sound Pattern of English*. New York: Harper and Row.

Corley, S., M. Corley, F. Keller, M. W. Crocker, and S. Trewin. 2000. Finding syntactic structure in unparsed corpora: The Gsearch corpus query system. *Computers and the Humanities* .

Croft, W. 1995. Intonation units and grammatical units. *Linguistics* 33(5):839–882.

Donohue, C. and I. Sag. 1999. Domains in Warlpiri. Paper presented at HPSG'99, Edinburgh, 6–8 August 1999.

Gazdar, G., E. Klein, G. Pullum, and I. Sag. 1985. *Generalized Phrase Structure Grammar*. London: Basil Blackwell.

Gee, J. P. and F. Grosjean. 1983. Performance structures: a psycholinguistic and linguistic appraisal. *Cognitive Psychology* 15:411–458.

Hayes, B. 1989. The prosodic hierarchy in meter. In P. Kiparsky and G. Youmans, eds., *Phonetics and Phonology*, vol. 1, pages 201–260. San Diego: Academic Press.

Hitzeman, J., A. W. Black, P. Taylor, C. Mellish, and J. Oberlander. 1998. On the use of automatically generated discourse-level information in a concept-to-speech synthesis system. In *ICSLP'98*, pages 2763–2768.

Hogg, R. and C. B. McCully. 1987. *Metrical Phonology: A coursebook*. Cambridge: Cambridge University Press.

Kathol, A. 1995. *Linearization-Based German Syntax*. Ph.D. thesis, Ohio State University.

Koenig, J.-P. 1999. *Lexical Relations*. Stanford Monographs in Linguistics. Stanford: CSLI Publications.

Ladd, D. R. 1996. *Intonational Phonology*. Cambridge: Cambridge University Press.

Liberman, M. and A. Prince. 1977. On stress and linguistic rhythm. *Linguistic Inquiry* 8:249–336.

Miller, P. 1992. *Clitics and Constituents in Phrase Structure Grammar*. Outstanding Dissertations in Linguistics. New York: Garland Publishing.

Nespor, M. and I. Vogel. 1986. *Prosodic Phonology*. No. 28 in Studies in Generative Grammar. Dordrecht: Foris Publications.

Pierrehumbert, J. B. and M. E. Beckman. 1988. *Japanese Tone Structure*. No. 15 in Linguistic Inquiry Monographs. Cambridge, MA: The MIT Press.

Reape, M. 1994. Domain union and word order variation in German. In J. Nerbonne, K. Netter, and C. J. Pollard, eds., *German in Head-Driven Phrase Structure Grammar*, no. 46 in CSLI Lecture Notes, pages 151–197. CSLI Publications.

Sag, I. A. 1997. English relative clause constructions. *Journal of Linguistics* 33:431–483.

Sag, I. A. 1999. Deconstructing phrasal construction. Ms., Stanford University.

Selkirk, E. O. 1981. On prosodic structure and its relation to syntactic structure. In T. Fretheim, ed., *Nordic Prosody II: Papers from a Symposium*. Trondheim: Tapir.

Selkirk, E. O. 1984. *Phonology and Syntax: The Relation between Sound and Structure*. Current Studies in Linguistics. Cambridge, Mass.: MIT Press.

Selkirk, E. O. 1986. On derived domains in sentence phonology. *Phonology Yearbook* 3:371–405.

Selkirk, E. O. 1996. The prosodic structure of function words. In J. L. Morgan and K. Demuth, eds., *Signal to Syntax: Bootstrapping from Syntax to Grammar in Early Acquisition*, pages 187–213. Mahwah, NJ: Lawrence Erlbaum Associates.

Selkirk, E. O. and T. Shen. 1990. Prosodic domains in Shanghai Chinese. In S. Inkelas and D. Zec, eds., *The Phonology-Syntax Connection*, pages 313–338. Chicago: CLSI/University of Chicago Press.

Shattuck-Hufnagel, S. and A. E. Turk. 1996. A prosody tutorial for investigators of auditory sentence processing. *Journal of Psycholinguistic Research* 25(2):193–247.

Steedman, M. 1991. Structure and intonation. *Language* 67(2):260–296.

Taglicht, J. 1998. Constraints on intonational phrasing in English. *Journal of Linguistics* 34:181–211.

Zwicky, A. M. 1982. Stranded *to* and phonological phrasing in English. *Linguistics* 20(1/2):3–57.

Zwicky, A. M. 1986. The unaccented pronoun constraint in English. In A. M. Zwicky, ed., *Interfaces*, vol. 32 of *Ohio State University Working Papers in Linguistics*, pages 100–114. Ohio State University Department of Linguistics.

11

A Head-Driven Account of Long-Distance Case Assignment

ROBERT MALOUF

11.1 Introduction

In virtually every syntactic framework, case assignment is considered a local phenomenon. That is, while many languages with so-called 'quirky case' have verbs which assign dative case to their subject, it would be very surprising to find a verb which, say, assigned dative case to its subject's specifier's complement. Roughly speaking, a head assigns case under government. While frameworks may differ wildly in the technical elaboration of notions like 'head', 'assigns case', and 'government', the essential insight remains the same: case assignment is a local relationship between a head and a dependent.

While in, e.g., Government and Binding Theory (Chomsky, 1981), the local nature of case assignment is stipulated, one attraction of the Head-Driven Phrase Structure Grammar treatment of case is that the locality of case assignment can be made to follow as a corollary of more general locality principles. Pollard and Sag (1994) treat case assignment as a matter of lexical selection. That is to say, there is no case assignment operation per se. Instead, case is simply one of the properties of a dependent which a head can subcategorize for. Generalizations about case assignment, like any other subcategorization patterns, can be expressed as constraints on types in the lexical hierarchy. Under this view, the domain of case assignment follows as a consequence of the locality of subcategorization, which in turn follows from geometry of feature structures.

Unfortunately, Pollard and Sag's (1994) original conception of case assignment, while simple and elegant, was not quite general enough to

Grammatical Interfaces in HPSG.
Ronnie Cann, Claire Grover and Philip Miller.

be applied to languages with more complex case systems than English. In particular, since it treated case assignment as a purely lexical matter, it was unable to provide an account of phenomena in which case is associated with a particular structural position rather than a particular lexical head. In order to account for structural case assignment, Pollard (1994) and Heinz and Matiasek (1994) shifted at least some case assignment from individual lexical entries to individual constructions. One side effect of this configurational theory of case assignment was that separating case assignment from lexical subcategorization eliminated the locality predictions of the Pollard and Sag's original analysis. Under the configurational view, case assignment was still local to the combination of a single head with its dependents, but only as a matter of convention. This locality did not follow from any more general principles.

In more recent work, Przepiórkowski (1999a,1999b) has reconciled these two positions, arguing that the appropriate locus of case assignment is a slightly enriched dependents list. Przepiórkowski takes from the configurational approach to case assignment the distinction between lexical and structural cases and the recognition that some information about the structural realization of a dependent is necessary to determine proper case assignment. However, since the domain of case assignment is a single head's dependents list, Przepiórkowski's analysis makes the same locality predictions as Pollard and Sag's purely lexical proposal.

To see how Przepiórkowski's analysis works, let us consider an example. In German, a finite verb like *hilft* '(he/she/it) helps' generally takes a nominative subject, unless the subject is realized as a complement of some higher verb in a raising construction. In this respect, it is like any other finite verb in German. Unlike most finite verbs, however, *hilft* assigns dative case rather than accusative case to its direct object. Therefore, *hilft* would have the following (partial) lexical specification:

(1) $\begin{bmatrix} \text{PHON} & \langle \textit{hilft} \rangle \\ \text{DEPS} & \langle \text{NP}[\textit{str}], \text{NP}[\textit{dat}] \rangle \end{bmatrix}$

This entry selects for the case assigned to the direct object but leaves the case of the subject specified only as *structural,* as the actual case assigned to the subject depends on its structural realization.

To account for the constructional nature of structural case assignment while still preserving the locality of case assignment, Przepiórkowski introduces the feature RAISED into the dependents list, which identifies those dependents which are realized locally and those that are realized non-locally via some kind of raising construction. This introduces just enough structural information into DEPS to allow structural case to be determined by the non-configurational Case Principle, given in (2).[1]

(2) CASE PRINCIPLE (Przepiórkowski, 1999a)

a. $$\begin{bmatrix} \text{HEAD} & \textit{verb} \\ \text{DEPS} & \left\langle \begin{bmatrix} \text{ARG} & \text{NP}[\textit{str}] \\ \text{RAISED} & - \end{bmatrix} \right\rangle \oplus \boxed{1} \end{bmatrix} \rightarrow$$

$$\begin{bmatrix} \text{DEPS} & \langle \text{NP}[\textit{snom}] \rangle \oplus \boxed{1} \end{bmatrix}$$

b. $$\begin{bmatrix} \text{HEAD} & \textit{verb} \\ \text{DEPS} & \boxed{2}\ \textit{nelist} \oplus \left\langle \begin{bmatrix} \text{ARG} & \text{NP}[\textit{str}] \\ \text{RAISED} & - \end{bmatrix} \right\rangle \oplus \boxed{1} \end{bmatrix} \rightarrow$$

$$\begin{bmatrix} \text{DEPS} & \boxed{2}\ \textit{nelist} \oplus \langle \text{NP}[\textit{sacc}] \rangle \oplus \boxed{1} \end{bmatrix}$$

These constraints ensure that a non-raised dependent which is lexically assigned a structural case receives nominative case if it is the subject, otherwise is receives accusative case.

Przepiórkowski's Case Principle is non-lexical, in the sense that it depends on constructional information which not available in any single lexical entry. However, the domain of the constraints in (2) is the DEPS list of a lexical head. Therefore, (2) preserves the strong locality predictions made by the earlier purely lexical treatment of case assignment. In particular, it predicts that a head cannot assign case at a distance, selecting for a dependent which itself has a dependent in a particular case, as no single DEPS list includes both dependents and dependents of dependents. In this instance, *hilft* requires a dative object, but as we see in (3b), dependents of dependents are not assigned dative case by the verb:

(3) a. Der Mann hilft mir.
The man.NOM helps me.DAT
'The man is helping me.'

b. Der Mann hilft dem Freund meines Vaters.
The man.NOM helps the friend.DAT my father.GEN

[1]In this paper I will be assuming Bouma et al.'s (2001) version of Argument Structure Extension and so the Case Principle must make reference to the DEPS list. Since Przepiórkowski (1999a) assumes a slightly different formulation of Argument Structure Extension, he states this as a constraint on ARG-ST, not DEPS.

'The man is helping my father's friend.'

Rather, *meines Vaters*, a dependent of *Freund*, is assigned genitive case locally by *Freund*, as in (4).

(4)

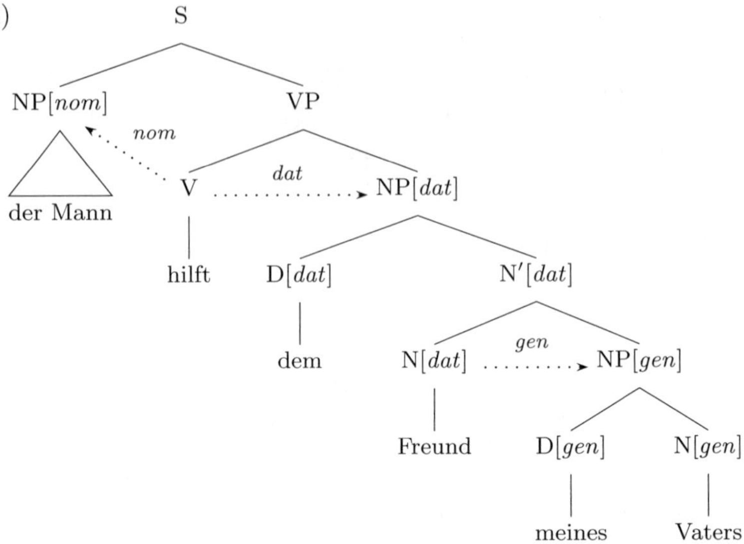

The dative determiner *dem* shows concord with the head noun, but does not receive case directly from the main verb.

11.2 A Problem

Przepiórkowski's Case Principle can account for structural case marking while still making the same strong locality predictions as Pollard and Sag (1994). Unfortunately, however, a few languages do seem to exhibit exactly the kind of long-distance case marking that is predicted not to occur under this analysis. This phenomenon can be found throughout the languages of the world, though it is particularly well attested in the languages of Australia (Dench and Evans, 1988; Blake, 1994; Plank, 1995). For instance, consider this Gumbaynggir sentence:

(5) Ba:ba-gu gunuy-gundi-yu ju:ngu jala:ny jamay
father-ERG child-GEN-ERG say.FUT tongue-NOM too
barway.
big-NOM.

'The child's father will say "(Your) mouth is too big".'
(Eades, 1979, 277)

The possessor *junuygundiyu* 'child' is locally assigned genitive case by the noun *ba:bagu* 'father', and is also assigned ergative case by the verb *ju:ngu* 'say'. Since the possessor is not directly a dependent of the verb, it is surprising to see ergative case marking on the embedded constituent. In Gumbaynggir, multiple case marking is largely restricted to combinations of genitive case with grammatical cases like the ergative, but in other languages we also find the same kind of multiple case marking on possessors in NPs bearing a 'semantic' case which functions like a PP would in an English sentence. For example, consider this example from Kayardild:

(6) dan-karra-nguni maku-karra-nguni mirra-nguni mijil-nguni
this-GEN-INSTR woman-GEN-INSTR good-INSTR net-INSTR
'...with this woman's good net' (Evans, 1995a, 119)

The NP as a whole functions as an adverbial and is marked with the instrumental case. The subconstituent *dankarranguni makukarranguni* 'this woman' is also assigned genitive case by the head noun *mijilnguni* 'net', so its components bear both genitive and instrumental case endings.

In many languages that show classical 'suffixaufnahme', this kind of multiple case marking is limited to genitive NPs. However, in a few, long distance case marking can be extended even further, as in these Martuthunira examples:

(7) Ngayu nhuwa-lalha tharnta-a kupuyu-marta-a
1SG.NOM spear-PAST euro-ACC little-PROP-ACC
thara-ngka-marta-a.
pouch-LOC-PROP-ACC
'I speared a euro with a little one in its pouch.'
(Dench and Evans, 1988, 7)

(8) Ngunhu wartirra puni-lha ngurnu-ngara-mulyarra
the woman go-PAST that-PL-ALL
kanyara-ngara-mulyarra kapunmarnu-marta-ngara-mulyarra
man-PL-ALL shirt-PROP-PL-ALL
jirli-wirra-marta-ngara-mulyarra.
arm-PRIV-PROP-PL-ALL
'That woman went towards those men with shirts without sleeves.' (Andrews, 1996, 19)

In (7) each word in the object NP is marked with accusative case in agreement with the head noun *tharntaa* 'euro (a kind of kangaroo)'. In addition to receiving accusative case, the modifier *kupuyumartaa* 'little (one)' is marked with the propriative case, indicating the relationship between it and the head noun. *Tharangkamartaa* 'pouch' carries three case markers: accusative case in concord with *tharntaa*, propriative case in concord with *kupuyumartaa*, and locative case indicating its role as a modifier. With effort, this can be carried even further: in the elicited example (8), *jirliwirramartangaramulyarra* 'arm' has four case markers![2]

While this kind of case stacking has received some attention in the Lexical-Functional Grammar literature (Simpson, 1991; Andrews, 1996; Nordlinger, 1998b), it has not yet received an adequate treatment in other frameworks. In the remainder of this paper, I will show how the HPSG theory of case assignment can be extended to account for this kind of case marking.

11.3 A Solution

The most straightforward way to model case stacking in HPSG is to generalize the value of the CASE feature to be a list of morphosyntactic cases.[3] This allows us to preserve the generalization that case is assigned locally via the argument structure of a lexical head, and that the case of the head of a phrase determines the case of the phrase as a whole. What case stacking in languages like Gumbaynggir shows is that a concord constraint also propagates the case of the head onto all of its dependents, even those that locally receive a different case. If we adopt the position that at least some adjuncts appear on the DEPS list of the head they modify (see, e.g., van Noord and Bouma 1994; Bouma et al. 2001), then this Case Concord Principle, like the Case Principle itself, can be formalized as a constraint on DEPS:

(9) CASE CONCORD PRINCIPLE

$$\begin{bmatrix} \text{HEAD}\,|\,\text{CASE} & \boxed{0} \\ \text{DEPS} & \boxed{2} \oplus \left\langle \begin{bmatrix}\text{ARG} & \text{NP}\begin{bmatrix}\text{L-CASE} & \boxed{1}\ \textit{list}(\textit{case})\end{bmatrix}\end{bmatrix}\right\rangle \oplus \boxed{3} \end{bmatrix} \rightarrow \begin{bmatrix}\text{DEPS} & \boxed{2}\oplus\left\langle\begin{bmatrix}\text{ARG} & \text{NP}\begin{bmatrix}\text{CASE} & \boxed{1}\oplus\boxed{0}\end{bmatrix}\end{bmatrix}\right\rangle\oplus\boxed{3}\end{bmatrix}$$

This constraint ensures that the CASE value of each dependent will consist minimally of the CASE value of the head which selects for it, with

[2]The plural suffix *ngara* operates much like a semantic case marker in Martuthunira; see Andrews 1996.

[3]Tseng (1999) makes essentially the same suggestion.

the addition of any locally assigned case at the head of the list. When the argument is a nominal modifier or demonstrative, such as *dankarranguni* 'this' in (6), the L-CASE value is empty and the CASE value is identical to that of the selecting head. When the dependent is itself an NP, it will be assigned a grammatical or semantic case, and the CASE value of the dependent will be that assigned case plus the CASE value of the head.

Finally, in addition to the constraint in (9) and a language-particular Case Principle similar to (2), there must be a constraint on words which relates the value of CASE to the morphological form of the word:

(10) CASE REALIZATION PRINCIPLE

word→

$$\begin{bmatrix} \text{PHON} & f_c(\boxed{1}, \boxed{2}) \\ \text{STEM} & \boxed{1} \\ \text{HEAD}|\text{CASE} & \boxed{2} \end{bmatrix}$$

The function f_c maps the morphosyntactic cases in CASE into their morphophonological realization. The order of affixes generally reflects the order of cases in the CASE value, but the order is sometimes determined by purely morphological factors, as in this Kayardild example:

(11) Ngada balmbi-wu kurri-ju kilwan [barraki-n-ku
I.NOM morrow-MOD watch-FUT them-MOD chop.NOM-MOD
kurda-wuu-nth].
coolamon-MOD-OBL

'Tomorrow I will watch them chopping (making) a coolamon.'
(Evans, 1995b, 412)

Here the verb *kurriju* 'watch' assigns a modal case to each of its non-subject dependents. On *kurdawuunth* 'coolamon', this modal case marking precedes the oblique case marking assigned by the nominalized verb *barrakinku* 'chopping', even though the oblique case precedes the modal case on the noun's CASE list.

These constraints taken together provide a completely general head-driven account of case stacking and long distance case assignment. To see how they work, consider again the example in (5). If we assume that ergative and genitive are both lexical cases in Gumbaynggir, *ju:ngu* 'say' and the noun *ba:ba* 'father' would have the following lexical entries:

(12)
$$\begin{bmatrix} \text{STEM} & \langle \textit{ju:ngu} \rangle \\ \text{DEPS} & \langle \text{NP}[\ \text{L-CASE}\ \langle \textit{erg} \rangle], \text{CP} \rangle \end{bmatrix}$$

(13) $\begin{bmatrix} \text{STEM} & \langle \textit{ba:ba} \rangle \\ \text{DEPS} & \langle \text{NP}[\ \text{L-CASE}\ \langle \textit{gen} \rangle] \rangle \end{bmatrix}$

When combined with the principle in (9), this yields the partial lexical descriptions in (14) and (15), respectively.

(14) $\begin{bmatrix} \text{STEM} & \langle \textit{ju:ngu} \rangle \\ \text{HEAD}\,|\,\text{CASE} & \boxed{1} \\ \text{DEPS} & \langle \text{NP}[\langle \textit{erg} \rangle \oplus \boxed{1}],\ \text{CP} \rangle \end{bmatrix}$

(15) $\begin{bmatrix} \text{STEM} & \langle \textit{ba:ba} \rangle \\ \text{HEAD}\,|\,\text{CASE} & \boxed{2} \\ \text{DEPS} & \langle \text{NP}[\langle \textit{gen} \rangle \oplus \boxed{2}] \rangle \end{bmatrix}$

When combined to construct the sentence in (5), these lexical descriptions combine to yield the structure in (16).

(16)

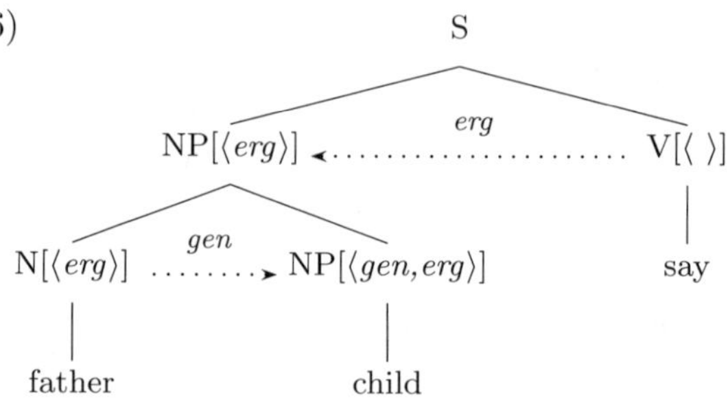

If we follow Bouma et al. (2001) in allowing a head's DEPS list to be extended to include adjuncts as well as arguments, the Case Concord Principle and the Case Realization Principle also provide a natural account of case stacking with semantic cases, as in (7). To see how this would work, we first need to consider a modification of Argument Structure Extension. As originally formulated in (17), this constraint states that the DEPS list is the ARG-ST plus zero or more adjuncts:

(17) ARGUMENT STRUCTURE EXTENSION:

verb$\rightarrow$

$$\begin{bmatrix} \text{HEAD} & \boxed{3} \\ \text{DEPS} & \boxed{1} \oplus \textit{list}\left(\begin{bmatrix} \text{MOD} \begin{bmatrix} \text{HEAD} & \boxed{3} \\ \text{KEY} & \boxed{2} \end{bmatrix} \end{bmatrix}\right) \\ \text{ARG-ST} & \boxed{1} \\ \text{CONT}\,|\,\text{KEY} & \boxed{2} \end{bmatrix}$$

Each adjunct is constrained to modify the semantic content of the head, but nothing is said about the particular relation introduced by the adverbial phrases. In English, the content of the modifier is introduced in the lexical entry of the preposition or adverb that heads the modifier, so there is no need for Argument Structure Extension to say anything about the content of the modifier. In some languages with semantic case, like Polish and Korean, semantic cases behave very much like morphologically bound prepositions, so the content of the adverbial can be determined by the semantic case ending in the same manner as a preposition (see, e.g., Bratt 1996; Tseng 1999).

In the languages under consideration here, however, dependents agree with the head that selects for them in both grammatical and semantic case. That means that the adverbial relation cannot be associated with the semantic case ending itself. Otherwise, in an example like (6), the *with* relation would be introduced not only on the head of the phrase as a whole, but also on each of the words in the phrase that bears instrumental case marking. We could assume that these case markers are systematically ambiguous between a semantic case that introduces an adverbial meaning and a grammatical case that merely shows concord (following Simpson 1991), or that there is some other mechanism for disregarding the adverbial relation introduced by concord uses of semantic case markers (as does Andrews 1996). However, a solution closer to the spirit of Bouma et al.'s (2001) approach to adjunction is to associate the adverbial meaning of the semantic case not with the case ending itself, but with the constraint that licenses the appearance of the adjunct:

(18) ARGUMENT STRUCTURE EXTENSION (MARTUTHUNIRA):

$$
\textit{word} \rightarrow
\begin{bmatrix}
\text{HEAD} & \boxed{3} \\
\text{DEPS} & \boxed{1} \oplus \left(\begin{bmatrix} \text{L-CASE} & \langle \textit{prop} \rangle \\ \text{CONT}\,|\,\text{KEY} & \textit{with-rel} \\ \text{MOD} & \begin{bmatrix} \text{HEAD} & \boxed{3} \\ \text{KEY} & \boxed{2} \end{bmatrix} \end{bmatrix} \right) \oplus \\
 & \left(\begin{bmatrix} \text{L-CASE} & \langle \textit{loc} \rangle \\ \text{CONT}\,|\,\text{KEY} & \textit{in-rel} \\ \text{MOD} & \begin{bmatrix} \text{HEAD} & \boxed{3} \\ \text{KEY} & \boxed{2} \end{bmatrix} \end{bmatrix} \right) \oplus \ldots \\
\text{ARG-ST} & \boxed{1} \\
\text{CONT}\,|\,\text{KEY} & \boxed{2}
\end{bmatrix}
$$

Rather then allowing adjuncts to be freely added to the DEPS list, this language-specific variant of Argument Structure Extension licenses the optional addition of specific kinds of adverbials. One possibility is to add an adjunct which bears propriative case and has the appropriate semantics, another is to add an adjunct which bears locative case and has the appropriate semantics, and so on.

This constraint will apply to the lexical entry for the noun stem *tharnt-* 'euro' to produce the partial lexical specification:

(19)
$$\begin{bmatrix} \text{STEM} & \langle \textit{tharnt} \rangle \\ \text{HEAD} & \begin{bmatrix} \textit{noun} \\ \text{CASE} & \boxed{1} \end{bmatrix} \\ \text{DEPS} & \boxed{2} \oplus \langle \text{NP}[\langle \textit{prop} \rangle \oplus \boxed{1}] \rangle \\ \text{ARG-ST} & \boxed{2}\langle\ \rangle \end{bmatrix}$$

Similarly, this constraint will license a version of the lexical entry for *kupuyu-* 'little' which selects for a locative modifier. Finally, the lexical entry for the verb *nhuwalalha* 'spear' includes the constraint:

(20)
$$\begin{bmatrix} \text{PHON} & \langle \textit{nhuwalalha} \rangle \\ \text{HEAD} & \begin{bmatrix} \textit{verb} \\ \text{CASE} & \boxed{1}\langle\ \rangle \end{bmatrix} \\ \text{DEPS} & \boxed{2} \oplus \langle\ \rangle \\ \text{ARG-ST} & \boxed{2}\langle \text{NP}[\langle \textit{nom} \rangle \oplus \boxed{1}],\ \text{NP}[\langle \textit{acc} \rangle \oplus \boxed{1}] \rangle \end{bmatrix}$$

When combined, these lexical specifications will yield the structure in (21).[4]

(21)

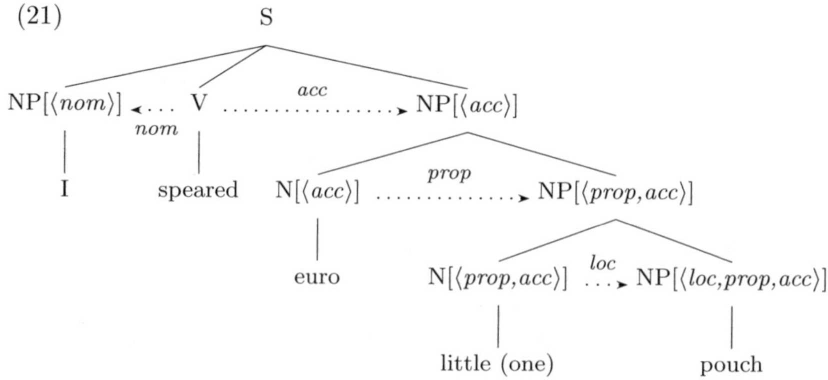

[4]Here I follow Dench (1995) on the structure of the Martuthunira noun phrase.

The verb selects for a nominative subject and an accusative object. The head of the object selects for an NP whose CASE value is a list containing an adnominal case (propriative) and the case value of the head (accusative). The head of that modifier NP itself selects for a modifier NP whose CASE value consists of an adnominal case (in this case, locative) and the case value of the head (propriative and accusative).

11.4 Consequences and Conclusions

This head-driven account of case concord can also be applied straightforwardly to other types of case agreement. For example, the oblique case or the locative case can be used to mark finite complement clauses in Kayardild:[5]

(22) a. Ngada murnmurdawa-th ngijin-inja thabuju-ntha
1SG.NOM be.glad-ACT my-OBL brother-OBL
thaa-thuu-nth.
return-POT-OBL
'I am glad that my brother is coming back.'
(Evans, 1995a, 490)

b. Dan-kurrka ri-in-kurrka thardawankawuru-ntha
here-LOC.OBL east-FROM-LOC.OBL airplane-OBL
burri-jurrk.
emerge-IMMED.OBL
'(I can hear) the airplane is coming in, here from the east now.' (Evans, 1995a, 525)

As (22) shows, the oblique can also be used with 'insubordinated' main clauses, which presumably involve (at least diachronically) elision of an epistemic main clause. Since under this proposal verbs carry a (usually empty) CASE value, the behavior of 'complementizing case' is predicted. Modal case and associating case in Kayardild could be given an analogous treatment (see Nordlinger 1998a, 1998b for more discussion of this and related phenomena).

The analysis presented here also has the potential to shed some light on a number of 'case attraction' phenomena, in which a constituent bears the case of a larger constituent of which it is a part rather than its locally assigned case. For example, in Classical Armenian, a possessor can sometimes bear the case of the head of which it is a dependent rather than the expected genitive:

[5] In (22), *-kurrka* is a portmanteau realization of the locative and the oblique case endings.

(23) i knoǰ-ê t'agawor-i-n
by wife-ABL.SG king-GEN.SG-DEF
'by the wife of the king' (Plank, 1995, 20)

(24) i knoǰ-ê t'agawor-ē-n
by wife-ABL.SG king-ABL.SG-DEF
'by the wife of the king' (Plank, 1995, 20)

Suppose that case concord in Classical Armenian obeys the Case Concord Principle in (9). Then the value of CASE on *t'agawor-* 'king' will be ⟨*gen, abl*⟩. While the morphological resources of Armenian do not allow multiple case suffixes on a single word, the Case Realization Principle in (10) will potentially allow either case to surface.

Another kind of case attraction is found in relative clauses, in which the relative word shows either the internal case assigned to it inside the relative clause or the external case assigned to the relative clause construction as a whole. Often, as in these Gothic examples, the choice of which case is realized depends on the relative obliqueness of the cases involved:

(25) iþ [þamm-ei leitil fraletada] leitil friod
but whom-DAT little is.forgiven little loves
'But (the one) whom little is forgiven loves little
(Harbert, 1992, 111)

(26) [þo-ei ist us Laudeikaiou] jus ussggwaid
which.ACC-COMP is from Laodicea you read
'And read (the one) which is from Laodicea'
(Harbert, 1992, 111)

In (25), the relative pronoun receives dative case inside the relative clause and nominal case from the main clause. Since dative is more oblique that nominative, the relative pronoun appears in the dative form. On the other hand, in (26), the internal case of the relative pronoun, nominative, is less oblique than its external case, accusative, so the relative pronoun appears in the accusative form. This sort of interaction is exactly what we would expect if case attraction phenomena arise from the Case Realization Principle's need to express multiple cases using limited morphological resources.

The analysis that I have outlined here contrasts with previous approaches in that it is completely head-driven. Andrews (1996) and Nordlinger (1998b) claim that adnominal case stacking can only be adequately accounted for using inside-out constraints. For example, the propriative affix *-marta* would be associated with a lexical entry along the lines of (27).

(27) *-marta* (ADJ $\uparrow$)
(↑ CASE) = LOC

This entry can be interpreted to mean that the f-structure of the word this affix is attached to contains the feature/value pair [CASE *loc*], and that the f-structure of that word is the value of the feature ADJ in some higher f-structure.

The approach described here on the other hand is able to account for case stacking without the addition of new formal mechanisms beyond those needed for case marking in other languages. Furthermore, since the inside-out approach to case stacking treats case marking as an essentially non-local phenomenon, additional constraints on the scope of a case marker's inside-out functional equations are required to capture the 'successive cyclic' nature of case stacking and to restrict the kinds of non-local case marking dependencies that can be introduced. In contrast, under the current analysis the scope of case marking is strictly controlled by independently motivated locality conditions. So, while it is possible to enrich the HPSG description language to include inside-out constraints (Koenig, 1999), it is not clear that it is either necessary or desirable to do so to handle case stacking.

References

Andrews, A. D. 1996. Semantic case-stacking and inside-out unification. *Australian Journal of Linguistics* 16:1–55.

Blake, B. J. 1994. *Case.* Cambridge University Press.

Bouma, G., R. Malouf, and I. A. Sag. 2001. Satisfying constraints on extraction and adjunction. *Natural Language and Linguistic Theory* 19:1–65.

Bratt, E. O. 1996. *Argument Composition and the Lexicon: Lexical and Periphrastic Causatives in Korean.* Ph.D. thesis, Stanford University.

Chomsky, N. 1981. *Lectures on Government and Binding.* Dordrecht: Foris.

Dench, A. 1995. Suffixaufnahme and apparent ellipsis in Martuthunira. In F. Plank, ed., *Double Case*, pages 380–395. New York: Oxford University Press.

Dench, A. and N. Evans. 1988. Multiple case-marking in Australian languages. *Australian Journal of Linguistics* 8:1–47.

Eades, D. 1979. Gumbaynggir. In R. M. W. Dixon and B. J. Blake, eds., *Handbook of Australian Languages*, vol. 1, pages 244–361. Canberra: ANU Press.

Evans, N. 1995a. *A Grammar of Kayardild.* Berlin: Mouton de Gruyter.

Evans, N. 1995b. Multiple case in Kayardild: Anti-iconic suffix ordering and the diachronic filter. In F. Plank, ed., *Double Case*, pages 396–428. New York: Oxford University Press.

Harbert, W. 1992. Gothic relative clauses and syntactic theory. In I. Rauch, G. F. Carr, and R. L. Kyes, eds., *On Germanic Linguistics: Issues and Methods*, pages 109–146. Berlin: Mouton de Gruyter.

Heinz, W. and J. Matiasek. 1994. Argument structure and case assignment in German. In J. Nerbonne, K. Netter, and C. Pollard, eds., *German in Head-driven Phrase Structure Grammar*, pages 199–236. Stanford: CSLI Publications.

Koenig, J.-P. 1999. Inside-out constraints and description languages for HPSG. In G. Webelhuth, A. Kathol, and J.-P. Koenig, eds., *Lexical and Constructional Aspects of Linguistic Explanation*, pages 265–280. Stanford: CSLI Publications.

Nordlinger, R. 1998a. The case of subordinate clauses in australian languages: a constructive approach. Paper presented at the 1998 LFG Conference.

Nordlinger, R. 1998b. *Constructive Case: Evidence from Australian Languages*. Stanford: CSLI Publications.

Plank, F. 1995. (Re-)introducing suffixaufnahme. In F. Plank, ed., *Double Case*, pages 4–110. New York: Oxford University Press.

Pollard, C. 1994. Towards a unified account of passive in German. In J. Nerbonne, K. Netter, and C. Pollard, eds., *German Grammar in HPSG*, pages 273–296. Stanford: CSLI Publications.

Pollard, C. and I. A. Sag. 1994. *Head-Driven Phrase Structure Grammar*. Chicago and Stanford: University of Chicago Press and CSLI Publications.

Przepiórkowski, A. 1999a. *Case assigment and the complement/adjunct dichotomy*. Ph.D. thesis, Universität Tübingen.

Przepiórkowski, A. 1999b. On case assignment and 'adjuncts as complements'. In G. Webelhuth, A. Kathol, and J.-P. Koenig, eds., *Lexical and Constructional Aspects of Linguistic Explanation*, pages 231–246. Stanford: CSLI Publications.

Simpson, J. 1991. *Warlpiri Morpho-syntax: a Lexicalist Approach*. Dordrecht: Kluwer.

Tseng, J. 1999. Grammatical marking in HPSG. In G.-J. M. Kruijff and R. T. Oerhle, eds., *Proceedings of Formal Grammar 1999*, pages 155–164. Utrecht.

van Noord, G. and G. Bouma. 1994. Adjuncts and the processing of lexical rules. In *Proceedings of the Fifteenth International Conference on Computational Linguistics (COLING '94)*. Kyoto, Japan.

12

German Particle Verbs and the Predicate Complex

STEFAN MÜLLER

12.1 Introduction

In German there is a class of verbs that can appear discontinuously (1). The part that appears to the left of the main verb in verb final position and that is stranded when the finite verb is in initial position is traditionally called a separable prefix. Since prefixes are by definition not separable, the terms particle and preverb are used in more recent work.

(1) a. Setzt der Fährmann Karl über?
takes the ferryman Karl across
'Does the ferryman take Karl across?'

b. daß der Fährmann Karl übersetzt.
that the ferryman Karl across.takes

In (1a), where the verb is in initial position, the preverb is stranded.

Below I will argue that separable verbs in German behave like other elements in the predicate complex. This view is supported by the following facts: Preverbs are serialized like verbal or predicative adjectival complements in the right sentence bracket (the right periphery of a clause that does not contain extraposed elements), they can be fronted as can be done with single verbs or predicative adjectives. If preverbs are analyzed as part of the predicate complex, the fronting data can be accounted for as an instance of complex fronting (Partial Verb Phrase Fronting (PVP)). The inability of particles and predicates in resultative constructions to co-occur and the non-iterability of preverbs will be explained by the fact that particles and resultative predicates occupy a designated valance position that does not allow more than one particle

Grammatical Interfaces in HPSG.
Ronnie Cann, Claire Grover and Philip Miller.

or resultative predicate.

12.2 The Phenomena

12.2.1 Fronting

Preverbs can be fronted, although this is often denied. Different claims about non-frontability have been made by Bierwisch (1963, p. 103), Kiss (1994, p. 100), Olsen (1997, p. 307), Zifonun (1999, p. 227), Eisenberg (1999, p. 306), and others. Due to space limitations I cannot discuss all claims here, but see Müller Submitted. Usually fronted particles are contrasted, or a focus (on the complete verb) is established.

(2) a. Los ging es schon in dieser Woche.[1]
PART went it already in this week
'It already started this week.'

b. Vor hat er das jedenfalls.[2]
PART has he that in any case
'But he does plan this.'

c. Entgegen kam der EuGH den Streitkräften, indem er der Regierung die Entscheidung überlässt, welche Verwendungsbereiche sie von dem Gleichbehandlungsgebot ausnehmen wollen.[3]

'The European Court of Justice accommodated the troops by leaving it to the government to decide which areas to exclude from the equal treatment ruling.'

d. Auf fällt, daß ...[4]
PART falls that
'It is noticed that ...'

In Müller 1999, Ch. 19.1.2 and Müller Submitted, I provided more fronting examples with preverbs that are related to nouns, adjectives, and adverbs.

A non-finite particle verb cannot be fronted without its preverb (Uszkoreit, 1987, p. 104):

(3) * Schlafen wird Karl ein.
sleep will Karl PART
Intended: 'Karl will fall asleep.'

[1] taz, 11.10.95, p. 4. The *taz* is a newspaper that appears nation-wide in Germany.
[2] taz, 07.15.1999, p. 19
[3] taz, 01.12.2000, p. 1
[4] (Duden, 1991, p. 62)

The examples of particle fronting in (2) are parallel to examples where verbs or adjectives are fronted.

(4) a. Erzählen wird er seiner Tochter ein Märchen.[5]
tell will he his daughter a fairy tail
'He will tell his daughter a fairy tale.'

b. Treu will Karl seiner Frau sein.
faithful wants Karl his wife be
'Karl wants to be faithful to his wife.'

In (4a) only the verb *erzählen* is fronted. The complements of this verb remain in the *Mittelfeld*. (4b) is an example of a fronted adjective. The example in (3) is parallel to (5).

(5) a. * Müssen wird er ihr ein Märchen erzählen.
must will he her a story tell

b. * Sein will Karl seiner Frau treu.
be wants Karl his wife faithful

The generalization about these ungrammatical examples is that if parts of the predicate complex are fronted (alone or with adjuncts or complements), all parts of the predicate complex that are governed by fronted heads have to be fronted together with this head. So in (5a) *müssen* governs *erzählen*. If *müssen* is fronted *erzählen* has to move as well. If particles are analyzed as parts of the predicate complex, the ungrammaticality of (3) is explained.

12.2.2 Linearization

Finally, it can be observed that preverbs behave similarly to verbs and adjectives in respect to serialization. They are located in the right sentence bracket.[6] The control verb *vorschlagen* can appear discontinuously.

(6) a. Karl schlägt der Frau vor zu gehen.
Karl beats the woman PART to go
'Karl suggests to the woman to go.'

b. daß Karl der Frau vorschlägt zu gehen.

c. * Karl schlägt vor, der Frau zu gehen.

If serializations of the preverb in adverb positions were possible, orders like those in (6c) should also be possible, since they are possible with adverbs, as (7) shows.

[5](Haftka, 1981, p. 720–721). For more data see Müller 1999, Chapter 18.
[6]Cf. (Drach, 1937, p. 55)

(7) a. Karl überredete die Frau gestern zu gehen.
Karl persuaded the woman yesterday to go
b. Karl überredete gestern die Frau zu gehen.

But this is not the case. (6c) is totally out since it would be an instance of multiple extraposition with an NP and a VP. NP extraposition as such is rather marked, but together with an extraposed infinitive the sentence becomes unacceptable. This suggests that preverbs occupy the same position as that occupied by non-finite verbs in sentences like (8), that do not contain a finite particle verb.

(8) Er hat den Hund geschlagen.
he has the dog beaten
'He beat the dog.'

The particle marks the right sentence boundary. If the preverb + verb combination in (7) is licensed by the same grammar rule as the auxiliary + verb combination in (8), the facts can be explained easily.

In Dutch, preverbs can be separated from their main verb (Koster, 1975, p. 126) and the same is true for some variants of German. Grewendorf (1990, p. 99) gives the German example in (9).

(9) Daß ich an zu weinen fing[7]
that I PART to cry caught
'that I started to cry'

It is tempting to count this example as an intentional breach of the rules, but such orders are attested to be possible in some German dialects:

(10) a. a ... hot aa ze schimpfm gfanga
he has PART to get.angry caught
'He started to get angry.'
b. die ham ... auf zu arwettn ghört
they have PART to work heard
'They stopped working.'

Werner (1994, p. 356) gives the examples in (10), which are quoted from Sperschneider and were spoken in the northwest of Sonneberg/Thuringia.

Furthermore, Werner (1994, p. 355) discusses data like those in (11).

(11) Wos da sich ölles aahotmüßhör!
what the REFL all PART.has.must.hear
'All these things he had to listen to!'

[7] Joseph von Eichendorff, *Erinnerung, Gedichte*, Eichendorff-W. Vol. 1, p. 77

He argues that these orderings follow the pattern in (12).

(12) a. , weil er in die Stadt / fort geht.
because he in the town away goes
'because he goes to town / away.'

b. , weil er in die Stadt / fort hat müssen gehen.
because he in the town away has must go
'because he had to go to town / away.'

Particle verbs historically developed from adverb+verb combinations. The canonical position of adverbs is in front of the verbal complex. Most of these adverbs changed their meaning and the combinations became lexicalized. In the East Franconian/Thuringian dialect the canonical order in respect to modals is preserved. In head final sentences the preverb has to be immedeately to the left of the verbal material, the adverbial elements got reanalyzed as parts of the verbal complex.

12.2.3 Resultative Constructions

Resultative constructions and object predicatives share a lot of properties with particle verbs. In this and the next subsection, I will give a short overview of these constructions in order to be able to sketch analyses in sections 12.3.2 and 12.3.3.

The formation of resultative constructions in German is a process of transitivization that takes an intransitive verb as input and produces a transitive verb + predicate (Oppenrieder 1991, Chapter 1.5.3.7.4; Wunderlich 1997).[8]

(13) Sie fischen den Teich leer.
they fish the pond-ACC empty

The accusative object in (13) has to be an object of the verb since it can appear in the nominative in passive constructions. However, no selectional restrictions are imposed on this kind of object by the matrix verb. The only restriction is that the result state might be caused by the verb.

Again, the predicate can be fronted, but the fronting of the verb that governs the predicate is out.

(14) a. Klein müssen Sie das Fleisch schneiden.
small must you the meat cut
'You have to cut the meat into small pieces.'

[8] German resultative constructions differ from English ones in several respects. For analyses and data see Rothstein 1985; Wechsler 1997. Some notes about the differences between English and German can be found in Wunderlich 1997. Due to space limitations it is impossible to give more details here.

b. ?? Schneiden müssen Sie das Fleisch klein![9]
cut must you the meat small

c. * Das Fleisch schneiden müssen Sie klein!
the meat cut must you small

As Keyser and Roeper (1992, p. 97), Neeleman and Weermann (1993), Lüdeling (1998, p. 129–130) and others observed, resultative constructions are impossible with particle verbs.

12.2.4 Object Predicatives

Verbs like *nennen* ('call') and *finden* ('find') embed a predicate. The subject of this predicate is raised to the object of the matrix verb (Pütz, 1982, p. 353).

(15) Man findet ihn gut.
one finds him-ACC good

As the object of the matrix verb, the subject of the embedded predicate is marked accusative. In passive constructions it functions as the subject and is marked nominative.

Again, the fronting of the matrix verb without the embedded predicate is impossible:

(16) * Gefunden hat er ihn gut.
found has he him good

There are also particle verbs that embed predicates:

(17) Das kam ihm dumm vor.
this came him silly PART
'This seemed silly to him.'

To sum up, one can conclude that the preverbs behave in a way that is known from other elements in the predicate complex.

12.3 The Analysis

For the analysis I use a variant of Head-Driven Phrase Structure Grammar (HPSG) as the grammar framework. The standard grammar by Pollard and Sag (1994) is extended by word order domains Reape (1990). Word order domains are lists that contain dependants of a head in a serialization that corresponds to the surface order. These word order domains are used by Reape, Kathol (1995) and Müller (1999) to account for the relatively free constituent order in German. Domain elements may be permutated freely provided no linear precedence rule (LP rule)

[9](Oppenrieder, 1991, p. 127)

is violated. I assume that all grammar rules are binary branching. If a head is combined with an adjunct, with a complement, or with a filler, the non-head element is inserted into the domain of the head (Müller, 1999, Ch. 11). Furthermore, I follow Hinrichs and Nakazawa (1994) in assuming a special schema for the formation of a verbal complex. In Müller 1997, I suggested extending the notion of verbal complex to a predicate complex and analyzing adjectives as parts of this predicate complex. The non-head daughter that is licensed by the predicate complex schema is also inserted into the domain of its head. The head selects its complex forming complement via a special valence feature called VCOMP (Chung, 1993; Rentier, 1994).

12.3.1 Particle Verbs

Due to the data in section 12.2, it seems reasonable to treat preverbs as elements that take part in complex formation.[10] In the following subsections, I will provide the basic lexical entries for non-transparent particle verbs. Analyses for the verb position, for the fronting of particles and for the verbal complex in Franconian/Thuringian will be provided.

(18) shows the lexical entry for *vorhaben* ('to plan'). I assume that

(18) (*vor*) *hat* ('plans'):

$$\begin{bmatrix} \text{SUBCAT} \left\langle \text{NP}[\textit{nom}], \text{NP}[\textit{acc}] \right\rangle \\ \text{VCOMP} \left\langle \text{PV}[\textit{vor}] \right\rangle \\ \textit{cat} \end{bmatrix}$$

the subject is represented at the subcat list for finite verbs only. For non-finite verbs and other predicates it is represented as a head feature (Kiss 1995). The preverb is selected like other complements that take part in complex formation via VCOMP. For the productive formations of particle verbs I assume a lexical rule that adds the appropriate particle to verbs without a particle. This lexical rule is very similar to the lexical rule for resultative constructions that will be discussed in the next section.

Figure 1 shows the analysis for (19), where the verb is in final position.

(19) , weil er das vorhat?
because he that PART.has
'because he plans to do this'

An H stands for head, a C for complement, an F for filler, and a CL

[10]Höhle (1982) suggested using the same rule for the combination of preverb and verb as for the verbal complex. Höhle deals mainly with morphological problems. The syntactic properties of the particle verb constructions are not explored in detail.

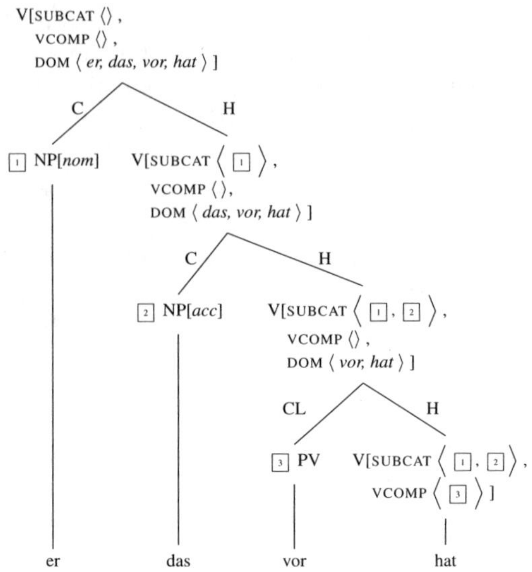

FIGURE 1 Analysis of *weil er das vorhat?*

for cluster daughter. I assume that preverb and verb are two separate syntactic objects that are merely serialized in adjacent positions.

The dominance structure for the sentence (20) is entirely the same, only the serialization of the main verb differs.

(20) Hat er das vor?
has he that PART
'Does he plan to do this?'

Instead of being serialized to the right of the complements and the preverb, the verb is serialized sentence initially.

The sentence (2b) gets the structure in (21).

(21) [Vor]$_j$ hat er das jedenfalls $\__j$.

Since I do not assume that the base verb in (20) is extracted out of the complete verb *vorhat*, I do not have to assume that the base verb is scrambled back somehow into the *Mittelfeld*, as is done in some GB analyses. The analysis of (2b) is shown in figure 2. Note that in HPSG there are no restrictions on the phrasehood of the fronted constituent (the filler daughter). The filler in figure 2 is a word. In theories that assume that only maximal projections may be fronted, it has to be assumed that preverbs are projected to maximal phrases (see Lüdeling 1998 for such an approach). There is no evidence whatsoever that pre-

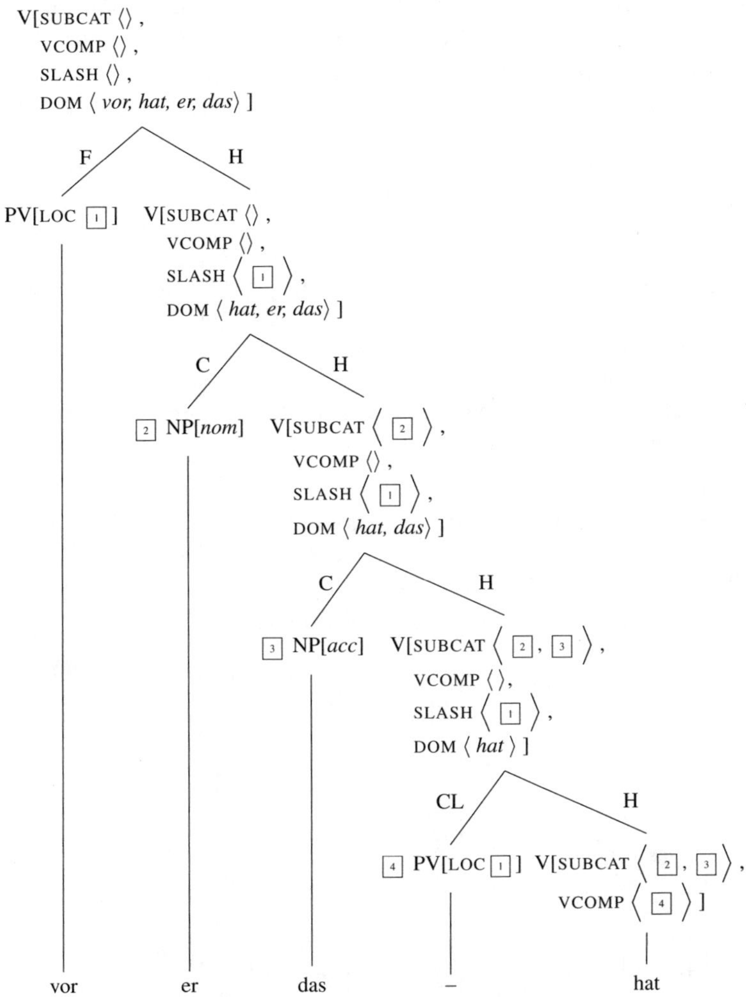

FIGURE 2 Analysis of *Vor hat er das.*

verbs like *vor* or preverbs that are related to bare nouns do project to full phrases.

12.3.2 Object Predicatives

The lexical entry in (22) for object predicative taking verbs like *finden* is similar to the entry for the copula *sein* ('be') that was formulated in Müller 1999, p. 314.

(22) *findet* ('finds'):

$$\begin{bmatrix} \text{SUBCAT} & \left\langle \text{NP}, \boxed{2} \right\rangle \\ \text{VCOMP} & \left\langle \text{AP}[\ \text{SUBJ}\ \left\langle \boxed{2}\,\text{NP} \right\rangle,\ \text{SUBCAT}\ \langle\rangle,\ \text{VCOMP}\ \langle\rangle\ ] \right\rangle \\ \textit{cat} & \end{bmatrix}$$

As Pütz (1982, p. 353) observed, this kind of object predicate construction is a raising construction: The object predicate is embedded under VCOMP (*gut* in (15)). The subject (*ihn*) of the embedded predicate is raised to the object of the matrix verb. The matrix verb does not assign a semantic role to the raised NP, and therefore the embedding of expletive constructions is possible.

(23) Ich finde es hier zu kalt.
I find it-EXPL here too cold

12.3.3 Resultatives

The lexical rule in (24) shows how resultatives are formed:

$$\text{(24)}\quad \begin{bmatrix} \text{SYNSEM|LOC} & \begin{bmatrix} \text{CAT} & \begin{bmatrix} \text{HEAD|SUBJ} & \left\langle \text{NP} \right\rangle \\ \text{SUBCAT} & \langle\rangle \\ \text{VCOMP} & \langle\rangle \end{bmatrix} \\ \text{CONT} & \boxed{1} \end{bmatrix} \end{bmatrix} \Rightarrow$$

$$\begin{bmatrix} \text{SYNSEM|LOC} \\ \begin{bmatrix} \text{CAT} & \begin{bmatrix} \text{SUBCAT} & \boxed{2} \\ \text{VCOMP} & \left\langle \begin{bmatrix} \text{L} & \begin{bmatrix} \text{C} & \begin{bmatrix} \text{H} & \begin{bmatrix} \text{PRD} & + \\ \text{SUBJ} & \boxed{2}\ \left\langle \text{NP}_{ref} \right\rangle \\ \textit{adj-or-prep} & \end{bmatrix} \\ \text{SUBCAT} & \langle\rangle \\ \text{VCOMP} & \langle\rangle \end{bmatrix} \\ \text{CONT} & \boxed{3} \end{bmatrix} \end{bmatrix} \right\rangle \end{bmatrix} \\ \text{CONT} & \textit{cause}(\boxed{1}, \textit{become}(\boxed{3})) \end{bmatrix} \end{bmatrix}$$

An intransitive verb is the input for this rule. The output is a verb that selects a predicate via its valance feature VCOMP. The subject of this predicate ($\boxed{2}$) is identical to the object of the matrix verb. The subject of the embedded predicate has to be referential since it is the nature of these resultative constructions that an entity is affected by the action expressed by the matrix verb. The resultative meaning of the whole construction is represented under CONT in the output of the rule. For the example in (13), the lexical rule is applied to the intransitive verb *fischen*, and the valance information for a predicate and an object that is raised from the subject of the predicate is added.

(25) *fischen* ('fish' as is used in 'fish empty'):

$$\begin{bmatrix} \text{SUBCAT} \left\langle \text{NP}, \boxed{2} \right\rangle \\ \text{VCOMP} \left\langle \text{A/PP}[\,\text{SUBJ} \left\langle \boxed{2}\text{NP}_{ref} \right\rangle, \text{SUBCAT} \langle\rangle, \text{VCOMP} \langle\rangle\,] \right\rangle \\ \textit{cat} \end{bmatrix}$$

The predicate gets saturated by *leer* in (13) and the object by *ihn*.

Since the output of the rule does not match the input specification, it follows that at most one result predicate per verb is allowed. It is also clear that the rule cannot be applied to particle verbs or other verbs that select a complement via VCOMP. The rule for the productive particle formations cannot be applied to resultative constructions for the same reason. Therefore, the iteration of resultative predicates and of particles, and the combination of particles and resultatives or other complex predicates, is correctly ruled out. The only way for more than one element to get into VCOMP is by direct specification in the lexicon. Examples for such cases are the object predicate verb *vorkommen* (see (17)) and the phase verb *anfangen* (see below).

12.3.4 Phase Verbs and the Verbal Complex in Thuringian

Phase verbs like *anfangen* ('start') and *aufhören* ('stop') are raising verbs. They are able to form a verbal complex with the verb they embed. Space considerations preclude a detailed justification here of this kind of verb, but see Kiss 1995; Müller 1999 for details. The important thing to focus on here is the relation between base verb and particle, and how the order in the verbal complex in the examples in (10) can be accounted for. (26) shows the relevant CAT features of *anfangen* (see also Kathol 1995, p. 244–248).

(26) (*an*) *fang-* (finite form):

$$\begin{bmatrix} \text{SUBCAT } \boxed{1} \oplus \boxed{2} \\ \text{VCOMP } \left\langle \text{V[SUBJ } \boxed{1}\text{, SUBCAT } \boxed{2}\text{, } \textit{inf}\text{, LEX+]:} \boxed{3}\text{, PV[}\textit{an}\text{]} \right\rangle \\ \textit{cat} \end{bmatrix}$$

Figure 3 shows how the sentence in (27) can be analyzed.

(27) , daß ich zu weinen anfing.
that I to cry started
'that I started to cry.'

A verbal complex is built from *an* and *fing*. This complex is combined with the infinitive *zu weinen*. All three elements are serialized in the same order domain. (9) can be analyzed completely analogously: Since

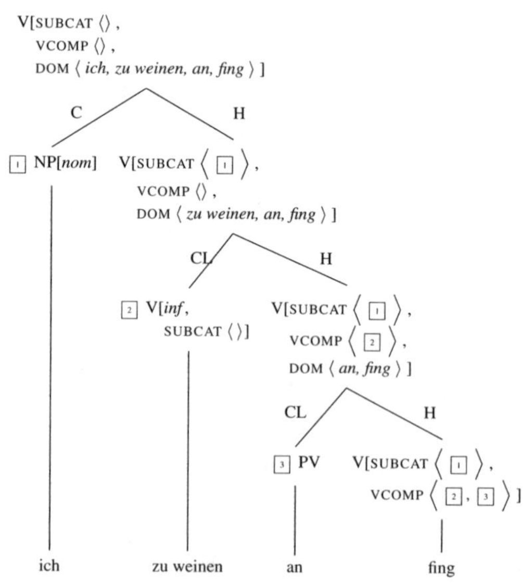

FIGURE 3 Analysis of *daß ich zu weinen anfing?*

an, *zu weinen*, and *fing* are in the same word order domain, the serialization of *an* to the left of the verbal complex is possible if required by the ordering rules of the specific variant of German. For standard German, an LP rule with high preference states that preverb and verb have to be adjacent in verb final sentences.

12.4 Conclusion

An account of particle verbs has been developed that treats preverbs as part of the verbal complex. Preverb fronting can be analyzed as an instance of complex fronting. No new mechanisms have to be introduced. In particular no extraction of the finite verb from the fronted constituent as is needed in other theories is necessary. The preverb is selected by the same valence feature as other complements that form a complex with their head. Therefore, similarities with object predicatives and resultative constructions can be explained. The impossibility of resultative constructions with particle verbs also follows from the valance specification of the latter. Since preverbs are selected via VCOMP the resultative formation lexical rule cannot introduce a resultative predicate because VCOMP is filled already. It is difficult to see how approaches that use just one valance feature (SUBCAT) to represent complements, verbal complements, and preverbs, as for instance that of Bouma and van Noord (1998), can account for the non-iterability of preverbs. Accounts that assume different valence features for preverbs (PART) and verbal elements (AUX), as for instance that of Ackerman and Webelhuth (1998), cannot capture the similarities between the constructions.

Finally, it was shown how word order in the verbal complex in some variants of German can be handled. Since the preverb is selected in the same way as other parts of the verbal complex, the position of the preverb can be accounted for with linear precedence rules. If the preverb were analyzed as a part of the word in verb final constructions, the separability which is also possible in head final constructions could not be explained.

Of course there is a lot more to say about resultatives and other predicative constructions in general, but due to space limitations this could not be done in this paper. Nevertheless, I hope to have made clear both the commonalities of the discussed phenomena, and that they should be treated in the same way.

Acknowledgements

Thanks to Kordula De Kuthy, Walter Kasper, and Anke Lüdeling for discussion, two anonymous reviewers for comments, and to Kordula De Kuthy, Detmar Meurers, and Anke Lüdeling for the supplying me with relevant literature. I want also to thank Uta Waller who helped me translate sample sentences from newspapers.

References

Ackerman, F. and G. Webelhuth. 1998. *A Theory of Predicates*. No. 76 in

CSLI Lecture Notes. Stanford, California: CSLI Publications.

Bierwisch, M. 1963. *Grammatik des deutschen Verbs*. studia grammatica II. Berlin: Akademie Verlag.

Bouma, G. and G. van Noord. 1998. Word order constraints on verb clusters German and Dutch. In E. W. Hinrichs, A. Kathol, and T. Nakazawa, eds., *Complex Predicates in Nonderivational Syntax*, pages 43–72. San Diego: Academic Press.

Chung, C. 1993. Korean auxiliary verb constructions without VP nodes. In *Proceedings of the 1993 Workshop on Korean Linguistics*, pages 274–286. Cambridge: Massachusetts: Harvard University, Department of Linguistics.

Drach, E. 1937. *Grundgedanken der deutschen Satzlehre*. Darmstadt: Wissenschaftliche Buchgesellschaft.

Duden. 1991. *Die deutsche Rechtschreibung*, vol. 1. Mannheim, Leipzig, Wien, Zürich: Dudenverlag.

Eisenberg, P. 1999. *Grundriß der deutschen Grammatik*, vol. 2. Der Satz. Stuttgart, Weimar: Verlag J. B. Metzler.

Grewendorf, G. 1990. Verb-Bewegung und Negation im Deutschen. *Groninger Arbeiten zur Germanistischen Linguistik* 30:57–125.

Haftka, B. 1981. Reihenfolgebeziehungen im Satz (Topologie). In K. E. Heidolph, W. Fläming, and W. Motsch, eds., *Grundzüge einer deutschen Grammatik*, pages 702–764. Berlin: Akademie Verlag.

Hinrichs, E. W. and T. Nakazawa. 1994. Linearizing AUXs in German verbal complexes. In Nerbonne et al. (1994), pages 11–38.

Höhle, T. N. 1982. Über Komposition und Derivation: zur Konstituentenstruktur von Wortbildungsprodukten im Deutschen. *Zeitschrift für Sprachwissenschaft* 1:76–112.

Kathol, A. 1995. *Linearization-Based German Syntax*. Ph.D. thesis, Ohio State University.

Keyser, S. J. and T. Roeper. 1992. Re: The abstract clitic hypothesis. *Linguistic Inquiry* 23(1):89–126.

Kiss, T. 1994. Obligatory coherence: The structure of German modal verb constructions. In Nerbonne et al. (1994), pages 71–108.

Kiss, T. 1995. *Infinite Komplementation. Neue Studien zum deutschen Verbum infinitum*. No. 333 in Linguistische Arbeiten. Tübingen: Max Niemeyer Verlag.

Koster, J. 1975. Dutch as an SOV language. *Linguistic Analysis* 1(2):111–136.

Lüdeling, A. 1998. *On Particle Verbs and Similar Constructions in German*. Ph.D. thesis, Universität Tübingen.

Müller, S. 1997. Yet another paper about partial verb phrase fronting in German. Research Report RR-97-07, DFKI, Saarbrücken. A shorter version appeared in *Proceedings of COLING 96*, pages 800–805.

Müller, S. 1999. *Deutsche Syntax deklarativ. Head-Driven Phrase Structure Grammar für das Deutsche*. No. 394 in Linguistische Arbeiten. Tübingen:

Max Niemeyer Verlag.

Müller, S. Submitted. *Complex Predicates: Verbal Complexes, Resultative Constructions, and Particle Verbs in German.* Habilitationsschrift, Universität des Saarlandes, Saarbrücken.

Neeleman, A. and F. Weermann. 1993. The balance between syntax and morphology: Dutch particles and resultatives. *NLLT* 11:433–475.

Nerbonne, J., K. Netter, and C. J. Pollard, eds. 1994. *German in Head-Driven Phrase Structure Grammar.* No. 46 in CSLI Lecture Notes.

Olsen, S. 1997. Prädikative Argumente syntaktischer und lexikalischer Köpfe: Zum Status der Partikelverben im Deutschen und Englischen. *Folia Linguistica* 31:3–4.

Oppenrieder, W. 1991. *Von Subjekten, Sätzen und Subjektsätzen.* No. 241 in Linguisitische Arbeiten. Tübingen: Max Niemeyer Verlag.

Pollard, C. J. and I. A. Sag. 1994. *Head-Driven Phrase Structure Grammar.* Studies in Contemporary Linguistics. Chicago, London: University of Chicago Press.

Pütz, H. 1982. Objektsprädikate. In W. Abraham, ed., *Satzglieder im Deutschen*, pages 331–367. Tübingen: Gunter Narr Verlag.

Reape, M. 1990. Getting things in order. In H. Bunt and A. van Horck, eds., *Discontinuous Constituency*, pages 209–253. Berlin, New York: Mouton de Gruyter. Appeared 1996.

Rentier, G. 1994. Dutch cross serial dependencies in HPSG. In *Proceedings of COLING 94*, pages 818–822. Kyoto, Japan.

Rothstein, S. D. 1985. *The Syntactic Forms of Predication.* Ph.D. thesis, Bar-Ilan University. Reproduced by the Indiana University Linguistics Club.

Uszkoreit, H. 1987. *Word Order and Constituent Structure in German.* No. 8 in CSLI Lecture Notes. Stanford: Center for the Study of Language and Information.

Wechsler, S. 1997. Resultative predicates and control. In *Texas Linguistic Forum 38: The Syntax and Semantics of Predication. Proceedings of the 1997 Texas Linguistics Society Conference*, pages 307–321.

Werner, O. 1994. Was da sich ölles aahotmüßhör! ‚Was der sich alles hat anhören müssen!‘ Auxiliar-Inkorporation im Ostfränkisch-Thüringischen. In H. Löffler, K. Jakob, and B. Kelle, eds., *Texttyp, Sprechergruppe, Kommunikationsbereich*, pages 343–361. Berlin, New York: Walter de Gruyter.

Wunderlich, D. 1997. Argument extension by lexical adjunction. *Journal of Semantics* 14(2):95–142.

Zifonun, G. 1999. Wenn *mit* alleine im Mittelfeld erscheint: Verbpartikeln und ihre Doppelgänger im Deutschen und Englischen. In H. Wegener, ed., *Deutsch kontrastiv. Typologisch-vergleichende Untersuchungen zur deutschen Grammatik.* Stauffenberg Verlag.

13

A Constraint-Based Semantics for Tenses and Temporal Auxiliaries

FRANK VAN EYNDE

13.1 Introduction

Combining ideas from Donald Davidson, Hans Reichenbach and Discourse Representation Theory (DRT), I will develop a constraint-based semantics for the Dutch tenses and temporal auxiliaries which is fully integrated in the HPSG framework. The semantics will be inspired to a large extent by DRT, but the syntax is squarely based on the lexicialist surface-oriented approach of HPSG, and so is the treatment of the relation between syntax and semantics. Instead of DRT's construction rules which map syntactic structures onto discourse representation structures, I will use lexically anchored constraints on the relation between syntactic, semantic and pragmatic properties of signs. Since the constraints which I will use are monotonic, the resulting treatment is non-directional, in contrast to DRT's construction rules, which are unidirectional (from syntax to semantics) and irreversible. Next to this technical advantage, there is also a conceptual one: since the construction rules of DRT have the unlimited power which was once characteristic of transformations in the Standard Theory, they allow for such a broad range of stipulations and arbitrarily complex conditions that the linguist is not encouraged to strive for maximum transparency in the formulation of relations between syntax and semantics/pragmatics. The constraint-based approach, on the other hand, imposes a much tighter discipline on the formulation of such relations, and thus enhances the possibility of arriving at computationally viable analyses.

The paper starts with a section on the representation of tensed verbs in general, and then covers the Dutch tenses, the auxiliaries of the perfect

Grammatical Interfaces in HPSG.
Ronnie Cann, Claire Grover and Philip Miller.

(*hebben* and *zijn*) and the auxiliary of the future (*zullen*).

13.2 The Semantic Representation of Tensed Verbs

Most versions of the Predicate Calculus (PC) use only one type of variables, as in the following representation of *John bought a horse.*

(1) ∃x [horse(x) & bought(j,x)]

This style of analysis has been challenged by Donald Davidson. In Davidson (1967) he argued for the use of event variables in the analysis of action sentences, as in

(2) ∃x ∃e [horse(x) & bought(e,j,x)]

This notation is somewhat more verbose and assumes a richer ontology than standard PC, but it facilitates the treatment of VP modification. The modifier in *John bought a horse in Egypt*, for instance, is a constraint on the location of the buying event, and not on the location of either John or the horse. The first argument of *in* should, hence, be identified with the event of buying, as in

(3) ∃x [horse(x) & in(bought(j,x),egypt)]

While brief and plausible, this representation is less appropriate for modelling inferences; the fact, for instance, that *John bought a horse in Egypt* necessarily implies that *John bought a horse* would require a separate statement. By contrast, in the notation with an event variable, this simply follows from the logic of conjunction (p & q → p).

(4) ∃x ∃e [horse(x) & bought(e,j,x) & in(e,egypt)]

Another argument for the use of event variables concerns the fact that natural languages allow for quantification over events and for pronominal reference to events, as in

(5) Whenever it rains, John sneezes.

(6) Mary is going out with George. Bill does not like it.

For a good survey of the major arguments in favor of the event type analysis, see (Parsons, 1990, 13-19) and (Kamp and Reyle, 1993, 504–10).

In HPSG, where the PC variables roughly correspond to indices, it is standard practice to limit the use of indices to the representation of nominal projections, see Pollard and Sag (1994). For a variety of reasons, however, many authors have argued for a wider use of indices and also employ them for the representation of verbal projections, see a.o. Sanfilippo (1990), Van Eynde (1998) and Sag and Wasow (1999).

Adopting this Davidsonian style, the CONTENT values of verbal signs can be given the same general format as the ones of nominal signs.

(7)
$$\begin{bmatrix} \text{CATEGORY}\,|\,\text{HEAD} & \textit{noun} \\ \text{ARG-ST} & \langle\ \rangle \\ \text{CONTENT} & \begin{bmatrix} \text{INDEX} & \boxed{1}\ \textit{ref} \\ \text{RESTR} & \left\{ {}_{\textit{horse}}\begin{bmatrix}\text{INST} & \boxed{1}\end{bmatrix} \right\} \end{bmatrix} \end{bmatrix}$$

(8)
$$\begin{bmatrix} \text{CATEGORY}\,|\,\text{HEAD} & \textit{verb} \\ \text{ARG-ST} & \langle \text{NP}_{\boxed{1}}, \text{NP}_{\boxed{2}} \rangle \\ \text{CONTENT} & \begin{bmatrix} \text{INDEX} & \boxed{3}\ \textit{ref} \\ \text{RESTR} & \left\{ {}_{\textit{buy}}\begin{bmatrix}\text{INST} & \boxed{3} \\ \text{BUYER} & \boxed{1}\ \textit{ref} \\ \text{BOUGHT} & \boxed{2}\ \textit{ref}\end{bmatrix} \right\} \end{bmatrix} \end{bmatrix}$$

In both cases there is a referential index which is further constrained by at least one restriction.

The introduction of verbal indices also facilitates the analysis of the tenses. The temporal meaning of a past tense verb, for instance, could be analyzed as a precedence relation between its index and the time of utterance. While basically sound, many authors have argued that this relation is somewhat more complex. Reichenbach (1947), for instance, claimed that the relation between events and utterance times should be mediated by event and reference times, and similar claims can be found throughout the vast literature on tense and aspect, see Binnick (1991) for a good survey. Also in Pollard and Sag (1994) it is clearly suggested—in a footnote—that the semantic analysis of tense requires more than events and utterance times: "... we assume that the proper way to handle it [= tense, FVE] is in terms of an additional LOCATION role in the CONTENT value together with certain *context* attributes concerning temporal location, corresponding (say) to Reichenbach's utterance time, reference time, and event time. For example, present tense might be treated by structure sharing the EVENT-TIME value in the CONTEXT with the index of the LOCATION value in the CONTENT, and adding a BACKGROUND psoa [= paramatrized-state-of-affairs, FVE] restricting the EVENT-TIME value to temporally overlap the UTTERANCE-TIME value." (o.c., 29) Following this suggestion, the present tense forms of *buy* can be analyzed as follows.

(9)
$$\begin{bmatrix} \text{CATEGORY}\,|\,\text{HEAD} & \textit{verb} \\ \text{CONTENT} & \begin{bmatrix} \text{INDEX} & \boxed{1}\ \textit{ref} \\ \text{RESTR} & \left\{ {}_{\textit{buy}}\begin{bmatrix} \text{INST} & \boxed{1} \\ \text{BUYER} & \textit{ref} \\ \text{BOUGHT} & \textit{ref}\end{bmatrix}, {}_{\textit{at}}\begin{bmatrix}\text{INST} & \boxed{1}\\ \text{LOC} & \boxed{2}\end{bmatrix} \right\} \end{bmatrix} \\ \text{CONTEXT} & \begin{bmatrix} \text{C-INDICES} & \begin{bmatrix} \text{EVENT-TIME} & \boxed{2}\ \textit{temp} \\ \text{REF-TIME} & \textit{temp} \\ \text{UTT-TIME} & \boxed{3}\ \textit{temp}\end{bmatrix} \\ \text{BACKGROUND} & \left\{ \boxed{2} \bigcirc \boxed{3} \right\} \end{bmatrix}\end{bmatrix}$$

The verbal index $\boxed{1}$ is related to a location $\boxed{2}$, which is an object of type *temporal* and which is introduced in the CONTEXT attribute, more specifically as the value of EVENT-TIME.[1] Though sketchy, this format provides a useful starting point for a constraint-based analysis of the Dutch tenses and temporal auxiliaries.

13.3 The Dutch Tenses

Like English, Dutch has two tenses: the present and the past. For their analysis I will combine insights from the Reichenbachian tradition with some more recent developments in Discourse Representation Theory (DRT), as described in Kamp and Reyle (1993).

13.3.1 The Past Tense

In contrast to Reichenbach (1947), who provides a uniform analysis of the simple past (E = R, R < S), DRT emphasizes that its interpretation in event describing sentences is fundamentally different from its interpretation in state describing sentences. Compare

(10) John bought a horse yesterday.

(11) Bart was ill yesterday.

The first sentence is only true if the buying event is temporally included in yesterday, whereas the second sentence is also true if Bart's illness extends beyond yesterday: it may have started earlier and it may

[1] The LOCATION attribute could also be treated as an extra-role in the *buy*-predicate itself, but the advantage of the present—more modular—structure is that it enables us to refer to the temporal properties of the predicate, without having to mention its other semantic roles.

go on after yesterday. In order to capture this difference DRT stipulates that the relation between the described situation and the time of utterance is mediated by a time of location. More specifically, if a past tense sentence describes an event (e), then the event is included in a time of location (t) which precedes the time of utterance ($e \subseteq t$ and $t < u$), and if it describes a state (s), then the state overlaps a time of location (t) which precedes the time of utterance ($s \bigcirc t$ and $t < u$). As is clear from this formulation, the location time of DRT does not stand for the temporal location of the situation itself, but rather for a time with respect to which the situation's location is defined. In Reichenbach's terms, it would be more like the reference time than like the event time.

The distinction between states and events is also relevant for the analysis of the Dutch past. More specifically, the observations about the difference between *bought* and *was* also apply to their Dutch equivalents.

(12) Jan kocht gisteren een paard.
John buy.PAST yesterday a horse
'John bought a horse yesterday.'

(13) Bart was gisteren ziek.
Bart be.PAST yesterday ill
'Bart was ill yesterday.'

In order to model this in the constraint-based style of HPSG I will make use of three implicational constraints. The most general one (IC-VERB) applies to all substantive verbal signs, both lexical and phrasal ones.[2]

$$
{}_{subst}\begin{bmatrix}\text{CAT}\mid\text{HEAD} & \textit{verb}\end{bmatrix} \rightarrow
\begin{bmatrix}
\text{CONT} & \begin{bmatrix} \text{INDEX} & \boxed{1}\ \textit{ref} \\ \text{RESTR} & \left\{ {}_{at}\begin{bmatrix} \text{INST} & \boxed{1} \\ \text{LOC} & \boxed{2} \end{bmatrix} \right\} \end{bmatrix} \\
\text{CONX} & \begin{bmatrix} \text{C-INDS} & \begin{bmatrix} \text{SIT-TIME} & \boxed{2}\ \textit{temp} \\ \text{LOC-TIME} & \boxed{3}\ \textit{temp} \end{bmatrix} \\ \text{BACKGROUND} & \left\{ \boxed{2} \bigcirc \boxed{3} \right\} \end{bmatrix}
\end{bmatrix}
$$

In words, every substantive verbal sign has a referential index which is related to a temporal location, more specifically its situation time,[3]

[2]The relevance of the restriction to substantive signs will become apparent in the section on the past time perfect.

[3]The situation time is comparable to Reichenbach's event time. I prefer the term *situation* since it generalizes over states, events and other types of actions.

and the latter is required to overlap the time of location.

The second constraint (IC-PAST) applies to the substantive past tense verbs.[4]

$$_{subst}\begin{bmatrix}\text{CAT}\,|\,\text{HEAD}\,|\,\text{VFORM} & past\end{bmatrix} \rightarrow \begin{bmatrix}\text{C-INDS} & \begin{bmatrix}\text{LOC-TIME} & \boxed{1}\ temp \\ \text{UTT-TIME} & \boxed{2}\ temp\end{bmatrix} \\ \text{BACKGROUND} & \left\{\boxed{1} < \boxed{2}\right\}\end{bmatrix}$$

The third constraint (IC-EVENT) only applies to event describing predicates, adding the requirement that the event's location be included in the time of location. To model this I start from the assumption that the main distinguishing characteristic of event type predicates is that they present a situation as bounded in time.[5] The temporal extension of a predicate like *wrote this letter*, for instance, is bounded, since writing this letter takes a specifiable amount of time: once the letter is finished, the event is over. By contrast, the temporal extension of *wrote letters* is unbounded, since the action can go on indefinitely: there is no built-in termination point. A well-known test for drawing this distinction is based on the form which the durational adjunct takes: if the predication's location is unbounded, the adjunct is introduced by *for*, and if it is bounded, the adjunct is introduced by *in*, cf. *wrote letters for/*in the whole afternoon* vs. *wrote this letter in/*for half an hour*. Since the bounded/unbounded dichotomy applies to temporal objects, it seems natural to associate it with the objects of type *temporal*.

(14) $_{temp}\begin{bmatrix}\text{BOUNDED} & boolean\end{bmatrix}$

In the lexicon, the LOC value of most verbs is the underspecified *boolean*, since they can just as well head a bounded VP as an unbounded one. It is only after the addition of the complements and/or adjuncts that *boolean* can be replaced with a more specific value, cf. the bounded

[4]In DRT, the relation between the location time and the time of utterance is mediated by a temporal point of perspective. The relevance of this extension, though, is limited to the analysis of some rather marked discourse phenomena, such as flashbacks, free indirect speech and inner monologues. For the purpose of this paper, I will make the simplifying assumption that the point of perspective coincides with the time of utterance. For an analysis which also covers contexts in which the perspective time is dissociated from the utterance time, see Van Eynde (1998).

[5]The familiar distinction between telic and atelic predicates is a special case of this: telic predicates have a built-in termination point and are hence bounded at the end, whereas atelic predicates lack such a point and are hence unbounded at the end.

wrote this letter vs. the unbounded *wrote letters*. For a detailed formal account of how this can be done in a compositional way, see Verkuyl (1993). Assuming that this can also be modeled in terms of a lexicalist framework as HPSG, and admitting that this still needs to be worked out, we can formulate IC-EVENT as follows.

$$
{}_{subst}\left[\begin{array}{ll}
\text{CATEGORY} & \left[\begin{array}{ll}\text{HEAD} & \textit{verb}\\ \text{COMPS} & \langle\ \rangle\end{array}\right]\\
\text{CONTENT} & \left[\begin{array}{ll}\text{INDEX} & \boxed{1}\ \textit{ref}\\ \text{RESTR} & \left\{ {}_{at}\left[\begin{array}{ll}\text{INST} & \boxed{1}\\ \text{LOC} & \boxed{2}\ {}_{temp}\left[\text{BOUNDED}\quad +\right]\end{array}\right]\right\}\end{array}\right]
\end{array}\right]
$$

$$
\rightarrow \left[\begin{array}{ll}
\text{CONTEXT} & \left[\begin{array}{ll}\text{C-INDS} & \left[\begin{array}{ll}\text{SIT-TIME} & \boxed{2}\\ \text{LOC-TIME} & \boxed{3}\ \textit{temp}\end{array}\right]\\ \text{BACKGROUND} & \left\{\boxed{2} \subseteq \boxed{3}\right\}\end{array}\right]
\end{array}\right]
$$

In words, if a verbal sign with an empty COMPS list has a bounded temporal location, then the latter is included in the time of location. Since inclusion is a special case of overlap, this constraint does not contradict the more general IC-VERB; it only provides more specific information.

An interesting property of this analysis is that it correctly predicts the contrast in

(15) Bart was gisteren al een week ziek.
Bart be.PAST yesterday already a week ill
'Bart had been ill for a week yesterday.'

(16) ? Laura schreef gisteren een sonnet in een week.
Laura write.PAST yesterday a sonnet in a week

The state describing sentence is well-formed, since a state is only required to overlap the time of location, so that its temporal extension (a week) may exceed the one of the time of location (yesterday). The event describing sentence, on the other hand, is not well-formed, since an event is required to be included in the time of location.

This greater flexibility in the interpretation of temporally unbounded predications does not mean that they cannot be constrained in other ways. In the following sentence, for instance, Bart's stay in Brussels is not meant to overlap with yesterday, but rather to be included in it.

(17) Bart was twee uur in Brussel gisteren.
Bart be.PAST two hour in Brussels yesterday
'Bart was in Brussels for two hours yesterday.'

This more specific interpretation is due to the semantic contributions of the temporal adjuncts. For a proposal on how this can be modelled in the present framework, see Schelkens et al. (2000).

13.3.2 The Present Tense

Semantically, the Dutch present is complementary to the Dutch past. Whereas the latter expresses precedence, the former expresses simultaneity or futurity, i.e., non-precedence.

(18) Greta is ziek vandaag.
Greta be.PRES ill today
'Greta is ill today.'

(19) Morgen loopt Jan de 100 meter.
tomorrow run.PRES Jan the 100 meter
'Jan runs the 100 meter tomorrow.'

The combination with a past time adjunct is highly unusual and stylistically marked, like in English.

(20) ? Gisteren loopt Jan de 100 meter.
yesterday run.PRES Jan the 100 meter

The semantic contribution of the Dutch present can, hence, be characterized as follows (IC-PRESENT).

$$
_{subst}\Big[\text{CAT} \mid \text{HEAD} \mid \text{VFORM} \quad \textit{present}\Big] \rightarrow \begin{bmatrix} \text{C-INDS} & \begin{bmatrix} \text{LOC-TIME} & \boxed{1} \\ \text{UTT-TIME} & \boxed{2} \end{bmatrix} \\ \text{BACKGROUND} & \left\{ \boxed{1} \nprec \boxed{2} \right\} \end{bmatrix}
$$

How the time of location relates to the situation time is specified by IC-VERB and IC-EVENT.[6] As a consequence, we expect that the tem-

[6]In contrast to the English present, the Dutch present is compatible with event type predicates, also if they stand for a single ongoing event. The sentence *Jan eet een hamburger*, for instance, can refer to a single event of eating which is going on at the time of utterance. In English, the expression of this meaning requires the use of the present progressive, as in *John is eating a hamburger* (Kamp and Reyle, 1993, 537).

poral extension of a state type predicate may exceed the length of the location time, whereas the one of an event type predicate may not. This expectation is indeed borne out.

(21) Morgen wonen we hier precies twee jaar.
tomorrow live.PRES we here precisely two year
'Tomorrow we will have lived here for precisely two years.'

(22) ? Morgen schrijf ik een boek in twee jaar.
tomorrow write.PRES I a book in two year

In the state describing sentence it does not matter that the period of two years cannot be interpreted as part of tomorrow, since it is sufficient that they overlap, but in the event describing sentence, the resulting combination is not well-formed, since events require inclusion.

13.4 The Dutch Perfect

The formation of the Dutch perfect involves the use of two verbs: the auxiliary of the perfect, which is either *hebben* ('have') or *zijn* ('be'), and the past participle of the main verb. Syntactically, the auxiliary is the head; it takes the participle as its most oblique argument, and inherits its other arguments from that participle.[7]

(23)
$$\begin{bmatrix} \text{CATEGORY}\,|\,\text{HEAD} & \textit{verb} \\ \text{ARG-ST} & \boxed{1} \oplus \left\langle \begin{bmatrix} \text{V}[\textit{psp}],\ \text{ARG-ST} & \boxed{1} \end{bmatrix} \right\rangle \end{bmatrix}$$

Semantically, I will distinguish between two uses of the perfect.

13.4.1 The Aspectual Perfect

Some typical examples of the aspectual perfect are

(24) Om tien uur had ik al drie klanten bezocht.
at ten hour have.PAST I already three clients visit.PSP
'At ten o'clock I had already visited three clients.'

(25) Ik heb nu al drie klanten bezocht.
I have.PRES now already three clients visit.PSP
'I have already visited three clients now.'

These sentences describe a state which results from a completed event. In contrast to what happens in the simple tenses, the adjuncts

[7]Since only words have an ARG-ST feature, this analysis implicitly assumes that the participial complement is a lexical sign, rather than a phrasal one. This is compatible with the analysis of the Dutch *Mittelfeld* in van Noord and Bouma (1994).

om tien uur ('at ten o'clock') and *nu* ('now') do not specify the location time of the visits themselves, but rather the time at which the state of having paid the visits holds; the visits themselves are, hence, said to have taken place at some earlier time. Interestingly, this more complex interpretation can be derived in a purely compositional way.

For a start, let us assume that the auxiliary of the aspectual perfect has the following AVM.

(26)
$$\begin{bmatrix} \text{CATEGORY} \mid \text{HEAD} & \textit{verb} \\ \text{ARG-ST} & \boxed{1} \oplus \left\langle \begin{bmatrix}\text{V, ARG-ST } \boxed{1}\text{ , SIT-TIME } \boxed{4}\ \textit{temp}\end{bmatrix}_{\boxed{3}} \right\rangle \\ \text{CONTENT} & \begin{bmatrix} \text{INDEX} & \boxed{2}\ \textit{ref} \\ \text{RESTR} & \left\{ \begin{bmatrix} \text{INST} & \boxed{2} \\ \text{SOA-ARG} & \boxed{3}\ \textit{ref} \end{bmatrix}_{\textit{result-of}} \right\} \end{bmatrix} \\ \text{CONTEXT} & \begin{bmatrix} \text{C-INDS} \mid \text{SIT-TIME} & \boxed{5}\ \textit{temp} \\ \text{BACKGROUND} & \left\{ \boxed{4} < \boxed{5} \right\} \end{bmatrix} \end{bmatrix}$$

The name of the predicate (*result-of*) is meant to generalize over *hebben* and *zijn*; it takes the index of the participle $\boxed{3}$ as its argument, and since the result of an action necessarily succeeds the action itself, its situation time $\boxed{5}$ is required to follow the one of the participle $\boxed{4}$.[8] The latter is furthermore bounded, since the event is presented as completed; the former, on the other hand, is unbounded, since it denotes a state.

Since the AVM of the auxiliary unifies with the left hand side of IC-VERB, the situation time of the result state is related to a time of location, and if the auxiliary is tensed, the latter is further related to the time of utterance by either IC-PAST or IC-PRESENT. Incidentally, since the Dutch present allows for a futurate interpretation, we predict that the present perfect is compatible with future time adjuncts, and this prediction is indeed borne out.[9]

(27) Morgen heb ik het gevonden; dat is zeker.
tomorrow have.PRES I it find.PSP; that is sure
'I will have found it by tomorrow; that is for sure.'

The participle, for its part, has its own AVM. If substantive, it will have its own index, situation time and location time, and—given IC-

[8]This corresponds to Reichenbach's constraint that E precede R in the perfect tenses.

[9]In English, this combination sounds awkward, since the English present is hardly ever used to express futurity in state describing sentences.

VERB—this time of location will be required to overlap the situation time. Moreover, since the participle describes a completed event, its situation time is bounded, and hence included in the location time, as required by IC-EVENT. As will be argued below, this is not only a property of the participle in aspectual perfect constructions, but a property of the Dutch past participle in general. To capture it I add the constraint IC-PSP.

$$_{subst}\left[\text{CAT}\,|\,\text{HEAD}\,|\,\text{VFORM} \quad psp\right] \rightarrow \begin{bmatrix} \text{C-INDS} & \begin{bmatrix} \text{SIT-TIME} & \boxed{2}\ temp \\ \text{LOC-TIME} & \boxed{3}\ temp \end{bmatrix} \\ \text{BACKGROUND} & \left\{\boxed{2} \subseteq \boxed{3}\right\} \end{bmatrix}$$

This is a formal expression of the intuition that the Dutch past participle presents an eventuality as completed.[10]

Having specified the information which is carried by the auxiliary and the participle, we can now turn to their combination. The following tree, for instance, shows how the past participle interacts with the present forms of the perfect auxiliary.

(28)

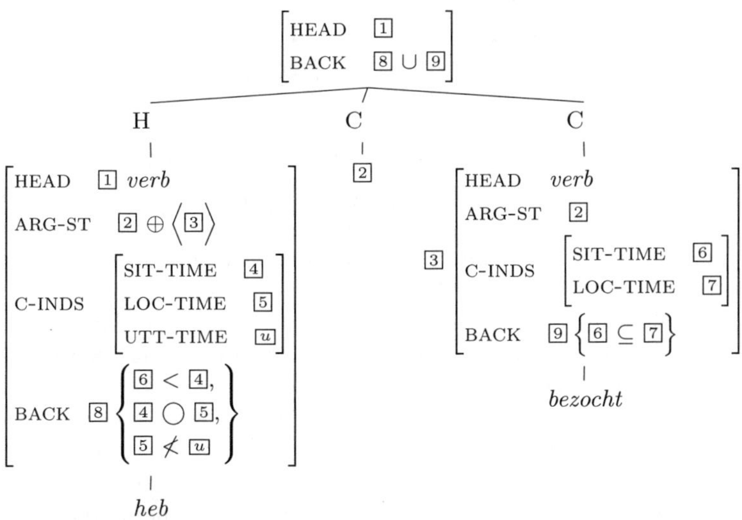

The temporal constraints of the present tense auxiliary and of the participle are included in their respective background values and passed on to the mother node, as stipulated in the Principle of Contextual Consistency: "The CONTEXT|BACKGROUND value of a given phrase is the

[10]Significantly, the standard term of the past participle in Dutch grammars is *voltooid deelwoord* ('completed participle').

union of the CONTEXT|BACKGROUND values of the daughters.” (Pollard and Sag, 1994, 333) In this case, the four background restrictions are mutually compatible, so that the resulting temporal interpretation is consistent.

Since the resulting feature structure contains two times of location, the addition of a temporal adjunct may lead to ambiguity, as in

(29) Ze had om vier uur al een hamburger gegeten.
she have.PAST at four hour already a hamburger eat.PSP
‘She had already eaten a hamburger at four o’clock.’

In this sentence, the adjunct can apply to the location time of the auxiliary, meaning that the state of having eaten the hamburger held at four, but it can also apply to the location time of the participle, meaning that the eating itself took place at four.

Further evidence for this compositional analysis of the aspectual perfect can be extracted from the contrast in

(30) Het sneeuwt nu al vier dagen.
it snow.PRES now already four days
‘It has been snowing for four days now.’

(31) Het heeft nu al vier dagen gesneeuwd.
it have.PRES now already four days snow.PSP
‘It has already snowed for four days by now.’

The meanings of these sentences are similar, but their semantic analysis reveals a subtle difference. In the simple present sentence, there is only one situation time and this has to overlap the time of location, which is specified by *nu* (‘now’); as a consequence, the sentence is only true if it is snowing at (part of) the location time. For instance, if uttered on November 28, it will only be true if it started snowing on November 25 and is still snowing on the 28.

In the present perfect sentence, on the other hand, there are two situations, i.e., the process of snowing and the state which results from four days of snowing, and since it is only this state which has to overlap the location time of the auxiliary, it follows that the sentence can also be true if it is not snowing at the time of location. If uttered on November 28, for instance, the sentence is also true if the snowing took place in a period from say November 23 till November 26.

Summing up, this lexicalist analysis of the Dutch aspectual perfect does not only have the advantage of being strictly compositional, it also captures a salient but previously unnoticed contrast with the simple present.

13.4.2 The Past Time Perfect

As demonstrated in the previous paragraph, the aspectual present perfect expresses non-precedence, and is hence compatible with present and future time adjuncts, but not with past time adjuncts. In practice, though, the Dutch present perfect does combine with such adjuncts.

(32) Hij heeft gisteren een verklaring afgelegd.
he have.PRES yesterday a declaration make.PSP
'He made a declaration yesterday.'

In contrast to the combination of the simple present with a past time adjunct, this combination is not unusual or marked.

To model this past time use of the present perfect we could stick to the analysis of the aspectual perfect and add the stipulation that the adjunct *gisteren* ('yesterday') does not specify the location time of the auxiliary here but rather the one of the participle. This would not only solve the incompatibility problem, it would also capture the fact that yesterday specifies the time of the declaration itself, rather than the temporal location of the state which results from that declaration.

In spite of these assets, though, the resulting analysis is not entirely satisfactory, since it still includes a result state, even though sentences like the above do not make any reference—neither implicit nor explicit—to a result state. They simply present some action as having taken place in the past. Significant in this respect is the fact that the English equivalent of this use of the present perfect is the simple past. Moreover, if the semantic analysis of a sentence like the above would include a non-past state, next to the past event, then it should be possible to add a present time adjunct, next to the past time *gisteren* ('yesterday'), without creating any contradictions, but this is not the case: adding the adverb *nu* ('now'), for instance, results in inconsistency.

More appropriate would be an analysis which contains only one time of location. In order to achieve this effect I will assume that the past time perfect lacks descriptive content. Unlike the aspectual perfect, which introduces a new verbal index and which denotes a predicate (*result-of*), the past time perfect simply relates the location time of its participial complement to the time of utterance without contributing any descriptive content of its own. In terms of the HPSG type hierarchy, its contribution concerns the CATEGORY and CONTEXT attributes, but not the CONTENT attribute. Technically, this can be implemented by distinguishing between two types of *local* objects.

(33) *local*
substantive *nonsubstantive*

While all objects of type *local* have the attributes CATEGORY and CONTEXT, only the substantive ones have the CONTENT attribute.

(34) $$_{local}\begin{bmatrix} \text{CATEGORY} & \textit{category} \\ \text{CONTEXT} & \textit{context} \end{bmatrix}$$

(35) $$_{substantive}\begin{bmatrix} \text{CONTENT} & \textit{content} \end{bmatrix}$$

Being nonsubstantive, the auxiliary of the past time perfect is not subject to any of the implicational constraints which have been introduced so far. Instead, its contribution is specified lexically.

(36) $$_{nonsubst}\begin{bmatrix} \text{CATEGORY}\,|\,\text{HEAD}\,|\,\text{VFORM} & \textit{present} \\ \text{ARG-ST} & \boxed{1} \oplus \left\langle \begin{bmatrix} \text{V, ARG-ST } \boxed{1}\text{, LOC-TIME } \boxed{2} \end{bmatrix} \right\rangle \\ \text{CONTEXT} & \begin{bmatrix} \text{C-INDS}\,|\,\text{UTT-TIME} & \boxed{3}\ \textit{temp} \\ \text{BACKGROUND} & \left\{ \boxed{2} < \boxed{3} \right\} \end{bmatrix} \end{bmatrix}$$

The location time of the participle is not related to the auxiliary's situation time (for the simple reason that the auxiliary has no situation time), but directly to the time of utterance. When combined with a past participle, the auxiliary is the syntactic head, but since it lacks a CONTENT attribute, it is the participle which functions as the semantic head.[11]

(37)

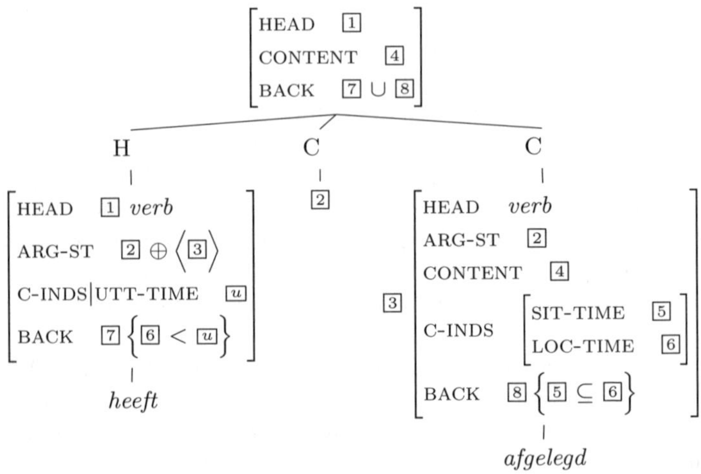

[11]The dissociation of syntactic and semantic heads is by no means exceptional. In Pollard and Sag (1994), for instance, the adjuncts are treated as the semantic head in HEAD-ADJUNCT combinations.

Interestingly, the BACKGROUND value of the combination is identical to the one for the English simple past in event describing sentences.

Because of the nonsubstantive nature of the auxiliary, the combination has only one situation time and one location time. This explains why the past time perfect fails to show the scope ambiguities which are typical of the aspectual perfect: the adjunct *om vier uur* ('at four o'clock') in the next example, for instance, can only be understood as specifying the time of eating, i.e., the location time of the participle.

(38) Gisteren heeft hij om vier uur een hamburger gegeten.
yesterday have.PRES he at four hour a hamburger eat.PSP
'Yesterday he ate a hamburger at four o'clock.'

The absence of a second time of location also helps to explain the contrast in

(39) Het heeft nu al vier dagen gesneeuwd.
it have.PRES now already four days snow.PSP
'It has been snowing for four days now.'

(40) ? Het heeft gisteren al vier dagen gesneeuwd.
it have.PRES yesterday already four days snow.PSP

While the aspectual present perfect allows the combination of a temporal adjunct with a durational adjunct which exceeds its length, the past time perfect does not. This can be explained as follows: the constraint of the past participle that the situation time be included in the location time, can be satisfied in the first sentence, since the location time of the auxiliary, specified by *nu* ('now'), is distinct from the location time of the participle, but in the second sentence, this requirement cannot be met, since there is only one location time.

Because of its simpler semantic structure, the past time perfect has more in common with the simple past than with the aspectual perfect, but in spite of this similarity, their meanings are not identical. In state describing sentences, for instance, the past tense requires overlap with the location time, whereas the past time perfect requires inclusion, because of IC-PSP. This explains the contrast in

(41) Hij was gisteren al een week ziek.
he be.PAST yesterday already a week ill
'He had been ill for a week (by) yesterday.'

(42) ? Hij is gisteren al een week ziek geweest.
he be.PRES yesterday already a week ill be.PSP

In sum, the past time perfect cannot be treated in the same compositional manner as the aspectual perfect, but this does not imply that we have to resort to non-monotonic techniques. All we need is a distinction between substantive and nonsubstantive signs, and the addition of a separate AVM for the auxiliary.

13.5 The Dutch Future

The Dutch auxiliary of the future is *zullen*. Syntactically, it is similar to the one of the perfect; the main difference is that it requires an infinitival complement instead of a participial one. Semantically, *zullen* is ambiguous in a way which resembles the perfect. In its substantive use, it is a modal verb, which contrasts with other modal verbs, such as *moeten* ('must'), *mogen* ('may') and *kunnen* ('can'). In its nonsubstantive use, it is the auxiliary of the future. Some typical examples of the future *zullen* are

(43) Willy zal om vier uur de klokken luiden.
Willy will.PRES at four hour the bells toll.INF
'Willy will toll the bells at four o'clock.'

(44) Morgen zullen we het weten.
tomorrow will.PRES we it know.INF
'We will know it tomorrow.'

Morphologically, the auxiliaries are in the present tense, but semantically they do not express non-precedence, but rather futurity.[12] They should, hence, be exempted from IC-PRESENT, and the way to do this is by now familiar. Instead of treating the auxiliary as a substantive verb with its own index and time of location, it is treated as a nonsubstantive verb, whose main function is to relate the location time of its complement to the time of utterance, as in

(45)
$$\begin{bmatrix} \text{CATEGORY}\,|\,\text{HEAD}\,|\,\text{VFORM} & \textit{present} \\ \text{ARG-ST} & \boxed{1} \oplus \left\langle \begin{bmatrix} \text{V, ARG-ST } \boxed{1}\text{, LOC-TIME } \boxed{2} \end{bmatrix} \right\rangle \\ \text{CONTEXT} & \begin{bmatrix} \text{C-INDS}\,|\,\text{UTT-TIME} & \boxed{3}\ \textit{temp} \\ \text{BACKGROUND} & \left\{ \boxed{2} > \boxed{3} \right\} \end{bmatrix} \end{bmatrix}_{\textit{nonsubst}}$$

Since a combination of this auxiliary with an infinitive contains only one time of location, it is predicted that there cannot be any scope

[12] The present tense of the modal *zullen* expresses non-precedence, as is normal for a substantive verb. The modal use of the auxiliary will not be analyzed in this paper.

ambiguities for the temporal adjuncts, depending on whether they apply to the entire finite VP or only to the infinitive. This prediction is indeed borne out. In the sentence above, for instance, *om vier uur* can only be understood as the time at which the bells will be ringing, and not as a time which precedes that event.

The analysis of the future auxiliary closely resembles the one of the past time perfect, but apart from the obvious difference in meaning (future vs. past), there is another more subtle difference. For, since its complement is an infinitive instead of a participle, the situation time need not be included in the time of location; instead, given IC-VERB, all that is required is overlap, at least in sentences with an unbounded temporal extension, and this explains why the following sentence is well-formed.

(46) Morgen zullen we hier precies tien jaar wonen.
tomorrow will.PRES we here precisely ten year live.INF
'Tomorrow we will have lived here for precisely ten years.'

Ten years cannot be included in a day, but this does not matter, since temporal overlap is sufficient.

When the auxiliary of the future is combined with the aspectual perfect, one gets the so-called future perfect, as in

(47) Voor het einde van de dag zal de haan drie maal
before the end of the day will.PRES the cock three time
gekraaid hebben.
crow.PSP have.INF
'Before the end of the day the cock will have crowed three times.'

This combination contains two substantive verbs, and hence two times of location. The one of the perfect auxiliary is specified by *voor het einde van de dag* ('before the end of the day'), and marks the time at which the state obtains which results from the three crowing events. The function of the nonsubstantive future auxiliary is to relate that time of location to the time of utterance.

13.6 Conclusion

Combining insights from Davidson, Reichenbach and Discourse Representation Theory, I have developed a constraint-based semantics for the Dutch tenses and temporal auxiliaries, and integrated it in the HPSG framework. The core of the analysis is a set of five implicational constraints (IC-VERB, IC-EVENT, IC-PAST, IC-PRESENT, IC-PSP), which, when applied to the AVMs of individual verbal signs, specify their temporal meanings. If a clause contains more than one verb, its temporal meaning can be derived compositionally from the temporal constraints which are associated with the individual verbs. Apparent counterexamples, such as the past time perfect and the future, were brought into line, by the introduction of a sortal distinction between substantive and nonsubstantive signs, the stipulation that the implicational constraints only apply to substantive verbs, and the addition of two lexical AVMs. Further evidence for the distinction between substantive and nonsubstantive signs is provided in Van Eynde (2000), where it is applied to the English auxiliaries.

When compared to the rule-based treatment of the syntax/semantics interface in DRT, this constraint-based treatment has the advantages of being non-directional, fully explicit and comparatively simple. More specifically, DRT's irreversible construction rules which are a mixture of formal notation and prose, and which often take a full page of text, have been replaced by a small set of fully formalized implicational constraints and lexical specifications.

References

Binnick, R. 1991. *Time and the verb. A guide to tense and aspect.* New York/Oxford: Oxford University Press.

Davidson, D. 1967. The logical form of action sentences. In N. Rescher, ed., *The logic of decision and action*. University of Pittsburgh Press.

Kamp, H. and U. Reyle. 1993. *From Discourse to Logic. Introduction to Modeltheoretic Semantics of Natural Language, Formal Logic and Discourse Representation Theory.* Dordrecht/Boston/London: Kluwer Academic Publishers.

Parsons, T. 1990. *Events in the Semantics of English*, vol. 19 of *Current Studies in Linguistics*. MIT Press.

Pollard, C. and I. Sag. 1994. *Head-driven Phrase Structure Grammar*. Stanford/Chicago: CSLI and University of Chicago Press.

Reichenbach, H. 1947. *Elements of Symbolic Logic.* New York: The Free Press. reprint (1966).

Sag, I. and T. Wasow. 1999. *Syntactic Theory. A formal introduction.* CSLI Publications.

Sanfilippo, A. 1990. *Grammatical Relations, Thematic Roles and Verb Semantics*. Ph.D. thesis, University of Edinburgh.

Schelkens, N., F. Van Eynde, and S. Verdoolaege. 2000. The Semantics of Temporal Adjuncts. In P. Monachesi, ed., *Computational Linguistics in the Netherlands 1999*. Utrecht: University of Utrecht.

Van Eynde, F. 1998. Tense, Aspect and Negation. In F. Van Eynde and P. Schmidt, eds., *Linguistic Specifications for Typed Feature Structure Formalisms*, vol. 10 of *Studies in Machine Translation and Natural Language*

Processing, pages 209–280. Luxembourg: Office for Official Publications of the European Communities.

Van Eynde, F. 2000. Figure Heads in HPSG. In F. Van Eynde, I. Schuurman, and N. Schelkens, eds., *Computational Linguistics in the Netherlands 1998*, pages 161–178. Amsterdam/Atlanta: Rodopi.

van Noord, G. and G. Bouma. 1994. Adjuncts and the Processing of Lexical Rules. In *Proceedings of the 15th International Conference on Computational Linguistics (Coling)*, pages 250–256. Kyoto: University of Kyoto.

Verkuyl, H. 1993. *A Theory of Aspectuality. The Interaction between Temporal and Atemporal Structure*, vol. 64 of *Cambridge Studies in Linguistics*. Cambridge University Press.

14

Spanish Psychological Predicates

CARL VOGEL AND BEGOÑA VILLADA

14.1 Introduction

This paper examines syntactic valency, semantic argument structure and subject/verb agreement in Peninsular Spanish psychological predicates, and related constructions in other languages. We formalize our approach in HPSG. We also propose solutions to some HPSG theory-internal problems connected to interfaces between these aspects of grammar.

Spanish is an SVO language. Our operational definition of a subject NP is that it be a nominal satisfying the following conditions: A) it requires nominative case upon pronominal substitution; B) it appears as the first NP in an unmarked finite clause; C) it is semantically coindexed with the "logical subject"; D) it exhibits agreement coindexing with the finite V. However, certain emotion verbs in Spanish test this definition. In (1a), *apetecer* accepts the object of fancy as a canonical subject, but this is a highly marked structure; (1b) is more acceptable. It has as its first NP a dative NP (*A mí*) rather than a nominative, and agreement features are shared between the verb and the nominative NP which follows it, even though the dative is the logical subject. If the first NP is the subject, then conditions A and D are violated, and if the postverbal NP is the subject then conditions B and C are violated.

(1) a. ? Tus pasteles me apetecieron.
Your pies DAT-CL-1SG fancy-3RD-PL-PAST
'I fancied your pies.'

b. A mí me apetecieron tus pasteles.
To me DAT-CL-1SG fancy-3RD-PL-PAST your pies
'I fancied your pies.'

From similar data Zaenen et al. (1985) conclude that 'quirky' case

Grammatical Interfaces in HPSG.
Ronnie Cann, Claire Grover and Philip Miller.

predicates in Icelandic have dative subjects, while related dative structures in German do not count as subjects. Dative subjects in Icelandic are not active agreement controllers (Zaenen et al., 1985, p. 107).

Head-Driven Phrase Structure Grammar (HPSG; Pollard and Sag 1994) provides the wherewithal to neatly account for the behavior of this class of verbs. We assume a lexical relation between the two syntactic valency patterns. As a first pass, in (1a), the verb's SUBJ list specifies a nominative NP with a semantic index that is argument to a function which determines agreement morphology on the verb (Kathol, 1994), and the verb's COMPS list specifies a dative NP whose index is the logical subject. In (1b), the verb's SUBJ list specifies a dative NP whose semantic index is the logical subject, and the verb's COMPS list requires a nominative NP whose semantic index is shared by the function that determines the verb's agreement features.

Psychological predicates are among the data which suggest that "subject" is a problematic notion. Therefore, we dispense with it and revert to the original way Pollard and Sag (1987) handled valency, using a single SUBCAT list rather than a SUBJ–COMPS partition, and propose an alternative solution to the problems pointed out by Borsley (1989). We examine the details and ramifications of this and alternative HPSG analyses for other aspects of the grammar (e.g., control and raising).

14.2 Psychological Verbs

14.2.1 Overview of the Data

The constructions under discussion follow five different valency patterns.

1. Verbs falling in this category are: *aburrir* 'to bore', *molestar* 'to disturb', *enojar* 'to annoy', *alegrar* 'to cheer', *divertir* 'to amuse', *agradar* 'to please', etc.

Nominative NP	V	Dative/Accusative NP
Cause		Experiencer
AGR: [1]	AGR: [1]	

2. The same verbs as in Type 1 but with different word order: the experiencer dative-NP occurs in initial position along with an agreeing clitic pronoun; the nominative agreement controller is postverbal.

Dative/Accusative NP	dat/acc-clitic	V	nom-NP
Experiencer			Cause
AGR: [2]	AGR: [2]	AGR: [1]	AGR: [1]

3. Verbs representative of this type are: *apetecer* 'to fancy', *gustar* 'to like', *encantar* 'to charm', *interesar* 'to interest', *doler* 'to ache' and *apasionar* 'to fascinate'. These predicates resemble Type 2

constructions, but extremely rarely appear in a Type 1 form.

Dative NP	dative-clitic	V	Nominative NP
Experiencer			Cause
AGR: [2]	AGR: [2]	AGR: [1]	AGR: [1]

4. 'Pronominal verbs': *aburrirse* 'to get bored', *molestarse* 'to get cross', *ofenderse* 'to take offense', *enojarse* 'to get angry', *alegrarse* 'to rejoice', *divertirse* 'to amuse oneself', *apenarse* 'to grieve', etc.

Nominative NP	pronominal–*se*	V	(PP)
Experiencer			Cause
AGR: [1]		AGR: [1]	

5. Finally, a 'normal' pattern of complementation corresponds to verbs such as: *temer* 'to fear', *odiar* 'to hate', *creer* 'to believe', *adorar* 'to adore', *confiar* 'to trust', *conocer* 'to know', *añorar* 'to long for', *anhelar* 'to wish for', *admirar* 'to admire', etc.

Nominative NP	V	NP/PP/that-clause
Experiencer		Stimulus
AGR: [1]	AGR: [1]	

Some of the structures attach greater importance to the experiencer of a psychological state and others give more relevance to the participant that induces such a state on the experiencer. Type 2 verbs could be seen as topicalizations of Type 1 predicates. However, because of their structural similarity to Type 3 constructions which lack Type 1 and Type 4 correlates, we consider Type 2 predications as related to Type 1 predicates via lexical rule, yet still distinct as constructions.

Type 2 predicates take one more syntactic constituent than Type 1 verbs. This is a dative or accusative clitic coindexed with the preceding NP agreeing in case, number, person and gender.[1] In Types 1, 2 and 3, the full NPs may be dropped once their referents have been presented in discourse but their coindexed clitics are still needed and they provide agreement information. Some studies on accusative doubling clitics (this does not entail that the clitics under discussion are accusative-marked in all predicates but their status is similar) claim that this clitic is simply an agreement marker and does not take a semantic role as that is exclusively given to the coindexed referential full NP (Suñer, 1988). However, the clitic takes a clear argument position in Type 4.

14.2.2 What is the Subject?

Alarcos Llorach (1994) argues that because the experiencer-NP in Type 3 constructions is embedded under the preposition *a*, it cannot be the syntactic subject of the sentence. In contrast, Fernández-Soriano (1999)

[1] Gender agreement is marked only for the accusative.

claims that it is possible to analyze "*a*-PPs" as dative NPs eligible to be grammatical subjects. For Alsina (1996) the dative does not have enough subject properties. Moure (1995; p. 101) argues that the subject of the verb *gustar* is the postverbal nominative NP and the initial constituent is an indirect object. Belletti and Rizzi (1988) claim that the constructions involve two nonsubject arguments. In their analysis of psychological predicates in Italian, Belletti and Rizzi (1988) classify the verbs into three groups: *temere* ('to fear') type (our Type 5 verbs), *preoccupare* ('to worry') verbs (our Types 1 and 2) and *piacere* ('to please') (our Type 3). Belletti and Rizzi (1988) analyze the first type as having a logical and syntactic subject, but the latter types as double object constructions with "derived" subjects that cannot occupy the external argument position of the VP because it is assigned inherent (rather than structural) case. Because the Type 3 ordering is unmarked, yet with the experiencer in the position the logical subject is usually in, they conclude that the dative is a quirky subject, analyzed as object.

Grimshaw (1990) classifies psych verbs into two main groups: *fear* type stative verbs and *frighten* type causative and eventive predicates. She faults the Belletti and Rizzi (1988) analysis as not explaining why the categories are what they are. *Fear* type verbs have an external argument; passivization and nominalization provide the proof. Grimshaw argues that *frighten* predicates do not have external arguments, although they do have underlying logical subjects. Grimshaw comments about a third type of psych predicate (Grimshaw, 1990, p. 29): *please* and *concern* in English (the Spanish versions of these are in our Type 3 verbs; *piacere* in Italian). Grimshaw argues that these verbs resemble the *fear* type according to their thematic argument structure and ordering of thematic arguments, although configurationally they are like the *frighten* type (thus, lack an external argument). Grimshaw's analysis is attractive in explaining differences between her two main types through the interaction of an aspectual hierarchy and the hierarchy of theta roles, but does not explain the behavior of Type 3 predicates.

Despite the apparent clarity of pretheoretic intuitions, there is not a clear analytic definition of "subject", although there is a family of properties that correlate with being a subject (Keenan, 1976). It is interesting to observe how these predicates interact with other phenomena that are arguably sensitive to grammatical functions. We present data on control and raising in Spanish, along with our analysis in §14.4.2; an interesting fact is that Spanish does admit object control but not object raising, yet Type 3 dative NPs can raise to subject position without controlling agreement. Vogel and Villada (1999) present more data on causatives, control in general, raising, nominalization, passivization, binding, reflexivization and deverbal adjectives. Our evaluation of the raising data differs from that of Alsina (1996; p. 182) and is more compatible with the reasoning of Zaenen et al. (1985) about Icelandic—in Type 3 predicates the datives raise but do not control agreement on the raising verb. Some tests argue for subject status of the dative, some against, for each type of psychological predicate.

Odd agreement patterns that we have described for the psychological predicates also hold for certain other verbs that are not considered psychological predicates. For example, Fernández-Soriano (1999) discusses stative verbs (*constar* 'to state', *bastar* 'to be enough', *faltar* 'to lack', *sobrar* 'to have extra' and existential *haber* 'there is/are'), eventive verbs (*suceder, ocurrir* 'to happen') and weather verbs (*llover* 'to rain', *nevar* 'to snow') among others with odd case and agreement control patterns. Masullo (1992) presents additional predicates.

14.2.3 Odd Case and Agreement in English

While the English correlates of Type 3 predicates behave as ordinary (SVO) predicates with respect to agreement and case assignment, certain constructions in English act differently. Consider the data in (2–5). Examples (2–3) demonstrate that the agreement controller in these constructions is the non-expletive NP following the verb. (4–5) show that the postverbal agreement controller is also in nominative case.[2]

(2) There is/*are a book on the table.

(3) There are/*is three books on the table.

(4) Who laughs loudly?
There is she/*her who laughs last.

(5) Who eats junk food?
There is she/*her who McDonald's targets successfully.

The existential sentences in English have properties similar to the Type 3 predicates in Spanish. They lack Type 1 counterparts: inverting the arguments yields a strictly demonstrative reading for *there*. Consider raising, using (2) for reference, and (6) as its raised counterpart.

(6) There seems/*seem to be a book on the table.

(7) There seem/?seems to be three books on the table.

Examples (6) and (7) demonstrate that in English (like Spanish; see (17)) it is not necessary for an NP raised to "subject" to control agreement on

[2]Both subject and object relatives are used to demonstrate that the case does not arise from the relative clause.

the raising verb. Pollard and Sag (1994; p. 154) analyze this expletive raising data by taking the expletive as subject of 'be' yet with a NUM value that is coindexed with the NUM value of the post copular noun. In contrast, our account is entirely parallel with our account of raising in Type 3 predicates. The NPs may have incompatible NUM values, and grammaticality results provided that the raising verb and embedded verb share agreement controllers.

Locative inversion and dative shift are additional cases discussed in the literature as providing examples in English in which subjects are assigned quirky case (e.g., see den Dikken and Næss 1993).

14.2.4 Summary

Neither the data nor theorists are univocal on whether the constructions have a subject. We favor a version of HPSG in which that question is moot. Linearization and agreement control properties are indisputable: in the relevant Spanish cases (Type 3) the logical subject is in leftmost position, is marked dative and does not control agreement.

14.3 Background Debate in HPSG

Pollard and Sag (1994; Chr. 9) accept arguments from Borsley that there is a problem with the theory as originally formulated, and this inspired the partitioning of SUBCAT into SUBJ and COMPS. In English, case marking PPs provide an example of the problem. Such a preposition subcategorizes for one argument, but that argument is an oblique argument, not a subject. The preposition is a lexical head expecting its sole argument to occur to its right; this is what the LP constraint dictates, but the ID schema don't allow lexical heads to combine with *all* of their complements unless they are inverted. Under the revision suggested by Borsley, valency features on such heads specify the SUBJ list to be empty, and the COMPS list to contain one element. The ID schema and valency reduction principle are adjusted accordingly.

A simple solution for the problem would be to mark nonpredicative prepositions as [INV+]. However, a number of other aesthetic reasons are provided by Pollard and Sag (1994; Chr. 9) to further motivate the change. Many of these boil down to the convenience of being able to refer to 'subject' rather than 'least oblique element of the SUBCAT list'. A net increase in linguistic ontology ensues when a head is deemed to possess a least oblique complement that does not count as a subject. Our view is that the constructions typically thought of as subjectless have enough subject properties to make the assertion contentious (if one accepts "subject" as a contentful syntactic notion in the first place). Our solution is to drop the notion of syntactic subject from linguistic ontology, reverting to a position in which explanations are based upon less disputable properties of linguistic types.[3]

We propose the alternative ID and LP constraints in (8) and (9). Our alternative solution suggests a feature called POS associated with lexical heads. The subcategorization frame of a verb is the local domain in which the head occurs, and a head declares its position within that domain as at the beginning, the end, or somewhere in the middle (cf. Reape 1990, 1994). We posit POS as a feature of lexical items which can take one of three values: *b*, *m* or *e*. We omit detail of the relation between this and other proposals that suggest positional features (e.g., Nerbonne and Mullen 1999). We suppose that the feature is appropriate only to lexical signs (just as DTRS is appropriate only to phrasal signs), because we cannot imagine a calculus without epicycles that determines phrasal head placement on the basis of lexical head placement. The POS feature is specified on heads and nonheads, but our theory interprets the feature as specified only on nonvacuously subcategorizing elements.

(8) a. $\begin{bmatrix}\text{LEX: } - \\ \text{SUBCAT: } \langle\rangle\end{bmatrix} \rightarrow \text{H} \neg\begin{bmatrix}\text{POS: m}\end{bmatrix} \text{C}^{+}$

b. $\begin{bmatrix}\text{LEX: } - \\ \text{SUBCAT: } \langle\_\rangle\end{bmatrix} \rightarrow \text{H}\begin{bmatrix}\text{POS: m}\end{bmatrix} \text{C}^{+}$

(9) a. $\text{C} < \text{H LEX}-$

b. $\text{H} \begin{bmatrix}\text{LEX: } + \\ \text{POS: } \neg\ \text{e}\end{bmatrix} < \text{C}$

c. $\text{C} < \text{H} \begin{bmatrix}\text{LEX: } + \\ \text{POS: e}\end{bmatrix}$

d. $\text{C}^{1} \leq \text{C}^{2}$

As the POS feature is appropriate only to lexical signs, it is obviously not a head feature, nor is it shared between mother and head daughter by other means. The first rule can apply to [LEX +] or [LEX −] heads. The second applies only to [LEX +] heads because of the appropriateness constraints on POS. Realizing no complements is not an option (no unary branches). The ID rules are mutually exclusive due to their specification of POS. The negation in the LP rules is just a value negation, but the negation in (8) can be satisfied by a head lacking the POS feature as well as one that is either [POS b] or [POS e].

The following table indicates how standard phrase structure rules for English correspond to applications of these ID and LP constraints.

[3]For clarity we keep the term in description of phenomena like "subject raising".

Structure	Example	Schema	LP
NP ⟶ D N	my car	a	c
PP ⟶ P NP	to the child	a	b
PP ⟶ P NP	on the highway	b	b
VP ⟶ V NP	drove my car	b	b
S ⟶ NP VP	Val drove my car	a	a
S ⟶ V NP VP	Did Val drive my car	a	b, d
S ⟶ NP V	The child slept	a	c

Predicative and nonpredicative PPs each depend on different rule schema. Inverted clauses and clauses with intransitive verbs fall under the same ID schema. In fact, it is the same schema that puts a subject together with a transitive VP and which builds a nonpredicative PP. We have shown the structure of an NP analysis, but DPs could also be realized (using ID schema a and LP constraint b); whichever analysis is taken requires the corresponding POS marking on the head. Vacuous applications of rules through unary branching structures are unnecessary in the construction of predications using intransitive verbs.

14.4 Spanish Psychological Predicates in HPSG

14.4.1 Semantic and Syntactic Argument Structure

HPSG does not require that the agreement controller of the verb have canonical subject properties. Pollard and Sag (1994; p. 82) note that verbs in some languages have non-initial SUBCAT elements participating in agreement relations. Our syntax-semantics interface for Type 3 predicates is such that the dative experiencer-NP is the first element of SUBCAT and the nominative cause-NP second.

We propose an additional HEAD feature on signs. The feature is AGRC, for agreement controller. We presume this to be a SYNSEM valued feature (risking no violation of locality constraints).[4] The head feature principle ensures that AGRC is token identical between head daughter and root sign. It is a property of an unsaturated lexical head that its AGRC is coindexed with one of its SUBCAT elements (if it has any). Whether phonological/morphological consequences follow depends on further structure sharing of that value with, for example, PHON values.

We propose a lexical entry for *gustar* ('to like') in (10).[5] The con-

[4]INDEX values are an alternative but SYNSEM values account for differences in control and raising (see §14.4.2).Vogel and Villada (1999) consider list values.

[5]The entry is a simplification that omits clitics. The assertions in the following section hold even when clitics are fully accounted for, however we do not mention them there for the sake of clarity and compactness. It is necessary to have a theory of clitics which allows that some are affixes (Miller and Sag, 1997) and that some occupy argument positions (for such a theory, see Monachesi, 1998). Vogel and

straints require that the logical subject (the X-ER) of the verb *gustar* be an NP bearing dative case; no constraints are imposed on the INDEX of that NP. This verb subcategorizes for a second complement bearing nominative case. The CONTENT value states the *gustar* relation also has an X-ED role structure shared with the referential index of the nominative. For comparison, in (11) we offer a lexical entry for *molestar* (to bother) as well, a Type 1 predicate. The advantage of this theory is that it entails no connection between AGRC and the leftmost element of SUBCAT.

$$\text{(10)}\quad \left[\begin{array}{l} \text{PHON: } f(\textit{gustar}, \boxed{2}, \boxed{4}) \\ \text{CAT: } \left[\begin{array}{l} \text{HEAD: } {}_{\textit{verb}}\left[\begin{array}{l}\text{VFORM: } \boxed{4}\ \text{fin}\\ \text{AGRC: } \boxed{3}\end{array}\right] \\ \text{SUBCAT: } \langle \textit{np}[\textit{dat}]\text{: } \boxed{1}, \boxed{3}\,\textit{np}[\textit{nom}]\text{: } \boxed{2}\rangle \end{array}\right] \\ \text{CONTENT: } \left[\begin{array}{l}\text{RELN: } \textit{gustar}\\ \text{LIKER: } \boxed{1}\\ \text{LIKED: } \boxed{2}\end{array}\right]\end{array}\right]$$

$$\text{(11)}\quad \left[\begin{array}{l} \text{PHON: } f(\textit{molestar}, \boxed{2}, \boxed{4}) \\ \text{CAT: } \left[\begin{array}{l} \text{HEAD: } {}_{\textit{verb}}\left[\begin{array}{l}\text{VFORM: } \boxed{4}\ \text{fin}\\ \text{AGRC: } \boxed{3}\end{array}\right] \\ \text{SUBCAT: } \langle \boxed{3}\,\textit{np}[\textit{nom}]\text{: } \boxed{2}, \textit{np}[\textit{dat}]\text{: } \boxed{1}\rangle \end{array}\right] \\ \text{CONTENT: } \left[\begin{array}{l}\text{RELN: } \textit{molestar}\\ \text{BOTHERER: } \boxed{2}\\ \text{BOTHERED: } \boxed{1}\end{array}\right]\end{array}\right]$$

The AGRC feature, as a head feature, and unlike the SUBJ feature, is not a valency feature and thus does not get reduced between levels of constituency. Phonological consequences of AGRC depend on the PHON value. AGRC has systematic relations to the Borsley-Pollard-Sag SUBJ feature. For most constructions in English, the leftmost SUBCAT element and AGRC element coincide with the usual notion of subject. In Spanish there is a divergence of SUBCAT elements from the usual position for the AGRC in the case of psychological predicates.[6] The verbs which diverge from the norm do so in a systematic way which abets generalization across lexical entries.

Villada (1999) provide a version of the entries with clitics. For Type 2 and Type 3, the clitic is coindexed with an adjacent dative element on the SUBCAT list; in Type 4, the clitic is the sole entity coindexed with the X-ER in CONTENT.

[6]In an analysis along these lines that keeps a SUBJ/COMPS distinction, the AGRC can be among the COMPS; however, such an analysis must defend why SUBJ is discriminated at all when AGRC is acknowledged as distinct.

14.4.2 Embedded Contexts

Here we provide relevant data from control and raising predicates along with our analysis. The AGRC feature turns out to be a useful mechanism for capturing the fact that Spanish admits both subject and object control, but only subject raising, not object raising (yet for Type 3 predicates it is possible to raise the dative marked experiencer which does not control agreement on either predicate). In (12–15) we provide lexical entries for Spanish control verbs showing the interactions with Type 1 and Type 3 embedded predicates.

(12)

$$\begin{bmatrix} \text{PHON: morph(permitir, }\boxed{1}, \boxed{6}\text{)} \\ \text{SS: } \begin{bmatrix} \text{LOC: } \begin{bmatrix} \text{CAT: } \begin{bmatrix} \text{HEAD: } \begin{bmatrix} \text{VFORM: } \boxed{6} \\ \text{AGRC: } \boxed{3} \end{bmatrix} \\ \text{SUBCAT: } \boxed{A} \end{bmatrix} \\ \text{CONTENT: } \begin{bmatrix} \text{RELN: } \textit{permitir} \\ \text{X-ER: } \boxed{1} \\ \text{X-ED: } \boxed{2} \\ \text{TO-Y: } \boxed{5} \end{bmatrix} \end{bmatrix} \end{bmatrix} \end{bmatrix}$$

$$A = \langle \boxed{3}\text{NP:}\boxed{1}, \text{NP:}\boxed{2}, \text{VP-Y} \begin{bmatrix} \text{FIN: } - \\ \text{AGRC: } \boxed{4} \\ \text{SUBCAT: } \langle \text{NP} : \boxed{2} \rangle \end{bmatrix} : \boxed{5} \rangle$$

* Leslie le permitió a Val gustar los músicos diabólicos
Leslie DAT-CL permitted to Val to like the musicians evil
'Leslie permitted Val to like the evil musicians'

(13)

$$\begin{bmatrix} \text{PHON: morph(permitir, }\boxed{1}, \boxed{6}\text{)} \\ \text{SS: } \begin{bmatrix} \text{LOC: } \begin{bmatrix} \text{CAT: } \begin{bmatrix} \text{HEAD: } \begin{bmatrix} \text{VFORM: } \boxed{6} \\ \text{AGRC: } \boxed{3} \end{bmatrix} \\ \text{SUBCAT: } \boxed{A} \end{bmatrix} \\ \text{CONTENT: } \begin{bmatrix} \text{RELN: } \textit{permitir} \\ \text{X-ER: } \boxed{1} \\ \text{X-ED: } \boxed{2} \\ \text{TO-Y: } \boxed{5} \end{bmatrix} \end{bmatrix} \end{bmatrix} \end{bmatrix}$$

$$A = \langle \boxed{3}\text{NP:}\boxed{1}, \text{NP:}\boxed{2}, \text{VP-Y} \begin{bmatrix} \text{FIN: } - \\ \text{AGRC: } \boxed{4} \\ \text{SUBCAT: } \langle \boxed{4}\text{NP} : \boxed{2} \rangle \end{bmatrix} : \boxed{5} \rangle$$

Leslie permitió a Val molestar a los músicos diabólicos.
Leslie permitted to Val to bother the musicians evil
'Leslie permitted Val to bother the evil musicians.'

Example (12) shows object control of Type 3 experiencer, and (13) shows object control of Type 1 cause. A generalization is evident: the agreement controller of the embedded VP must be coindexed with something in the same SUBCAT list as the embedded VP. The sentence in (12) is ill-formed because the AGRC value of the embedded VP ($\boxed{4}$) is realized insided the embedded VP and not coindexed with its sister. Example (14) demonstrates the case of subject control of cause in a Type 1 predicate, and (15) illustrates subject control of Type 3 experiencer. Both (12) and (15) violate the principle of complement control.

(14)
$$\begin{bmatrix} \text{PHON: morph(prometer, }\boxed{1},\boxed{5}\text{)} \\ \text{SS: } \begin{bmatrix} \text{LOC: } \begin{bmatrix} \text{CAT: } \begin{bmatrix} \text{HEAD: } \begin{bmatrix} \text{VFORM: } \boxed{5} \\ \text{AGRC: } \boxed{3} \end{bmatrix} \\ \text{SUBCAT: } \boxed{A} \end{bmatrix} \\ \text{CONTENT: } \begin{bmatrix} \text{RELN: } \textit{prometer} \\ \text{X-ER: } \boxed{1} \\ \text{X-ED: } \boxed{2} \\ \text{TO-Y: } \boxed{4} \end{bmatrix} \end{bmatrix} \end{bmatrix} \end{bmatrix}$$

$$A = \langle \boxed{3}\text{NP:}\boxed{1}, \text{NP:}\boxed{2}, \text{VP-Y} \begin{bmatrix} \text{FIN: } - \\ \text{AGRC: } \boxed{3} \\ \text{SUBCAT: } \langle \boxed{3}\text{NP} : \boxed{1} \rangle \end{bmatrix} : \boxed{4} \rangle$$

Leslie le prometió a Val molestar a sus padres.
Leslie DAT-CL promised Val to bother to his parents
'Leslie promised Val to bother his parents.'

(15)
$$\begin{bmatrix} \text{PHON: morph(prometer, }\boxed{1},\boxed{6}\text{)} \\ \text{SS: } \begin{bmatrix} \text{LOC: } \begin{bmatrix} \text{CAT: } \begin{bmatrix} \text{HEAD: } \begin{bmatrix} \text{VFORM: } \boxed{6} \\ \text{AGRC: } \boxed{3} \end{bmatrix} \\ \text{SUBCAT: } \boxed{A} \end{bmatrix} \\ \text{CONTENT: } \begin{bmatrix} \text{RELN: } \textit{prometer} \\ \text{X-ER: } \boxed{1} \\ \text{X-ED: } \boxed{2} \\ \text{TO-Y: } \boxed{5} \end{bmatrix} \end{bmatrix} \end{bmatrix} \end{bmatrix}$$

$$A = \langle \boxed{3}\text{NP:}\boxed{1}, \text{NP:}\boxed{2}, \text{VP-Y} \begin{bmatrix} \text{FIN: } - \\ \text{AGRC: } \boxed{4} \\ \text{SUBCAT: } \langle \text{NP} : \boxed{1} \rangle \end{bmatrix} : \boxed{5} \rangle$$

* Leslie prometió a Val gustar las uvas
Leslie promised Val to like the grapes
'Leslie promised Val to like the grapes'

(16) **Principle of Complement Control**
The AGRC value of a nonfinite VP embedded as a complement in a control predicate shares its semantic index with a less oblique constituent on the same SUBCAT list as the embedded VP.

The raising data is easily accommodated. We provide a lexical entry for *parecer* ('to seem') (17). The raised SUBCAT list is nonempty: *parecer*, in combination with weather predicates that do not subcategorize, requires the embedded predicate to be in finite form under a complementizer; thus the complement of *parecer* in that case is saturated.

(17)
$$\begin{bmatrix} \text{PHON: morph(parecer, } \boxed{4}, \boxed{5}) \\ \text{SS: } \begin{bmatrix} \text{LOC: } \begin{bmatrix} \text{CAT: } \begin{bmatrix} \text{HEAD: } \begin{bmatrix} \text{VFORM: } \boxed{5} \\ \text{AGRC: } \boxed{3}:\boxed{4} \end{bmatrix} \\ \text{SUBCAT: } \boxed{A} \end{bmatrix} \\ \text{CONTENT: } \begin{bmatrix} \text{RELN: } \textit{parecer} \\ \text{X-ED: } \boxed{1} \end{bmatrix} \end{bmatrix} \end{bmatrix} \end{bmatrix}$$

$$\text{A} = \boxed{2} \oplus \langle \text{ VP-Y } \begin{bmatrix} \text{FIN: } - \\ \text{AGRC: } \boxed{3} \\ \text{SUBCAT: } \boxed{2}\,\textit{ne-list} \end{bmatrix} : \boxed{1} \rangle$$

Leslie pareció molestar a sus padres.
Leslie$_i$ seemed$_i$ to bother$_i$ to his parents
'Leslie seemed to bother his parents.'

A Leslie le parecieron gustar los regalos.
To Leslie DAT-CL-3SG seemed$_i$ to like$_i$ the presents$_i$
'Leslie seemed to like the presents.'

We propose an additional clause to the raising principle which constrains lexical entries given by Pollard and Sag (1994; p. 140).

(18) **Raising Principle**
If E is a lexical entry whose SUBCAT list L contains an element X not specified as expletive.

1. Then X is lexically assigned no semantic role in the content of E if and only if L also contains a (nonsubject) Y[SUBCAT⟨X⟩]
2. AGRC on E is identical to the AGRC on Y.

This principle rules out lexical entries like (19) which involve semantically two-place object raising verbs. The entry is ruled out because although the first condition of the Raising Principle is met—the verb subcategorizes for an NP whose index is not an argument to the finite verb semantics and also for a nonfinite VP subcategorizing for the NP—but the second condition is not: the agreement controller of the embedded predicate is not agreement controller of the raising verb. The corresponding sentence is ungrammatical. On the other hand, if the agreement controller of *creer* were $\boxed{3}$ instead of $\boxed{5}$, then ungrammaticality would result because it would agree with the wrong NP. The principle correctly predicts which examples are correct for subject raising as well as why *creer* does not function as an object raising verb in Spanish (the constraint does not apply to English lexical elements, but as a lexical principle, its parochial restriction is easy to fathom). A subject raising instance of *creer* is correctly accepted, as in (20); the corresponding subject raising entry of *creer* is parallel to that for *parecer* in (17) but has an additional semantic argument for the believer.

(19)

$$\left[\begin{array}{ll} \text{PHON: } \text{morph(creer, }\boxed{4},\boxed{6}) & \\ \text{SS:} & \left[\text{LOC:} \left[\begin{array}{ll}\text{CAT:} & \left[\begin{array}{ll}\text{HEAD:} & \left[\begin{array}{ll}\text{VFORM:} & \boxed{6}\\ \text{AGRC:} & \boxed{5}\end{array}\right]\\ \text{SUBCAT:} & \boxed{\text{A}}\end{array}\right]\\ \text{CONTENT:} & \left[\begin{array}{ll}\text{RELN:} & \textit{creer}\\ \text{X-ER:} & \boxed{4}\\ \text{X-ED:} & \boxed{1}\end{array}\right]\end{array}\right]\right]\end{array}\right]$$

$$\text{A} = \langle\, \boxed{5}\text{NP:}\boxed{4}\,\rangle \oplus \boxed{2} \oplus \langle\, \text{VP-Y} \left[\begin{array}{ll}\text{FIN:} & -\\ \text{AGRC:} & \boxed{3}\\ \text{SUBCAT:} & \boxed{2}\langle\boxed{3}\text{NP}\rangle\end{array}\right] : \boxed{1}\rangle$$

* Jose cree Kim divertir a los niños
Jose$_i$ believes$_i$ Kim$_j$ to amuse$_j$ to the children
Jose believes Kim amuses the children

(20) Jose cree divertir a los niños.
Jose$_i$ believes$_i$ to amuse$_i$ to the children
Jose believes himself to amuse the children.

We believe the solution of adding an agreement controller to the head features on signs is a good one. It enables a predicate's lexical head to indicate exactly which of its arguments co-varies in agreement features, without prejudice to the linear position of that argument. In particular, the agreement controller need not be the subject. The solution integrates the analysis of expletive raising with raising of "quirky subjects" where the raised element has a NUM value that may differ from the value the PHON value of raising verb depends on. A unified account is not possible for the solution to expletive raising given by Pollard and Sag (1994).

14.5 Conclusions

We have examined a range of predications which have been examined in the literature as having no subject at all or having quirky subjects. We have argued not that the predicates are subjectless in a world of otherwise subjectful clauses, but that subject is not an explanatory notion, and that these predicates supply the evidence for this. We argue instead that observable quantities are explanatory: position and agreement control, cause and experiencer. We have offered a theory of raising and control in Spanish which explains the data and makes correct predictions.

The theory we presented is formalized in a version of HPSG with just a SUBCAT list, rather than a SUBJ/COMPS distinction. However, our main proposal could be integrated in the split valency account as well. Our account involves keeping track of the agreement controller.[7] A lexical head selects one of its SUBCAT elements (hence, a SYNSEM) as the value of AGRC. As AGRC is a head feature, this value is shared through all phrasal projections of the head. Principles of control and raising dictate how the AGRC value of an embedded predicate interacts with the value of the embedding verb itself and sisters of the embedded predicate. With raising, the AGRC of the embedded verb must be the same as that of the embedding verb. For control, the AGRC of the embedded verb must be coindexed with a less oblique sister on the SUBCAT list of the embedding verb (in the case of "subject" control this element will also be the AGRC of the embedding verb as well). If AGRC is instead taken as congruent to SUBJ then linearization principles must be significantly augmented.

Given that we have maintained an obliqueness ordered SUBCAT list, we have also proposed an alternative solution to the SUBJ/COMPS dis-

[7]Heinz and Matiasek (1994) offer an account of German case assignment and argument structure in HPSG, noting that the SUBCAT list on its own does not supply sufficient information to determine what counts as an internal or external argument. Their approach is more conservative than splitting the SUBCAT list into SUBJ and COMPS to indicate what the external argument is. Instead they propose a feature for the Designated Argument (DA). While this seems likely to be identical to AGRC, it is not. The DA feature picks out the external argument of predications to distinguish ergative predicates (those which have an empty DA list are ergative). However, even ergative structures have agreement controllers. Heinz and Matiasek (1994) make use of the DA value as a trigger to lexical rules that reduce argument structure (e.g., passivization). The idea is to capture case constraints in languages like German in which assignment of case can be structural (case of an NP varying with its syntactic context) or lexical (invariant case). Related work by Kathol (1994) marks not the DA but ERG: the ERG value is the list containing the accusative argument of a predication. The intention is to capture the fact that only those base entries with a nonempty ERG value are available for passivization. Unergative verbs have a nonempty SUBJ feature, but an empty ERG feature. Thus, the function of ERG is the complement of the function of DA. Pollard (1994) also addresses passivization in German and provides an analysis heavily influenced by that of Kathol (1994); it is different in certain respects (lexical rules vs. inheritance hierarchies for the lexicon) but uses the main idea of the ERG feature with only minor modifications. Przepiórkowski (1999; Chr. 4) also adopts the ERG feature but substantially refines the theory of case assignment in HPSG. However it is clear that neither DA nor ERG is coextensive with AGRC.

tinction for constructions like nonpredicative PPs problematic to earlier versions of HPSG. The solution proposed reduces the number of phrase structure schema and eliminates unary branching structures. The proposal is to dispense with the INV feature in favor of a POS feature which has three possible values for beginning, middle and end. We assume that a lexical head declares its position, but that as this feature is appropriate only to words, phrasal heads do not. Thus, a transitive verb indicates that it appears in the middle of its complements, and an intransitive at the end, and a nonpredicative preposition at the beginning, and so on.

Acknowledgements

We are grateful for remarks from an anonymous reviewer. This research is supported by Forbairt Basic Research Grant SC/97/623.

References

Alarcos Llorach, E. 1994. *Gramática de la Lengua Española*, chap. XXI, pages 266–276. Madrid: Espasa–Calpe.

Alsina, A. 1996. *The Role of Argument Structure in Grammar*. Stanford, CA: CSLI Publications.

Belletti, A. and L. Rizzi. 1988. Psych-verbs and θ-theory. *Natural Language & Linguistic Theory* 6:291–352.

Borsley, R. 1989. An HPSG Approach to Welsh. *Journal of Linguistics* 25:333–54.

den Dikken, M. and A. Næss. 1993. Case Dependencies: The Case of Predicate Inversion. *The Linguistic Review* 10:303–36.

Fernández-Soriano, O. 1999. Two Types of Impersonal Sentences in Spanish: Locative & Dative Subjects. *Syntax* 2(2):101–140.

Grimshaw, J. 1990. *Argument Structure*. Cambridge, Mass: MIT Press.

Heinz, W. and J. Matiasek. 1994. Argument Structure and Case Assignment in German. In J. Nerbonne, K. Netter, and C. Pollard, eds., *German in Head-driven Phrase Structure Grammar*, pages 199–236. CSLI Publications: Stanford.

Kathol, A. 1994. Passives without Lexical Rules. In J. Nerbonne, K. Netter, and C. Pollard, eds., *German in Head-driven Phrase Structure Grammar*, pages 237–72. CSLI Publications: Stanford.

Keenan, E. 1976. Towards a Universal Definition of 'Subject'. In C. Li, ed., *Subject and Topic*, pages 304–33. Academic Press: London.

Masullo, P. J. 1992. Quirky Datives in Spanish & the Non-nominative Subject Parameter. In A. Kathol and J. Beckman, eds., *Papers from the Fourth Student Conference in Linguistics*, vol. 16 of *MIT Working Papers in Linguistics*, pages 89–104.

Miller, P. H. and I. A. Sag. 1997. French Clitic Movement without Clitics or Movement. In *Natural Language and Linguistic Theory*, vol. 15, pages 573–639.

Monachesi, P. 1998. Decomposing Italian Clitics. In S. Balari and L. Dini, eds., *Romance in HPSG*, pages 305–57. Stanford: CSLI Publications.

Moure, T. 1995. Sobre el Controvertido Perfil del Complemento Directo. *Moenia* 1:47–110.

Nerbonne, J. and T. Mullen. 1999. Empty-headed NPs in German and English. In *Proceedings of Computational Linguistics in the Netherlands*.

Pollard, C. 1994. Toward a Unified Account of Passive in German. In J. Nerbonne, K. Netter, and C. Pollard, eds., *German in Head-driven Phrase Structure Grammar*, pages 273–96. CSLI Publications: Stanford.

Pollard, C. and I. Sag. 1987. *Information-Based Syntax and Semantics, Volume 1: Fundamentals*. Centre for the Study of Language and Information, Stanford University, CA.

Pollard, C. and I. Sag. 1994. *Head-Driven Phrase Structure Grammar*. University of Chicago Press and CSLI Publications.

Przepiórkowski, A. 1999. *Case Assignment and the Complement-Adjunct Dichotomy: A Non-Configurational Constraint-Based Approach*. Ph.D. thesis, Universität Tübingen, Germany.

Reape, M. 1990. Getting Things in Order. In W. Sijtsma and A. van Horck, eds., *Proceedings of the Symposium on Discontinuous Constituency*. Institute for Language Technology and Artificial Intelligence, Tilburg University, Holland.

Reape, M. 1994. Domain Union and Word Order Variation in German. In J. Nerbonne, K. Netter, and C. Pollard, eds., *German in Head-driven Phrase Structure Grammar*, pages 151–97. CSLI Publications: Stanford.

Suñer, M. 1988. The Role of Agreement in Clitic Doubled Constructions. *Natural Language & Linguistic Theory* 6:391–434.

Vogel, C. and B. Villada. 1999. An HPSG Analysis of Grammatical Relations, Syntactic Valency and Semantic Argument Structure in Spanish Psychological Predicates and other Instances of Quirky Case and Agreement. TCD-CS-1999-77, Computational Linguistics Lab. Department of Computer Science. Trinity College, University of Dublin.

Zaenen, A., J. Maling, and H. Thráinsson. 1985. Case & Grammatical Functions: The Icelandic Passive. *Syntax and Semantics* 24:95–136.

15

A Bistratal Approach to the Prosody-Syntax Interface in Japanese

KEI YOSHIMOTO

15.1 Introduction

The recent progress in constraint-based phonology (see Bird 1995, Coleman 1998, and Matui 1999) underscores the possibility of an integrated unification-based grammar subsuming the phonological aspects of language. The investigation of prosody along this line is of particular interest owing to the interwoven relationship between prosody, morphology, syntax, semantics, and discourse. In pursuing this goal, Pierrehumbert and Beckman's (1988) underspecified approach can be applied to represent prosodic information.

One of the essential difficulties in addressing this issue is that in many languages, the constituent structure standardly required by semantics is inconsistent with the grouping manifested by prosody. As we will see later, in Japanese a structure built on prosodic criteria is discrepant with a semantics-based one. The phenomenon known as METRICAL BOOST, an effect of the syntactic structure on the pitch of the modifying phrase, also poses a complicated problem in formulating the interaction between the two structures. Furthermore, it has been observed that the prosodic structure can exert an influence in the opposite direction on syntax.

This paper proposes an HPSG-based approach that integrates information from the standard syntactic structure and independently represented prosodic information. In resolving the difficulties, minimal interfaces are posited that keep the distinction between syntax and phonology on the whole intact.

Grammatical Interfaces in HPSG.
Ronnie Cann, Claire Grover and Philip Miller.

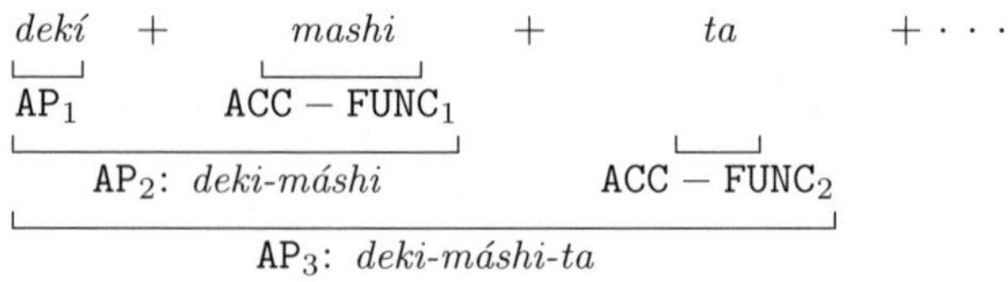

FIGURE 1 Recursive Formation of Accentual Information

15.2 Prosody in Japanese

15.2.1 Accentual Phrase

Essential to the construction of Japanese prosody is a tonal domain, corresponding to a phonological word, which is called 'accentual phrase' (AP) in this paper. It is the fundamental locus of phonological formation—pauses are inserted at the beginning and end of the AP, and the portion near the end of the AP tends to be weakened and devocalized. Each AP exhibits either a tone pattern with a sharp fall from high pitch or a relatively flat pattern without a fall. The first is phonologically interpreted as ACCENTED and the second as UNACCENTED. The variation contributes partly to the disambiguation of lexical meanings.

An AP is formed by recursively attaching a closed-class GRAMMATICAL WORD—i.e., a postposition, clitic complemetizer, or conjugational ending—to an open class FULL WORD, that is, a noun, verbal or adjectival stem, or adverb. Grammatical words encompass both independent words, i.e., auxiliary verbs and postpositions, and conjugational suffixes of verbs, adjectives, and auxiliary verbs. It is known that the information on whether an AP is accented and which mora in an AP is accented (this is called 'accentual information') is obtained by combining information from two sources: the 'accentual function' associated with the right-most grammatical word and the accentual information of the sequence immediately to the left of it. The regularity in combinations has been formalized as the Accent Assignment Rule that applies recursively. Figure 1 is an example. In the figure, a full word *dekí*, a verb for 'be made/be possible', has an accent (i.e., a sharp fall from high pitch marked by '´') on its last mora when pronounced alone. A grammatical word attached to it, an addressee-oriented honorific auxiliary verb *mashi*, has an accentual function that shifts the accent of the whole AP to its own first mora, whatever the accentual information of the preceding sequence may be. The outcome is *deki-máshi*. The second grammatical word, a past auxiliary verb *ta*, has an accentual function that maintains the accentual information of the preceding sequence regardless of its own accentual information. Accordingly, the verb *dekí*

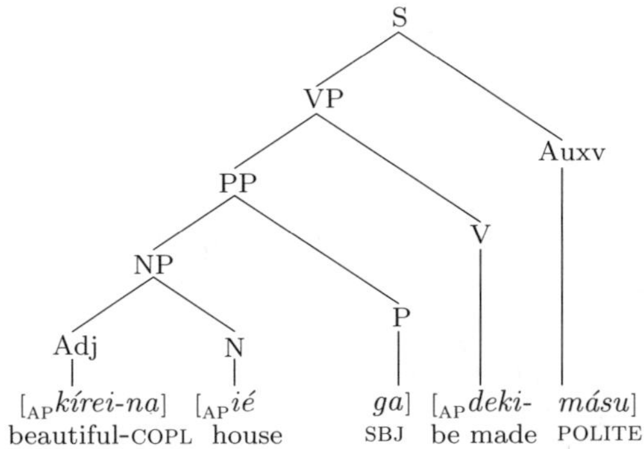

'A beautiful house is built.'

FIGURE 2 Syntactic Tree and AP Segmentation

followed by the two auxiliary verbs is pronounced *deki-máshi-ta*.

Figure 2 illustrates how a sentence is segmented into APs. Note that there is an obvious dicrepancy between the conventional parsing indicated as the tree diagram and the segmentation into APs shown in brackets. For example, in the tree the adjective *kírei-na* ('beautiful') and the noun *ié* ('house') form together an NP, to which a subject–marking postposition *ga* is attached. This contrasts sharply with the AP segmentation: *kírei-na* forms a single AP, and *ié* and *ga* together constitute an AP. Furthermore, in the tree the verb *deki* ('be made') is first concatenated with the subject NP *kírei-na ié ga* to form a verbal phrase, to which the auxiliary verb for politeness *masu* is suffixed; in the AP segmentation *deki* and *masu* constitute one unit.

So far, speech processing researchers have adopted an AP-based analysis, referred to as P(ROSODIC)-STRUCTURE in this paper, while syntacticians, semanticists and NLP researchers have employed the syntactic structure based on the standard chunking of meanings as shown in the tree diagram in Figure 2, called C(ONSTITUENT)-STRUCTURE.[1] The two structures have been used separately for different purposes and have usually been considered to be mutually exclusive.

15.2.2 Metrical Boost

Evidence has been brought forward by Kubozono (1987) that even in processing prosody, C-Structure must be taken into account. He has shown in his statistical phonetic experiments that an adnominal adjunct has different pitch levels, depending on whether the phrase structure is

[1] This is distinct from C-structure in Lexical Functional Grammar (Bresnan, 1982).

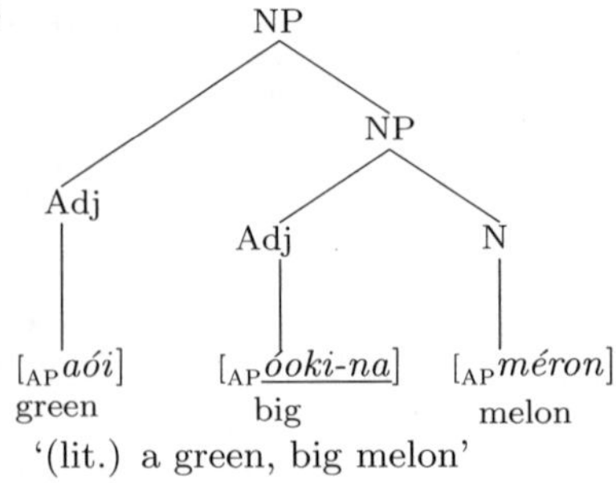

FIGURE 3 Right-Branching Structure

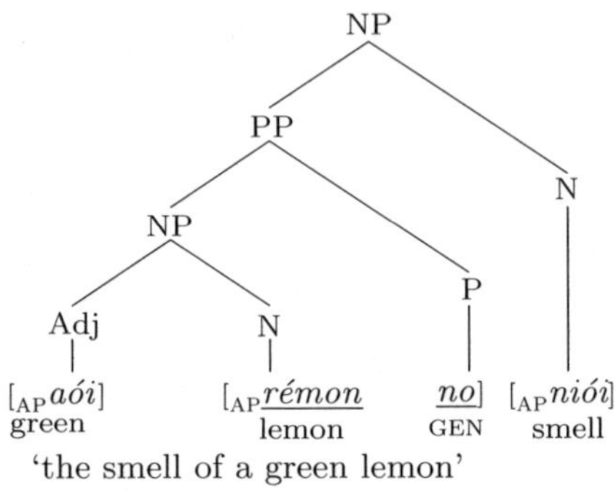

FIGURE 4 Left-Branching Structure

right-branching or left-branching. He calls this phenomenon METRICAL BOOST. In the examples in Figures 3 and 4 each with two modifiers, the peak of the second AP *óokina* ('big'), which occurs in the right-branching structure in Figure 3, is significantly higher than that of *rémon no* ('lemon-GENITIVE'), an adjunct on the left-branching structure in Figure 4. Likewise, in NPs with three adjuncts, modifiers in right-branching subtrees receive a significantly higher pitch value; furthermore, the second adjunct which involves a double opening bracket (i.e., which is by two branching nodes deeper than the first one), A_2 in (1), is the highest in all the possible structures:

(1) $[A_1\ [[\mathbf{A}_2\ A_3]\ H]]$

Choi et al. (1995) observe a similar difference in peaks of adverbial phrases in a syntactically ambiguous sentence and demonstrate that the pitch difference is used to disambiguate the sentence. They also report that Korean, Mongolian, and Turkish employ prosodic means to resolve the ambiguity in sentences with structures parallel to their Japanese examples. Moreover, Schafer (1997) shows that prosody is used for the resolution of English ambiguous sentences, arguing that models of sentence processing must incorporate a module of prosodic structure. Traditionally, it has been assumed that the syntactic structure has a strictly limited influence on prosody by way of intonational phrasing. The findings cited above show that the influence is much more direct and the formulation of an interface that transmits information on the syntactic hierarchy to phonology is called for.

15.2.3 Prosodic Effects on Syntax

An influence in the other direction is also attested: the prosodic hierarchy can constrain the syntactic structure. By the principle of 'Phonology-Free Syntax' Pullum and Zwicky (1988) prevented the syntax from having access to phonological information. Evidence against this principle in Serbo-Croatian and Hausa has been given by Zec and Inkelas (1990), who argue that information on the prosodic hierarchy, if not the phonology as a whole, affects the syntactic structure in these languages. Examples of the same sort are found in Japanese as well.

It is a widely accepted view that the location at which the Japanese interjectional particles *ne*, *yo*, etc. can be placed is determined purely *structurally*.

(2)	[$_{AP}$ Kirei-na	**ne**],	[$_{AP}$ ie	ga	**ne**],	[$_{AP}$ at-te	**ne**], ...
	beautiful	INTJ-P	house	SUBJ	INTJ-P	exist	INTJ-P

'There is, you see, a beautiful house, and ...'

In the spoken sentence above, the interjectional postposition *ne*, which is used to confirm what has been said up to that point, can be inserted at any right-most position of an AP regardless of the AP's syntactic category. The necessary and sufficient condition for its distribution is that it occurs *immediately after an AP*; no other phonological factors, pitch, pause or whatever, are relevant.

Admittedly, 'Phonology-Free Syntax' proposed by Pullum and Zwicky (1988) is crucial in maintaining the division between the two components. In terms of the above-mentioned case, however, this hypothesis must be slightly relaxed, keeping in line with Zec and Inkelas.

15.3 Review of Previous Research

Whitelock (1991) proposes to handle the 'bracketing paradox' in Japanese expounded in Section 15.2, the inconsistency in structures required by semantic and phonological criteria applied to the same sequence, within the framework of Categorial Unification Grammar (Uszkoreit, 1986), assuming an implementation based on PATR-II (Shieber, 1985). He posits that phrase structures form structures that partly reflect P-Structure and partly C-Structure. He then stipulates prosody-related information by feature constraints. Figure 5 depicts

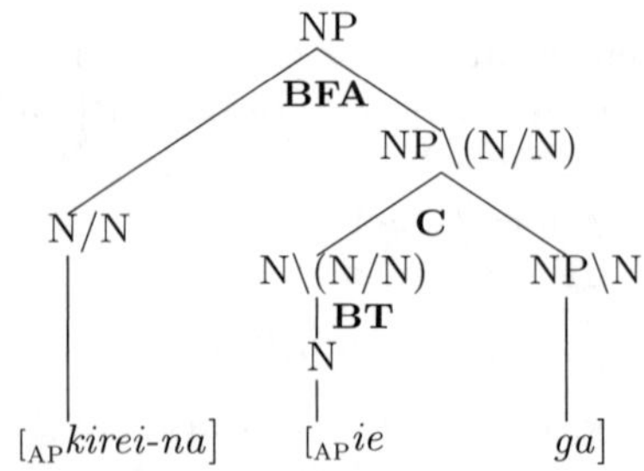

FIGURE 5 Analysis of *kirei-na ie ga*

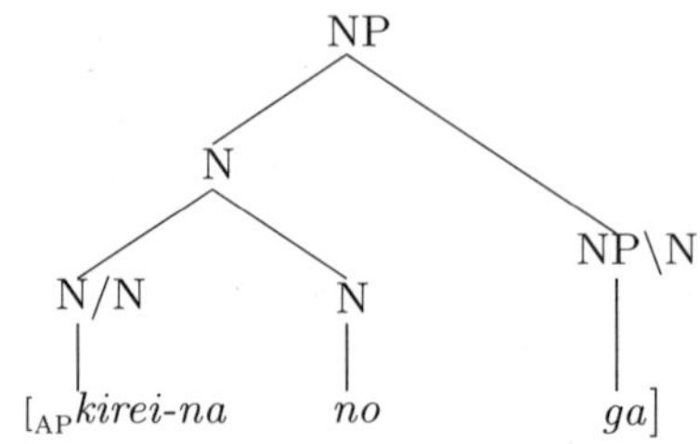

FIGURE 6 Analysis of *kirei-na no ga*

how the PSG rules analyze the subject *kirei-na ie ga* ('a beautiful house-SUBJ') consisting of two APs in Figure 2. Note that this is just one of a number of possible interpretations on Whitelock's grammar about which precise details are unknown, but this fact is irrelevant to the following discussion. Of all the information assigned to each node, expressed as feature structures in the original paper, only syntactic categories are represented here. Following the notation in Categorial Grammar, a complex category encoding a function from X to Y is written 'X/Y' if the argument stands to the right of the functor and 'X\Y' if the other way round.

The set of rules proposed assigns a parse tree deviating from the standard one shown as the tree in Figure 2, whenever combination of two adjacent words is given priority for the sake of forming an AP. This happens when the phrase to be formed is made up of multiple APs (as in *kirei-na ie ga*) and the grammatical word (e.g., *ga*) first concatenates with just one full word which stands immediately to the left of it (e.g., *ie*), while the adjunct (i.e., *kirei-na*) constitutes an independent AP.

In order to produce such syntactic structures forming a compromise between C-Structure and P-Structure, Whitelock proposes the chaining rule and merging rule. In Figure 5, the noun *ie* ('house'), to which a category N is assigned in the lexicon, is turned into N\(N/N) by the Backward Type-raising rule below (application of the rule is indicated by **BT** in the figure) in order to be combined with *ga*.

(3) Backward Type–raising: T\(T/X) $\longrightarrow$ X

Instead of the cancellation rules standard in Categorial Grammars, here the rules are laid down in the form of PS-rules. N\(N/N) in turn can be linked up with NP\N, the category of the postposition *ga*, by the Chaining rule (indicated by **C** in the figure):

(4) Chaining: X\Z $\longrightarrow$ Y\Z X\Y

At this stage, an AP status is given to *ie ga* by adding the [minor +] feature. Furthermore, the Backward Functional Application rule (**BFA** in the figure) is used to concatenate the two APs into an NP. This solution is analogous to that by Steedman (1991) who adopts a similar syntax to cope with English prosody.

It is beyond the scope of this paper to compare Categorial Grammar and HPSG, which take totally different theoretical approaches to language. The discussion here is limited to an application of Whitelock's proposal to Unification Grammars, specifically to the Typed Unification formalism, postulating that computational complexity has no great importance and what is shown in Figure 5 is a syntactic structure represented as a phrase structure or a feature structure. When applied to HPSG, the rules (3), (4) will be embodied directly in lexical descriptions or lexical rules; the resulting tree is relatively flat, with APs as direct daughters of the root node. On this assumption, problems are pointed out and an alternative solution is offered.

First, in this approach the syntactic structure does not reflect faithfully the construction of meaning as is standardly understood. For instance, the noun phrase *kirei-na no ga* ('beautiful FORMAL-NOUN SUBJECT' i.e., 'a beautiful one-SUBJECT') undergoes an analysis in Figure 6 that is different from the structure illustrated in Figure 5 for *kirei-na ie ga*. This is because the formal noun *no*, which is analogous to the English pronoun *one*, is phonologically dependent on the adnominal full word immediately before it (unlike normal nouns), and accordingly the Backward Type-raising rule is not applied. This is against the standard practice in Japanese linguistics that gives *no* the same syntactic status as other nouns, since no difference is observed between them except in phonology. In the HPSG framework too, to assign the same syntactic structure to both cases is considered, to say the least, to be highly advantageous, for it makes easier and more understandable the extension of

$$
{}_{ap}[\ \ ] \longrightarrow \begin{bmatrix} \text{PHON} & \begin{bmatrix} \text{MORA} & \boxed{1} \oplus \boxed{2} \\ \text{ACC-LOC} & \boxed{3} \\ \text{ACC-PROPERTY} & \begin{bmatrix} \text{L-EDGE} & \boxed{4} \\ \text{BOOST} & \boxed{5} \end{bmatrix} \end{bmatrix} \\ \text{AP-DTRS} & \begin{bmatrix} \text{BODY|PHON} & \begin{bmatrix} \text{MORA} & \boxed{1} \\ \text{ACC-LOC} & \boxed{6} \end{bmatrix} \\ \text{ENDING|PHON} & \begin{bmatrix} \text{MORA} & \boxed{2} \\ \text{ACC-FUNC} & \boxed{7} \end{bmatrix} \end{bmatrix} \end{bmatrix}
$$

$$
\text{Conditions:}\quad \textit{acc-assign}(\boxed{7}, \boxed{6}) = \boxed{3},\quad \textit{get-boost}(\boxed{4}) = \boxed{5}
$$

FIGURE 7 Type Specification for *ap*

the grammar to cope with other syntactic and/or semantic phenomena.

Second, to look at this from a slightly different perspective, the syntax proposed essentially depends on the phonology. This impairs the modularity in grammar.

Third, since Whitelock's formalization lacks information about the C-Structure, it cannot explain the metrical boost. In fact, he tries to accommodate it by adding simple features, which are unsuccessful.

In the following I shall propose an HPSG-based grammar with an independent representation of the P-Structure that resolves the difficulties pointed out above.

15.4 A Bistratal Approach

15.4.1 A Basic Framework

In order to overcome the paradox illustrated in Section 15.2, a new attribute P-STR(UCTURE) taking a list of *ap*s as its value is introduced as a representation of the P-Structure orthogonal to the syntactic information. The proposed HPSG grammar differs from the standard version in that all *signs* are specified for the attributes P-STR and (ORDER-)DOM(AIN). The latter, following Reape (1994) and Kathol (1995), processes the word order by representing linear properties parallel to the phrase structure. P-STR is constructed in close relation to DOM, since the value of P-STR depends on the word order, and it is a subset of APs that can be scrambled. However, in the abridged grammar presented here, P-STR is defined as if it could stand on its own. Of the information provided by P-STR, that part which involves the prosodic hierarchy is shared by syntax. Henceforth they are construed as parallel representations overlapping in terms of this syntactic information and are called STRATA in a sense close to Ladusaw's (1988).

Information about an AP is expressed by a type specification *ap* in

Figure 7. The value of the feature path PHON(OLOGY)|MORA is a list of moras providing segmental information. The value of MORA of an *ap* is obtained by appending (indicated by '$\oplus$') the MORA value of the right-most grammatical word of the AP, called the 'ending,' to that of the rest of the AP, called the 'body.' The value of ACC(ENT)-LOC(ATION), a natural number or 0, indicates on which mora the accent falls (0 means unaccented). As illustrated in Subsection 15.2.1, this value is determined by the accentual information of the body and the ending's accentual function. The latter is encoded by the value of ACC(ENTUAL)-FUNC(TION).

Let us return to the case of the AP *deki-máshi-ta* ('be made-POLITE-PAST') cited in Subsection 15.2.1. The full word *dekí* bears an ACC-LOC value 2. The grammatical word *mashi* has an ACC-FUNC value *ending-dominant-1*, a kind of accentual function that shifts the accent to its own first mora irrespective of the body's ACC-LOC value. The Accent Assignment Rule *acc(ent)-assign(ment)* applies the value of ACC-LOC to that of ACC-FUNC as in λ-conversion. The ACC-LOC value of *deki-máshi* is counted by adding 2, the number of the body's moras, to 1, the number indicating the accent location in the ending (the encoding of both numbers are omitted in the figure): the sum comes to 3. Next, the grammatical word *ta* has an ACC-FUNC value *body-dominant-5*, which in this case just identifies the ACC-LOC value of the whole phrase with that of the body. Thus, the accent of an AP is calculated recursively by *acc-assign* on the basis of the values of ACC-LOC and ACC-FUNC. An AP is also a domain where various suprasegmental and segmental rules apply (see Matui 1999 and Coleman 1998).

The value of P-STR is built up by the P-STRUCTURE Principle shown in Figure 8. An *ap-clitic* embedded in the P-STR list corresponds to a grammatical word. The first item (i) of the Principle combines a complement or an adjunct with a grammartical word head. In this case, the last *ap* of the complement/adjunct's P-STR value and the *ap-clitic* of the head constitute an *ap*, which is added to the end of the mother's P-STR value. The other elements of the list are identical with the *aps* in the P-STR value of the complement/adjunct save the last one. Note that a *sign* to which an *ap* is assigned may in the derivation process be further suffixed by an ending to form a larger AP. In (ii), the P-STR value of the head is a list of APs. Then the mother's P-STR value is obtained by appending those of the complement/adjunct and the head. This principle is similar to Gunji's (1999) 'biclausal' approach to the discrepancy between syntax and morphology/phonology in Japanese causatives. As explained in Subsection 15.2.1, both an independent word and a conjugational suffix can be a grammatical word. Accordingly, the P-STRUCTURE Principle applies both to a syntactic phrase and the inner

In both complement-head and adjunct-head structures of the form,

$$\textbf{M:}\begin{bmatrix}\text{P-STR} & \boxed{1}\end{bmatrix}$$

$$\textbf{C/A:}\begin{bmatrix}\text{P-STR} & \boxed{2}\end{bmatrix} \qquad \textbf{H:}\begin{bmatrix}\text{P-STR} & \boxed{3}\end{bmatrix}$$

(i) if $\boxed{3} = \langle\boxed{4}\text{: } \textit{ap-clitic}\rangle$, $\boxed{1}$ is a list of *ap*s obtained by replacing the last *ap* of $\boxed{2}$, $\boxed{5}$, by

$$_{ap}\begin{bmatrix}\text{AP-DTRS} & \begin{bmatrix}\text{BODY} & \boxed{5}\\ \text{ENDING} & \boxed{4}\end{bmatrix}\end{bmatrix}$$

(ii) otherwise (i.e., if $\boxed{3} = \textit{list}(\textit{ap})$), $\boxed{1}=\boxed{2}\oplus\boxed{3}$

FIGURE 8 P–STRUCTURE Principle

construction of a word.

Now let us examine how the subject phrase *kírei-na ié ga* ('a beautiful house-SUBJ') of the example in Figure 2 is analyzed by the P-STRUCTURE Principle. First, in combining the adjective *kírei-na* and *ié*, each being an independent AP, (ii) of the Principle applies to produce the following feature structure for the NP *kírei-na ié*.

(5)
$$_{np}\begin{bmatrix}\text{P-STR} & \left\langle \begin{matrix}\boxed{1}\,_{ap}\begin{bmatrix}\text{PHON}|\text{MORA} & \langle \textit{ki re i na}\rangle\\ \text{AP-DTRS} & \begin{bmatrix}\text{BODY} & \boxed{3}[\text{PHON}|\text{MORA}\ \langle \textit{ki re i}\rangle]\\ \text{ENDING} & \boxed{4}[\text{PHON}|\text{MORA}\ \langle \textit{na}\rangle]\end{bmatrix}\end{bmatrix},\\ \boxed{2}\,_{ap}\begin{bmatrix}\text{PHON}|\text{MORA} & \langle \textit{i e}\rangle\end{bmatrix}\end{matrix}\right\rangle\end{bmatrix}$$

Next, the lexical description for the subject-marking postposition *ga* is as shown below:

(6)
$$_{p\text{-}word}\begin{bmatrix}\text{P-STR} & \langle\boxed{5}_{ap\text{-}clitic}[\ \text{PHON}|\text{MORA}\ \ \langle \textit{ga}\rangle]\rangle\\ \text{SUBCAT} & \langle \textit{np}\ \rangle\end{bmatrix}$$

Its P-STR value is a list with only one element of type *ap-clitic*. Therefore, when this is put together with (5) to form a postpositional phrase, (i) in the Principle constructs a P-STR list whose first element is an *ap* for *kírei-na*, $\boxed{1}$ in (5), and whose second element is an *ap* composed of the phonological information for *ié* as body and that for *ga* as ending.

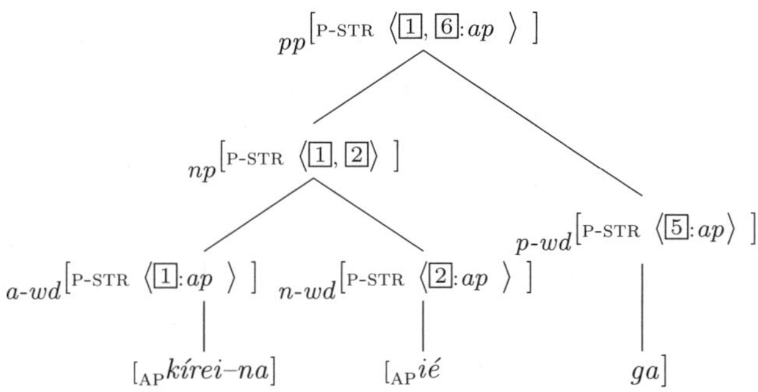

FIGURE 9 P-STR of *kírei–na ié ga*

(7)
$$\left[\text{P-STR}\ \left\langle \begin{array}{l} \boxed{1}\left[\begin{array}{ll}\text{PHON}|\text{MORA} & \langle ki\ re\ i\ na\rangle \\ \text{AP-DTRS} & \left[\begin{array}{ll}\text{BODY} & \boxed{3}[\text{PHON}|\text{MORA}\ \langle ki\ re\ i\rangle] \\ \text{ENDING} & \boxed{4}[\text{PHON}|\text{MORA}\ \langle na\rangle]\end{array}\right]\end{array}\right]_{ap}, \\ \boxed{6}\left[\begin{array}{ll}\text{PHON}|\text{MORA} & \langle i\ e\ ga\rangle \\ \text{AP-DTRS} & \left[\begin{array}{ll}\text{BODY} & \boxed{2}[\text{PHON}|\text{MORA}\ \langle i\ e\rangle] \\ \text{ENDING} & \boxed{5}[\text{PHON}|\text{MORA}\ \langle ga\rangle]\end{array}\right]\end{array}\right]_{ap} \end{array}\right\rangle\right]_{pp}$$

Figure 9 outlines how the relevant information is processed in a tree diagram. The numbers of the tags in the figure correspond to those in (5–7). From the value of P-STR thus obtained, further phonological information of a sentence is inferred. For example, the Accent Assignment Rule *acc-assign* is triggered each time a type *ap* is evaluated. In the following subsection I shall give a further account of this.

15.4.2 Defining an Interface: from C-Structure to P-Structure

The phenomenon of metrical boost discussed in Subsection 15.2.2 is captured by percolating the branching information in C-structure to P-structure. For this purpose, a binary feature R(IGHT)-BRANCH(ING), one of the LOCAL features, is introduced. Only if its value is +, the value in addition has a feature structure with an attribute L(EFT)-EDGE and a value, either zero or a natural number. The Branching Principle in Figure 10 is proposed which forms an appropriate R-BRANCH feature on each node, whenever an adjunct is combined with its head.

The first conjunct of this principle constrains the R-BRANCH value of the head to be a +-typed feature structure with an attribute L-EDGE and

$$
{}_{phrase}[\text{DTRS } \textit{head-adj-str}] \longrightarrow
\left[\begin{array}{ll}
\text{DTRS|HEAD-DTR} & {}_{phrase}[\text{SYNSEM|LOC|R-BRANCH} \quad {}_{+}[\text{L-EDGE} \quad 0]\,] \\
 & \vee\ {}_{word}[\text{SYNSEM|LOC|R-BRANCH} \quad -\,]
\end{array}\right]
$$

$$
\wedge \left(\left[\begin{array}{ll}
\text{SYNSEM|LOC|R-BRANCH} & {}_{+}[\text{L-EDGE} \quad \boxed{1}] \\
\text{DTRS|ADJ-DTR|SYNSEM|LOC|R-BRANCH} & {}_{+}[\text{L-EDGE} \quad add(1,\boxed{1})]
\end{array}\right]
\vee \left[\begin{array}{ll}
\text{SYNSEM|LOC|R-BRANCH} & - \\
\text{DTRS|ADJ-DTR|SYNSEM|LOC|R-BRANCH} & -
\end{array}\right] \right)
$$

FIGURE 10 Branching Principle

a value 0 if the head is a *phrase*, viz., if it is right-branching; otherwise R-BRANCH has an atomic value $-$. The second conjunct specifies the R-BRANCH value of the adjunct daughter on the basis of that of its mother. If the mother has a $+$-typed R-BRANCH value, the adjunct also has a $+$ in its R-BRANCH with an L-EDGE value larger than that of the mother by one. If the mother's R-BRANCH has $-$, that of the adjunct is also $-$. The R-BRANCH value of the root node is always set to $-$.

The value of L-EDGE is percolated to PHON|ACC(ENTUAL)-PROPERTY|L-EDGE of an *ap* defined in Figure 7 by a constraint on a full word:

(8) $${}_{fullword}[\text{ SYNSEM|LOC|R-BRANCH} \quad {}_{+}[\text{L-EDGE} \quad \boxed{1}]\,]$$
$$\longrightarrow [\text{ P-STR} \quad \langle {}_{ap}[\text{PHON|ACC-PROPERTY|L-EDGE} \quad \boxed{1}\,]\rangle]$$

Based on the value of L-EDGE thus transmitted to an *ap*, the relation *get-boost* calculates the value of BOOST, as specified in Figure 7. The latter value, represented as a constant, is 1 if the value of L-EDGE is 0 or unspecified, b if 1, and b' if 2, where $1 < b < b'$.

This paper draws on Pierrehumbert and Beckman's (1988) theory modeling prosody by underspecified representations. Major factors determining the pitch, e.g., metrical boost, focus, and catathesis (i.e., the effect of an accented AP on the following AP), are presented as constants calculated on the basis of information from syntax and semantics. They are introduced as values of new attributes added under PHON|ACC-PROPERTY in Figure 7, which will not be further discussed in this paper. Following Pierrehumbert and Beckman, it is assumed that the prosodic contour for the whole utterance can be synthesized from the pitches of underspecified tones, to which the above-mentioned factors make the most crucial contributions.

Figure 11 gives an overview of how BOOST values for the right-branching phrase *aói óokina méron* ('a green, big melon') in Figure 3 are

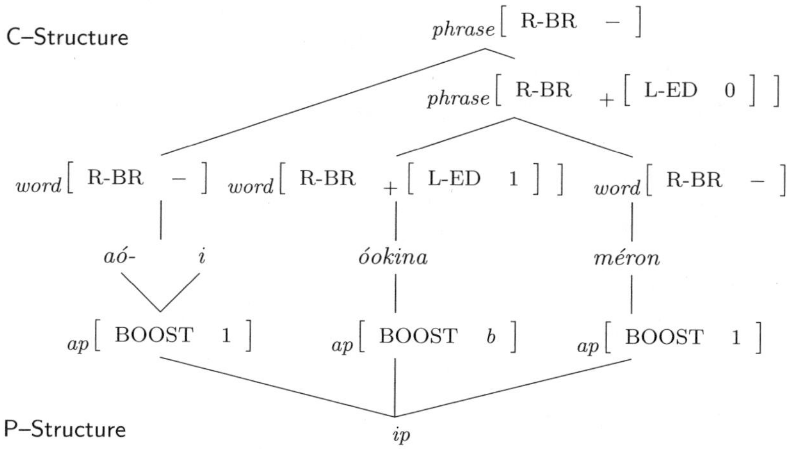

FIGURE 11 BOOST Value of the Right-Branching Structure

derived. The upper tree in the figure is an abbreviation of the DAUGHTERS feature, while the tree below is for the P-STR feature. The second AP *óokina* has *b* as its BOOST feature, and thus the occurrence of a metrical boost is explained. By contrast, in a left-branching phrase such as *aói rémon no niói* ('the smell of a green melon') in Figure 4, the Branching Principle assigns to every node in the C-structure a feature structure [R-BRANCH –] which leads to the unmarked BOOST value, 1; in this case no APs are boosted.

Phrases with triple modifiers, mentioned in Subsection 15.2.2, are also captured by this principle. In particular, the second adjunct A_2 in (1), which involves a double opening bracket, is given an L-EDGE value 2, and as a result its BOOST value is set to b', a value higher than the value b for the other boosted APs.

In order to capture the phenomenon of metrical boost, it is thus essential for the phonology to refer to the shape of the syntactic tree. Even the theory with P-Structure-based syntax (Whitelock, 1991) must accommodate this kind of information, presumably in the form of feature structures. This will mean the adoption of a significant portion of my proposal.

15.4.3 Defining an Interface: from P-Structure to C-Structure

Next, let us consider how we can constrain the position of interjectional postpositions *ne* and *yo* discussed in Subsection 15.2.3. As accounted for there, the structural specification that they 'subcategorize for an AP' is necessary and sufficient. However, this should not lead to its SUBCAT attribute taking a value $\langle[\text{P-STR } \langle ap \rangle]\rangle$; in HPSG, heads are prohibited from imposing conditions on their complements other than the values of SYNSEM (Pollard and Sag, 1994, p. 23).

Henceforth, what we need is a *skeleton* of the P-STR information as an interface, and the SUBCAT feature should refer to it along the SYNSEM|LOC path. In order to derive this from P-STR, the PROSODIC-HIERARCHY Principle is defined as follows:

(9) $${}_{phrasal\text{-}sign}[\;] \longrightarrow \begin{bmatrix} \text{P-STR } \langle {}_{ap}[\text{ AP-INDX } \boxed{1}{:}\,acc\text{-}ph\ ],\ {}_{ap}[\text{ AP-INDX } \boxed{2}{:}\,acc\text{-}ph\ ],\ \ldots,\ \\ \quad {}_{ap}[\text{ AP-INDX } \boxed{n}{:}\,acc\text{-}ph\ ] \rangle \\ \text{SYNSEM|LOC|P-HIER } \langle \boxed{1}, \boxed{2}, \ldots, \boxed{n} \rangle \end{bmatrix}$$

This Principle requires that the value of the SYNSEM|LOC|P(ROSODIC)-HIER(ARCHY) path be the concatenation of the AP-IND(E)X values of the *ap*-type elements (if any) of the P-STR list under preservation of order. The value of AP-INDX, *acc(entual)-ph(rase)*, is distinct from *ap*.

Based on this principle, the lexical description for the interjectional postposition *ne* is given as follows:

(10) $${}_{p\text{-}word}\begin{bmatrix} \text{P-STR} & \langle {}_{ap\text{-}cl}[\text{PHON|MORA} \quad ne] \rangle \\ \text{SYNSEM|LOC|SUBCAT} & \langle [\text{LOC|P-HIER} \quad \langle acc\text{-}ph \rangle]\ \rangle \end{bmatrix}$$

The SUBCAT attribute checks if the complement consists of a single AP without access to further contents of the phonology. Thus, for example, SUBCAT constraints are prohibited from requiring a complement with an initial consonant that is not [b] (Pullum and Zwicky, 1988). According to this specification, a relaxation of the principle of 'Phonology-Free Syntax' required by the data is limited to a minimum.

15.5 Conclusions

Advantages of the presented approach are as follows:

First, in distinction from Whitelock's (1991), this approach is based on the syntactic structure reflecting the intuition-based construction of meaning. This has great importance in extending the grammar to cope with other phenomena in syntax and semantics, although the difference might not be an absolute one.

Second, a mechanism is available which predicts the influence of the C-Structure on the P-Structure, i.e., a metrical boost. Whitelock's grammar as it stands is unable to do this.

Third, the influence of the P-Structure on the C-Structure in terms of the position of the interjectional postpositions can be accounted for by defining an interface without profoundly contravening the principle of 'Phonology-Free Syntax'; the separation between the two components is on the whole maintained. By contrast, Whitelock's formalization completely blurs the distinction by basing its syntax solely on phonology.

To sum up, the approach proposed posits bistratal representations and limits their interactions to the interfaces represented as hierarchical information in local syntactic features, observing the standardly acknowledged distinction between syntax and phonology.

Acknowledgements

I would like to thank David Bogdan, Francis Bond, Hiroyuki Maeda, Yoshiki Mori, Hiroaki Nakamura, Shigeru Satō, and two anonymous reviewers for suggestions and comments.

References

Bird, S. 1995. *Computational Phonology*. Cambridge: Cambridge University Press.

Bresnan, J., ed. 1982. *The Mental Representation of Grammatical Relations*. Cambridge, Mass.: MIT Press.

Choi, Y.-S., S. Satō, and G.-J. Min. 1995. Tōgo–teki ni Aimaina Bun no Seisei ni okeru Inritsu–teki Yōso no Bunseki. *Proceedings of the Phonetic Society of Japan 1995 Annual Convention* pages 26–31.

Coleman, J., ed. 1998. *Phonological Representations: Their Names, Forms and Powers*. Cambridge: Cambridge University Press.

Gunji, T. 1999. On Lexicalist Treatments of Japanese Causatives. In R. D. Levine and G. M. Green, eds., *Studies in Contemporary Phrase Structure Grammar*, pages 119–160. Cambridge University Press.

Kathol, A. 1995. *Linearization–Based German Syntax*. Ph.D. thesis, Ohio State University.

Kubozono, H. 1987. *The Organization of Japanese Prosody*. Ph.D. thesis, University of Edinburgh. Published 1993 by Kuroshio Publishers.

Ladusaw, W. A. 1988. A Proposed Distinction between *Levels* and *Strata*. In The Linguistic Society of Korea, ed., *Linguistics in the Morning Calm 2*, pages 37–51. Hanshin Publishing Co.

Matui, M. 1999. An Overview of the JPSG Phonology. In T. Gunji and K. Hasida, eds., *Topics in Constraint-Based Grammar of Japanese*, pages 99–140. Kluwer Academic Publishers.

Pierrehumbert, J. and M. Beckman. 1988. *Japanese Tone Structure*. Cambridge, Mass.: MIT Press.

Pollard, C. and I. Sag. 1994. *Head–Driven Phrase Structure Grammar*. Chicago: The University of Chicago Press.

Pullum, G. K. and A. M. Zwicky. 1988. The Syntax-Phonology Interface. In F. J. Newmeyer, ed., *Linguistics: The Cambridge Survey, vol. 1*, pages 255–280. Cambridge University Press.

Reape, M. 1994. Domain Union and Word Order Variation in German. In J. Nerbonne, K. Netter, and C. Pollard, eds., *German in Head-Driven Phrase Structure Grammar*, pages 151–197. CSLI Publications.

Schafer, A. J. 1997. *Prosodic Parsing: The Role of Prosody in Sentence Comprehension*. Ph.D. thesis, University of Massachusetts Amherst.

Shieber, S. M. 1985. Criteria for Designing Computer Facilities for Linguistic Analysis. *Linguistics* 23:189–211.

Steedman, M. 1991. Structure and Intonation. *Language* 67:260–296.

Uszkoreit, H. 1986. Categorial Unification Grammars. *Proceedings of COLING 1986*, pages 187–194.

Whitelock, P. 1991. What Sort of Trees Do We Speak?—A Computational Model of the Syntax–Prosody Interface in Tokyo Japanese. *Fifth Conference of the European Chapter of the ACL* pages 75–82.

Zec, D. and S. Inkelas. 1990. Prosodically Constrained Syntax. In S. Inkelas and D. Zec, eds., *The Phonology-Syntax Connection*, pages 365–378. The University of Chicago Press.

Subject Index

accent, 268
Accent Assignment Rule, 268, 277
accent-assignment (acc-assign), 275, 277
ACCENT-LOCATION (ACC-LOC), 274
ACCENTED, 268
accentual function, 268, 274
accentual information, 268, 274
accentual phrase (AP), 268, 274
ACCENTUAL-FUNCTION (ACC-FUNC), 274
accentual-phrase (acc-ph), 280
ACCENTUAL-PROPERTY (ACC-PROPERTY), 278
adjunct, 270, 275
    pre-head, 195
adjunct extraction, 161
adjuncts as complements, 57
adjuncts as dependents, 104
adverbial relativization, 160
aff, 24
agreement, 252, 255
agreement controller (AGRC), 258, 259, 262–264
ambiguity, 270
AP, 273, 278, 280
ap, 274, 276, 278, 280
ap-clitic, 275, 276
AP-INDEX (AP-INDX), 280
ARG-ST, 23–25, 139
argument inheritance, 68
argument raising, 97
Argument Realization Constraint, 156
Argument Realization Principle, 24, 57, 104
    Prepositional, 62, 63
argument structure, 57, 65
Argument Structure Extension, 203, 208–210
Argument Structure Extension Principle, 57, 104
    Passive, 70
    Verbal, 57, 70
argument-raising source, 102, 106
Armenian, 211
aspectual perfect, 240
auxiliary contraction, 17–31
auxiliary verb, 177, 179, 218

BACKGROUND, 117
Backward Functional Application rule, 273
Backward Type-Raising Rule, 273
be
    valence patterns, 28
Bech's problem, 52, 72, 73
Bengali, 177
biclausal approach, 275
Bind R-Pronoun Principle, 66
binding theory, 25
bistratal representation, 281
blocking, 19, 21, 27

body, 274
BOOST, 278
boundary
  Intonational Phrase, 171
  within metrical trees, 174
bracketing paradox, 271
branching information, 277
Branching Principle, 277, 278

c-ppro (covert personal pronoun), 139
canonical, 24
case, 251, 254
case assignment, 201
case attraction, 211, 212
Case Concord Principle, 206, 208, 212
Case Principle, 203, 204, 206, 207
Case Realization Principle, 207, 208, 212
case stacking, 205–207, 212
Categorial Unification Grammar, 271
chaining rule, 273
clitic, 176, 252, 253, 258
clitic placement, 77, 79, 83, 85–87, 92, 94
coindexing relation, 166
Combinatory Categorial Grammar, 170
complement, 275
complementizing case, 211
Complex Noun Phrase Constraint, 154, 165
COMPS, 139
connective particles, 119
Constituent-Structure (C-Structure), 269, 271–274, 277, 278, 280
constraint
  ext-pr, 193
  base-pr, 191, 192
  ext-pr, 191
constraint-based phonology, 267
construction, 182, 187
  hd-cx, 182
  head-final, 193
  head-initial, 191
CONTENT, 130
CONTEXT, 116
CONTEXT Inheritance Principle, 129
contextual factors, 116
contraction, 17–31
control, 254, 260, 261
conversational implicature, 117, 126, 127
Cooperative Principle, 117
cross-classification, 191, 197

dative, 252, 254, 255
DAUGHTERS, 278
default prominence, 173
dependency structure, 53, 57
dependent raising, 97
Dependent Realization Principle, 161
Description Level Lexical Rule (DLLR), 8–10
Designated Terminal Element, 173, 185, 186
disambiguation, 270, 271
discourse anaphora, 6, 7
discourse markers, 119–120
Discourse Representation Theory, 232
DOM, 185
domain union, 186
Donno So, 142
double nominative construction, 162
DTE, *see* Designated Terminal Element
Dutch, 51

easy-construction, 60, 66
EHRC, *see* externally headed relative clause
enclisis, 79, 80, 83, 84, 89
end-based mapping, 195

ending, 274
English, 209, 254–256
    relative clause, 138
English auxiliaries, 17–31
ERG, 145
existential construction, 52–56, 69–72
existential sentence, 255, 263
externally headed relative clause
    and unbounded dependencies, 138
    vs. internally headed relative clause, 141
extraction, 51, 53, 56, 58–60, 63, 64, 66, 68, 69

f-structure, 213
finitivization lexical rule, 103
focus, 163, 173, 179, 188
focused specifier, 165
formal noun, 273
Fox, 89, 94
Franconian, 219
free, 24
French, 36, 49, 77, 86, 87
fronting, 216–217
full word, 268, 272, 275, 278
function word, 176
future *zullen*, 246

gap, 24
genitive relative clause, 162
German, 202, 203, 264
German syntax, 97
get-boost, 278
Gothic, 212
grammatical word, 268, 272, 275
Gumbaynggir, 204, 206, 207

Hakha Chin (Lai), 137
Hausa, 271
head, 29–30
    c-structure, 29
    f-structure, 29
    m-structure, 29
Head Feature Principle, 19, 21, 258
head movement, 99
Head-driven Phrase Structure Grammar, 56, 57, 68, 267, 274
Head-Filler Construction, 70
Head-Filler-Comps Structure, 57
Head-Subj-Comps Schema, 59
hierarchy
    of constructions, 182, 183
    of prosodic constructions, 191
    of prosodic types, 187
honorifics, 125–127

IHRC, *see* internally headed relative clause
illocutionary force, 120–124
immediate dominance, 256, 257
impersonal passive, 71
incorporation, 1
    classificatory, 5
    compounding, 5
    morphological, 1, 5
indexical, 115, 130
induction
    of prosodic structure, 185
inferential pronominalization, 6
infinitive, 83–85, 94
    inflected infinitive, 83, 85
information focus, 163
inside-out equations, 18
inside-out unification, 212, 213
institutionalized activity, 5
intention, 120
interface, 267, 270, 271, 277, 280, 281
interjectional postposition, 271, 279, 281
internally headed relative clause, 141–142
    and LF movement, 149
Intonational Phrase, 171, 172, 181
IP, *see* Intonational Phrase
island-violating relativization, 154
Italian, 48, 77, 79, 86, 87, 92, 176, 254

Japanese, 174
juncture, 169, 174–176

Kanjobal, 7
Kayardild, 205, 207, 211
Korean, 153, 209
Korean relatives, 154

Lai, 137
  absence of unbounded dependencies, 138
  unrealized arguments, 138
  verbal form alternation, 146
leaner, 176, 179, 194
leaner group, 176, 182
left-association, 194–196
left-branching, 270
LEFT-EDGE (L-EDGE), 277, 278
Lexical Argument-Raising Principle (LARP), 102
Lexical Dependent-Raising Principle (LDRP), 105
Lexical Head Association Constraint, 195, 196
lexical Integrity, 94
lexical rule, 45, 46
Lexical-Functional Grammar, 17–31, 206
LEXICAL-STRESS, 10
linear precedence, 256, 257
linearization, 77, 83, 84, 86, 89, 90, 92, 94
  order domain, 77, 92–94
linearization approach, 100
literal meaning, 130
locality, 19, 21, 202
locative adverb, 52–57, 70, 71, 74
Locative Subject Constraint, 71

major categories, 61
Mam, 7
Martuthunira, 205, 206, 210
merging rule, 273
mesoclisis, 79, 80, 89
metrical boost, 267, 270, 274, 277, 278, 280
metrical grid, 10
metrical phonology, 10
metrical tree, 172, 176, 185, 187
  n-ary, 174, 179
  binary-branching, 172
Middle Field, 65, 66
minor categories, 61
modal verb, 177, 179
modal *zullen*, 246
modularity in grammar, 274
Mokilese, 7
mora, 268, 274
MORA, 274
morphological dependency, 27–29
morphophonology, 87–90
morphotactics, 87–90
mutation, 33, 37
mutual belief, 116

n-word, 33, 34, 36, 42, 43, 46, 48
ne, 271, 279
negative adverb, 36–38, 43
negative concord, 35
negative object, 44
negative quantifier, 38–42
negative subject, 38, 44, 45
negative verb, 42, 43, 46–48
nominal object sort, 61
noncanonical, 24
normal belief, 126
normal meaning, 132
NSR, *see* Nuclear Stress Rule
Nuclear Stress Rule, 172, 173
null context, 131

object predicative construction, 220, 224
operation
  polymorphic, 187
ORDER-DOMAIN, 274

P-STRUCTURE (P-STR), 274, 275, 277, 278, 280
P-STRUCTURE Principle, 275, 276
parasitic gap, 56
partial constituent fronting, 97

partial verb phrase fronting, 215
particle verb, 215–227
partitive interpretation, 41, 44
passive, 70
  impersonal, 52–56, 69–71
past time perfect, 243
PATR-II, 271
performative verb, 120
phase verb, 225–226
PHON, 182, 183, 185, 192
Phonological Phrase, 171, 175, 176
phonological phrasing, 2
Phonological Word, 172, 176
phonological word, 268
phonology
  in HPSG, 182
PHONOLOGY, 9
phonology-free syntax, 271, 280
pitch, 268, 278
Polish, 77, 209
politeness, 118
Portuguese
  European, 77–81, 83–88, 90, 92–94
predicate complex, 215–227
predicative, 10, 11
preposition phrase, 51–56, 61, 62, 65, 67, 69, 72
presupposition, 127
Principle of Complement Control, 261
Principle of Contextual Consistency, 242
PRO, 25
proclisis, 79–85, 93
projection of contextual information, 127–128
prominence, 172, 174, 179, 185
pronominal, 115
  covert, 115
Pronoun Incorporation Lexical Rule, 22
prosodic bracketing, 2, 11
prosodic contour, 278
prosodic domain, 185
  nested, 185
prosodic flattening, 177, 181
prosodic hierarchy, 170, 271
Prosodic Isomorphism Hypothesis, 169, 172, 192
prosodic performance model, 181
prosodic promotion, 179, 193
prosodic relation, 183
prosodic weight, 172
PROSODIC-HIERARCHY Principle, 280
Prosodic-Structure (P-Structure), 269, 271–274, 277, 280
psychological predicate, 251, 252, 254, 258
PVP-Slash-Introduction Schema (Adjunct), 100

quantifier, 80–84, 90, 91
quirky case, 201, 252, 263

R-pronoun, 51–56, 61, 64–67, 69, 72
  daar, 55
  er, 52, 53, 55, 56, 61, 69, 70
  hier, 55
raising, 254, 260, 262
Raising Principle, 262
reanalysis, 105
reflexive intentions, 116
rel-pro (relativizable pronominal), 140
relative clause, 153
  and grammatical construction, 150
Relative Clause Constraint, 158
relative pronoun, 153
relativization, 153
RELATIVIZER (REL), 155
respect, 126
resultative construction, 219–220, 224–225
right-branching, 270, 277, 278
RIGHT-BRANCHING (R-BRANCH), 277, 278

Samoan, 7
sandhi, 176
SEGMENT, 274
segmentation into APs, 269
SEGMENTS, 9–11
semantic case, 208, 209
sentence final particles, 118–119
separable prefix, 215
Serbo-Croat, 77, 271
sign, 185
Slash Amalgamation, 60
Slash Inheritance Constraint, 157
Spanish, 251–256, 258–263
specificity, 5, 10
specifier, 162
stratum, 274
stress, 2, 3, 10
Strict Layer Hypothesis, 171, 186
SUBCAT, 280
SUBJ, 139
subject, 195, 196, 251–254, 256, 264
subject extraction, 158
subordinate relation, 163
suffixaufnahme, 205
SYNSEM, 280
syntactic chunk, 170
syntactic noun incorporation (SNI), 1
syntax/semantics Interface, 232

temporal adjuncts, 238
temporal auxiliaries, 232
tense, 115, 232
θ-role, 254
Thuringian, 219, 225–226
Trace Principle, 100
traceless vs. trace-based extraction, 105
traces, 26
transformational grammar, 52
type
    parametrised, 185
Type I Incorporation, 1, 7
type variable, 186, 188
typed unification formalism, 273

Udi, 94
UNACCENTED, 268
unbounded dependencies
    absence in Lai, 138
underspecification, 267, 278
Unification Grammar, 273
unrealized arguments, 139

Valence Principle, 19, 21
verb movement, 26
Verb Phrase Ellipsis, 25
VSO, 33, 42

weak determiner, 194
weak function word, 175, 185, 186
weak pronominal object, 192
weight, 8
Welsh
    colloquial, 33–49
    literary, 33
wh-expression, 80, 84, 93, 94
wh-question, 84, 85

Xiamen, 171

Yapese, 7
yo, 271, 279

Name Index

Abeillé, A., 1, 3, 8, 13, 24
Abney, 170
Ackerman, F., 227
Alarcos Llorach, E., 253
Alsina, A., 254, 255
Andrews, A. D., 19, 27, 205, 206, 209, 212
Askedal, J. O., 107
Asudeh, A., 1, 11, 192
Atterer, M., 181
Austin, J. L., 120
Awbery, G., 48

Bach, E., 80
Bachenko, J., 181, 196
Bar-Hillel, Y., 113, 116
Barbosa, P., 85
Barron, J., 18–21, 26–29
Barwise, J., 80
Basbøll, H., 1, 3
Bech, G., 52, 72, 107
Beckman, M., 171, 173, 174, 267, 278
Belletti, A., 254
Bender, E. M., 17
Bennis, H., 52, 56
Bierwisch, M., 216
Bird, S., 1, 9, 267
Bittner, M., 6
Black, A. W., 170
Blake, B., 204
Blevins, J., 27
Borsley, R. D., 33, 36, 37, 43, 46, 47, 252, 256
Bouma, G., 46, 51, 53, 57–59, 65, 69, 72, 98, 104, 110, 156, 160, 192, 203, 206, 208, 209, 239
Branco, A., 81, 83, 90, 92
Bratt, E., 209
Bresnan, J., 269
Butt, M., 29, 177, 185

Cardelli, L., 187
Chen, M. Y., 171
Choi, Y.-S., 270
Chomsky, N., 173, 201
Chung, C., 221
Cohen, P. R., 117
Cole, P., 139, 142, 149
Coleman, J., 267, 275
Cooper, R., 80
Copestake, A., 90, 91
Corley, M., 170
Corley, S., 170
Crain, S., 131
Crocker, M. W., 170
Croft, W., 170
Crysmann, B., 77, 78, 81, 83, 87, 89, 90, 92, 94
Culy, C., 142

Davidson, D., 232, 248
De Kuthy, K., 97, 98, 102, 103, 105, 109

Den Besten, H., 97
Den Dikken, M., 256
Dench, A., 204, 205, 210
Donohue, C., 182
Drach, E., 217
Duarte, I., 78, 79

Eades, D., 204
Eisenberg, P., 216
Engdahl, E., 163
Evans, N., 204, 205, 207, 211

Faria, I., 78
Fernández-Soriano, O., 253, 255
Fischer-Jørgensen, E., 3, 10
Fitzpatrick, E., 181, 196
Flickinger, D., 13, 90, 91
Fodor, J. D., 157
Frank, A., 59
Fraser, B., 120

Gazdar, G., 128, 129, 177
Gee, J. P., 169, 174, 175, 181, 196
Gerdts, D. B., 5
Godard, D., 1, 3, 8, 13, 24
Green, G. M., 113, 116, 117, 122, 126, 128–132
Grewendorf, G., 218
Grice, H. P., 117, 119, 126–130, 132
Grimshaw, J., 254
Grosjean, F., 169, 174, 175, 181, 196
Gunji, T., 275

Haeseryn, W., 53
Haftka, B., 217
Halle, M., 173
Halpern, A., 77
Han, J.-I., 155, 165, 166
Harbert, W., 212
Hasegawa, N., 166
Hayes, B., 10, 14, 171, 173
Heinz, W., 202, 264
Hentze, R., 1, 11
Herslund, M., 4
Hinrichs, E., 97, 104, 221
Hitzeman, J., 170
Hogg, R., 173
Horn, L., 81, 118, 122
Huck, G., 163, 165–167
Höhle, T., 221

Iida, M., 57
Inkelas, S., 271

Jelinek, E., 80
Jespersen, O., 3, 5
Jones, B. M., 33, 36, 46

Kamp, H., 232, 234, 238
Kang, M.-Y., 155, 165
Kathol, A., 87, 90, 92, 94, 98, 137, 145, 146, 151, 186, 220, 225, 252, 264, 274
Keenan, E., 254
Keller, F., 170
Keyser, S., 220
Kim, J.-B., 33, 36, 42, 45, 153–155, 157, 162, 163, 165
King, T. H, 177, 185
Kiparsky, P., 115
Kiss, T., 216, 221, 225
Klein, E., 1, 9, 169, 177
Koenig, J.-P., 46, 88, 191, 213
Koster, J., 218
Kratzer, A., 80
Krieger, H.-U., 88
Kubozono, H., 269
Kuno, S., 164
Kupść, 48, 77

Ladd, R., 173
Ladusaw, W., 92, 274
Lakoff, R. L., 120
Lappin, S., 129
Lee, Y.-S., 160
Levesque, H. J., 117
Levine, B., 22
Levinson, S., 115
Liberman, M., 10, 172–174
Lu, W.-Y., 118

Lüdeling, A., 220

Maling, J., 252, 255
Malouf, R., 53, 57–59, 65, 104, 110, 156, 160, 192, 201, 203, 206, 208, 209
Mann, T., 107
Manning, C., 57, 70, 139
Martins, A., 81
Masullo, P. J., 255
Matiasek, J., 202, 264
Matos, G., 78
Matsumoto, Y., 153
Matui, M., 267, 275
McCawley, J. D., 115
McCully, C. B., 173
Mellish, C., 170
Melnik, N., 146
Meurers, D., 1, 8, 97, 98, 102, 103, 105–107, 109
Mikkelsen, L. H., 1, 192
Miller, P., 24, 57, 68, 77, 86, 87, 104, 110, 192, 258
Mithun, M., 1, 5, 7
Model, J., 52, 56
Monachesi, P., 9, 68, 77, 79, 86, 87, 258
Morgan, J. L., 116, 117, 127–129
Moure, T., 254
Mullen, A., 257
Müller, G., 97
Müller, S., 98–100, 109, 110, 215–217, 220, 221, 224, 225

Na, Y., 163, 165–167
Nakazawa, T., 97, 104, 221
Nedergaard Thomsen, O., 1, 5
Neeleman, A., 220
Nerbonne, J., 88, 98, 257
Nespor, M., 171, 173, 175, 176, 185
Niño, M.-E., 29
Nordlinger, R., 29, 206, 211, 212
Nunberg, G., 116, 130, 132
Næss, A., 256

Oberlander, J., 170
Olsen, S., 216
Oppenrieder, W., 219, 220

Pafel, J., 110
Park, B.-S., 153, 162, 165
Parsons, T., 232
Partee, B., 80, 115
Penn, G., 77
Peterson, D., 144, 146
Pierrehumbert, J., 171, 173, 174, 267, 278
Pirker, H., 88
Plank, F., 204, 212
Pollard, C., 13, 22, 52, 57, 59, 61, 98, 100, 103–106, 113, 128, 129, 142, 145, 150, 201, 202, 204, 220, 232, 233, 242, 244, 252, 256, 258, 262–264, 280
Prince, A., 10, 172–174
Przepiórkowski, A., 44, 48, 57, 202–204, 264
Pullum, G., 20, 77, 271, 280
Pullum, G. K., 177
Pütz, H., 220, 224

Radford, A., 26
Reape, M., 186, 220, 257, 274
Reichenbach, H., 233, 234, 248
Rentier, G., 56, 221
Reyle, U., 232, 234, 238
Richter, F., 44
Rischel, J., 1, 3, 5
Rizzi, L., 254
Roeper, Th., 220
Ross, J. R., 120
Rothstein, S., 219
Rouveret, A., 42
Rowlett, P., 41
Ruhl, C., 130

Sadler, L., 17–21, 25–29
Sadock, J. M., 120
Sag, I. A., 11, 17, 22, 24, 33, 36, 42, 45, 52, 53, 57–59, 61, 65, 68, 70, 77, 84, 86, 87, 90,

91, 100, 104, 105, 110, 113, 128, 129, 139, 142, 150, 155–158, 160, 170, 177, 182, 191, 192, 197, 201–204, 206, 208, 209, 220, 232, 233, 242, 244, 252, 256, 258, 262–264, 280
Sailer, M., 44
Sanfilippo, A., 233
Schafer, A., 270
Schelkens, N., 238
Schmerling, S. F., 131
Schourup, L., 120
Searle, J., 120
Segond, F., 29
Selkirk, E. O., 14, 20, 170–172, 175–177, 185, 195, 196
Shattuck-Hufnagel, S., 171
Shen, T., 175
Shieber, S., 271
Simpson, J., 206, 209
Spencer, A., 17–19, 77, 79
Sperber, D., 115
Stampe, D., 120
Steedman, M., 13, 131, 169, 185, 196, 273
Suzuki, Y., 118
Suñer, M., 253
Sweet, H., 20

Taglicht, J., 171, 185
Taylor, P., 170
Thiersch, C., 97
Thráinsson, H., 252, 255
Trewin, S., 170
Truckenbrodt, H., 13
Tseng, J., 206, 209
Turk, A., 171

Uszkoreit, H., 216, 271

Van Eynde, F., 61, 231, 233, 236, 238, 248
Van Geenhoven, V., 5, 7
Van Noord, G., 57, 69, 72, 98, 104, 110, 206, 239
Van Riemsdijk, H., 51, 52, 56
VanBik, K., 146, 151
Verdoolaege, S., 238
Verkuyl, H., 237
Villada, B., 251, 254, 258
Vogel, C., 251, 254, 258
Vogel, I., 171, 173, 175, 176, 185

Warner, A. R., 33, 36, 42, 46
Wasow, T., 13, 233
Webelhuth, G., 97, 227
Wechsler, S., 160, 219
Weermann, F., 220
Wegner, P., 187
Werner, O., 218
Whitelock, P., 271, 279, 280
Wilson, D., 115
Wunderlich, D., 219

Yang, D.-W., 165
Yoshimoto, K., 267

Zaenen, A., 252, 255
Zec, D., 271
Zifonun, G., 216
Zwicky, A., 20, 77, 176, 193, 271, 280